"Don Carson is one of the most productive and capable evangelical scholars in the English-speaking world, and this volume by former students and teaching colleagues reflects the breadth of his interests and especially his concern for the development of biblical studies in a global context. Alongside fresh personal contributions to New Testament study, there are informative surveys of developments in New Testament studies in Africa and Asia, as well as in North America and Europe. This solid volume thus offers not only a worthy tribute to its honoree but also valuable assessments of the state of New Testament scholarship worldwide."

I. Howard Marshall, Professor Emeritus of New Testament,
University of Aberdeen, Scotland

"D. A. Carson is the Renaissance man of North American evangelicalism. He is a biblical scholar of the highest caliber, a preacher and evangelist of renown, and a theologian of unswerving commitment to the gospel. His teaching ministry has spanned the globe; in fact, I've heard his sermon on Matthew 27 on three different continents and found it equally stirring each time. This book is a snapshot of issues in the international New Testament scene as it stands today. This erudite collection of essays is rightly dedicated to one who has committed his life to serving the global church."

Michael F. Bird, Lecturer in Theological Studies,
Crossway College, Brisbane, Australia

"This lively book of essays represents a fitting tribute to the life of Don Carson, one of the liveliest and most learned biblical scholars of our time. It will only suit its honoree, however, if it leads its varied readers to the Scriptures he has studied for so long, increasing devotion and fidelity to the gospel they proclaim. I pray that God will make this so for Jesus' sake."

Douglas A. Sweeney, Professor of Church History and the History
of Christian Thought, Trinity Evangelical Divinity School; Director,
Carl F. H. Henry Center for Theological Understanding

"This is a remarkable series of studies in honor of a remarkable man. Carson's influence has been extraordinary, and this book explores a number of his particular interests with great skill."

Simon Gathercole, Senior Lecturer in New Testament,
Cambridge University; editor, *Journal for the Study of the New Testament*

"Anyone impressed with the scope of Don Carson's work will likewise be impressed with this volume of essays. It has something for every student of the New Testament. Readers of Carson in particular will not be disappointed."

Nicholas Perrin, Franklin S. Dyrness Professor of Biblical Studies,
Wheaton College

Understanding
the Times

Understanding
the Times

NEW TESTAMENT STUDIES
IN THE 21ST CENTURY

ESSAYS IN HONOR OF D. A. CARSON
ON THE OCCASION *of* HIS 65TH BIRTHDAY

Edited by Andreas J. Köstenberger
and Robert W. Yarbrough

CROSSWAY
WHEATON, ILLINOIS

Understanding the Times: New Testament Studies in the 21st Century:
Essays in Honor of D. A. Carson on the Occasion of His 65th Birthday
Copyright © 2011 by Andreas J. Köstenberger and Robert W. Yarbrough
Published by Crossway
              1300 Crescent Street
              Wheaton, Illinois 60187

Cover design: Studio Gearbox
Interior design and typesetting: Lakeside Design Plus

First printing 2011
Printed in the United States of America

Hardcover ISBN:	978-1-4335-0719-9
PDF ISBN:	978-1-4335-0720-5
Mobipocket ISBN:	978-1-4335-0721-2
ePub ISBN:	978-1-4335-2237-6

Crossway is a publishing ministry of Good News Publishers.

LB		22	21	20	19	18	17	16	15	14	13	12	11
14	13	12	11	10	9	8	7	6	5	4	3	2	1

Contents

Editors' Preface   9

Abbreviations   13

Part 1: New Testament Studies and Ancillary Disciplines

1. Greek Linguistics and Lexicography   19
   Stanley E. Porter

2. Hermeneutics and Theological Interpretation   62
   Grant Osborne

3. The Church: A Summary and Reflection   87
   Mark Dever

4. Evangelical Self-Identity and the Doctrine of Biblical
   Inerrancy   104
   John D. Woodbridge

Part 2: Special Topics in New Testament Studies

5. Lifting Up the Son of Man and God's Love
   for the World: John 3:16 in Its Historical, Literary,
   and Theological Contexts   141
   Andreas J. Köstenberger

6. Justification in Galatians   160
   Douglas J. Moo

7. God as the Speaking God: "Theology" in the Letter
   to the Hebrews   196
   Peter T. O'Brien

8. The Language of Baptism: The Meaning of Βαπτίζω
   in the New Testament   217
   Eckhard J. Schnabel

Part 3: New Testament Studies around the World

9. New Testament Studies in Africa   249
   Robert W. Yarbrough

10. New Testament Studies in North America   277
    Craig L. Blomberg

11. New Testament Studies in Asia   300
    David W. Pao

12. New Testament Studies in Europe   324
    Robert W. Yarbrough

Appendix: D. A. Carson: His Life and Work to Date   349
   Andreas J. Köstenberger

Selected Writings of D. A. Carson   370

Contributors   379

Bible Permissions   381

General Index   383

Scripture Index   393

Editors' Preface

A t a recent lecture, a cameraman planted himself close to Don Carson's podium, palpably distracting the audience from Carson's message. With only a moment's hesitation, Carson paused and asked the man to move, explaining, "We are talking about the *gospel*. The gospel is a lot more important than media." During the same lecture, Carson also referred to an e-mail exchange he had with his daughter Tiffany, who gently chided her dad that he was the only one who sent his daughter e-mails that required the use of a dictionary. These vignettes reveal two vital aspects of Don Carson's life and passion: the gospel and his family.

Over the years, Carson has been a close student of evangelicalism. He has taken a keen interest in the doctrine of Scripture, which is one of the most significant benchmarks of the evangelical movement. He has engaged in a worldwide teaching, preaching, and writing ministry that has had a large impact on God's kingdom, both on a church-wide level and on many servants of God and students of Scripture individually. Don Carson truly has proved to be one who exemplifies "understanding the times," like the men of Issachar in Old Testament days, "who understood the times and knew what Israel should do" (1 Chron. 12:32, NIV).

Those who desire to know what the church should do today would do well to listen to Don Carson. Transcending narrow areas of specialization, Carson has not only authored numerous scholarly contributions—including commentaries on Matthew and John, with several others in various stages of production—he has also contributed significantly to a wide variety of current issues in the contemporary church. Whether the issue is gender-inclusive Bible translation, the emergent church, or postmodernism, to name but a few, Don Carson has provided a judicious assessment of the relevant issues and has prescribed a sensible, constructive way forward.

This volume is but a small token of appreciation for D. A. Carson at the occasion of his sixty-fifth birthday by some of his colleagues, former students, and friends. Our focus here—spanning only part of the vast area of Don's interests—is the state of New Testament studies at the beginning of the twenty-first century. The volume is divided into three parts. The first deals with New Testament studies and ancillary disciplines—Greek linguistics and lexicography, hermeneutics and theological interpretation, the church, and evangelical identity—and features essays by Stanley Porter, Grant Osborne, Mark Dever, and John Woodbridge. The second part is devoted to special topics in New Testament studies. Andreas Köstenberger conducts an in-depth study of the well-known verse John 3:16; Douglas Moo deals with justification in Galatians (against the backdrop of the "New Perspective" on Paul); Peter O'Brien contributes an essay on "the speaking God" in the book of Hebrews; and Eckhard Schnabel provides a thorough study of the language of baptism in Greek, Jewish, and Christian literature. The third part takes the reader on a tour of New Testament studies around the world: Africa, North America, Asia, and Europe, with contributions by Robert Yarbrough, Craig Blomberg, and David Pao.

An appendix discusses D. A. Carson's life and work to date, followed by a selected bibliography of his contribution to New Testament studies. We are well aware that this is but a small installment, with many significant contributions still to come.

A word on the genesis of this project is appropriate. While the idea of a Festschrift honoring Don Carson was an obvious one and had been contemplated for several years by both of the editors (along with others), Andy Naselli deserves credit for approaching us and making preliminary contact with Crossway and thus serving as a key catalyst for the project. Andy also compiled a comprehensive bibliography that formed the basis of the "Selected Writings" included at the end of this volume. In addition, Andy made early contributions in the form of possible authors and topics. The editors are very grateful to Andy for the important impetus he provided.

The editors wish to express appreciation to the Henry Center for Theological Understanding, its director, Dr. Douglas A. Sweeney, and its board members. Without their support, this project would not have been possible.

The editors and contributors to this volume join in expressing our profound gratitude to you, Don, for your tireless work in God's kingdom and for your immeasurable impact on the church and on all of us. May God give you and your dear wife, Joy, many more years of fruitful labor, and may the gospel continue to spread, to God's greater glory and for the good of his people. *Soli Deo gloria.*

Andreas J. Köstenberger, Wake Forest, North Carolina
Robert W. Yarbrough, Deerfield, Illinois
May 1, 2010

Abbreviations

A. J.	*Jewish Antiquities* (Josephus)
AB	Anchor Bible
BBR	*Bulletin for Biblical Research*
BDAG	Bauer, Danker, Arndt, and Gingrich
BECNT	Baker Exegetical Commentary on the New Testament
BLG	Biblical Languages: Greek
BTB	*Biblical Theology Bulletin*
BZNW	Beihefte zur Zeitschrift für die neutestamentliche Wissenschaft
CBET	Contributions to Biblical Exegesis and Theology
CBR	*Currents in Biblical Research*
CSL	Cambridge Studies in Linguistics
CTL	Cambridge Textbooks in Linguistics
Did.	*Didache*
EKK	Evangelisch-Katholischer Kommentar
EQ	*Evangelical Quarterly*
ESV	English Standard Version
FilNeot	*Filologia neotestamentaria*
FRLANT	Forschungen zur Religion und Literatur des Alten und Neuen Testaments
GNB	Good News Bible
Haer.	*Against Heresies* (Irenaeus)
HNT	Handbuch zum Neuen Testament
HTKNT	Herders theologischer Kommentar zum Neuen Testament
ICC	International Critical Commentary

IEJ	*Israel Exploration Journal*
JB	Jerusalem Bible
JBL	*Journal of Biblical Literature*
JETS	*Journal of the Evangelical Theological Society*
JSNT	*Journal for the Study of the New Testament*
JSNTSup	Journal for the Study of the New Testament Supplement
JSOTSup	Journal for the Study of the Old Testament Supplement
KEK	Kritisch-Exegetischer Kommentar über das Neue Testament
LCL	Loeb Classical Library
Louw-Nida	*Greek-English Lexicon of the New Testament Based on Semantic Domains*
LXX	Septuagint
MT	Masoretic Text
NAC	New American Commentary
NASB	New American Standard Bible
NET	The NET Bible
NICNT	New International Commentary on the New Testament
NIGTC	New International Greek Testament Commentary
NIV	New International Version
NIVAC	NIV Application Commentary
NLT	New Living Translation
NRSV	New Revised Standard Version
n.s.	new series
NSBT	New Studies in Biblical Theology
NTD	Das Neue Testament Deutsch
NTM	New Testament Monographs
NTS	*New Testament Studies*
NTTS	New Testament Tools and Studies
OTL	Old Testament Library
OTM	Oxford Theological Monographs
PNTC	Pillar New Testament Commentary
RB	*Revue biblique*
RSV	Revised Standard Version
SBG	Studies in Biblical Greek

SBJT	*Southern Baptist Journal of Theology*
SBL	Society of Biblical Literature
SBLDS	Society of Biblical Literature Dissertation Series
SBLRBS	Society of Biblical Literature Resources for Biblical Study
SBT	Studies in Biblical Theology
SNTG	Studies in New Testament Greek
SNTS	Society for New Testament Studies
SNTSMS	Society for New Testament Studies Monograph Series
SP	Sacra pagina
THKNT	Theologischer Handkommentar zum Neuen Testament
TNIV	Today's New International Version
TrinJ	*Trinity Journal*
TS	*Theological Studies*
TynBul	*Tyndale Bulletin*
WBC	Word Biblical Commentary
WMANT	Wissenschaftliche Monographien zum Alten und Neuen Testament
WTJ	*Westminster Theological Journal*
WUNT	Wissenschaftliche Untersuchungen zum Neuen Testament
WW	*Word and World*
ZNW	*Zeitschrift für die neutestamentliche Wissenschaft*
ZTK	*Zeitschrift für Theologie und Kirche*

New Testament Studies
and Ancillary Disciplines

1

Greek Linguistics and Lexicography

STANLEY E. PORTER

G reek linguistics and lexicography as applied to the Greek of
the New Testament have witnessed significant development
since the publication of James Barr's *The Semantics of Biblical
Language*,[1] in many ways a clarion call from within the biblical studies guild to more responsible treatment of the languages of the Bible.
Barr's book was not a theoretical treatise on linguistic method, but a
very practical treatment of a number of important issues concerning
understanding the Hebrew and Greek of the Bible. However, even
though the book is often acknowledged or even cited for its telling
conclusions, Barr's insights are still, I believe, widely ignored in much
language-related biblical research.

In response, a number of scholars have continued to draw attention to the potential and realized pitfalls that Barr addressed. One of
these scholars is the honoree of this volume, Don Carson, who has
made his own significant contributions to responsible handling of the
Greek language, in both his teaching of Greek grammar from a lin-

---

[1] James Barr, *The Semantics of Biblical Language* (Oxford: Oxford University Press, 1961).

guistic standpoint and his own publications. When I studied advanced Greek with him in 1981, he used the excellent volume by John Lyons, *Introduction to Theoretical Linguistics*,[2] among others, as the basis of some of his lectures. My first academic publication was a revised form of the term paper that I wrote for this grammar course, which provided an excellent foundation for my later doctoral research in Greek linguistics.[3] Don's own publications in the area, besides his exegetical studies and commentaries, include his book on Greek accents and his oft-cited and helpful *Exegetical Fallacies*,[4] as well as three volumes of essays, coedited with me, on various Greek and linguistic topics.[5]

In the course of my own study, however, I have repeatedly found that, despite the widespread availability of numerous linguistically informed resources to aid exegetes, there is still a woeful lack of their use, even in works that represent themselves as concerned with matters of language and linguistics. It is difficult to explain why this is so. One reason may simply be normal human lethargy or stubbornness that results in resistance to anything new or different. A further reason may be fear that new methods may threaten traditional or agreed-upon theological conclusions. Another may be the perceived difficulty of understanding a new technical vocabulary—as if traditional biblical studies did not have plenty of its own technical vocabulary already. A last might even be the perception that some of the treatments of topics do not introduce provocatively new insights, but only repackage previous understandings.

It is in tribute to Don's important teaching and research in these areas, and with the wish that the model that he has demonstrated will be continued by others, that I offer this essay as a further contribution to the fields of Greek linguistics and lexicography. I will treat Greek lexicography first, challenging some of the assumptions of traditional New Testament lexicography and making some new proposals, and

---

[2]Cambridge: Cambridge University Press, 1968.
[3]Stanley E. Porter, "The Adjectival Attributive Genitive in the New Testament: A Grammatical Study," *TrinJ* n.s. 4 (1983): 3–17.
[4]D. A. Carson, *Exegetical Fallacies*, 2nd ed. (Grand Rapids: Baker, 1996); Carson, *Greek Accents: A Student's Manual* (Grand Rapids: Baker, 1985).
[5]Stanley E. Porter and D. A. Carson, eds., *Biblical Greek Language and Linguistics: Open Questions in Current Research*, SNTG 1, JSNTSup 80 (Sheffield: JSOT, 1993); Porter and Carson, *Discourse Analysis and Other Topics in Biblical Greek*, SNTG 2, JSNTSup 113 (Sheffield: JSOT, 1995); Porter and Carson, *Linguistics and the New Testament: Critical Junctures*, SNTG 5, JSNTSup 168 (Sheffield: Sheffield Academic Press, 1999).

GREEK LINGUISTICS AND LEXICOGRAPHY

then examine the issue of Greek linguistics, proposing a new approach and assessing some recent trends.

Greek Lexicography

The field of New Testament lexicography has undergone only moderate development over the last fifty years or so, so that it is fair to say that most New Testament lexicography continues to refine the methods of traditional lexicography.[6] I will first survey the major works in Greek lexicography and then explore some new approaches.

The State of New Testament Greek Lexicography

The most widely used lexicon in New Testament study continues to be the various revisions of the one by Walter Bauer, recently revised in English by the New Testament scholar Frederick Danker.[7] There have no doubt been a number of significant improvements introduced into this lexicon by Danker, who was well suited to the task on the basis of his knowledge of German and his having worked with earlier English revisers of the lexicon. These improvements include revisiting the meanings and analyses of many of the words, a useful theoretical distinction between a meaning and a gloss resulting in added translational meanings, and a more logically ascertainable differentiation of meaning categories, among others.

However, there are still a number of readily obvious shortcomings of such a lexicon—besides individual instances where competent scholars would disagree on the specific gloss or translation of a given lexical item. One of these shortcomings is its continuation of the approach of traditional lexicography in its clear dependence upon previous lexicons, rather than beginning anew with lexical and syntactical information, in its analyses and formulations of meanings, a point that John Lee has so well documented in his study of lexicography.[8] Another is the confusion of categories within any given entry. Sometimes these entries are sense oriented, and other times reference oriented (θάλασσα); sometimes

---

[6] I will assume the information found in Stanley E. Porter, *Studies in the Greek New Testament: Theory and Practice*, SBG 6 (New York: Lang, 1996), 49–74, on lexicography.

[7] Walter Bauer, *A Greek-English Lexicon of the New Testament and Other Early Christian Literature*, 3rd ed., rev. and ed. Frederick William Danker (Chicago: University of Chicago Press, 2000); cf. Frederick William Danker, *Lexical Evolution and Linguistic Hazard* (privately printed, 1999). For a critique, see John A. L. Lee, *A History of New Testament Lexicography*, SBG 8 (New York: Lang, 2003), 166–70.

[8] See Lee, *History*, 139–51.

21

they reflect different submeanings of a single meaning (ἀνακύπτω), and other times different distinct meanings (polysemy) (ἀναλύω); sometimes they mix categories by introducing syntactical information for some entries (ἐναντίον), but not all. A third shortcoming is the organization of the lexicon alphabetically by lexical item, which isolates each individual lexical item. Some of these problems are more readily addressable than others, but the fundamental problem, it seems to me, revolves around the meaning of meaning. What does it mean for a word to mean in the Bauer-Danker lexicon? Are we differentiating sense and reference (or denotation and connotation in some parlance), or glosses and translations? What is the relationship between lexical meaning and syntactical meaning? How do we organize meaning in the most useful way? These are not easy questions to answer, though there have been various attempts in lexicography, New Testament lexicography included, to address them.

There have been two major attempts to address many of the shortcomings of traditional lexicography as found in a lexicon such as Bauer-Danker. I will treat each of these briefly. One of the major attempts to address the shortcomings of a traditional lexicon such as Bauer-Danker has been the semantic-domain lexicon produced by the classicist and text-linguist Johannes Louw and the linguist and translation theorist Eugene Nida.[9] There are many noticeable and noteworthy features of the semantic-domain lexicon. These include its organization by what are called semantic domains. These domains represent the semantic fields or meaningful groupings of items and concepts by which the lexical stock of the Greek of the New Testament is organized. Based on previous lexicography, Louw-Nida determined that there were ninety-three such domains in the Greek of the New Testament. Thus, rather than the lexicon being organized alphabetically, lexical items are placed within one or more domains, and meanings are provided for these lexemes, often with accompanying semantic and syntactical differentiations. The Louw-Nida lexicon represents a significant advance, not only in New Testament lexicography but in lexicography in general, as it is the first semantic-field dictionary completed for any language or dialect. Purportedly prepared to aid translators, who would

---

[9]Johannes P. Louw and Eugene A. Nida, *Greek-English Lexicon of the New Testament Based on Semantic Domains*, 2 vols. (New York: United Bible Societies, 1988); cf. Eugene A. Nida and Johannes P. Louw, *Lexical Semantics of the Greek New Testament*, SBLRBS 25 (Atlanta: Scholars Press, 1992). For critique, see Lee, *History*, 155–66.

be in particular need of translational tools designed to illustrate the semantic relations of different lexical items to aid in understanding and translating a given source language into a receptor language, the lexicon by virtue of its theoretical and organizational principles has potential to aid any student of the Greek text.

The question of whether the Greek of the New Testament constitutes a language or dialect, however, raises a number of further questions regarding the lexicon. Some have questioned the apparent dependence of the lexicon upon previous traditional lexicography for its meanings. Others have wondered about the basis of the establishment and population of the semantic fields, and whether these were established on the basis of ancient Greek categories or modern conceptual understandings. The question of appropriate taxonomies continues to be an item of debate regarding semantic-field theory. Some have called into question the categorization of various lexical items. This includes questioning both the placement of a given lexical item within a given category, and instances where words are given two or more distinct senses and hence placed in more than one category, and whether this constitutes polysemy or instances of homographs. Finally, there is criticism that the lexicon is limited in the scope of its completeness so that only a relatively small selection of examples is apparently used to arrive at the major semantic distinctions. Some of these criticisms—especially the one related to the basis of the semantic domains—are of significance and need to be addressed. Nevertheless, the Louw-Nida lexicon remains a significant advance in lexicography of the New Testament.

The second major effort to address the deficiencies of traditional lexicography, especially as found in Bauer-Danker, is the Spanish New Testament lexicon by the classicists and New Testament scholars Juan Mateos and Jesús Peláez.[10] This lexicon is still in development, but makes some major steps forward in lexicography. In a recent paper presented by the current editor of the lexicon, Professor Pelaez describes the approach of the lexicon in terms of the following four features:

---

[10]Juan Mateos and Jesús Peláez, *Diccionario Griego-Español del Nuevo Testamento*, 3 vols. to date (Córdoba: Ediciones El Almendro, Fundación Épsilon, and Cátedra de Filología Griega Universidad de Córdoba, 2000–); cf. Mateos, *Metodo de analisis semantico aplicado al Griego del Nuevo Testamento* (Córdoba: Ediciones El Almendro, 1989); Jesús Peláez, *Metodologia del diccionario Griego-Español del Nuevo Testamento*, Estudios de Filología Neotestamentaria 6 (Córdoba: Ediciones El Almendro, Fundación Épsilon, 1996).

> Systematic distinction between meaning and translation when drafting each entry: "Inclusion in each entry of the lexeme's definition and the corresponding senses or sememes"; "Indication of contextual factor or factors that influence the lexeme's change in meaning"; and "Verification of all the contexts in which the lexeme appears within the New Testament *corpus*."[11]

There is much to be applauded in this lexicon, because it attempts to bring rigor to the lexicographical process by defining various semantic case roles and then applying them to the valency structure of the various lexemes.[12] In this way, the analysis is very similar to the recently developed construction grammar of Charles Fillmore applied by Paul Danove to the Greek of the New Testament. However, there are also a number of shortcomings that have not yet been satisfactorily addressed. One is the question of defining meaning. It appears that once a meaning is determined, then the semantic framework is determined for the individual lexical item, rather than the valency structure determining the meaning. Another is that criteria for differentiating the various semantic case roles are not explicit, and the abbreviated notation system does not provide a means of querying the analysis. A third shortcoming is that meaning beyond the word, in terms of syntax and beyond, is not taken into explicit account, even though it is undoubtedly embedded implicitly in the valency structures proposed.

There have been a number of other works that have attempted to advance lexicography in New Testament studies. These can be categorized in roughly two major categories, one concerned with information retrieval and the other with lexical theory. The first, and one that I will not dwell upon, concerns complete lexical studies of a given lexeme, utilizing the resources of the Thesaurus Linguae Graecae. The TLG, as it is called, developed and presided over for years by Theodore Brunner of the University of California at Irvine, has been a successful attempt to take standard editions of various Greek authors and make them accessible in machine-readable form. There have been other

---

[11] Jesús Peláez, "A New Method of Semantic Analysis, Applied to New Testament Lexicography: Four Basic Premises for the Greek-Spanish New Testament Dictionary" (paper presented at SNTS meeting, Vienna, Austria, Aug. 4–7, 2009), 4.

[12] E.g., Paul L. Danove, *Linguistics and Exegesis in the Gospel of Mark: Applications of a Case Frame Analysis and Lexicon*, SNTG 10, JSNTSup 218 (Sheffield: Sheffield Academic Press, 2001), relying upon Charles J. Fillmore and Paul Kay, *Construction Grammar* (Stanford: Center for the Study of Language and Information, 1999).

attempts to provide similar databases, such as the Perseus Project on the web, but the TLG has been the most complete, with now over sixty million Greek words by authors from Homer to well into the late Byzantine period available in searchable form. This abundance of data, when it first became known in the 1980s, created great expectations regarding the kind of lexicography that could be performed on the Greek New Testament. Usage within the New Testament, for which there had been concordance search capacity for some time, first manually and then electronically, could now be conducted within a larger Greek-language context previously unrealizable except through excruciating and lengthy manual searching. There are a number of limitations to the TLG and most related databases.[13] These include the fact that they are morphologically tagged databases and so must be searched for each morphologically based form. Moreover, besides their individual authors being categorized by literary type, they include no further tagged information, including more advanced morphological categorization, and certainly no syntactical information beyond providing simple strings of words. Even if these limitations could be overcome, there is the problem that these lexical searches do not come with a lexical theory attached. There have been a few studies of the complete usage of given lexical items within the New Testament and the wider Greek language context (and no such search comes with a lexical theory attached),[14] but the abundance of data has no doubt discouraged much further study, to say nothing of limitations in terms of lexical method.

The second stream of investigation encompasses a number of attempts to bring insights of modern linguistics to bear on New Testament semantics and lexicography. Three works merit mention in this regard. The first is the essay on semantics by Anthony Thiselton first published in 1977.[15] This essay appeared in a very important volume that has set the standard for evangelical discussion of the

---

[13]See Matthew Brook O'Donnell, *Corpus Linguistics and the Greek of the New Testament*, NTM 6 (Sheffield: Sheffield Phoenix Press, 2005), 27 et passim.

[14]E.g., James M. Scott, *Adoption as Sons of God: An Exegetical Investigation into the Background of ΥΙΟΘΕΣΙΑ in the Pauline Corpus*, WUNT 2/48 (Tübingen: Mohr Siebeck, 1992); and Stanley E. Porter, Καταλλάσσω *in Ancient Greek Literature, with Reference to the Pauline Writings*, Ediciones de Filología Neotestamentaria 5 (Córdoba: Ediciones El Almendro, 1994).

[15]Anthony C. Thiselton, "Semantics and New Testament Interpretation," in *New Testament Interpretation: Essays on Principles and Methods*, ed. I. Howard Marshall (Grand Rapids: Eerdmans, 1977), 75–104.

issue of biblical interpretation. In his treatment, which is to a large extent predicated upon Ferdinand de Saussure's fundamental distinctions regarding language (e.g., synchrony vs. diachrony, language as structure, conventionality, and langue and parole),[16] Thiselton places his analysis in the context of both James Barr's important work in biblical studies and the work on semantics of John Lyons,[17] as well as drawing upon insights from philosophy. Thiselton lists a number of "false assumptions" that have hindered lexical study. Though most of these are valid criticisms—such as criticizing etymologizing, the search for conventionalized meaning, equation of logical and grammatical structures, that language is referential, the focus on propositions, and the external view of language—there is one that I believe merits further attention: the notion that "the *word, rather than the sentence or speech-act*, constitutes the basic unit of meaning to be investigated" in a lexical study.[18] Thiselton develops this idea by noting that "the meaning of a word depends not on what it is in itself, but on its relation to other words and to other sentences which form its context." However, he immediately qualifies this observation by noting that "words do indeed possess a stable core of meaning without which lexicography would be impossible, and there is also a legitimate place for word-study."[19] When it comes to laying out his view of how lexical study should be done, Thiselton draws upon semantic-field theory, in which the different senses of a word are determined on the basis of similarity, opposition, and various types of inclusiveness. These sense relations include synonymy (whether partial or otherwise), antonymy, converseness, and hyponymy, among others.

The major constructive work in lexical semantics to date in New Testament studies is the volume by Moisés Silva, *Biblical Words and Their Meaning*.[20] The first half of the book is on historical semantics, but the second is on descriptive semantics, where he treats issues of how to describe and determine the meanings of words. Drawing heavily

---

[16]Ferdinand de Saussure, *Course in General Linguistics*, ed. Charles Bally and Albert Sechehaye, trans. Wade Baskin (London: Fontana/Collins, 1960).

[17]John Lyons, *Structural Semantics: An Analysis of Part of the Vocabulary of Plato*, Publications of the Philological Society 20 (Oxford: Blackwell, 1963).

[18]Thiselton, "Semantics," 76, emphasis original.

[19]Ibid., 79.

[20]Moisés Silva, *Biblical Words and Their Meaning: An Introduction to Lexical Semantics*, 2nd ed. (Grand Rapids: Zondervan, 1994 [1983]). Silva's subsequent volume, *God, Language and Scripture* (Grand Rapids: Zondervan, 1990), 86–97, adds little to the discussion.

upon the terminology of Lyons,[21] Silva first admits that "most vocabulary items are linked to a more or less stable semantic core; indeed, without it, communication would be unimaginable."[22] However, he clearly wishes to point out the conventionality of meaning and the failure of denotation as the primary function of lexemes in the vast majority of instances, apart from theological terminology. Instead, Silva believes that lexical meaning "consists largely in the sets of (structural) relations obtaining between the senses of different symbols."[23] He defines these sense relations in some detail, including those based upon similarity (e.g., synonymy and hyponymy) and oppositeness (antonymy and incompatibility). When he turns to determination of meaning, Silva develops the notion of context and in effect takes a contextualist approach to meaning. As he states, "The principle of contextual interpretation is, at least in theory, one of the few universally accepted hermeneutical guidelines."[24] By this, he means that linguists "assign a determinative function to context; that is, the context does not merely help us understand meaning—it virtually makes meaning."[25] He cites Vendryes in support: "Among the diverse meanings a word possesses, the only one that will emerge into consciousness is the one determined by the context. All the others are abolished, extinguished, non-existent. This is true even of words whose significance appears to be firmly established."[26] The same, Silva asserts, is true of words with multiple meanings. He further defines the notion of context in terms of both immediate context and context of situation, inclusive of world knowledge.

Such is the state of play of New Testament Greek lexicography, with standard lexicography being supplemented in a few instances by some more linguistically informed approaches.

New Approaches to New Testament Greek Lexicography

In his recent, thorough study *Meaning in Language*, Cruse defines five approaches to lexical semantics: (1) one-level versus two-level approaches, which is a distinction between a more restrictive, formal

---

[21]Especially John Lyons, *Semantics* (Cambridge: Cambridge University Press, 1977).
[22]Silva, *Biblical Words*, 103.
[23]Ibid., 119.
[24]Ibid., 138.
[25]Ibid., 139.
[26]J. Vendryes, *Language: A Linguistic Introduction to History* (New York: Knopf, 1925), 177, cited in Silva, *Biblical Words*, 139.

semantics and a less formal and more cognitively based encyclopedic knowledge; (2) monosemic versus polysemic approaches, in which monosemy sees a limited number of senses motivating extensions of senses, while polysemy argues that these motivated extensions should be recorded as separate meanings; (3) a componential approach, in which smaller units of meaning are seen to constitute larger units of meaning; (4) holistic approaches, in which the meaning of a word is determined by its relationships with all of the other words in the language; and (5) conceptual approaches, in which the meaning of a word is the concepts that it gives access to within the user's cognitive system, often equated with prototype theory in which members are more or less representative of the category of meaning.[27]

Most New Testament lexicography, in which its lexical semantics is theory-based, rather than simply data-intensive or accumulative, including the work of Louw-Nida and the major theorists, such as Thiselton and Silva, takes what Alan Cruse has called a "holist" approach.[28] Cruse sees Lyons as one of the best representatives of holism. Based upon Saussure's notion of meaning as relational and contrastive, Lyons defines the sense of a lexical item in terms of the complex of sense relations it has within the language in relation to all of the potential lexical items available. It is not surprising, therefore, that, as words enter into a variety of sense relations, there are multiple meanings for individual words, or polysemy, as even a given word will have different sense relations.[29] Bauer-Danker differentiates senses within a given lexical entry, such as ἀγαθός with its two senses, one concerning quality and the other merit. Louw-Nida, with their placement of different words within semantic fields and in different semantic fields, illustrate this holistic approach in a clearly discernible way (see their index). Within a given semantic domain, a word will have various sense relations to the other words within that domain. The same grapheme placed in a different semantic domain illustrates a distinctly different sense, and this word is polysemous. The same type of approach is taken by Thiselton and Silva. However, both Thiselton

---

[27] Alan Cruse, *Meaning in Language: An Introduction to Semantics and Pragmatics*, 2nd ed., OTL (Oxford: Oxford University Press, 2004), 93–98.

[28] Ibid., 96–97.

[29] The notion of polysemy is variously defined. See D. A. Cruse, *Lexical Semantics*, CTL (Cambridge: Cambridge University Press, 1986), 80; William Croft and D. Alan Cruse, *Cognitive Linguistics*, CTL (Cambridge: Cambridge University Press, 2004), 109–40.

and Silva register a significant caveat to their sense-related holistic approach. As quoted above, after stating that words have their meaning in relation to the other words in the language, Thiselton endorses the notion of a stable core of meaning. Similarly, Silva notes that words have a semantic core, otherwise communication would not be possible. Their argument seems to be that a stable semantic core, even if minimal, would be necessary for communication to occur, because the interpreter assumes such a meaning—whether established by convention or otherwise—is necessary as a starting point for interpretation, even if context exerts a further pragmatic shaping force on the core meaning. There is an inherent logic to this approach.

Not all linguists believe, however, that communication would be impossible if words did not have a stable semantic core. Cruse himself admits to taking a highly polysemic view of meaning.[30] In various places throughout his volume, for example, he develops a notion of prototypical meaning. Cruse takes a conceptual view of meaning in which concepts are part of human cognition, organized into what he calls "bundles of stored knowledge."[31] These concepts are linked together, and linguistic forms, such as individual words, activate a concept and the concepts linked to it. Prototype theory enters into Cruse's analysis when it is realized that traditional equations of words and concepts are insufficient to elicit the meanings of any significant number of words. When it is recognized that conceptual categories have fuzzy boundaries and that they are structured hierarchically, a prototype approach begins to make sense. In the prototype approach, using the language of Wittgenstein, there is a "family resemblance" among items.

> The members of a human family typically resemble one another, but there may well not be any set of features that they all possess, and it may be possible to find two members who have no features in common. However, they will be linked by a chain of intermediate members with whom they do share features.[32]

The meanings closest to the prototype have been found to correlate with the order in which such categories are mentioned, their overall

---

[30]Cruse, *Meaning*, 94.
[31]Ibid., 125.
[32]Ibid., 130.

frequency, their order of acquisition, their enhancement of vocabulary learning, those that are verified more quickly, and those for which they are primed by other prototypical words. As a result, Cruse notes that such prototypical semantic categories have what he calls "intuitive unity," but "definitional polyvalence."[33] That is, they are seen to group together, but a single definition cannot be used to capture the meaning. Such categorical definitions have fuzzy boundaries, such that even prototypical members may not have all of the categories of meaning. However, there are a number of evident weaknesses to such an approach to word meanings, such as the lack of recognized category boundaries that make differentiation possible; the problem of saying that words have "degrees of membership" if there are no boundaries to categories and the further problem of inclusion and exclusion if there are such boundaries; and the difficulties of categories that are a combination of two or more basic categories.[34]

A further recent development in lexical semantics is what Cruse calls the "dynamic construal approach."[35] Cruse admits that most approaches to the semantics of words assume that each word has a stable meaning, while recognizing also that the notion of meaning is also highly dependent upon context, and that reconciling the two has proved highly problematic. In response to the question of how communication can occur if there are no stable meanings of words, Cruse notes that the dynamic construal approach holds "not that words have no stable semantic properties, but rather that these properties are not meanings."[36] Dynamic construal contends that individual words do not have individual meanings, but that meanings are what emerge out of a process of construal in which meaning is constructed. Each word does not have a meaning but has a purport, that is, a "body of conceptual content" that is associated with a word.[37] The concept of meaning is reserved not for the meanings of words, but for the result in context from a number of processes of unconscious construal activities. These construal activities are constrained by a number of conventional and contextual factors. Conventional constraints include those imposed

---

[33]Ibid., 131.
[34]Ibid., 134–36.
[35]Ibid., 262–72. For further development of this cognitive lexical model, see Croft and Cruse, *Cognitive Linguistics*, 141–94.
[36]Cruse, *Meaning*, 262.
[37]Ibid.

by society, and contextual constraints are more linguistic in nature, including linguistic, physical, and cognitive context, discourse type, and interpersonal relations. Cruse lists four advantages of this approach: (1) one can abandon the quest for the stable meanings of words, as they do not exist; (2) there is an explanation of the difference between dictionary meanings and experienced meanings; (3) sense relations can be clarified and simplified because of the construal process and constraints of context; and (4) properties that are either context dependent or independent can be accounted for. Nevertheless, as Cruse points out, questions remain regarding dynamic construal analysis, especially in terms of the notions of purport, construal, constraints, and the relation to constraints.[38]

Despite the positive features of these two major proposals, questions still remain regarding their usefulness in lexical semantics, especially in terms of meaning. In Cruse's analysis, there is the residual thought that he is trying too hard to advocate a polysemic view and downplay stable meaning, while at the same time creating strong arguments for it. For example, as he admits in his critique of prototypical meaning, to be useful the theory seems to require that meaningful boundaries be drawn. If they are drawn, then what is circumscribed becomes the core or stable meaning. It is not surprising if there is not contiguity with this boundary for many of the words, as the core or stable meaning does not purport to contain all of the meaning but the invariable core, with other attached meanings being either contextually dependent or connotations. Further, simply renaming lexical meaning as "body of conceptual content" does not make it any less a concept of meaning. One can argue that dynamic construal analysis assumes a strong concept of meaning (semantics) and then focuses upon a different type of meaning, contextual or pragmatic meaning.

As a result, it is worth considering whether the notion of monosemy ought to be revisited in New Testament lexical study. Cruse contends that the "majority view" in contemporary lexical semantics is "probably monosemic."[39] Whether this is true or not, I cannot say,[40] but I am virtually certain that most New Testament scholars who have studied

---

[38]Ibid., 271–72.

[39]Ibid., 94.

[40]I do not believe that Charles Ruhl, who has written the most significant book on monosemy, would think that this is the case (see below).

the issue in any way would not contend that they are monosemic in orientation. However, I believe that monosemy is worth considering as a means of understanding the major persistent issues in New Testament lexicography. I think that one can see monosemy, especially as so ably laid out by Charles Ruhl,[41] as possibly providing a way forward in a number of different issues of pertinence to New Testament study, in particular its lexicography.

In the distinction between semantic maximalists and semantic minimalists, monosemists are minimalists. In other words, whereas maximalists attribute maximal meaning to the word itself, minimalists see only minimal meaning in the word and attribute the rest to pragmatics or to the function or use of language.[42] In that sense, many contextualists, even in biblical studies, are oriented toward monosemy. This is what Ruhl calls the "monosemic bias," that is, "the hypothesis that a form . . . has a single meaning, and that all the complicating factors that make it appear polysemic have their sources in contextual contributions to meaning."[43] Traditional New Testament lexicography, as well as exegesis, has tended to take a maximalist method, in which a great amount of meaning, and in some cases developed theological meaning (i.e., theological lexicography), is attributed to individual words. The minimalist position does not assert a total minimalist semantics, which would mean that a word has no meaning, not even a minimal one, and gains all of its meaning from function, but that words have a minimal meaning, with the rest of the meaning gained from context. Traditional lexicography has struggled to find the balance between semantics and pragmatics. Much New Testament lexicography has traditionally erred toward semantics (maximalists), but much recent theorizing has ambiguously endorsed pragmatics, while retaining a core semantic meaning.

Thus, the study of monosemy, while being a study of the minimalist agenda in lexical meaning, is just as much a study of pragmatics. As Ruhl points out, much meaning that is often analyzed as semantic is actually pragmatic, based on function and use, rather

---

[41]Charles Ruhl, *On Monosemy: A Study in Linguistic Semantics* (New York: State University of New York Press, 1989).

[42]Ibid., vii, citing Roland Posner, "Semantics and Pragmatics of Sentence Connectives in Natural Language," in *The Signifying Animal*, ed. Irmengard Rauch and Gerald F. Carr (Bloomington, IN: Indiana University Press, 1980), 100.

[43]Ruhl, *On Monosemy*, viii.

than semantics. Lexical meaning in such a model is, to use Ruhl's term, "highly abstract," even to the point of being "remote from all ambient contingencies."[44] Thus the typical monosemic word can be said to be indeterminate or unspecified,[45] with its specification and determinateness coming from context of usage. A pertinent example in both Greek and English is prepositions. These function words are often seen to have basic local interpretations that give them concrete and substantial meanings. The argument of monosemy is that their single meaning is more abstract than even the local interpretation, and allows for both concrete local interpretations and other more metaphorical extensions.[46]

Let me take as an example the preposition ἐν.[47] Bauer-Danker offers twelve different senses of the preposition, while the Louw-Nida lexicon offers twenty-one identified meanings, with twenty-two supplementary syntactical identifications. This is quite a mass of meanings for what is identified in linguistic circles as a function or relation word, that is, a word with procedural, functional, and grammatical meaning, but not content or conceptual meaning.[48] A brief analysis of Louw-Nida's treatment helps us understand the use of this preposition. Virtually all of the supplementary syntactical identifications are found in semantic domains other than the ones in which the prepositions are usually classified (i.e., §89 and §90). This indicates that, at the least, it is the words in the other domains in syntactical configuration with the preposition that result in its supplementary meanings. The same applies to several of the identified meanings. The rest are in domains for spatial relations (§83), spatial extensions (§84), relations (§89), and case (§90)—all of which indicate some type of spatial or relational sense in a specified situation. Bauer-Danker offers insight into this situation before listing its twelve senses:

---

[44]Ibid., ix.

[45]Ibid., xi, citing Max Bierwisch, "Basic Issues in the Development of Word Meaning," in *The Child's Construction of Language*, ed. Werner Deutsch (New York: Academic Press, 1981), 347ff.

[46]Ruhl, *On Monosemy*, xiii–xiv.

[47]What follows is directly dependent upon several paragraphs in Stanley E. Porter, "Mark and Matthew: The Contribution of Recent Linguistic Thought," in *Mark and Matthew, Texts and Contexts I: Understanding the First Gospels in Their First Century Contexts*, ed. Eve-Marie Becker and Anders Runesson, WUNT (Tübingen: Mohr Siebeck, forthcoming).

[48]See Stephanie L. Black, *Sentence Conjunctions in the Gospel of Matthew: καί, δέ, τότε, γάρ, οὖν and Asyndeton in Narrative Discourse*, SNTG 9, JSNTSup 216 (Sheffield: Sheffield Academic Press, 2002), 43–54.

The uses of this prep. are so many and various, and oft. so easily
confused, that a strictly systematic treatment is impossible. It must
suffice to list the main categories, which will help establish the usage
in individual cases. The earliest auditors/readers, not being inconve-
nienced by grammatical and lexical debates, would readily absorb
the context and experience little difficulty.[49]

What Bauer-Danker states explicitly, and Louw-Nida exemplifies
throughout, is that the senses of the preposition are not in fact dif-
ferentiated on the basis of semantic distinctions. In all of the cases,
the differentiation is in terms of pragmatic and contextual usage. The
supplementary examples of Louw-Nida clearly indicate this, as do the
distinctions made within the spatial and other relational and case-
related categories. Bauer-Danker explicitly states that it is the "uses"
of the preposition that are many, not necessarily its senses, despite
their twelve categories. The original readers, the lexicon states, would
have been able to differentiate how the preposition was being used
with "little difficulty" on the basis of "context."

One can see how the "monosemic bias" would have an effect on
lexical semantics. As Ruhl indicates, the "monosemic bias" consists
of two major hypotheses: that a "word has a single meaning," and
that if "a word has more than one meaning, its meanings are related
by general rules."[50] Ruhl notes that Stephen Ullmann posited three
categories of meaning: shifts in application, where a word is applied
in different contexts; polysemy, with several senses of a given word;
and homonymy, where one set of sounds is two or more words.[51] Ruhl
labels all of these as "multiplicity," a continuum of categories Ruhl
believes can be explained through monosemy.

An example is the use of the word δικαιοσύνη. This word appears
seven times in Matthew and well over fifty in Paul's letters. Bauer-
Danker differentiates three senses of the word: (1) "the quality, state,
or practice of judicial responsibility w. focus on fairness"; (2) "quality
or state of juridical correctness with focus on redemptive action"; and
(3) "the quality or characteristic of upright behavior." Louw-Nida
offers a similar differentiation of four senses of the word: 88.13: "the
act of doing what God requires—'righteousness, doing what God

---

[49]Bauer-Danker, *Greek-English Lexicon*, 326.
[50]Ruhl, *On Monosemy*, 4.
[51]Ibid., 3, citing Stephen Ullmann, *The Principles of Semantics* (Oxford: Blackwell, 1957), 114.

requires, doing what is right'"; 34.46: "to cause someone to be in a proper or right relation with someone else—'to put right with, to cause to be in a right relationship with'"; 53.4: "observances or practices required by one's religion—'religious observances, religious require-ments'"; and 57.111: "charity." If we were to take a monosemic bias toward the meaning of δικαιοσύνη, we would, I think, be able to reduce this complexity significantly. Notable is the fact that, in both lexicons, the distinctions are made on the basis of pragmatic usage in context. Bauer-Danker identifies its second category in terms of a "focus on redemptive action," that is, contexts in which such action can be identified. Louw-Nida's fourth definition—charity—is clearly based on a specific context as found in Matthew 6:1 (although they admit that this could be an instance of the third category, 53.4), in which they see a metaphorical modulation (metonymy).

The specific contexts are the ones that give these specific meanings to what otherwise is the singular sense of the word. When the specifi-cally contextual factors are removed, the monosemous sense of right behavior, doing what is right, and the like, is what is left, a sense that can be modulated in the several different pragmatic contexts. For Matthew, such a context might include right behavior in terms of the expectations of formalized religion, while in a Pauline context such behavior might involve some type of redemptive or salvific action. The word itself is the same, but the pragmatic context in which it is used modulates the meaning from the more abstract to the specific contextual sense.

What these two examples illustrate is what Ruhl calls "modular-ity" and "systematicity." Modularity recognizes that what are often identified as

> solely lexical senses are actually complexes of a word's inherent content and contextual inference. What appears to be a number of separate senses, possibly highly different and unrelatable, can better be analyzed as a single general lexical meaning that can be variously "modulated" by a range of specific interpretations.[52]

Thiselton in his article uses the Greek noun πνεῦμα as an example of a word with what he appears to identify as eight different meanings. These eight are arranged under four types of agencies.[53] The monosemic

---

[52]Ruhl, *On Monosemy*, 6.
[53]Thiselton, "Semantics," 91.

bias would claim that there is one abstract notion of "wind" modulated in various contexts, so as to be a natural wind, or the human wind (breath), or internal wind (spirit), the wind of God (Spirit), and the like. One of the reasons that the word πνεῦμα has proved difficult in lexicography is that there has been a clear tendency to maximize its semantics by positing "spirit" as its core meaning, rather than relying upon function in context, or pragmatics, to determine its contextual meaning.

Systematicity is related to modularity. Ruhl defines systematicity as occurring along a continuum whereby on one end there is weak systematicity or modularity in which there are a number of related elements. Strong systematicity or mutuality occurs when the elements determine each other, so that change for one alters the others.[54] An example is the verb ἔχω. This verb is given eleven senses in Bauer-Danker's lexicon. These include various types of physical, emotional, and intellectual holding. The monosemic bias would indicate that the minimal semantics of the verb is concerned with holding on to some thing, person, or idea. The verb is the same in all of the Greek clauses, but it is the collocations and syntax that affect the nature and type of holding and its object. The verb exhibits fairly strong mutuality because it is used in a set of relations that are mutually defining in their completeness. As Ruhl points out, systematicity is an important concept when considering interlingual translation, because one of the purposes of translation is to attempt to capture not only the same balance in the target language between semantics and pragmatics as is found in the source language, but also the same systematicity, especially in systems of mutuality.[55] In this regard, English translation of most pragmatic uses of ἔχω with "have" is translationally deficient, because it does not capture this systematicity.

The above treatment at this point must remain a sketch of various practices, proposals, and possibilities. Much New Testament lexicography has been content to continue to repeat previous practices, when there are new, alternative lexicographical approaches that merit further examination. I believe that the concept of lexical monosemy may provide a useful and productive step forward as a means of preserving the integrity of the notion of lexical stability, while providing for the

---

[54]Ruhl, *On Monosemy*, 8.
[55]Ibid., 9.

widest pragmatic, functional contextual meaning. Further investigation is required to test this hypothesis.

Greek Linguistics
Recent Developments in Greek Linguistics
In 1989, I published an article in which I advocated studying ancient languages, the Greek of the New Testament in particular, from a modern linguistic perspective.[56] In that essay, I attempted three tasks. The first was to offer a definition of language and linguistics, and to identify four underlying principles of modern linguistics: that it is empirically based and explicit, that it is systematic in method and concerned for language structure, that it emphasizes synchrony over diachrony, and that it is descriptive, rather than prescriptive. These form the foundations of a linguistic approach to language. For the second task, I questioned whether linguists can agree on anything in light of the various linguistic models that are being practiced. I found that, rather than there being no consensus, linguists are agreed on a number of common assumptions concerning an empirical approach to language, the fact that language is individual and communal, and the importance of structure in language. These assumptions were designed, among other things, to show that linguistics is more about ways of examining language than about reaching certain conclusions. The third task was to distinguish modern linguistics from potentially competing or confusing alternatives, among which are traditional grammar and the ability to translate. My conclusion was not that there is only one modern linguistic approach, but that the various recognized linguistic approaches have common features that merit their consideration in the study of the Greek of the New Testament.

Since the writing of that article (though clearly not simply because of it), there have been mixed responses to taking a linguistic approach to the study of the Greek New Testament. One of those responses is, apparently, to ignore such research, and continue to publish articles, monographs, and even commentaries on the Greek text without showing any significant knowledge of linguistically informed methods or results that might have bearing on such research. I have come across

---

[56]Stanley E. Porter, "Studying Ancient Languages from a Modern Linguistic Perspective: Essential Terms and Terminology," *FilNeot* 2 (1989): 147–72.

far too many articles and sections of monographs that deal with such issues as syntax, lexis, and other linguistic elements where there is no reference to anything more recent than Blass-Debrunner's Greek grammar—hardly a linguistically current piece of research. There are several commentary series that purport to be concerned with the language of the Greek New Testament—some even linguistically oriented—that do little better in drawing upon the available linguistic resources. Authors in such series compromise the quality of their research and the significance of their findings by not utilizing such resources. No doubt in some instances the lack of attention is due to ignorance of the accessible linguistic resources. This is where their editors have a major role to play. Editors of journals or series that do not insist on their authors at least examining such work not only publish material that does not meet the highest academic standards available, but may well also be compromising the purported purposes of the very series they edit.

I think that New Testament scholarship as a whole has benefited greatly, however, from those scholars who have taken time to address questions of importance in New Testament studies by utilizing a variety of linguistic models. A major journal, *Filología neotestamentaria*, often and regularly includes linguistically informed articles, along with others on matters of Greek language. In terms of wider scholarship (I do not pretend to be complete here in my survey),[57] there have been insights gained into nominalized complementation and levels of constituent structure using forms of Chomskyan generative grammar, the case systems and case syntax using the insights of Charles Fillmore's case grammar and construction grammar, and the utilization of corpus linguistics modified to suit the finite corpus of the New Testament and Hellenistic Greek.[58] The three areas where there has been the greatest amount of linguistically informed

---

[57]I have surveyed such research on other occasions. See Stanley E. Porter, "Greek Grammar and Syntax," in *The Face of New Testament Studies: A Survey of Recent Research*, ed. Scot McKnight and Grant R. Osborne (Grand Rapids: Baker, 2004), 76–103; Stanley E. Porter and Andrew W. Pitts, "New Testament Greek Language and Linguistics in Recent Research," *CBR* 6, no. 2 (2008): 214–55.

[58]Representative work includes Daryl D. Schmidt, *Hellenistic Greek Grammar and Noam Chomsky*, SBLDS 62 (Atlanta: Scholars Press, 1981); Micheal W. Palmer, *Levels of Constituent Structure in New Testament Greek*, SBG 4 (New York: Lang, 1995); Simon S. M. Wong, *A Classification of Semantic Case-Relations in the Pauline Epistles*, SBT 9 (New York: Lang, 1997); Danove, *Linguistics and Exegesis*; O'Donnell, *Corpus Linguistics*.

research have been the fields of verbal aspect, discourse analysis, and translational theory.

Study of verbal aspect has not been dominated by any single linguistic model, though most of the research is, if not always linguistically astute, at least attempting to be language sensitive. However, the most linguistically informed work in the area has continued to provide constructive insights into the nature of the Greek verbal network. The forming consensus is that verbal aspect is the fundamental semantic category of tense-form usage. Even though there continue to be divergent opinions over temporality, the semantics of the future form, and the aspect of the perfect tense form, the fact that research continues to advance understanding attests to the usefulness of modern linguistics for gaining insight into ancient languages (see discussion below).

Discourse analysis draws upon a number of different linguistic models, although recent work in Hallidayan-based systemic-functional grammar and various methods being utilized by the Summer Institute of Linguistics appear to be the most productive of late.[59] Both continue to develop analyses of the various discourses of the New Testament, adding insights into their conceptual and grammatical structure. There has also been the development of eclectic methods that draw upon various elements of linguistics while also involving other areas of New Testament research, such as literary study.

Lastly, the area of Bible translation has shown a number of signs of new theoretical development, as the dynamic-equivalence model of Eugene Nida gives way to discussion of a number of other translational methods. These methods range over the various levels of language usage, from the clause complex to the contexts of situation and culture. Relevance theory is one such method that appears to have been embraced by a number of active translators, especially in the various Bible societies.[60]

In light of these recent and significant developments, I find it difficult to understand why there still remain interpreters who not

---

[59]See the survey of research in Stanley E. Porter, "Discourse Analysis and New Testament Studies: An Introductory Survey," in *Discourse Analysis*, ed. Porter and Carson, 14–35, supplemented by Porter and Pitts, "New Testament Greek Language," 235–41, on an eclectic model.

[60]For a survey of such research, see Stanley E. Porter, "Assessing Translation Theory: Beyond Literal and Dynamic Equivalence," in *Translating the New Testament: Text, Translation, Theology*, ed. Stanley E. Porter and Mark J. Boda, McMaster New Testament Studies (Grand Rapids: Eerdmans, 2009), 119–48.

only are ignorant or neglectful of Greek linguistics, but consciously distance themselves from it. I suspect that the few who express their opinions on the subject speak for a far larger number who simply choose to ignore the opportunities that linguistics provides. Daniel Wallace explicitly takes such a position. In his intermediate grammar, *Greek Grammar Beyond the Basics*, a work on Greek syntax, Wallace, without assuming any position on linguistics per se, consciously distances himself from discourse analysis, an area of advancement even before his book was published.[61] Wallace explicitly states that there is no discussion of discourse analysis in his book for four reasons. The first is that "DA is still in its infant stages of development. . . ."[62] The facts are that discourse analysis began to emerge in linguistics from the 1930s to the late 1960s. In view of dissatisfaction with Chomskyan linguistics and increased interest in meaning above the sentence, the year 1968 marks a significant turning point as discourse theories began to affect linguistics. By 1972, new theories of language were being developed, so that in the early 1980s two standard works in discourse analysis still valuable today could be published by Gillian Brown and George Yule, and by Robert de Beaugrande, with many more to follow.[63] Wallace notes that his grammar was begun in 1979 and had reached draft stage by 1982,[64] so it is perhaps understandable why he would have taken his position at that time—but it does not explain why he held the same position in 1996, when the volume was published. In support, he notes in a footnote:

> On a broader level, this [first objection to the use of discourse analysis] is analogous to Robinson's blistering critique, now two decades old, of Noam Chomsky's transformational grammar: "Fashions in linguistics come and go with a rapidity which in itself suggests something suspect about the essential claim of linguistics, that it is a science." . . .[65]

---

[61]Daniel B. Wallace, *Greek Grammar Beyond the Basics: An Exegetical Syntax of the New Testament* (Grand Rapids: Zondervan, 1996), xv.
[62]Ibid.
[63]The short history above is from Robert de Beaugrande, *Text, Discourse, and Process: Toward a Multidisciplinary Science of Texts* (London: Longman, 1980), xi–xiv. See also Gillian Brown and George Yule, *Discourse Analysis*, CTL (Cambridge: Cambridge University Press, 1983).
[64]Wallace, *Greek Grammar*, ix.
[65]Ibid., xv n13, citing Ian Robinson, *The New Grammarians' Funeral: A Critique of Noam Chomsky's Linguistics* (Cambridge: Cambridge University Press, 1975), x.

Nearly thirty-five years later, there is no sign that linguistics and Chomsky and discourse analysis are going away, that they are fads, or that there is a justification for avoiding them.

Wallace's second objection to discourse analysis is that methodologically it tends "not to start from the ground up."[66] Wallace does not seem to understand discourse analysis, as one of the major orientations to discourse study is in fact called "bottom up" processing, in which one begins with the lower-level linguistic phenomena such as syntax.[67]

The third objection is that, according to Wallace, his work is explicitly about syntax and that discourse analysis "by definition only plays at the perimeter of the topic and hence is not to be included."[68] This is an interesting reason for Wallace to use, when he has on the previous page just given the classroom illustration that context means, to quote his hypothetical teacher, "Everything." In fact, syntax, Wallace asserts (in italics), "cannot be understood apart from other features of the language." As discourse analysis includes both context and other features of the language, as well as syntax, it can hardly be excluded as peripheral on such grounds, but is arguably (or should be) central.

The fourth and final objection, a strange one in light of the above, is that discourse analysis "is too significant a topic to receive merely a token treatment, appended as it were to the end of a book on grammar."[69] This comment may have been directed at me, since the chapter I wrote on discourse analysis was the final chapter in my *Idioms of the Greek New Testament*.[70] He instead cites the work of Peter Cotterell and Max Turner and D. A. Black as "full-blown discussion[s]."[71] However, Cotterell and Turner's volume has one chapter on discourse analysis (26 pages, but with the major example of 6 pages from the

---

[66] Wallace, *Greek Grammar*, xv.

[67] Brown and Yule, *Discourse Analysis*, 234–36, and reiterated by many since.

[68] Wallace, *Greek Grammar*, xv. At this point, Wallace includes a footnote from Peter Matthews in which he states that syntax is distinct from stylistics and that he does not believe there is "syntax beyond the sentence" (*Syntax* [Cambridge: Cambridge University Press, 1981], xvix). First, this footnote is not entirely germane to the point Wallace is making and is potentially misleading to readers who might think it constitutes some form of support. Second, one does not have to hold to a theory of "syntax beyond the sentence" to be an advocate of discourse analysis. Many discourse analysts do not hold to such a position.

[69] Wallace, *Greek Grammar*, xv.

[70] Stanley E. Porter, *Idioms of the Greek New Testament*, 2nd ed., BLG 2 (Sheffield: Sheffield Academic Press, 1994), 298–307.

[71] Wallace, *Greek Grammar*, xv.

Old Testament) and one on conversation analysis (35 pages, with a New Testament example).[72] It is not clear whether Wallace means Black's introduction to linguistics for students (with one section on discourse of 3 pages) or his edited volume of fourteen essays by different scholars, none of them a complete treatment of discourse analysis.[73] None of these can be said to qualify as a full-blown treatment. This last argument appears to be special pleading.

In other words, Wallace clearly wishes to avoid discourse analysis, but for unconvincing reasons that do not warrant his lack of treatment. It is hard to know whether it is because Wallace's work was actually written so much earlier than its publication or because of his own linguistic and discourse-analytical limitations. In his recently published doctoral dissertation of 2009, completed in 1995, Wallace notes "three limitations in the *method* of this study. The first has to do with the imperfect state of linguistics—a discipline that is still in a state of flux."[74] I find it interesting that such a statement could be published in 2009. What does Wallace think that the field of linguistics has been doing for the last one hundred years? Whatever flux or tension or scholastic rivalry there may be has not hindered it from continuing to develop and make important observations on language.[75] He further says that, "because of such shifting currents, the approach taken in this work will not be tied to any one school."[76] My difficulty is finding reference to any school of linguistics, to say nothing of being tied to one or more. I suspect that the reason for these statements is found in his next limitation: Wallace admits to "my own lack of formal training in linguistics."[77] Again, Wallace resorts to special pleading to

---

[72]Peter Cotterell and Max Turner, *Linguistics and Biblical Interpretation* (London: SPCK, 1989), 230–56, 257–92.

[73]David Alan Black, *Linguistics for Students of New Testament Greek: A Survey of Basic Concepts and Applications* (Grand Raids: Baker, 1988), 138–41; Black with Katharine Barnwell and Stephen Levinsohn, eds., *Linguistics and New Testament Interpretation: Essays on Discourse Analysis* (Nashville: Broadman & Holman, 1992).

[74]Daniel B. Wallace, *Granville Sharp's Canon and Its Kin: Semantics and Significance*, SBG 14 (New York: Lang, 2009), 18, though he does acknowledge common ground and favorably cites Porter, "Studying Ancient Languages."

[75]There are a number of excellent histories of the development of linguistics, as well as compendia of accumulated thought. See, e.g., Peter Matthews, *Grammatical Theory in the United States from Bloomfield to Chomsky*, CSL 67 (Cambridge: Cambridge University Press, 1993); Geoffrey Sampson, *Schools of Linguistics* (Stanford: Stanford University Press, 1980).

[76]Wallace, *Canon*, 18.

[77]Ibid., 19. Justifying this position by citing his mentor's own admission of lack of linguistic knowledge hardly inspires confidence (Buist Fanning, *Verbal Aspect in New Testament Greek*,

minimize an obvious shortcoming in his treatment of discourse analysis, a discussion he should have avoided from the outset.

There are a number of reasons why a scholar may try to avoid linguistics. These include lack of formal training, lack of genuine curiosity or ambition, fear of the unknown, or, perhaps, fear of what might become known. Many discussions of linguistics assume a fairly sophisticated level of linguistic knowledge. This demand for technical competence has its own potential stultifying effect on linguistically informed research, because it puts an extra burden on the already overtaxed exegete, who has had to master all of the other areas of New Testament study, and who now is asked to master another as well. There is another means of approaching the issue of linguistically responsible Greek study.

What I wish to suggest is that one of the fundamentals that has been lacking in much New Testament language study has been an appropriate linguistic orientation to the Greek of the New Testament. In the development of Chomskyan forms of linguistics, there was a movement from his phrase-structure grammar to his standard theory, which was then expanded and then revised so as to become his revised expanded standard theory. Then later came his principles and parameters, known by others as government and binding. Then came the minimalist program.[78] The constant evolution and development eventuated a move to minimalism. At this point, it became clear to Chomsky that a reorientation was necessary. My purpose here is not to debate the value of his minimalist program, but to suggest that there is warrant for a fundamental reorientation to linguistically informed study of the New Testament along lines that will open up new avenues of thought for exegetes.

A Linguistic Proposal and Some Assessments

Rather than tackle a single specific problem in linguistics, as I have on other occasions, I wish to present an alternative orientation to linguistic problems. What I offer here is not a comprehensive theory of language, or more particularly of discourse or grammar, but a set of minimalist fundamentals for approaching the Greek of the New Testament.

OTM [Oxford: Clarendon, 1990], v–vi).

[78] On the history of Chomskyan linguistics, see Matthews, *Grammatical Theory*, 184–252; and on the minimalist program, Andrew Radford, *Syntactic Theory and the Structure of English: A Minimalist Approach*, CTL (Cambridge: Cambridge University Press, 1997).

Without reference to the internal characteristics of the Chomskyan program, I refer to this as minimalist formalized semantics.[79]

In a linguistic description, the analyst can approach the language from one of three legitimate initiatory vantages: semantics or meaning, hypothetical rules often related to language universals, or formal elements. These choices are not always or entirely exclusive of each other, but one must provide the entry point into analysis of the language system. Many functionalist models of language begin with semantics or extended theories of meaning, while various Chomskyan and derived forms of linguistics begin with hypothetical rules. I believe that the conditions of a "purely epigraphic language,"[80] where there are only (selective) written remains, warrant a formal-elements approach as the initiating step for analysis. "Formal elements" does not simply mean various individual or randomly considered morphemes, words or other units, but a categorical approach, in which formally identified and bounded categories are populated by members organized in systems or paradigms, and hence provide optional choices.[81] In the case of Greek, this often means beginning with inflectional morphology that places various words in one or more paradigmatically determined categories. Thus, a participle in Greek has morphological features of aspect, voice, person, number, and case, and these morphemes systemically indicate its inflectionally based paradigmatic relation to other similar forms. Formalization is the recognition that classes of inflected morphological features are to be grouped together, and that these classes of entities are to be seen as entering into comparative and contrastive relations with other similar classes of entities, and hence providing functionally and meaningfully significant choice. The role of semantics in relation to formalization entails the initial recognition that

[79]The description below is reflected in much of my earlier linguistic research, including (besides works mentioned previously) Stanley E. Porter, *Verbal Aspect in the Greek of the New Testament, with Reference to Tense and Mood*, SBG 1 (New York: Lang, 1989), 1–16; "In Defense of Verbal Aspect," in *Biblical Greek Language*, ed. Porter and Carson, 26–45; and "Aspect Theory and Lexicography," in *Biblical Greek Language and Lexicography: Essays in Honor of Frederick W. Danker*, ed. Bernard A. Taylor et al. (Grand Rapids: Eerdmans, 2004), 207–22, among others. See also Robert M. W. Dixon, *What Is Language? A New Approach to Linguistic Description* (London: Longmans, 1965).
[80]N. E. Collinge, "Some Reflections on Comparative Historical Syntax," *Archivum Linguisticum* 12 (1960): 79–101, here 79.
[81]See Carl Bache, *English Tense and Aspect in Halliday's Systemic Functional Grammar: A Critical Appraisal and an Alternative* (London: Equinox, 2008), 97–100; cf. Bache, *The Study of Aspect, Tense and Action: Towards a Theory of the Semantics of Grammatical Categories* (Frankfurt am Main: Lang, 1995), 49.

these various sets of formal features are to be equated with semantic properties. This is what Collinge has called inner semantics, that is, the code-based semantic features that attach to patterned morphology and provide the basis of outer semantics (or pragmatics).[82] As noted above in the discussion of monosemy and prototypicality for lexis, so with morphologically based formal categories, there is an associated meaning for each member of these sets of forms. Thus, any word in grammatical context will have not only its lexical meaning but also its inflectionally based meaning. The joining of words together into word groups, into simplex clauses, into clause complexes, into subparagraphs, into paragraphs, and then into discourses, encompasses a complex aggregation of formally realized meanings. These encoded meanings are constrained by the levels and types of associations of the various elements as they enter into larger formalized semantic units, until the level of the discourse is reached.

The minimalist agenda I am advocating here—without reference to Chomsky's program—entails that an explanation of a given meaningful element, and consequently of a given larger unit of structure as one moves up the various grammatical levels, always contributes semantic features as warranted by the particular form. In other words, formal categories are not to be multiplied without formal realization, and semantic categories that are propounded by these formal units are not to be multiplied or made more complex than is warranted by their use within the discourse structure. The discourse provides the overall constraint on semantics, as constraint is exercised over each decreasing level of structure. In one sense, this is a model of description, fundamental to both functionalists and others, that takes seriously the notion that form equals meaning and function (where meaning and function are linked). This entails both that there is no difference in meaning or function without a difference in form, and that a change in form indicates a difference in meaning and function.[83] In other words, the formal properties, including morphologically encoded meaning of words, or larger units such as word groups, clauses, and so forth, are constrained by their various semantic and formal features to evince

---

[82]N. E. Collinge, "N. E. Collinge," in *Linguistics in Britain: Personal Histories*, ed. Keith Brown and Vivien Law (Oxford: Blackwells, 2002), 67–77, here 74.
[83]Cf. Trevor Evans, *Verbal Syntax in the Greek Pentateuch: Natural Greek Usage and Hebrew Interference* (Oxford: Clarendon, 2001), 41, who recognizes the principle, but stumbles on an example that shows the importance of paradigmatic categories.

a singular, even if increasingly complex, meaning within the larger discourse. Translations are indicators of how these various features are construed and understood.

Let me illustrate how such a perspective might provide insight into the Greek of the New Testament. I will use two basic examples as test cases, one regarding verbal aspect and the other regarding case. In these instances, I assess two presentations of features of Greek, evaluating them against the minimalist formalized semantic model proposed above.

The Greek Perfect Tense Form

The Greek perfect tense form has generated interest in recent scholarly discussion. In my work on verbal aspect,[84] following the work of Ken McKay and Johannes Louw at that point,[85] I defined the perfect tense form as grammaticalizing stative aspect, within the tripartite aspectual system of Greek (the others being perfective and imperfective aspect). Buist Fanning, in his study that soon followed, argued that the perfect tense form was a type of perfective aspect.[86] The question regarding the perfect has recently been revived in the monograph of Constantine Campbell, who claims that the perfect tense form grammaticalizes two major semantic features: heightened proximity and imperfective aspect.[87] As we shall see, the questionable method by which he arrives at this conclusion necessitates calling into question this conclusion, as well as his entire linguistic program.

In the first of five stages of his argument, Campbell inverts the minimalist formalized semantic method by utilizing his own competing translations as the method by which definitions of aspect are evaluated. As Henry Gleason pointed out years ago, "Translation is a very inadequate means of expressing meanings and must always be used with great caution."[88] Translation should reflect meaning,

---

[84]Porter, *Verbal Aspect*, 245–90.

[85]K. L. McKay, *Greek Grammar for Students: A Concise Grammar of Classical Attic with Special Reference to Aspect in the Verb* (Canberra: Australian National University, 1974), 136–48; cf. now McKay, *A New Syntax of the Verb in New Testament Greek: An Aspectual Approach*, SBG 5 (New York: Lang, 1994), 31–34; and J. P. Louw, "Die semantiese waarde van die perfektum in hellenistiese grieks," *Acta Classica* 10 (1967): 23–32.

[86]Fanning, *Verbal Aspect*, 290–305.

[87]Constantine R. Campbell, *Verbal Aspect, the Indicative Mood, and Narrative: Soundings in the Greek of the New Testament*, SBG 13 (New York: Lang, 2007), 161–211 (hereafter *Verbal Aspect 1*).

[88]Henry A. Gleason Jr., *An Introduction to Descriptive Linguistics*, rev. ed. (New York: Holt, Rinehart and Winston, 1961), 77. In many ways, the situation comes down to trusting one

not determine it, and should come after the meaning is decided, not before it. In any case, Campbell first separates and then concentrates on the definitions of McKay and Louw/Porter.[89] Concerning McKay, many of Campbell's explanations verge on special pleading (e.g., John 1:18, 41), as if he almost intends to ridicule possible explanations. Further, these explanations often reflect a failure to understand the aspectual explanation being offered. For example, in his explanation of John 7:22, Campbell confuses aspect and reality by failing to note that McKay's emphasis is upon the state of the subject as a semantic characterization, not on the subject as morally responsible agent. Campbell evaluates the Louw/Porter viewpoint on a similar basis. Within the first stage of his argument, his four specific criticisms of this viewpoint reveal his linguistic difficulties.[90] His first criticism is grounded simply on the ability to render particular examples in ways that are convincing to him. As noted above, translation is meant to be a reflection of understanding, but Campbell uses it as a determiner of meaning. Campbell claims to be using an inductive method of analysis,[91] failing to note that one needs a hypothesis against which to evaluate data, that is, an abductive method,[92] although I must admit that Campbell's apparent induction seems to betray that he already has a viewpoint firmly in mind.

Second, Campbell claims that the Louw/Porter view is similar to that of the resultative perfect, because it emphasizes a state of affairs. Even if Campbell's characterization of the Louw/Porter view were correct (although he seems to have confused it for his own purposes), this conclusion would not follow. The resultative perfect—which I argue against at length[93]—transfers the emphasis of the action directly to

---

over the other. On the challenge of translation in aspectual studies, see Renate Rathmayr, *Die perfektive Präsensform im Russischen: Eine multilateral-kontrastive Funktionsanalyse der russischen Form anhand ihrer französischen und deutschen Entsprechungen*, OAW 310/1 (Vienna: Austrian Academy of Sciences, 1976), 33–35.

[89]I question whether Campbell has interpreted the differences between the two proposals sufficiently well, but I leave that aside for now.

[90]Campbell begins enumeration at three, so it is difficult to follow his argument (*Verbal Aspect* 1, 170–74).

[91]Ibid., 29–30, and elsewhere.

[92]Charles Peirce, *Philosophical Writings of Peirce*, ed. Justus Buchler (New York: Dover, 1955), 151–56, on induction and abduction. I wish to thank my doctoral student, Francis Pang, for encouraging me to think of Peirce's category of abduction through our discussion of the future form.

[93]Porter, *Verbal Aspect*, 273–81.

the verbal object, whereas the state of affairs is the one created by the semantics of the verb, regardless of whether it takes an object.

Third, Campbell claims that "perhaps most seriously, stativity is regarded by most linguists as an *Aktionsart* value rather than an aspect."[94] It is difficult to know whether Campbell can be taken seriously at this point, when he himself adopts categories that are not widely held by others (see below on heightened proximity and remoteness). Besides that fact, linguistics is not done by popular vote, and, in any case, the consensus that he claims simply is not to be found. Those Greek linguists who have endorsed the notion of stative aspect (or equivalent, such as state) include at least Pierre Chantraine (with some reservations), Paul Friedrich, McKay, Louw, Porter, Rodney Decker, Paula Lorente Fernandez, and Toshikazu Foley, among others.[95] Those general linguists who also do so include T. F. Mitchell and Shahir El-Hassan, Laura Michaelis, Henk Verkuyl, and James Clackson, among others.[96] The label "stative aspect" is an understandable one for those analyzing Greek, a language that morphologically encodes, as Clackson so clearly states, three major morphologically based aspectual distinctions (excluding the future form from discussion), including the perfect and pluperfect forms.[97] I also think that

---

[94]Campbell, *Verbal Aspect* 1, 172. Cf. Porter, *Verbal Aspect*, 259, where I recognize that usage of the notion of "stative" by some is lexical.

[95]Besides those mentioned elsewhere, see Pierre Chantraine, *Histoire du parfait grec* (Paris: Champion, 1927), 4 et passim; Paul Friedrich, "On Aspect Theory and Homeric Aspect," *International Journal of American Linguistics*, Memoir 28, 40 (1974): S1–S44; Rodney J. Decker, *Temporal Deixis of the Greek Verb in the Gospel of Mark with Reference to Verbal Aspect*, SBG 10 (New York: Lang, 2001); Paula Lorente Fernandez, *L'aspect verbal en grec ancien: Le choix des thèmes verbaux chez Isocrate* (Louvain-la-Neuve: Peeters, 2003); Toshikazu S. Foley, *Biblical Translation in Chinese and Greek: Verbal Aspect in Theory and Practice*, Linguistic Biblical Studies 1 (Leiden: Brill, 2009).

[96]T. F. Mitchell and Shahir El-Hassan, *Modality, Mood and Aspect in Spoken Arabic with Special Reference to Egypt and the Levant* (London: Kegan Paul International, 1994), 65, 78–90; Laura A. Michaelis, *Aspectual Grammar and Past-Time Reference* (London: Routledge, 1998), 172–88; Henk J. Verkuyl, *A Theory of Aspectuality: The Interaction between Temporal and Atemporal Structure*, Cambridge Studies in Linguistics 64 (Cambridge: Cambridge University Press, 1993), 11; James Clackson, *Indo-European Linguistics: An Introduction*, CTL (Cambridge: Cambridge University Press, 2007), 119–21.

[97]Cf. Campbell, *Verbal Aspect* 1, 175n53, where early in his discussion he dismisses the form and function equation through several unconvincing arguments: the equation was an assumption of the linguist Georg Curtius (the recognition of the perfect/pluperfect as distinct functional forms within the Greek verbal system goes back to the Greek grammarians themselves; see Porter, *Verbal Aspect*, 18–22) or it was attributable to Slavonic aspect (Old Russian was tri-aspectual, but modern Russian bi-aspectual, so it would appear that if there were influence, it was based upon understandable morphological similarities; see Neil Bermel, *Context and the Lexicon in the Development of Russian Aspect* [Berkeley: University of California Press, 1997]). Campbell

there is some misunderstanding by those, such as Campbell, who write off stativity as merely lexical. Lyons says the following:

> Stativity, then, is lexicalized, rather than grammaticalized, in English. . . . Whether a language grammaticalizes either stativity or progressivity (or both, or neither) is something that cannot be predicted in advance of an empirical investigation of the grammatical and semantic structure of the language.[98]

In other words, as Lyons states, there may well be languages that grammaticalize stative aspect. Linguists who confine themselves to bi-aspectual languages (such as modern Russian), or English translation, may well miss the grammaticalization of other languages, and hence fail to appreciate the aspect system of a language such as Greek. Thus, efforts simply to dismiss stativity are misguided from the start.

Fourth, Campbell uses as a criticism against the stative view that a number of Greek linguists consider the perfect form to grammaticalize perfective aspect. However, it is not clear what force this criticism has, as Campbell himself, following Evans, chooses not to follow the "consensus" in this case, but argues for imperfective aspect (see below). Bernard Comrie, however, addresses both of these errant views: "In Ancient Greek, the morphology of the Perfect precludes combination with the Aorist/Imperfect aspectual distinction, since different stems are used for the three verb forms."[99] In other words, "Alongside its peculiar morphological status, the perfect appears to have been semantically distinct."[100] None of Campbell's arguments in the first stage of his argument is close to definitive or conclusive. By not approaching the language from the standpoint of its paradigmatic categories, Campbell has failed to dislodge the stative view of the perfect as one grounded in the formal features of the language.

The second stage in Campbell's argument is to examine the usage of the perfect tense form in select narrative passages in the New Testament and some extrabiblical authors as a means of positing his own semantic

---

claims that the encoding of the perfect in relation to the present tense form is something other than aspect (though the aorist and present are aspectually distinct)—a conclusion that does not follow, is not convincing, and moves counter-linguistically, as I show.

[98]Lyons, *Semantics*, 706–7.

[99]Bernard Comrie, *Aspect: An Introduction to the Study of Verbal Aspect and Related Problems*, CTL (Cambridge: Cambridge University Press, 1976), 62.

[100]Clackson, *Indo-European Linguistics*, 121.

analysis. Concerning usage, he concludes that the perfect tense form, within the narrative texts that he examines, is overwhelmingly used in discourse. There are three major problems with this analysis. The first is that Campbell has only examined a very limited corpus, even within the New Testament, including the Gospels. The Gospels and Acts only include roughly half of the instances of usage of the perfect tense form in the New Testament (446 of 835 by my count). Thus any conclusion cannot claim to represent the Greek verbal system, at best perhaps only pragmatic usage in narrative, not semantics of the form as part of the Greek verbal system. The second limitation is that he has not examined usage outside of the indicative mood. There are roughly 673 instances of the perfect participle in the New Testament alone, with 348 of these in the Gospels and Acts.[101] The third shortcoming is that he has not sufficiently analyzed the usage in terms of the other indicative forms, especially the aorist and present tense forms. There are 2,917 instances of the present indicative in the Gospels and Acts alone, and 3,375 instances of the aorist indicative. The only conclusion that he can reach is that the perfect indicative is used predominantly in discourse. However, by Campbell's own calculations, the present indicative is used in narrative as well, as is the aorist indicative. It is unclear what this evidence indicates at this stage, but it is limited in terms of corpus, textual type, and mood form.

The third stage of the argument is to determine the aspectual value of the perfect tense form. Here it becomes overwhelmingly clear that Campbell has already decided the case for the perfect, at the expense of both his own purported method and a linguistically informed approach. He states:

> Having rejected stative aspect as a solution to the problem of the semantic qualities of the perfect indicative [see above, where this is questioned], it is necessary to determine which aspect best explains its usage. With two options before us, the perfect will be seen to be either perfective or imperfective in aspect.[102]

---

[101]Campbell, *Verbal Aspect and Non-Indicative Verbs: Further Soundings in the Greek of the New Testament*, SBT 15 (New York: Lang, 2008), 24–29, does not remedy this situation, as his discussion of the participle simply invokes his previous conclusions and then gives examples that show that the participle is not temporally constrained—a conclusion that was reached a hundred years ago and is not widely disputed in Greek studies.

[102]Campbell, *Verbal Aspect* 1, 184.

There are several question marks raised by this last statement. First, why are the aspectual options limited to two? So far as I can read in Campbell's volume, he never justifies there being only two aspects or *these* two. He accepts as uncontroversial that the aorist is perfective and the present/imperfect are imperfective.[103] As noted above in the quotations from Comrie and Clackson, he cannot have decided it on morphological grounds because that would clearly indicate three semantically distinct aspects. It cannot have been decided simply inductively because, as he admits also, the stative interpretation often makes sense,[104] and without a theory it is difficult to know what counts for evidence. So, while this remains unclear, I cannot help but think that Campbell already has his answer in mind on the basis of general linguistic studies of aspect that have concentrated upon bi-aspectual languages such as modern Russian.[105] This is clearly an inadequate basis for determining Greek verbal aspect and flies in the face of a linguistic method such as the minimalist formalized semantics proposed here.

Despite the problems of the inductive method, in the fourth stage of his argument Campbell forges ahead and claims that by being "as inductive as possible" he can determine the aspect of the perfect form.[106] He first analyzes imperfective aspect. The only argument he offers in defense of this conclusion is its use as a "discourse tense-form": "This fact alone immediately aligns the perfect with the present indicative."[107] Campbell claims this on the basis of the distribution of the perfect indicative paralleling that of the present but not the aorist indicative. However, this is not an entirely accurate or meaningful assessment, as Campbell himself admits. He makes a leap to saying that the distribution of the perfect is similar to the present. That is simply not true numerically, proportionately, in terms of density, or in terms of actual usage. Whereas it may be true that the perfect is also found almost exclusively in discourse (he calls it "an *even more exclusive level*"), the distribution is not the same, as there are many more presents than perfects, as well as presents that occur in narrative proper, and possibly even many more aorists in discourse, as well as many

---

[103]Ibid., 35, 103.
[104]Ibid., 184.
[105]Campbell appears to be influenced by his teacher, Trevor Evans (*Verbal Syntax*), who arrives at many similar conclusions for the Greek of the Pentateuch.
[106]Campbell, *Verbal Aspect* 1, 184.
[107]Ibid.

more aorists in the narrative proper, than there are perfects.[108] By his own numerical argument, Campbell should argue for three aspects: the aorist as predominantly found in narrative (but also in discourse), the present found mostly in discourse (but also in narrative), and the perfect found almost entirely in discourse.[109]

Campbell's complications are multiplied when he presents a circular argument to talk about aspect and discourse as a defense of the imperfective aspect of the perfect tense form.

> With the occurrence of discourse, . . . the skeletal framework of the narrative is interrupted and slowed down as the discourse is related. The narrative is slowed down as time is taken to present the content of speech before the eyes of the reader. Since the discourse is unfolded before the reader, it naturally creates an imperfective context.[110]

There are two questionable statements being made here. One is that immediate and present action is slowed down before the eyes. This seems to go against most conceptions of how events unfold before the eye, including Campbell's description of the observer of a parade with the parade immediately in front,[111] and seems to have fallen victim to an overliteral interpretation of what is meant by imperfective aspect. Typically, events that are "remote"[112] are less proximate and active, as Campbell himself admits.[113] Those events that are immediately before the eyes tend to be moving faster as they pass by. Campbell seems, despite his objections to the contrary, to want to read Comrie's definition of the imperfective aspect, in terms of its "internal temporal structure of a situation," into the perfect.[114] Besides the temporal conception that he introduces into his analysis of the imperfective aspect, Campbell also verges on adopting an *Aktionsart* view, in which the action is objectively characterized in terms of its pace. Campbell then strangely defends a stative interpretation of many instances of the perfect tense form, though noting that these are better treated as

---

[108]Ibid., 187.

[109]See Porter, *Verbal Aspect*, 245–46.

[110]Campbell, *Verbal Aspect* 1, 185; cf. 196.

[111]Ibid., 198–99; cf. 50–51. The parade image goes back to the study of Russian. See Porter, *Verbal Aspect*, 91.

[112]To use Campbell's characterization of one of the semantic features of the aorist indicative, as well as the imperfect tense forms.

[113]Campbell, *Verbal Aspect* 1, 50–51.

[114]Comrie, *Aspect*, 24, quoted in ibid., 36, but denied by Campbell.

instances of *Aktionsart*, a notion already questioned above. Besides his own confusion over whether his analysis is *Aktionsart* based or not, if one accepts with Lyons (above) that stativity can at least in theory be grammaticalized in a language, rather than dismissed *a priori*, then this stage of the argument also ends up providing evidence for the stative aspect of the perfect. This section by Campbell can hardly qualify as a robust defense of imperfective aspect for the perfect tense form.

The fifth and final major argument Campbell marshals is to identify the way in which the perfect tense form differs from the present and imperfect tense forms while sharing imperfective aspect. Rejecting tense as an explanation despite his temporal description, Campbell invokes his spatial analysis to claim that the perfect represents "heightened proximity." What he means by this is that "the perfect semantically encodes a higher level of proximity. . . . heightened proximity simply means that this spatial relationship is closer than regular proximity."[115] There are three major issues raised by this discussion. The first is the basis of Campbell's spatial analogy. I can find no place where he justifies its adoption. Lyons makes comments about remoteness and nonremoteness, and equates them with possible temporal values, but he does not extend them to proximity or heightened proximity.[116] Campbell's apparent creation is flawed in its conception and its execution, and therefore does not provide an analogical base for his aspectual system. Second, there is the difficulty of the resulting verbal system that he posits. Without going into detail on the other aspects and their spatial relations, I note that Campbell conceives of the Greek aspect system as consisting of the aorist as perfective aspect, and the present/imperfect and perfect/pluperfect consisting of imperfective aspect, and the future form as temporal.[117] It is hard to see internal or external logic to such a conception (I dare not call it a system) and how it would have functioned. The third and most telling issue, however, and the one that perhaps explains the lack of systemicity to Campbell's aspectual scheme is that he has essentially relegated the most important inductive observation—the presence of the perfect form itself, a distinct form to be distinguished from the present and aorist, and quite possibly nearly

---

[115]Campbell, *Verbal Aspect* 1, 197.

[116]Lyons, *Semantics*, 819–20.

[117]Campbell, *Verbal Aspect* 1, 243. Here is not the place to enter into critique of his entire "system," which is less a system than a set of posited values.

unique to Greek[118]—to an isolated final factor. In other words, after shunning morphological distinction of the perfect tense form throughout his discussion by subsuming it into discussion of the categories of imperfective and perfective aspect at the last stage, Campbell invokes morphological significance to distinguish the semantic feature of the perfect as heightened proximity. What he appears to be saying, at the end of his analysis, regardless of what other words are used to describe and label the forms, is that the perfect tense form is a marked form in relation to the present tense form.[119]

Observant readers will note that, in fact, that is what my systemic analysis of the Greek verbal system, beginning with the formal evidence of the language, concluded from the start. In other words, Campbell has apparently pursued a series of misleading trails simply to arrive at a conclusion that is very similar to the one that I arrived at earlier. The major difference is that I began with morphology and ended with a workable aspectual system in line with a minimalist formalized semantics. Campbell began with problematic notions rather than formal substance, but then finally needed to invoke the formal evidence of the language to arrive at a useful conclusion.

This example well illustrates the importance of taking a clear linguistic approach to the evidence of the Greek New Testament, especially one that begins with formally based categories. Not only has Campbell limited his evidence so that, at best, he has posited individual values for the various tense forms without a clear conception of their systemic interaction, but he has approached the entire topic backwards, ending with what should have been an initial, fundamental morphological distinction. As a result, he has not presented an analysis of the Greek verbal system that is linguistically grounded.

The Greek Genitive Case

The second example that I will examine is the genitive case. In my *Idioms of the Greek New Testament*, I use a tripartite differentiation of case semantics, syntax, and context to describe the fundamental sense of each case and then provide the basis for various uses in context, which I confine to ten.[120] In his exegetical syntax, Wallace identifies

---

[118]See Clackson, *Indo-European Linguistics*, 119–21.
[119]See Porter, *Verbal Aspect*, 109, where my systemic network clearly labels the semantic features of the tense forms.
[120]Porter, *Idioms*, 80–83, 92–97.

thirty-three different uses of the genitive. I believe that, rather than this simply being a matter of numerical difference, the failure to use a formalized semantic method may stand behind such differences in pragmatic application.

In his introduction to the genitive, before describing the thirty-three uses, Wallace offers both preliminary remarks and a section on the definition of the unaffected meaning of the genitive case. By unaffected meaning, he intends the meaning "unaffected by context, genre, lexical intrusions, etc. This is the meaning the gen. would have if it were seen in isolation."[121] His first preliminary remark concerns the relation of the genitive to the English preposition *of*, where he notes that "many of the uses of the Greek genitive are similar to our preposition 'of.'"[122] This is an unfortunate place to start a discussion of the meaning of the Greek genitive case in anticipation of identifying its syntax, because, rather than treating its relationship to the other Greek cases (as one paradigmatic choice within the system), the discussion immediately shifts the understanding to English translation and examples, and the ambiguous preposition *of*.[123] For example, in English one may use the phrases "house of cards," "love of life," "baptism of repentance," "love of God," or "Jesus of Nazareth," each with a different relation indicated by "of." Wallace's example of Romans 8:35 does not help the situation. He says that Paul's statement "Who shall separate us from the love of Christ" clearly indicates in Greek and English that Paul means "the love Christ has for us," not "the love we have for Christ."[124] The statement may mean this, but it is clear that it does not mean this on the basis of just the Greek statement behind the English translation, and certainly not on the basis of the English "of." The phrase could just as easily mean "the love we have for Christ." In this case, "of" does not help at all. Wallace has to import at least a wider context, and perhaps a significant set of theological assumptions, to arrive at his conclusion. Wallace goes further and recognizes that there are uses of the genitive that are not conducive to the "of" translation, but he urges caution in explaining these to others. This strange com-

---

[121]Wallace, *Greek Grammar*, 76n10. Wallace has three preliminary comments, but the third does not concern me here.
[122]Ibid., 73–74. I take it Wallace means that the uses of the Greek genitive are similar to uses of the English preposition "of."
[123]Wallace admits this later, in the second preliminary comment (ibid., 74–75).
[124]Ibid., 74.

ment seems to assume that the English "of" has the same interpretive status as the Greek genitive, when in fact any number of other English renderings may be faithful understandings of the genitive, such as "for" in the example above. This first set of comments does not help us arrive at the "unaffected meaning" of the genitive case because it begins not with Greek but with English, and a very rigid understanding of English at that. Translation is meant to reflect understanding, not to dictate it or, worse yet, hide problematic issues.

Wallace's second preliminary comment concerns the semantics and exegetical significance of the genitive case. He states that "learning the genitive uses well pays big dividends," in that the genitive has "a great deal of exegetical significance . . . because it is capable of a wide variety of interpretations."[125] He identifies three factors that cause this wide variety: elasticity, embedded kernels, and antithetical possibilities. Wallace is here apparently leaving behind semantics of the case and going directly to use. However, he makes a number of questionable linguistic statements along the way. The first is to claim that the "genitive is more elastic than any other case" because it stretches over what are often two cases in other languages. Elasticity is not a semantic value, so far as I know. It appears that Wallace has confused his set of thirty-three uses of the genitive with the meaning of the genitive. He further states that "language, by its nature, is compressed, cryptic, symbolic." His defense of this unwarranted assertion is a section in his "Approach to the Book" that makes the same claim on the basis of several other suppositions. One is that words "in isolation mean next to nothing."[126] I wonder what Wallace does if he ever gives a vocabulary test in Greek? Does putting down nothing next to the word get next to full credit? He notes further that, without context, not only words, but sentences, and even paragraphs, have ambiguities. Wallace has identified an important feature of language use—context— but that does not mean that language itself is compressed, cryptic, or symbolic.[127] There are two factors here. One is that language requires context for interpretation. The second is that Wallace is himself playing on different senses of "meaning." He seems to require a full and

---

[125]Ibid.

[126]Ibid., 7.

[127]Indeed, language is symbolic in the sense that the spoken or written words are not the things in themselves (except when linguists are talking about them), but that is not the sense in which Wallace is using the term.

complete, indisputable and quantifiable meaning before meaning has arrived. Hence he uses the example of entire books of the New Testament being problematic because of various hermeneutical factors, such as distanciation. Only with such a restricted meaning of "meaning" is there the difficulty that Wallace identifies.

I would argue that words have measurable and significant, if not exhaustive, meaning (note above discussion), as certainly does syntax (sentences), and even paragraphs and larger works, if by that we mean interpreters are able to make sense of such utterances in context. The extended meaning (theological, historical, etc.) may well be debatable, but that does not indicate that the various components do not have meaning (even if not inclusive) and does not prevent meaningful communication from taking place. In his discussion of embedded kernels, designed to show the hidden and cryptic nature of language, Wallace notes several English "of" statements that can be interpreted in different ways. He attributes this to "of" covering "a multitude of semantic relationships."[128] "Of" in English can be ambiguous, but that is not the source of the difficulty in the underlying Greek, but a reflection of English rendering that could be otherwise.[129] Wallace's final category, antithetical possibilities, claims that the genitive is particularly dependent upon a study of context, lexis, and other features, but that it can have antithetical meanings (e.g., "faith of Christ"). I am not sure why this statement is included, except to show that we have not yet arrived at a serviceable meaning of the genitive. As with the above comments, this set of questionable linguistic statements is predicated almost entirely on the ability to translate the Greek genitive, especially preserving "of" while recognizing that "of" is insufficient.

Wallace then turns to the definition of the genitive. He first briefly distinguishes the genitive from the accusative and dative cases. He states that both the genitive and accusative cases express "some kind of *limitation*."[130] I am unclear whether this is the "unaffected meaning" that Wallace is talking about or not. If it is, then it is not helpful because both cases have it. There is no argument given as to how one arrives at or is meant to view or understand such a meaning.

---

[128]Wallace, *Greek Grammar*, 75.

[129]Ibid., 75n6, apparently because he refers to "kernels," claims to have "benefited much from Chomsky." A Chomskyan analysis would have been a completely different formulation, so far as I am aware of Chomskyan linguistics. I see no evidence of Chomskyan influence here.

[130]Wallace, *Greek Grammar*, 76.

Wallace, however, goes on to provide two further limitations on the genitive. The genitive "limits as to *quality*," versus quantity for the accusative, and is "usually related to a noun," as opposed to a verb for the accusative.[131] Although Wallace does not define quality, this at least is an attempt at a semantic distinction (although not one that he explains or exemplifies), whereas the second feature is syntactical and not semantic. In his distinction of the genitive from the dative, however, Wallace further confuses the matter when he posits that "the force of the genitive is generally adjectival."[132] He does not say what that means in relation to the genitive being the case that limits as to quality. I must admit to being totally befuddled by such a set of explanations, especially as they are meant to provide the unaffected meaning of the genitive case.

In the next two sections, Wallace discusses the genitive in terms of the eight-case system and the five-case system, a topic he has already treated in his introduction to cases.[133] Here he defines the genitive as being "similar to an adjective, but . . . more emphatic."[134] However, he appears to dismiss the eight-case system for the five-case system, since "the genitive and ablative have the same form ('case' being defined as a matter of form rather than function)."[135] One notes that Wallace introduces the important formal characteristics of the genitive at this point in his argument. However, he then seems to retreat from this observation. As he states, "In some respects, the definition of the genitive case in the five-case system simply combines genitive and ablative from the eight-case system," with the ablative representing separation and rendered with "from."[136] He acknowledges that some linguists have a singular semantic conception of the genitive, but he rejects such an idea as "of greater interest to the philologist (and the field of diachronics) than the exegete."[137] This statement is troubling for two reasons. One is that Wallace claims to be seeking the unaffected meaning of the (unitary) genitive case, and to reject such an interest would seem totally contrary to his stated purpose. The second is that this is clearly not the interest of simply philologists

---

[131]Ibid.
[132]Ibid.
[133]Ibid., 32–34.
[134]Ibid., 76.
[135]Ibid., 77.
[136]Ibid.
[137]Ibid.

or diachronic linguistics, but that of synchronic linguists interested in the semantics of the genitive case, as Wallace should be. One perhaps sees why Wallace has retreated from engagement with the semantics of the genitive when he finally affirms both the "of" and the "from" ideas for the meaning of the genitive. As he states, "the genitive case may be defined as *the case of qualification (or limitation as to kind) and (occasionally) separation.*"[138] Despite his saying that this is a five-case-system definition, this looks like an eight-case-system definition, the first for the genitive and the second for the ablative.[139] In other words, Wallace appears to have abandoned altogether the task of finding an "unaffected meaning" for the genitive case and to have endorsed two definitions based on English translations for two cases, the genitive and the ablative.

Wallace then turns to what he calls the specific uses of the genitive (and ablative?) case—all thirty-three of them. He prefaces the list by noting that they are all important because they are governed by "the principles of *semantic reality* and *exegetical significance.*"[140] We know from the discussion above that they certainly are not based upon semantic reality and therefore must be based upon Wallace's perceived exegetical significance. These are two very different things. The first is appropriate to a syntax, but whether the second deserves to be called Greek syntax is another thing altogether. Because Wallace has failed to define the semantics of the genitive case, there is no semantic control on his categories, and I am surprised he has limited the categories to thirty-three, rather than multiplying them according to various exegetical instances.[141] Wallace is apparently aware of this difficulty, because he bristles at possible objections to his numerous categories on the basis that they are contextually realized and not semantically based. His reason is "because *context* is just as much a part of syntax as morphology or *lexeme.*"[142] Wallace has apparently forgotten his earlier introductory comments where he notes that he is "traveling

---

[138]Ibid.

[139]On the Greek five-case system, with syncretism of the earlier eight-case system, see Clackson, *Indo-European Linguistics*, 90–91.

[140]Wallace, *Greek Grammar*, 78.

[141]In fact, ibid., 78n18, admits that he could have arrived at more than a hundred categories.

[142]Ibid. Here he criticizes my *Idioms* (82), for distinguishing between case, syntax, and context. I would argue that this is exactly the right way to proceed: from case semantics, to syntax, to context. I believe that this is what Wallace claims he intended to do.

in the same direction" with Peter Matthews's statement that "syntax beyond the sentence," that is, context, is "meaningless."[143]

This treatment reveals no real sense of how to approach a linguistic phenomenon such as the genitive case in this treatment. Not only is Wallace ambivalent as to whether the genitive is really one or two cases (genitive and ablative); he fails to recognize the formally important feature of the singular paradigmatic case ending and to build a semantics of the case and cases on that minimal formal basis. Instead, he approaches the topic virtually entirely from the point of English translation, with the result that he fails to arrive at an adequate semantic description of the case, its relationship to the other cases, or even the relation of English translation to the Greek genitive.

For both Campbell and Wallace, the failure to approach the linguistic phenomena of the Greek language from a linguistically informed standpoint seriously hinders their ability to formulate meaningful and consistent, and, most importantly, linguistically grounded, analyses. Both of them put English translation and other factors before recognizing the elements of the language itself, utilizing the formal features of the language within a given category, and explaining the resulting paradigmatic arrangement.

Conclusion
The fields of Greek linguistics and lexicography are areas of continuing importance and interest. There are many avenues open to scholars who wish to pursue such areas further. I believe that the ideal situation would involve thorough linguistic knowledge; however, I also am convinced that a linguistically sound approach to the data can also provide much needed and useful analytical benefit. In this chapter, I have attempted to provide one such means to lexicography by taking seriously the notion that words do have meaning. The field of lexicography is ripe for a radical transformation that recognizes the monosemous nature of words and uses this monosemic bias as a new orientation for creating the next generation of lexicons. I am not entirely sure what such lexicons would look like, but my suspicion is that they would look a lot more like Louw-Nida's than the traditional lexicons that we are accustomed to using. The field of linguis-

---

[143]Wallace, *Greek Grammar*, xv n14, though I note that Wallace does try to include context elsewhere.

tics has already benefited from a number of recent treatments that have advanced knowledge. However, there is a residual tendency to approach the Greek language from a linguistically hindered perspective that rests too much on English translation or on failure to first grasp the semantic significance of meaningful formal categories. In this essay, I have attempted to provide a linguistically informed approach to the Greek of the New Testament, what I have termed a minimalist formalized semantic method. The approach is simple in its conception, elegant in its design, and functional in its conclusions—and helps to reveal where others have gone astray in not utilizing such an approach. What is necessary in further language study is a linguistic approach to linguistic phenomena, one that places semantics before pragmatics and meaning before significance.

2

Hermeneutics and Theological Interpretation

GRANT OSBORNE

Theological interpretation" has become virtually a semi-technical term for a movement that has taken place over the last couple of decades. For most of the twentieth century, it was assumed by critical scholars that exegesis (the aspect of historical meaning) and theology (the aspect of ecclesial significance) were antithetical, the one the job of the academy, the other of the church. Thus the true critical exegete would forego the theological aspect of interpretation and center only on the historical aspect, more often than not centering upon a tradition-critical reworking of the so-called history behind the surface statements of the text while eschewing theology as the church's later rereading of the stories.

More and more, the dichotomy established by this so-called critical consensus has been challenged.

In the Enlightenment/modernist view, critical historical enquiry dealt with "objective facts" (and so was worth pursuing) while "theology" belonged to the more subjective realm of "values" and "beliefs" (and so could be ignored by the academy), which we now realized led to a prison in the biblical past, filled with the clamor of discordant voices.[1]

No more. It is now increasingly recognized that true understanding of Scripture cannot be accomplished without considering the theological dimension, for both Israel and the early church were theological communities, and everything they wrote had a theological core. If one is seeking the meaning of a biblical text, the theological message is actually part of that meaning. Francis Watson calls for a "theological hermeneutic" that can provide a "framework" for exegesis, which he says means to "offer a theological justification for particular hermeneutical decisions."[2]

At the same time, the "theological interpretation" of this school goes one step further, believing that the search for the original "meaning" of the message of the author/text must be replaced or at the least enhanced by a "ruled reading" (see further in the next section) that sees the text in light of the traditional creedal truths that have guided the church. So the purpose of this essay is to develop both an epistemological matrix and a pragmatic set of guidelines for doing theological interpretation. This topic is very fitting in a Festschrift dedicated to D. A. Carson, since he has done so much to bridge the hermeneutical gap between exegesis and theology in our search for truth.

Keith Johnson provides a good summary of the "concerns" of this movement: "(1) a desire to attend to the subject matter of Scripture—namely the triune God; (2) a desire to read Scripture canonically as a coherent dramatic narrative; (3) a desire to read Scripture both within and for the church; and (4) a desire to read Scripture under the guidance of the creeds."[3] This is the approach of several recent works, as in the ongoing Brazos Theological Commentary series, the *Dictionary for Theological Interpretation of the Bible*, and similar publications.[4]

---

[1]Max Turner and Joel B. Green, "New Testament Commentary and Systematic Theology: Strangers or Friends?," in *Between Two Horizons: Spanning New Testament Studies and Systematic Theology*, ed. J. B. Green and M. Turner (Grand Rapids: Eerdmans, 2000), 7.

[2]Francis Watson, *Text, Church, and World: Biblical Interpretation in Theological Perspective* (Grand Rapids: Eerdmans, 1994), 221.

[3]Keith E. Johnson, "Augustine's Trinitarian Reading of John 5: A Model for the Theological Interpretation of Scripture?," *JETS* 52 (2009): 799 (cf. 799–810).

[4]Daniel J. Treier, *Introducing Theological Interpretation of Scripture* (Grand Rapids: Baker, 2008); Stephen F. Fowl, *Engaging Scripture: A Model for Theological Interpretation* (Oxford:

Of course, when we speak of "theology" in this light, we must realize the different levels at which it occurs. At the start, there is the theological underpinning of the actual texts, the delineation of which is one of the tasks of exegesis. Then there are the theological themes traced through a book or an author's corpus (the individual chapters of Old or New Testament theology). These first two take place at the level of "authorial intention" (see more on this below) and constitute the historical "meaning" of Scripture at the theological level. Old or New Testament theology (which together constitute biblical theology) is still a historical discipline, determining the beliefs of Israel and the early church, but it at the same time bridges to historical theology and systematic theology, which go beyond the exegetical task and demand our own correlation of passages and themes derived from exegesis into a current belief system. In fact, as we move from exegetical theology to biblical theology to historical theology to systematic theology, each field in turn builds upon its predecessors. Historical theology traces the models the various theological traditions derived from their study of Scripture and their attempts to put it together in determining a doctrinal system for the different ages and needs of the developing church. Systematic theology uses the results of all three to create a model for our day. Theological interpretation covers all five areas (passage, book, biblical, historical, and systematic theologies) and the issues are immense. There is only space to consider some of the major areas briefly, and the goal is to develop both a hermeneutic and a methodology for the program.

Precritical Interpretation: The Earliest Model

Many advocates of the new approach to theological interpretation argue that the church fathers got it right. In the Rule of Faith (*regula fidei*) and in the fourfold-sense approach of Irenaeus, Tertullian, and Augustine, later dominating the Middle Ages, the early Fathers made theological interpretation possible. The rule was the earliest form of a creed and was essentially Trinitarian in essence, playing a hermeneutical function, assuring "a correct reading of Scripture, indeed a

---

Blackwell, 1998); Fowl, ed., *The Theological Interpretation of Scripture: Classic and Contemporary Readings* (Oxford: Blackwell, 1997). Similar, but not quite using this same approach, is *Between Two Horizons*, ed. Green and Turner, and the Two Horizons series of commentaries that has flowed out of that.

Christological reading."[5] This meant that "Scripture cannot simply interpret Scripture, but the theological traditions of the church are necessary to establish a correct reading,"[6] namely, the theological teachings developed by the church. So the goal of all biblical study is to determine "the mind of Scripture" as found in the unity of the whole Bible supplemented by the traditions of the church. "Without the tradition summed up in the creed and lived in Christian practice, it is impossible to discern aright what Scripture is about."[7]

Robert Wall adds,

> The crucial assumption of this species of theological hermeneutics, which holds that the church's Rule of Faith constrains the theological teaching of a biblical text, is that Scripture's legal address is the church's worshipping community, where biblical interpretation helps to determine what Christians should believe and to enrich their relations with God and neighbor.[8]

Wall is primarily addressing the skeptical hermeneutic of critical scholars in the academy and arguing for the primacy of a church-reading–centered hermeneutic as opposed to the critical approaches of much of modern scholarship.[9] The academy has thereby "dislocated" Scripture from its primary goal of addressing church and world with God's redemptive plan.

Many who belong to this school today believe this method is superior to current approaches of historical-critical or historical-grammatical exegesis. David Steinmetz argues that whenever the meaning of a biblical text is restricted to its original author and situation, it can no longer have relevance for someone living in modern times in a culture vastly different from the biblical situation. Therefore the church fathers were correct to "contemporize" its meaning along the lines of the church's tradition to meet the needs of the church's people.

---

[5]Kathryn Greene-McCreight, "Rule of Faith," in *Dictionary for Theological Interpretation of the Bible*, ed. Kevin J. Vanhoozer (Grand Rapids: Baker, 2005), 703.
[6]Frances M. Young, "Patristic Biblical Interpretation," in *Dictionary for Theological Interpretation*, ed. Vanhoozer, 568–69.
[7]Ibid., 570.
[8]Robert W. Wall, "Reading Our Bible from within Our Traditions: The 'Rule of Faith' in Theological Hermeneutics," in *Between Two Horizons*, ed. Green and Turner, 90.
[9]For a good discussion of the place of the academy in biblical interpretation, see David Lyle Jeffrey and C. Stephen Evans, eds., *The Bible and the University*, Scripture and Hermeneutics (Grand Rapids: Zondervan, 2007).

This calls for preferential place being given to the Rule of Faith and to the medieval fourfold sense (the literal sense, the allegorical or spiritual sense, the tropological or moral sense, and the anagogical or eschatological sense—life in heaven) as the best way to read Scripture.[10] Such a "ruled reading" is preferable because it links us with the earliest approach to Scripture, makes a Spirit-led (rather than a scientific) reading to become central, and meets the needs of the church rather than of a few "informed" scholars. Yet one wonders whether the actual practice of Bible reading needs so radical a move. Once we have derived the meaning of a text (which includes its intended theological message), it is easily contextualized for these diverse situations. There is no need to replace historical interpretation with theological interpretation, for they are one and the same. The Rule of Faith is a perspective, not a hermeneutical axiom to replace exegetical method. But more on this later.

As we will see below, this for some means that the author is being replaced by church dogma as the generator of meaning. This type of "ruled reading" is equated by many with the "plain sense" of the text, seen as the "literal sense" of the church fathers and as superior to the historical sense demanded by historical-critical scholars. "Plain sense can mean anything from the community's reading to the interplay between verbal meaning and ruled reading," with the latter bearing "more fruit for theology and the life of faith."[11] This latter is seen as fully authoritative, because it blends the verbal meaning of the text with the understanding of the church at its earliest period. Actually, this is what we are calling for, namely, an interplay between the verbal meaning (with the original theological message behind the text) and the ruled meaning, that is, what the particular text highlights in the traditional dogma of the church and how it fits into that dogma. The problem is that many in this camp want to *replace* the historical dimension with the ruled approach rather than discover an interplay of factors.

---

[10]David C. Steinmetz, "The Superiority of Pre-Critical Exegesis," in *The Theological Interpretation of Scripture*, ed. Fowl, 28–38.
[11]Kathryn Greene-McCreight, "Literal Sense," in *Dictionary for Theological Interpretation*, ed. Vanhoozer, 456.

Daniel Treier finds three "dimensions" or values of the "precritical" approach:[12] (1) In all of its diversity it centers on the sacramental nature of Scripture, developing a "reading as piety" that looks at the Bible as "one book by way of figural connections between early and later texts"[13] and allows readers to be caught up in the "mysteries" of religious experience. (2) The typological approach of many of the Fathers (and the allegorical or spiritual approach of Origen and others) unified the Bible as a whole witness to Christ and provided an example of typological and allegorical approaches to Scripture that cannot be ignored. (3) The fourfold sense (literal, allegorical, anagogical, tropological—see above) is helpful, and as Augustine said (*On Christian Teaching*, 1.86–88, 3.54), if we find Christ in a passage without consulting the literal sense, it is all right. Treier concludes that this approach "makes possible spiritual participation in the realities of which Scripture speaks" and enables one to "imitate reading for application with theological, not just narrowly exegetical, guidance and restraint."[14]

The goal of theological understanding and participation in the divine mysteries is worthwhile, and the basic purpose of this school of thought is a worthy one. The problem I have with this is the seeming agreement that some of these theologians have with the world of critical scholarship that dominated the twentieth century, namely, that there exists an ugly divide between exegesis and theology, so that historical study of the text must be done without recourse to the theological ramifications of the text. This is an all-too-common false assumption, leading critical exegetes to ignore theology and many practitioners of the school of "theological interpretation" to ignore the historical dimension of the biblical text. In reality, study of any text must consider the text's communication of its significance, that is, the reason the reader should agree with the communication and adhere to its perlocutionary claims. In the Bible, that dimension is by nature theological, and it is a historical aspect.

The Matrix of Interpretation: Scripture or Tradition?

Another issue is whether the two—the original meaning and the tradition of the church—are equally authoritative, or whether one has

---

[12]Treier, *Theological Interpretation*, 41–55. See also his "The Superiority of Precritical Exegesis? *Sic et Non*," *TrinJ* n.s. 24 (2003): 77–103.
[13]Treier, *Theological Interpretation*, 42.
[14]Ibid., 54.

precedence. This is the difference between an evangelical approach to Scripture and an Orthodox approach.[15] The tradition of the church is very important and should be a critical informing factor when we study Scripture. Yet in Protestant hermeneutics it cannot be an *a priori* that determines the meaning of a text. The *regula fidei* must be understood first on the basis of the *analogia fidei* of Luther and then by the *analogia Scripturae* of Calvin. The final arbiter of truth is not the traditions of the church fathers or of my church (whether Lutheran or Reformed or Anabaptist or Arminian or charismatic). All such formulations must be heuristic at the core and continually scrutinized by our study of Scripture. A good example is the *descensus ad inferno* (descent into hades) of the Apostles' Creed. No major commentary in the last fifty years has supported that view of Christ's descent between his death and resurrection,[16] and many modern editions of that creed now omit that part. The point is that creedal statements and church tradition are secondary to the biblical text and so must continually be reexamined and, if necessary, reformulated; yet at the same time they are invaluable as part of our preunderstanding.

"Tradition" stems from the Greek *paradosis* and refers to beliefs "handed down" and then "received" from one generation to the next (1 Cor. 11:2, 23; 15:3; cf. 2 Thess. 2:15; 3:6), that which Paul called "the good deposit that was entrusted to you" (2 Tim. 1:14; cf. 1 Tim. 6:20).[17] At one level "traditions" can refer to a set of human ideas that stretch truth (Mark 7:3, 5, 8, 9), but in Paul it also referred to revelation of truths from God (Gal. 1:11–12, 15–17), and Paul wanted his followers to follow those same traditions (Col. 2:6–7 contra 2:8; 1 Thess. 4:1–2). From the beginning, then, there was an emphasis first on the Spirit's guidance and speaking and second on the predecessors in whose teaching Paul was immersed (Thompson names Old Testament traditions, Jesus traditions, and Christian traditions— confessions, creedal formulations, hymns, paraenetic teaching).[18] In the early church, tradition was connected to the Rule of Faith and then later identified with the creeds and the magisterium, the whole compendium

---

[15]See my "The Many and the One: The Interface between Orthodox and Evangelical Protestant Hermeneutics," *St. Vladimir's Theological Quarterly* 39, no. 3 (1995): 281–304.

[16]For a recent and good discussion, see Karen H. Jobes, *1 Peter*, BECNT (Grand Rapids: Baker, 2005), 242–51.

[17]Unless otherwise indicated, Scripture quotations in this chapter are from the TNIV.

[18]Michael B. Thompson, "Tradition," in *Dictionary of Paul and His Epistles*, ed. G. F. Hawthorne, R. P. Martin, and D. G. Reid (Downers Grove, IL: InterVarsity, 1993), 943–45.

of the church's teaching that was mandated for her adherents. Today, tradition is used to describe the official belief system of any Christian movement, not just Roman Catholic or Orthodox but also Lutheran, Reformed, Baptist, and so on.

Anthony Lane lists six positions that have developed in history regarding the relationship between Scripture and tradition:[19] (1) a harmony or "coincidence" exists between Scripture, tradition, and teachings (Irenaeus, Tertullian); (2) tradition supplements or adds truth to Scripture (*Didache*, Hippolytus); (3) tradition is ancillary or subordinate to Scripture (the Reformers); (4) Scripture has solitary authority, and any kind of tradition is wrong (Anabaptists, the Brethren of the nineteenth century); (5) both Scripture and tradition can only be interpreted on the basis of the official teaching of the church (Council of Trent of the Counter-Reformation); (6) tradition continually unfolds and must be contextualized in different cultural contexts (recent Protestants and Catholics). Alister McGrath concludes that evangelicals should dialogue with the "great tradition" of the past "without in any way being bound by that past. A right regard for tradition is to be nourished, encouraged, challenged, and excited by the witness of those who have wrestled with Scripture before us, without allowing those servants of the gospel to become our master."[20]

The history of dogma is an essential aspect of theological understanding, for it traces the developing doctrines of the church and provides the models of the great minds of the past both in interpreting individual texts and in developing the systems that allow us to correlate those texts into covering laws for doctrinal formulation today. Yet we must also recognize the limits of tradition. As Wentzel van Huyssteen says,

> Since confessions claim to follow the Bible interpretively—and not to become a timeless Bible in themselves—every credo reflects the theological and non-theological climate of its time and is as such already a theological model, regardless of the authority it has in the course of time acquired in its tradition.[21]

---

[19] Anthony N. S. Lane, "Tradition," in *Dictionary for Theological Interpretation*, ed. Vanhoozer, 809–12.
[20] Alister E. McGrath, "Engaging the Great Tradition: Evangelical Theology and the Role of Tradition," in *Evangelical Futures: A Conversation on Theological Method*, ed. John G. Stackhouse (Grand Rapids: Baker, 2000), 158 (139–58).
[21] Wentzel van Huyssteen, *Theology and the Justification of Faith: Constructing Theories in Systematic Theology*, trans. H. F. Snijders (Grand Rapids: Eerdmans, 1989), 184.

Janet Martin Soskice states that a model is an analogous representation of the reality it depicts.[22] As such, a model must be heuristic, frequently reexplored to determine its aptness to describe that reality.

> Models do not observe reality (the positivistic approach) or relate exact descriptions (the naïve realist approach) or provide dispensable approximations of a theory (the instrumentalist approach). Rather, models suggest and explore patterns that potentially depict the reality envisioned (the critical realist approach).[23]

Of course, this does not mean church tradition is doubtful, for it is an accumulation of wisdom that took centuries to form and has lasted down through the centuries. These tradition models "are in essence blueprints of a community's beliefs as well as representations of biblical truths" and so "shape as well as describe the belief system . . . demand adherence and assent," and form "the framework as well as the boundaries of the communities' acceptable dogma."[24] Yet at the same time, we must recognize that each denominational community has its own set of traditions, and these traditions often clash. There must be a set of criteria that will enable us to adjudicate between competing truth claims, and that is supplied by Scripture itself.

The danger comes when a particular paradigm community (i.e., a Christian movement such as Reformed or Arminian) begins to ascribe absolute status to its traditions and to interpret the biblical data on the basis of its own logic system derived from these traditions. When this happens, we have created "a canon within a canon,"[25] that is, placed our belief system above Scripture and determined the meaning of the text on the basis of our tradition rather than giving the text priority in our search for truth. The key is to work with and within our tradition but to place it in front of the text (guided by Scripture) rather than behind the text (determining the meaning of Scripture). The matrix of theological interpretation is first the exegesis of individual texts and then the correlation of those texts into dogmatic truths via biblical theology (see below). Tradition is an informative guide and

---

[22]Janet Martin Soskice, *Metaphor and Religious Language* (Oxford: Clarendon, 1985), 101–3.
[23]Grant R. Osborne, *The Hermeneutical Spiral: A Comprehensive Introduction to Biblical Interpretation*, 2nd ed. (Downers Grove, IL: InterVarsity, 2006), 392.
[24]Ibid.
[25]On this, see James D. G. Dunn, "Levels of Canonical Authority," *Horizons in Biblical Theology* 4 (1982): 26–27, 40–43.

provides the categories for our theological formulation, but Scripture provides the truth content.

The Place of the Author in Theological Interpretation

There is a strong tendency among several members of the "theological interpretation" school to follow Wimsatt and Beardsley, who said that "the design or intention of an author is neither available nor desired as a standard for judging the success of a work of literary art."[26] The center of this debate is the relationship between author, text, and reader. Who determines meaning? An author creates a text, and a reader interprets that text. Where is meaning generated? This becomes more complicated when we realize that biblical interpretation always has a theological as well as a linguistic set of factors, since the biblical writers always thought in theological terms. A statement like "he left the land of the Chaldeans and settled in Haran" in Acts 7:4 has a theological connotation that is part of the meaning of the text, for it describes Abraham's obedience to the command of God. Theology is part of textual meaning. But what role do author and text play in guiding the reader to the linguistic and (intimately connected) theological meaning? Does the author or the reader determine the theological interpretation?

Treier looks at the issue from the standpoint of a theologian. He says that those who choose to stress the author emphasize the historical aspect, and those who center on the text stress literary methods, while those who pursue theology do not focus so much on the text or reader as on the God who acts, thereby seeing author, text, and reader in a new light.[27] From a similar perspective, Stephen Fowl says,

> The ends for which Christians are called to interpret, debate, and embody Scripture are to be found in such manifestations as faithful life and worship and ever deeper communion with the triune God and with others, and . . . these ends neither necessitate any specific critical practice nor accord privilege to the intentions of a scriptural text's human author.[28]

---

[26]W. K. Wimsatt and Monroe C. Beardsley, "The Intentional Fallacy," in *On Literary Intention*, ed. David Newton-deMolina (Edinburgh: Edinburgh University Press, 1976), 1.
[27]Treier, *Theological Interpretation*, 135–36.
[28]Stephen E. Fowl, "The Role of Authorial Intention in the Theological Interpretation of Scripture," in *Between Two Horizons*, ed. Green and Turner, 73. See also his *Engaging Scripture*.

Neither denies the authors of Scripture any place whatsoever in the hermeneutical task; rather, theological understanding transcends their intentions. The point Treier and Fowl make is that a plurality of interpretations is inescapable, but all should be guided by tradition and community.

The movement away from the author was exacerbated in biblical studies (in literary studies, the new criticism had challenged the place of the author since the 1930s) by Hans-Georg Gadamer, whose *Truth and Method* (1965) argued that "coming to understanding" depends not on past intentions or previous interpretations of a text but rather on a "fusion of horizons" in the act of reading. As the horizon of the reader intersects the horizon of the text, the two come together in an act of understanding. It is like jumping into a stream, in this case the stream of tradition. However, it is the stream of the present rather than the stream of the past that is available to the interpreter. After an author has written a text, "meaning has undergone a kind of self-alienation" and must be "stated anew" by the reader.[29] He adds, "Texts do not ask to be understood as a living expression of the subjectivity of their writers. . . . What is fixed in writing has detached itself from the contingency of its origin and its author and made itself free for new relationships."[30] The biblical text is no longer the entity of the past that spoke to the Jewish people or the early church, but a present reality that must be encountered in the present.

Yet Gadamer argues that this does not lead to subjectivity, for the text as presently constituted determines the meaning; so interpretation is a historical act, a "placing of oneself within a process of tradition, in which past and present are constantly fused."[31] It is not "methods" of interpretation but the act of "disclosure" as the text opens itself to the reader and draws her in, opening up new horizons of possibility.[32] So it is not the past act of the author producing a text but rather the present act of a reader encountering a text where meaning is discovered. It is in the process of tradition where past and present are fused,

---

[29]Hans-Georg Gadamer, *Truth and Method*, trans. and ed. G. Broden and J. Cuming (New York: Seabury, 1975), 354–55.
[30]Ibid., 356–57.
[31]Ibid., 258. He says here that "understanding is not to be thought of so much as an action of subjectivity, but as the placing of oneself within a process of tradition, in which past and present are constantly fused. This is what must be expressed in hermeneutical theory, which is far too dominated by the idea of process, a method" (258–59).
[32]Ibid., 258–78.

as the accumulated theological understandings of our predecessors influence our present encounter.[33]

Poststructuralists went another step, arguing for an "epistemological shift," in which the text is seen as art, as only activity, a work that does not stop, with an infinite number of possible meanings as every text contains within itself other texts, wherein the author's intentions are no more than an unnecessary guest. The result is that reader and text collaborate in producing a new text that is owned by the reader, not the author.[34] For this school, the text is a playing field on which the readers are the players and get to choose what game they wish to play. The field contains only the possibility of play; the readers choose the game and the rules. As soon as I write a book, it ceases to belong to me. I may have had certain purposes or goals, but the reader has little access to those messages. Rather, the reader brings her own preunderstanding to my book, and it is no longer mine but hers. She decides what language games and interpretive strategies to employ as she interacts with the work that was formerly mine.

There are three different schools of thought in this movement. First, there is the text-centered understanding of Wolfgang Iser and Paul Ricoeur. Iser teaches that the text contains "indeterminacies" or gaps that draw the reader into its textual world and provide a perspective that enables the reader to "understand." The text is the impetus, providing strategies that guide the reader into that narrative world. There is a "repertoire" or configuration (plot, dialogue, etc.), a sentence structure and set of actions enabling the reader to reexperience its textual strategy and complete its meaning.[35] Ricoeur also places the text above the author as the generating force in hermeneutics. Autonomous from the author, a text possesses its own narrative world, containing its own metaphors, which draw readers out of their world and develop a discursive process, an extratextual new world that envelops the reader in a "reality-shaping" mode. This new encounter enables the reader to experience the text anew and unites the objective world of the text with the existential world of the self, thereby forging an encounter that becomes an interpretation.[36]

---

[33]See also Treier, *Theological Interpretation*, 130–31.

[34]Roland Barthes, "From Word to Text," in *Textual Strategies: Perspectives in Poststructuralist Criticism*, ed. J. V. Harari (Ithaca, NY: Cornell, 1979), 73–81.

[35]Wolfgang Iser, *The Act of Reading: A Theory of Aesthetic Response* (Baltimore: Johns Hopkins University Press, 1978), 24–25, 93–111.

[36]Paul Ricoeur, "The Narrative Function," *Semeia* 13 (1978): 8–10.

The second school of thought is the reader-response criticism of Stanley Fish. For him, meaning or understanding is phenomenological in nature: there is no epistemological choice between alternative meaning possibilities but rather an ontological union between reader and text in which the reader "creates" meaning. He theorizes "that the form of the reader's experiences are one, that they come into view simultaneously, and therefore the questions of priority and independence do not arise."[37] Fish introduces the centrality of the paradigm community for understanding. The reading strategy derived from the interpreting community leads the reader into meaning. The text is an empty page consisting of polyvalent meaning possibilities, and all the understanding stems from the act of reading. In fact, the text as a formal entity has no existence until actualized by the interpretive act.[38]

The final and most influential school is the deconstruction approach of Jacques Derrida. He defines his movement as a "decentering" that frees language and rhetoric from Western philosophy, a way of thinking that deconstructs itself because it lacks a "transcendental signified," an outside presence that anchors meaning. The result is an endless chain of significances as encounter with the text produces "negativity," where "the infinitely-other cannot be bound by a concept, cannot be thought of on the basis of a horizon, for the horizon is always the horizon of the same."[39] So the basic locus of a text that supposedly provides meaning and coherence is disrupted as "an infinite number of sign-substitutions come into play,"[40] and the symbols can no longer be identified. There is no closure, and "difference" is the result as meaning both "differs" and is "deferred" (Derrida's pun) by the endless play between sign and signified, and "absence" characterizes the act of interpretation.[41] Thus there is never any transfer of meaning, no presence of the author or of original intentions, and so the

---

[37]Stanley Fish, "Interpreting the Variorum," in *Reader-Response Criticism*, ed. J. P. Thompkins (Baltimore: Johns Hopkins Press, 1980), 177.

[38]Stanley Fish, *Is There a Text in This Class? The Authority of Interpretive Communities* (Cambridge, MA: Harvard University Press, 1980), 11–14.

[39]Jacques Derrida, "Violence and Metaphysics: An Essay in the Thought of Emmanuel Levinas," in *Writing and Difference*, trans. A. Bass (Chicago: University of Chicago Press, 1978), 92.

[40]Ibid., 280.

[41]Derrida, "Structure, Sign, and Play in the Discourse of the Human Sciences," in *Writing and Difference*, 278–93.

reader will also deconstruct herself from the past and enter a present interrogation and involvement with the text.

There is much to be said for this because the average act of reading is indeed a decentering, and readers will usually understand the text from the perspective of the reading strategies inherited from their paradigm community. This is the view of Fowl. He speaks of an author's "communicative intention" and recognizes that for Paul (as an example) that is arrived at by a basic knowledge of first-century literary conventions applied to his epistles.[42] However, he argues, the search for authorial meaning cannot be a primary concern and is normally the result of a desire for stability in light of fears regarding deconstruction rather than a proper strategy for interpretation. For him the issue is "what counts as textual meaning." To demand authorial intent as the sole or primary meaning to him is "arbitrary" and "question-begging," because we first have to decide what "textual meaning" actually is.[43] Fowl believes that the true implications of this search must include "later theological formulations" and not just be restricted to an author's original purposes.[44]

But are Fowl and others correct? I think the evidence proves them wrong and that seeking authorial intention provides the proper basis for theological interpretation. Nicholas Wolterstorff says that seeking the author's meaning in a text is what all of us do when we read works like historical or legal documents or home repair manuals. In the Bible (as the Word of God) God is speaking, not just in inspiring the writers, but in the very words of the text. Speech-act theory notes that the illocutionary act of asserting in all biblical statements asks to be understood, and in Scripture a "double agency discourse" occurs because the writer is speaking on behalf of God.[45] From this perspective, the reader is being asked to interpret what God was saying through the biblical writer. In this way, authorial meaning is at the heart of biblical and theological reflection.

---

[42]Fowl, "Authorial Intention," 74–75.

[43]Ibid., 79–80. For this view, see also Jorge J. E. Gracia, "Meaning," in *Dictionary for Theological Interpretation*, ed. Vanhoozer, 492–99.

[44]Ibid., 82.

[45]Nicholas Wolterstorff, "Authorial Discourse Interpretation," in *Dictionary for Theological Interpretation*, ed. Vanhoozer, 78–80. See also his *Divine Discourse: Philosophical Reflections on the Claim That God Speaks* (Cambridge: Cambridge University Press, 1995). Interestingly, George Lindbeck agrees with this in his "Postcritical Canonical Interpretation: Three Modes of Retrieval," in *Theological Exegesis: Essays in Honor of Brevard Childs*, ed. C. R. Seitz and K. Greene-McCreight (Grand Rapids: Eerdmans, 1999), 26–51.

Kevin Vanhoozer adds that biblical discourse constitutes a "communicative agent" that has established a "covenant of discourse" with people and so intends to speak and be understood. He calls his approach a "trinitarian hermeneutic" centered on the triad of author, text, and reader.[46] Utilizing a similar speech-act approach as Wolterstorff, Vanhoozer makes four points: (1) Language is more than simply referential but is also transformative by having pragmatic as well as semantic qualities. (2) It is not indeterminate, and the author is an essential component in interpretation. (3) Action as well as representation is essential, and the true paradigm for biblical communication is promise and covenant; in other words, understanding the original communication event is critical. (4) Readers are not free to manipulate the text however they wish; there is a moral and ethical responsibility to try to ascertain what the author is saying.[47]

Let me summarize the point. Biblical interpretation results from a trialogue among author, text, and reader. Yet when we use the term "authorial intention," we are not trying to get into the author's mind or even to derive his intentions. Readers are simply studying the text the author has written. We want to discern what the author "intended" to say in the text he or she wrote, no more. The author's text is the object of study, not the author's mind.[48] The place of the reader is to use the exegetical tools to get back to what Paul or Peter was saying in his first-century setting. At the same time, we readers come to the texts with certain preunderstandings we have inherited from our community. Ian Barbour recognizes the centrality of the shared assumptions between a paradigm community and a reader. Yet he recognizes that observation of data and critical assessment maintain a certain control over such reading strategies, and correction of assumptions can occur.[49] This is where the larger community is essential. When I am challenged by another interpretation, this drives me back to the text

[46]Kevin J. Vanhoozer, *Is There a Meaning in This Text? The Bible, the Reader, and the Morality of Literary Knowledge* (Grand Rapids: Zondervan, 1998), 213.

[47]Kevin J. Vanhoozer, *First Theology: God, Scripture, and Hermeneutics* (Downers Grove, IL: InterVarsity, 2002), 164–67.

[48]Many, as noted in Treier, *Theological Interpretation*, 112–15 (who especially notes Childs), see an antithetical relationship between author and text, regarding the first as historical and the second as canonical. I would dispute that distinction. The interpreter studies author-text, not either in distinction from the other.

[49]Ian G. Barbour, "Paradigms in Science and Religion," in *Paradigms and Revolutions*, ed. G. Gutting (Notre Dame, IN: Notre Dame University Press, 1980), 223–45.

and to question my original understanding. In that ongoing dialogue, the text and what the author has said become ever clearer.

Moreover, many who deny the place of the author do so on the basis that the results are so inconclusive. Scholars disagree, and doubt is always present. However, that is always true of such decisions. Scholars are paid to come up with different interpretations; they are all Athenians, seeking some new idea (Acts 17:21)! In philosophy, it has been realized for some time that in the quest for knowledge probability, theory must have priority over necessary knowledge, lest the search for truth be negated before it can begin. We simply do not attain certainty.[50] The basis for this probability approach is critical realism, which holds that in such searches there is a reality to be discovered and that it can be attained through critical assessment. N. T. Wright says that "initial observation is challenged by critical reflection but can survive that challenge and speak truly of reality," as this reflection moves from observation to hypotheses that are then refined by critical reflection, leading to verification or falsification of the hypotheses.[51]

Let us apply this to the point of this article, theological interpretation. We begin with the study of individual texts, seeking to discern the author's communicative purpose and message. In doing so, we are not just ascertaining the brute propositions (the locutionary aspect), but also studying what the author is doing in the text (the illocutionary aspect), and the theological message that asks the readers to react (the perlocutionary aspect). All three are part of the original meaning, and we are looking for the meaning of Isaiah or Paul, not for what we or our communities can do with that. The next step is to collate the passages that have similar theological themes in the book, in the corpus of the author, and in the Bible as a whole (biblical theology). These still entail a historical study because we are developing the theology of Paul, of Israel (Old Testament theology), or of the early church (New Testament theology). Yet in theological interpretation there are two more levels, and these move away from biblical to historical and systematic theology. Yet these form a "trinitarian hermeneutic" (see

---

[50]See Roderick Firth, "The Anatomy of Certainty," and John L. Pollock, "Criteria and Our Knowledge of the Material World," *Philosophical Review* 76 (1967): 3–27, 28–60. For this in the area of religious dialogue, see James Ross, "Ways of Religious Knowing," in *The Challenge of Religion: Contemporary Readings in the Philosophy of Religion*, ed. F. Ferré (New York: Seabury, 1982), 83–104.

[51]N. T. Wright, *The New Testament and the People of God* (Minneapolis: Fortress, 1992), 36 (cf. 32–37).

above) as well, for there is a continuous trialogue between biblical, historical, and systematic theology. In light of the theology of Israel and the early church, we note the various models supplied in the history of dogma and try to construct a systematic theology for today that is true to biblical teaching and cognizant of the historical developments of that teaching. This leads us to the next section.

The Place of Biblical Theology in Theological Interpretation

D. A. Carson defines biblical theology as "that branch of theology whose concern it is to study each corpus of Scripture in its own right, especially with respect to its place in the history of God's unfolding revelation," recognizing the larger unity of Scripture and the place of each corpus in its Testament and in the whole of Scripture.[52] Yet this traditional view has come under considerable attack, beginning with its roots early in the last century. After the growth of the biblical theology movement in the 1940s and '50s (building on Barth), two works caused a virtual collapse of the movement. First, Langdon Gilkey observed that it was half modern (accepting higher criticism) and half orthodox (centering on a God who speaks and acts in redemptive history). He said the movement cannot accept the antisupernatural view of the world and yet declare a God who speaks.[53] Then, James Barr noted additional weaknesses in the movement's views of revelation and language, arguing that the Bible does not fit its use of history and that the movement committed the error of "illegitimate totality transfer" in seeing a full-fledged biblical theology in individual words.[54] The result was Brevard Childs's *Biblical Theology in Crisis*, calling for a renewal based on canonical criticism, the unity of the Bible as canon, and a new emphasis on the final form of the text/traditioning process in the canon.[55]

---

[52]D. A. Carson, "Unity and Diversity in the New Testament: The Possibility of Systematic Theology," in *Scripture and Truth*, ed. D. A. Carson and J. D. Woodbridge (Grand Rapids: Baker, 1992), 69. See also his "Systematic Theology and Biblical Theology," in *New Dictionary of Biblical Theology*, ed. T. D. Alexander et al. (Downers Grove, IL: InterVarsity, 2000), 89–104.

[53]Langdon Gilkey, "Cosmology, Ontology, and the Travail of Biblical Language," *Journal of Religion* 41 (1961): 194–205.

[54]James Barr, *The Concept of Biblical Theology: An Old Testament Perspective* (Minneapolis: Fortress, 1999). Against this, see Frances Watson, *Text and Truth: Redefining Biblical Theology* (Grand Rapids: Eerdmans, 1997), 23–26, who shows that words do carry theological meaning when interpreted carefully in cognizance of their diverse usage.

[55]Brevard S. Childs, *Biblical Theology in Crisis* (Philadelphia: Westminster, 1970). For an excellent succinct presentation of this, see Craig G. Bartholomew, "Biblical Theology," in *Dictionary for Theological Interpretation*, ed. Vanhoozer, 84–90.

Heikki Räisänen[56] provides a recent critique of the possibility of a biblical theology, providing four reasons why it is invalid. Let me respond to each in turn: (1) History and theology are incompatible fields of study, and a scholar must deal with the descriptive, the history of the early church, and not the prescriptive, its theology. Yet my entire article has intended to show that theology is historical, as we are elucidating the original beliefs of Israel and the early church that flow out of the biblical texts. This demarcation is no longer seen as valid by the majority of scholars.[57] (2) In keeping with the first reason, Räisänen argues that the nature of the biblical material restricts us to writing a history of religions rather than a biblical theology. However, this scholarly perspective stems from William Wrede and Rudolf Bultmann nearly a century ago and also is no longer held today.

(3) Such a study must center on the canon of Scripture, and that was a later decision on the part of Israel and the church that cannot guide a valid historical study. Yet Childs has demonstrated the validity of a canonical approach. I. Howard Marshall argues strongly for the viability of the New Testament canon as the basis:[58] a consensus developed regarding these twenty-seven documents by the end of the second century, and they were the product of the earliest followers (many of them eyewitnesses). These constitute the whole of first-century Christian literature, and there is a demonstrable unity of themes among them.[59]

(4) There are too many contradictions between the biblical books to provide a basis for a unified theology. Marshall responds to this as well:[60] It is true that much of the literature is occasional, and portions of these writings may not be formally theological in nature, but this does not mean it is impossible to reconstruct developing themes. The "variety and diversity" among them do contain some points that

---

[56]Heikki Räisänen, *Beyond New Testament Theology: A Story and a Program* (London: SCM, 1990).

[57]On history and theology, see Grant R. Osborne, "History and Theology in the Synoptic Gospels," *TrinJ* n.s. 24 (2003): 5–22.

[58]I. Howard Marshall, *New Testament Theology: Many Witnesses, One Gospel* (Downers Grove, IL: InterVarsity, 2004), 18–20. See also David Dunbar, "The Biblical Canon," in *Hermeneutics, Canon, and the Word of God*, ed. D. A. Carson and J. D. Woodbridge (Grand Rapids: Zondervan, 1986); and R. T. Beckwith, "The Canon of Scripture," in *New Dictionary of Biblical Theology*, ed. Alexander et al., 27–34.

[59]On "unity" between the Testaments, see Carson, "Systematic Theology and Biblical Theology," 95–97.

[60]Marshall, *New Testament Theology*, 20–23.

could be construed as contradictory, and they represent a development of thinking on the part of early Christians. Nevertheless, out of this "rich tapestry of changing and developing ideas" one can construct a biblical theology.

Daniel Treier notes three further issues that must be addressed.[61] (1) What is the scope of the project, as various scholars would restrict it to individual authors or to one Testament or the other? A true "biblical theology" must be holistic, uniting the Testaments and bringing together the Bible as a whole, but doing so is a daunting task.[62] (2) How does one organize such a theology? Is it done thematically, perhaps under a unifying or central theme like covenant or kingdom, or tracing themes historically, or centering upon each corpus in turn (poetry, wisdom, prophecy, etc.)? (3) What method should be chosen? Should we utilize a synthetic or analytical or tradition-critical or literary or christological approach? All have been used at one time or another, and the results could cancel each other in the final analysis. Such issues are certainly problematic, but they are not fatal to the cause of constructing a biblical theology. Rather, they provide parameters. Biblical theology can and should be done at all levels, studying the themes of a single book, of an author or corpus of literature, or of Scripture as a whole. Works have been written successfully at each of these levels and also with each of the methods. Craig Bartholomew is correct when he says, "There is surely room for a range of biblical theologies, operating along topical, dogmatic, great ideas, redemptive-historical, story lines, and so on" so long as they recognize "the Bible as canonical and the ancient sense of an inner unity that comes from Christian faith."[63]

Biblical theology as a discipline provides the bridge from exegetical analysis to theological interpretation. As stated above, there are five levels to theological interpretation in terms of Scripture itself: individual communicative utterances in a text; the theology of an author in a book; the theology of the whole corpus of an author; the theology of Israel or the church in the two Testaments; and the theology of the

---

[61]Treier, *Theological Interpretation*, 107–10.
[62]J. D. G. Dunn, "The Problem of Biblical Theology," in *Out of Egypt: Biblical Theology and Biblical Interpretation*, ed. Craig Bartholomew et al. (Grand Rapids: Zondervan, 2004), 172–84, considers the tension between the two Testaments the primary problem for biblical theology, calling this "the interface between a Jewish biblical theology and a Christian biblical theology."
[63]Bartholomew, "Biblical Theology," 89.

Bible as a whole. Each of these levels deals with "what it meant," that is, the historical task of delineating what the sacred writers of Scripture and the ancient people of God believed. Of course, this does not connote a strict bifurcation between past and present, for each of these contains theological significance for the present. Brian Rosner defines biblical theology as

> theological interpretation of Scripture in and for the church. It proceeds with historical and literary sensitivity and seeks to analyze and synthesize the Bible's teaching about God and his relations to the world on its own terms, maintaining sight of the Bible's overarching narrative and Christocentric focus.[64]

This discipline seeks a blend of each author's own theological emphases, the larger emphases of the communities of which they were a part, and the significance of those historical theologies for the church today. Theology has a historical dimension (the task of biblical theology) that leads to contemporary reflection and action.

Conclusion: Hermeneutical Guidelines for Theological Interpretation

R. R. Reno says, "The distance between the literal sense and theological abstractions is the single greatest failure of earnest and well-meaning attempts by modern exegetes of the NT to produce theological exegesis."[65] He means that modern exegetes are so tied to the text and its import that they fail (deliberately) to emulate the church fathers in the richness of their intratextual breadth as they discuss the theological import of passages. The new movement calls for a return to the Rule of Faith and rich theological imagery coming out of the "precritical" period. We have already discussed several of the issues (e.g., the importance of authorial message, the place of biblical theology), yet the problem is real. What does it mean to move from the Bible to theology? Several have spoken of theological interpretation as "beyond the Bible,"[66] but they are discussing current theological issues

---

[64]Brian Rosner, "Biblical Theology," in *New Dictionary of Biblical Theology*, ed. Alexander et al., 10.
[65]R. R. Reno, "Biblical Theology and Theological Exegesis," in *Out of Egypt*, ed. Craig Bartholomew et al., 391–92.
[66]I. Howard Marshall, *Beyond the Bible: Moving from Scripture to Theology* (Grand Rapids: Baker, 2004); Gary T. Meadors, ed., *Four Views on Moving Beyond the Bible to Theology* (Grand Rapids: Zondervan, 2009).

and application rather than theological reflection on biblical texts as a whole. I disagree that "intratextual echoes" are missing from modern exegesis; I for one am constantly moving through Scripture to find parallel texts that develop the concept in a certain text. The difference is that I take a semantic-field approach and seek to amplify the point of the text, but the intratextual richness is distinctly there.

Once more we need to note the levels of theological reflection. Let me use an example to illustrate this, Mark 1:21–22. The christological implications are clear in this. Mark is making an illocutionary assertion and is communicating the unique *exousia* of Jesus ("not as the scribes" [ESV]; level one), and when we trace this through Markan theology, it is part of Mark's emphasis on Jesus as teacher (interestingly, he uses both *didaskalos* and *exousia* as often as Matthew; level two). Jesus is seen as exercising a new level of teaching that includes his miracles, for after he casts the demon out of the man in the synagogue in Mark 1:23–26, the people are again amazed at his authority and call it "a new teaching" (1:27, undoubtedly because of his authoritative command that the demon "be quiet" and "come out"). Mark has a much higher christology than is often thought.

In New Testament theology (level three), this is part of the christological emphasis on Jesus as the voice of God and related to the passages on his divinity. For biblical theology (level four), one of the themes that unites the Testaments is Jesus as the new voice of Yahweh. The absolute authority of God "speaking" in the Old Testament is replicated in the words and teaching of Jesus in the New Testament. In fact, there is a Trinitarian aspect as all three—Father, Son, Spirit—speak with the same authority (on the Spirit, see John 14:26–27; 15:26; 16:12–15). This is where the Rule of Faith comes in. An important point is that at all these levels we are dealing with historical meaning (author's message, theology of the early church, theology of the Bible as a whole) with present implications for our belief systems today. Too many establish a false dichotomy between historical meaning and theological implications.

Two elements of biblical theology bridge the Testaments: first, promise-fulfillment, as the Old Testament points forward to Christ. As in Romans 10:4, Christ is "the end of the law" (ESV) in terms of completing or fulfilling it. This does not call for a complete christological approach to the Old Testament, as if its only value were in pointing forward to Christ. The Old Testament is canon in and of itself. Still,

Christ unites the Testaments. Second, there is progressive revelation, which assumes that there is a complete continuity of thought between Old and New Testaments, as exemplified in the *New Dictionary of Biblical Theology*, which seeks to treat New Testament articles in light of Old Testament antecedents and Old Testament articles in terms of further New Testament developments.[67] We are ascertaining how these truths have been progressively revealed through the unfolding of salvation history.

In historical and systematic theology we do move "beyond the Bible," yet not fully. In one sense, historical theology is the study of the history of dogma, namely, the belief systems developed throughout church history. Yet in another sense it studies also how these theologians used and understood Scripture in the development of their theologies.[68] The value of historical theology is that it "studies the way later paradigm communities understood the biblical doctrines and enables us to understand current theological debates by placing them in bold relief within the history of dogma."[69] Richard Muller notes the value of this discipline:[70] through it, we can understand current systems by noting their roots in past models, so it provides a foundation for present doctrine. These models also help us to understand the complexity of applying Scripture in widely different cultural and historical situations and thereby to realize the critical importance of history in current doctrinal decisions. We cannot think too highly of our facility in formulating doctrines when we realize our dependence on the past in doing so.

Systematic theology flows out of (1) exegetical decisions regarding the theological meaning of individual passages, (2) the collation of the meaning of passages on an issue in biblical theology, and (3) the use of models (good and bad) provided by a study of the history of dogma on that issue. In constructing a theology for today, four components form the "raw materials"—Scripture, tradition (both the creedal traditions of the church as a whole and the individual traditions of the theological

---

[67]See Rosner, "Biblical Theology," 8.

[68]See Michael S. Horton, "Historical Theology," in *Dictionary for Theological Interpretation*, ed. Vanhoozer, 293. Horton describes it as "the *history of exegesis* (descriptive)" and sees its goal as determining "what the church has in fact said in its dogmatic formulations through their organic development."

[69]Osborne, *Hermeneutical Spiral*, 352.

[70]Richard A. Muller, *The Study of Theology: From Biblical Interpretation to Contemporary Formulation* (Grand Rapids: Zondervan, 1991), 104–8.

systems), experience (personal experience, corporate experience in a local church, and the community of scholars whose works challenge and inspire us), and reason (ways of organizing the data into coherent patterns for the current culture).[71] Tradition, experience, and reason together form our preunderstanding, that set of hermeneutical awareness and beliefs that guide us when we study a text and draw theological meaning from it. This compendium of the reader's strategies must be consciously held, lest they become an *a priori* that determines the textual meaning rather than a perspective from which we make decisions. Once again, the competing schools of thought are our friend, for they force us away from presuppositional readings.

There is general agreement that Scripture must provide the basis for all theological formulation. The debate centers on what part it must play and what place we give to church tradition in developing our belief system. The thesis of this essay is that Scripture has absolute primacy, and tradition is supplemental, informing us and providing models for the way Scripture has been utilized through the centuries, but not determining our present system. As Carson says, "The primary authoritative source for that theological synthesis is the Bible" and "systematic theology attempts to organize what the Bible says according to some system." While at a certain level that system is an outside organizing force imposed on the Bible's teaching, at the same time when scholars do include the input of "seminal theologians" (e.g., Irenaeus, Augustine, Calvin), and when the process does truly engage with the culture in a Scripture-defining way, it will lead to "worldview formation, worldviews transformation."[72] For the relationship of exegesis to theology, Watson uses the analogy of a "hermeneutical circle or spiral," with the two in an ongoing dialectic in which "exegesis of the parts (individual biblical texts) presupposes some sense of the whole (an interpretation of the basic content of Christian faith)." This theological sense itself stems "from prior exegesis," while exegesis will "develop, clarify, and correct a given theological position."[73]

In this light, the purpose of systematic theology as "queen of the sciences" is to reexamine the biblical precedent and reformulate its teaching, utilizing the tradition-centered truths inherited from the his-

---

[71]See Kevin J. Vanhoozer, "Systematic Theology," in *Dictionary for Theological Interpretation*, ed. Vanhoozer, 776; and Osborne, *Hermeneutical Spiral*, 376–86.

[72]Carson, "Systematic Theology and Biblical Theology," 101–2.

[73]Watson, *Text, Church, and World*, 222.

tory of dogma, as well as to reformulate these truths in a system based upon the patterns of thinking of our day. The goal is to form a Christian understanding and a Christian worldview that is Bible-centered and at the same time speaks clearly to this culture. The Rule of Faith is essential, with its Trinitarian and christological core, as are the creedal truths that so clearly state the essentials of theological thinking. This does not mean we accept every part of the creeds (e.g., the "descent into hades" of the Apostles' Creed), but they provide critical guides. We also work with the conceptual patterns inherited from our paradigm community and allow these to inform our systemic models.

We must at the same time recognize the different models of Scripture controlling the understanding of the widely divergent Christian movements today (Catholic, Orthodox, Reformed, Anabaptist, etc.).[74] As Vanhoozer notes, the Reformation principle of *sola Scriptura* demands the primacy of the biblical material, yet the fact is that doctrinal differences remain, and "ecclesial practice" often dictates the results. Thus, the "community of interpretation" for a growing number is the only path to theological interpretation. For Vanhoozer, the answer is to enter the "theo-drama" of the Word: "For this reason Scripture is the church's authoritative script, the final criterion for theological understanding. At the same time, the script needs to be taken into new situations. What is called for is not mere repetition, but creative understanding."[75]

In conclusion, theological interpretation first is part of the exegetical task itself, with theology part of the reader's preunderstanding and at the same time a natural part of the process of "coming-to-understanding" with respect to the meaning of the text itself. This includes exegesis and biblical theology, for both are aspects of the study of the original/historical meaning of the text. Second, theological interpretation is also a result of exegesis, as the church collates biblical texts and uses the models derived from historical theology to fashion its current belief system. Thus biblical theology is the bridging mechanism, constructing the theology of Israel and the early church and thereby providing the archetypal blueprint by which current approaches are judged. The error of some practitioners of "theological interpreta-

[74]See David S. Kelsey, *The Uses of Scripture in Modern Theology* (Philadelphia: Fortress, 1975).
[75]Vanhoozer, "Systematic Theology," 778.

85

tion" is their placing tradition alongside Scripture as equal partners in theological interpretation. We must keep each participant in dogmatic formulation in its proper place: "Scripture remains the supreme authority for systematic theology, not as an epistemic norm that caters to modernity's craving for theoretical certainty and completeness, but as a sapiential norm that provides direction for fitting participation in the ongoing drama of redemption."[76]

---

[76]Ibid., 779. By "sapiential" Vanhoozer means "practical wisdom," a theology that is enacted in daily life, practiced more than merely discussed.

3

The Church

A Summary and Reflection

MARK DEVER

Someone has said, "I admire the church. I love the church. I would even be willing to *die* for the church. I just don't want to join the church." Many people today feel like that. They take the "I like Jesus, but I just don't like the church" position. Here's my concern, however: if you don't like the church, you may not really like Jesus (1 John 4:20; 2 Cor. 13:5).

Statistically, local churches don't tend to be as gender-balanced as the population as a whole; churches tend to be, in that sense, very female (and have been forever). American churches in particular have long been marked by individualism and consumerism, often in fairly crass ways. And this has left the local church as a whole often appearing like a spiritual invalid. It is a supplicant looking for consumers, not a herald creating converts.

In places with a high percentage of confessing Christians—like the United States—it is traditional to ascribe a lot of the problems in our society to the church. So it is no surprise that we Christians—especially those of us who are pastors—want to improve churches. But what does "improve" mean? Often, it means increasing our church membership and attendance. And we'll do it however we can, taking methods from business, or planning activities for minorities—like men—or applying the homogenous-unit principle. This principle states that churches will grow faster if they are composed of all the same kind of people in ethnic and other demographic terms. So our churches are often split along all the same lines our community is. And the church, instead of being the question mark in the midst of the community the way it is supposed to be, becomes a pale religious reflection of it.

Some of the church's harsher critics wonder whether the church will even survive in an increasingly atheistic, hedonistic, and secular world. Will we survive the grand assault of comic vitriol from the likes of Bill Maher, biting critiques from Christopher Hitchens, not to mention the atheistic bus signs? Should we survive?

Only if we remember why we're here. The church is important in God's plans—we read in Acts 20:28 that he purchased it with his own blood—and so, if we would be Christ's followers, the church must be important to us. In this essay, we consider seven basic questions about the church, all revolving around the twin concerns of what the church is called to be, and how our churches can be like that today.

What Is the Church?

A dry "Starbucks"? An ancient "third space"? A social club? A non-profit charity? A religious enthusiasts society?

The church is the body of people called by God's grace through faith in Christ to glorify him together by serving him in his world.

God's eternal plan has always been to display his glory not just through individuals but also through a corporate body. In creation, God made not one person but two, and two who had the ability to reproduce more. In the flood, God saved not one person, but a few families. In Genesis 12, God called Abram and promised that Abram's descendants would be as numerous as the stars in the sky or the sand at the seashore. In the exodus, God dealt not only with Moses, but also with the nation of Israel—twelve tribes comprising hundreds of thousands of people, yet bearing one corporate identity (Ex. 15:13–16). He gave laws and ceremonies that should be worked out not only in the lives of individuals, but also in the life of the whole people. And throughout the Old Testament, we see that God continued to work with the nation of Israel. How does this relate to the church? Through Jesus Christ. Christ is the fulfillment of all that Israel pointed toward (2 Cor. 1:20), and the church is Christ's body.

In the New Testament, the people of God are called by the name "church." Our English word *church* can be used to describe a local congregation or all Christians everywhere. Of course, we also use it to describe buildings and denominations. So our English word *church* doesn't exactly parallel the Greek word in the New Testament. To make clear the personal, and usually local, way that the New Testament speaks of the church, William Tyndale preferred translating the Greek word as "congregation."

A church is fundamentally an assembly. So in Acts 7:38 and Hebrews 2:12, *ekklēsia* is used to describe Old Testament assemblies. Luke uses *ekklēsia* three times in Acts 19 to describe the riot that flared up in an amphitheater in Ephesus in response to Paul (Acts 19:32, 39, 41). The remaining 109 uses of the word in the New Testament refer to a Christian assembly.

The images used in the New Testament explain more of what the church is. The church is the people of God, the new creation, the fellowship, and, of course, the body of Christ. In this fellowship are those people who have accepted and entered into the reign of God. It's interesting and important that this reign is not entered into by nations, or even families, but by individuals (Mark 3:31–35; cf. Matt. 10:37). According to Jesus' parables in Matthew 21 (the parables of the two sons and of the tenants), the kingdom of God was taken from the Jews and given to a people, as Jesus said, "who will produce its fruit" (Matt. 21:43; cf. Acts 28:26–28; 1 Thess. 2:16).[1] God's rule and reign in the world has begun in a special way with the coming of Jesus, and this is called "the kingdom of God." It is this kingdom of God that creates the church. Louis Berkhof puts it this way: true Christians "constitute a kingdom in their relation to God in Christ as their Ruler, and a church in their separateness from the world in devotion to God, and in their organic union with one another."[2]

This is something of what the church is.

---

[1] Unless otherwise indicated, Scripture quotations in this chapter are from the NIV.
[2] Louis Berkhof, *Systematic Theology* (Grand Rapids: Eerdmans, 1938), 569.

What Is the Church Like?

For over sixteen hundred years, Christians have summarized at least part of the Bible's teaching on the church by saying that it is the "one holy [universal] and apostolic church" (Nicene Creed). Basically, the church is like God. We reflect his nature and character.

The reality today, however, too often falls far short of this spiritual understanding. The letters of Jesus Christ to the seven churches of Asia Minor in Revelation 2–3 stand as a stark reminder of how churches can fail to live up to their own nature. Consider the following description of what the church is to be like, and then reflect on the reality that is your congregation.

The church is *one* and is to be one because God is one. In the book of Acts we see that Christians have always been characterized by their unity (e.g., Acts 4:32). The unity of Christians in the church is to be a sign for the world, reflecting the unity of God himself. The church on earth experiences this unity only as we are united in God's truth as revealed in Scripture. Do we appear to the world strangely and inexplicably united?

The church is *holy* and is to be holy because God is holy (Lev. 11:44–45; 19:2; 20:7; 1 Pet. 1:14–16). God has declared us to be holy in Christ, and he is making us holy by his Spirit. Both the Old and New Testaments emphasize the importance of holiness among the people of God so that we might be and do what God calls us to (Deut. 14:2; 1 Corinthians 5–6; 2 Cor. 6:14–7:1). Certainly a church that resigns itself to evil fails dismally. Are we, in our congregations, marked by holiness, a holiness like God's, which distinguishes us from the world around us?

The church is *universal* and is to be universal because God is the "Lord of all the earth" (Josh. 3:11, 13; Ps. 97:5; Mic. 4:13; Zech. 4:14; cf. Jer. 23:24) and "King of the ages" (Rev. 15:3). The church is universal, then, in that it stretches across space and time. "Universality" isn't taught by name in the New Testament, but, like "Trinity," it expresses biblical truth. "Catholic" is the older English word used to describe this. But because of that word's association with the Church of Rome, "universal" is a better English translation of the Greek word originally used in the creeds. The church in every place is fundamentally the same. Such universality marks all truly Christian congregations. In his letter to the Smyrneans in the early second century AD, Ignatius of Antioch wrote that "where Jesus Christ is, there is the universal church." The continuity of the church across space and time prevents the church from being held captive to any one segment of it. So the church—every local congregation *and* the church universal—belongs to Christ, and Christ alone. Our churches today must ask questions and explore in what ways our concern for contextualizing our witness to the gospel makes us more a church of our century or our country than we are a Christian church.

The church is *apostolic* and is to be apostolic because it is founded on and is faithful to the Word of God given through the apostles. Early in his public ministry, Jesus "called his disciples to him and chose twelve of them, whom he also designated apostles" (Luke 6:13). Toward the end of his ministry, Jesus then prayed "for those who will believe in me through their [the apostles'] message" (John 17:20). But what does it mean for us today to say that the church is apostolic, since the apostles are long gone? It means that their teaching must be our teaching. How can we be sure it is? By the careful, faithful teaching of the Bible. The physical continuity of a line of pastor-elders back to Christ's apostles is insignificant compared with the continuity between the teaching in churches today and the teaching of the apostles. Only with the apostles' teaching is the church, as Paul described it to Timothy, "the pillar and foundation of the truth" (1 Tim. 3:15).

This is the sense in which the church, then, is and is to be one, holy, universal, and apostolic.

What Makes a Church "Good"?

Over the centuries, the four attributes just considered have been joined and sometimes even replaced by two marks that define a local church. These two marks are the right preaching of the Word of God and the right administration of baptism and the Lord's Supper. In fact, the Bible's teaching on the church can largely be organized under these two marks, since God uses preaching, baptism, and the Lord's Supper to create his church and to preserve it. The preaching is the fountain of God's truth, which God uses to give life to his people. And the church—marked out by baptism and the Lord's Supper—is the lovely vessel to contain and display this glorious work. The fountain pours out, the bowl collects, and it can display its contents. The church is generated by the right preaching of the Word. And the church is distinguished and contained by the right administration of baptism and the Lord's Supper. To practice the Lord's Supper as we should presumes and implies the practice of accountability, including church membership and discipline.

Biblical Preaching

The right preaching of God's Word, and especially the gospel, is the most important mark of a true Christian church. A distorted church often coincides with a distorted gospel. The correct preaching of the Word of God accurately presents the teaching of the Bible with the gospel at the center. God's people in Scripture are created by God's revelation of himself. His Spirit accompanies his Word and brings life. The theme of life-through-the-Word is clear in both the Old and New Testaments. The first man and woman fall away from God, rebelling against him, and God sustains them and their descendants by his Word. Ezekiel 37 presents a dramatic picture of re-creation by God's Word.

Again, we find in the New Testament that God's Word plays the central role as bringer of life. So the eternal Word of God, the Son of God, becomes incarnate for the salvation of God's people (John 1; cf. Rom. 10:17). The consistent message of Scripture is that God creates his people and brings them to life through his Word. When God's people hear about God and what he requires, they *will* respond. Jesus said in John 6:37, "All that the Father gives me will come to me." So the right preaching of the Word of God is central to the church and is the basis and core of it.

Observance of the Ordinances

Another mark of a true church, a church that follows Christ, is the correct practice of the sacraments, or ordinances. This, of course, was not the idea of any church or later theologian. Jesus himself gave two visible signs of his special presence to his people. These signs are baptism (the initial sign) and the Lord's Supper (the continuing sign). Christ himself ordained these practices both by example and by command. When a church practices baptism and the Lord's Supper, it obeys Christ's teaching and example. On the other hand, when a church neglects either of these two signs, it fails to obey Christ's command. Practicing these signs correctly means especially that those who are baptized and those who come to the table give a credible profession that they are trusting in Christ alone for their salvation.

Baptism is intended for all Christians (Matt. 28:18–20; Rom. 6:1–5; Eph. 4:5). While it is generally understood to have been practiced by immersion in the New Testament church, believers have disagreed over the significance of the mode or manner of baptizing. Some (e.g., the Eastern Orthodox churches and many Baptist churches) insist on immersion; others say that the particular mode isn't essential. Also controversial has been the question of the proper subjects of baptism, that is, who should be baptized. Everyone has agreed that previously unbaptized believers are appropriate subjects for baptism. But there has been dispute whether the children of Christians may be baptized. Either way, the Bible teaches that baptism functions as both a confession of sin and a profession of faith for the believer. Faith in Christ is professed by the believer (or through a proxy, paedobaptists maintain), and the objective realities of Christ's death, the gift of the Spirit, and the final resurrection, are all depicted in baptism. All evangelical Christians recognize that water baptism does not create the reality of saving grace or faith in the one being baptized. Rather, it is the way Christ has ordained that Christians are to publicly profess that they wish to be known as Christ's followers.[3]

Christ also commanded his followers to celebrate *the Lord's Supper*. "Do this in remembrance of me," he said (Luke 22:19; 1 Cor. 11:24). The Bible does not provide an exact form of how we are to do this. Scripture gives us no precise form of words, nor does it tell us exactly what our posture must be, whether we should use bread or crackers, or whether we should come forward to partake. Scripture's silence here is suggestive. Is simplicity implied, so that *how* the supper is celebrated never distracts from *why* it is celebrated? The elements presented by the New Testament for the Lord's Supper are bread and wine, "the fruit of the vine" (Matt. 26:29; Mark 14:25; Luke 22:17).

Again, as with baptism, the question of who should participate in the Lord's Supper is far more important than the question of how to participate in the supper. Instructing the Corinthians, Paul teaches that participating in the supper testifies to participating in Christ's body and blood. It is the believer's subjective identification with Christ's saving work, represented objectively by the elements on the table. The one who takes the bread and the cup testifies to sharing in the fruits

[3]Cf. John Calvin, *Institutes*, 4.15.13.

of Christ's death, including a communion with both God and fellow Christians through the Spirit. Clearly, then, as Berkhof says, "The church must require of all those who desire to celebrate the Lord's Supper a credible profession of faith."[4]

The right preaching of God's Word—especially the gospel—and the right administration of baptism and the Lord's Supper are the components, the marks of a good church, even of a real or a true Christian church.

Who Should Regularly Take the Lord's Supper at a Church?

On the question of who should take the Lord's Supper, the short answer is: the members of the assembly, the congregation. Church members are those who should regularly take the Lord's Supper when a local church celebrates it. In today's world, the concept of membership suggests clubs or Costco. Sometimes, well-meaning Christians will look in the Bible and say, "I don't see anything like church membership there! Isn't this just a modern idea we're reading back into the Bible?"

I don't think so. First of all, the idea wasn't foreign to the people of the New Testament. There were membership organizations in the world of the Bible, too. So, in Acts 6:9, we find "the Synagogue of the Freedmen"; there were the Pharisees and Sadducees, and various other courts, councils, and guilds to which people belonged. In the Old Testament, there were members of brotherhoods of priests (the Levites) and of warriors (e.g., David's thirty men) or prophets.

In fact, the idea of membership is even more basic to humankind. Households and families have members. Races and tribes and clans have members. So also do communities and parties. And a still more basic meaning of "member" refers to the human person. Our bodies have members (Rom. 6:12–19; 7:23; 12:4–5; 1 Cor. 6:15; 12:12–27). The Bible uses the concept of member and membership in all these ways.

The Bible also represents churches as composed of members. From the earliest of times, local Christian churches were congregations of specific, identifiable people. The idea of a clearly defined community of people is central to God's action in both the Old and the New Testaments. The lives of Christians together display visibly the gospel they proclaim audibly. We Christians are supposed to look like we sound.

---

[4] Berkhof, *Systematic Theology*, 657.

If the church, in fact, presents a glorious climax in God's plan, several questions arise: How does an individual know he or she belongs to the church? How can I become a part of it? What is entailed by membership? The responsibilities and duties of members of a Christian church are simply the responsibilities and duties of Christians.[5]

But Christians also have particular duties in relation to the congregation. As Millard Erickson notes, "Christianity is a corporate matter, and the Christian life can be fully realized only in relationship to others."[6] The most fundamental duty Christians have in relation to the congregation is the duty to attend its regular gatherings.

Consider the Eighty-fourth Psalm. C. H. Spurgeon called this "the sweetest psalm."

> How lovely is your dwelling place,
>   O LORD of hosts!
> My soul longs, yes, faints
>   for the courts of the LORD;
> my heart and flesh sing for joy
>   to the living God.
>
> Even the sparrow finds a home,
>   and the swallow a nest for herself,
>   where she may lay her young,
> at your altars, O LORD of hosts,
>   my King and my God.
> Blessed are those who dwell in your house,
>   ever singing your praise!
>
> Blessed are those whose strength is in you,
>   in whose heart are the highways to Zion.
> As they go through the Valley of Baca
>   they make it a place of springs;
>   the early rain also covers it with pools.
> They go from strength to strength;
>   each one appears before God in Zion.

---

[5]For traditional teaching on the duties of church members in the North American context, see works by Benjamin Keach, Benjamin Griffith, the Charleston Association, Samuel Jones, W. B. Johnson, Joseph S. Baker, and Eleazer Savage, all reprinted in Mark Dever, ed., *Polity* (Washington, DC: 9Marks, 2001), 65–69, 103–5, 125–26, 148–51, 221–22, 276–79, 510–11.
[6]Millard Erickson, *Christian Theology*, 2nd ed. (Grand Rapids: Baker, 1998), 1058.

> O LORD God of hosts, hear my prayer;
>> give ear, O God of Jacob!
> Behold our shield, O God;
>> look on the face of your anointed!
>
> For a day in your courts is better
>> than a thousand elsewhere.
> I would rather be a doorkeeper in the house of my God
>> than dwell in the tents of wickedness.
> For the LORD God is a sun and shield;
>> the LORD bestows favor and honor.
> No good thing does he withhold
>> from those who walk uprightly.
> O LORD of hosts,
>> blessed is the one who trusts in you! (ESV)

Ultimately, of course, God is our hope. To his Old Testament people he especially testified to his presence at the temple in Jerusalem. The psalmist here testifies that he loves to meet with others who put their hope in God. We see that especially in verses 4 and 10 (cf. Ps. 27:4). Among Christians in the New Testament, we find this same desire for fellowship with other Christians. So we read in Acts 2:42: "They devoted themselves to the apostles' teaching and to the fellowship, to the breaking of bread and to prayer." The presence of God was among God's people, no longer in any special building. The building pointed to Christ. Christ had come and taught, he had been rejected, crucified, and buried, and he had risen and ascended. Now God's presence was to be found without a physical building as its locus. Now God's presence was to be found in his people, upon whom he had poured out his Spirit. What does Paul say later, in Acts 17:24? God "does not live in temples built by hands." The point is not that Christians are supposed to come regularly to a building we call the church. No, rather it is the local congregation with whom we are regularly to assemble. We assemble out of a sense of our duty sometimes, but we desire that it would always be delight. And the writer to the Hebrews warns against giving up this practice. He says in Hebrews 10:25, "Let us not give up meeting together, as some are in the habit of doing, but let us encourage one another—all the more as you see the Day approaching."

Those early Christians met regularly together on Sunday. That's why they called it "the Lord's Day" (Rev. 1:10). Though there was a millennium and a half of Jewish practice in keeping the seventh day, Christians immediately began to meet on the first, presumably because of a special connection they understood it to have to "the Lord" Jesus Christ, specifically. And that connection is, of course, that it was on the morning of the first day of the week that he arose. So, Christians from then until now have assembled on the first morning of the week. And this regular meeting is a congregation. It is those who are regularly in attendance who are known, and those are the ones who should regularly participate in the Lord's Supper in the assembly.

But membership includes not only privileges—like the Lord's Supper—it also includes duties. There are the duties and responsibilities we have toward one another as we experience the life of the new society that is the church. A great summary of all our duties as followers of Jesus Christ is that we are obliged to love one another (John 13:34–35; 15:12–17; Rom. 12:9–10; 13:8–10; Gal. 5:15; 6:10; Eph. 1:15; 1 Pet. 1:22; 2:17; 3:8; 4:8; 1 John 3:16; 4:7–12; cf. Ps. 133). And this makes sense when we consider how close we are to one another. Indeed, Christians are members of one family, even of one another. Look at what Paul wrote in 1 Corinthians 12:12–27:

> For just as the body is one and has many members, and all the members of the body, though many, are one body, so it is with Christ. For in one Spirit we were all baptized into one body—Jews or Greeks, slaves or free—and all were made to drink of one Spirit.
>
> For the body does not consist of one member but of many. If the foot should say, "Because I am not a hand, I do not belong to the body," that would not make it any less a part of the body. And if the ear should say, "Because I am not an eye, I do not belong to the body," that would not make it any less a part of the body. If the whole body were an eye, where would be the sense of hearing? If the whole body were an ear, where would be the sense of smell? But as it is, God arranged the members in the body, each one of them, as he chose. If all were a single member, where would the body be? As it is, there are many parts, yet one body.
>
> The eye cannot say to the hand, "I have no need of you," nor again the head to the feet, "I have no need of you." On the contrary, the parts of the body that seem to be weaker are indispensable, and on those parts of the body that we think less honorable we bestow the

greater honor, and our unpresentable parts are treated with greater modesty, which our more presentable parts do not require. But God has so composed the body, giving greater honor to the part that lacked it, that there may be no division in the body, but that the members may have the same care for one another. If one member suffers, all suffer together; if one member is honored, all rejoice together.

Now you are the body of Christ and individually members of it. (ESV)

Thus we find that church members are also obliged to seek peace and unity within their congregation (Rom. 12:16; 14:19; 1 Cor. 13:7; 2 Cor. 12:20; Eph. 4:3–6; Phil. 2:3; 1 Thess. 5:13; 2 Thess. 3:11; James 3:18; 4:11). And this love is expressed and unity is cultivated when church members actively sympathize with one another and go out of their way to care for each other, or as one church covenant says "carry each other's burdens and sorrows."

Church members, of course, also have particular responsibilities toward the leaders of the church. Pastors should be regarded, Paul says, "as servants of Christ and as those entrusted with the secret things of God" (1 Cor. 4:1). And therefore, as Hebrews 13 teaches, church members should remember their leaders and imitate their life and faith (Heb. 13:7; cf. 1 Cor. 4:16; 11:1; Phil. 3:17).

Jesus taught in John 13:34–35, "A new command I give you: Love one another. As I have loved you, so you must love one another. By this all men will know that you are my disciples, if you love one another." It is the living out of our Christian duties to one another that God uses to show himself real in an authentically Christian community. And it is those who are known to be doing that who are members of a local congregation. They have asked for membership, and the congregation has found their profession of Christian faith evidenced in their life. That is what formal membership is—a commitment of Christians in the name of God to one another. And it is those who are committed in this fashion who should regularly come to the Lord's Table.[7]

How Should a Church Be Run?
Though it seems like a minor matter to many, how the church is led is both an essential and important part of its life. Christians have

---

[7]The question of occasional communion by visitors is a distinct issue from the query of who should regularly commune.

disagreed about who runs the church. Various positions have been advocated. Should it be finally run by a congregation, or by some assembly within a congregation (elders), or by an assembly outside a congregation (like a presbytery), or by a bishop? Who has the final say in matters of the church's life together? The fact that such questions have caused divisions between Christians does not allow us to avoid them. As with any gathered body of people, the church must be led. Universally and locally, the head and chief shepherd of the church is Christ (Eph. 4:1–16; Heb. 13:20; 1 Pet. 5:4). And nowhere in the Gospels do we see Christ establishing—explicitly or implicitly—any sort of leadership structure for the *universal* church. But the local church is different. In the local congregation, church leaders are to be recognized. And as the elders lead and the deacons serve, the congregation is prepared to live as the witness God intends his church to be.

Notice especially that, according to the Bible, the congregation is the last and final court of appeal in matters of the life of the local church. This seems to be evidenced by the New Testament in matters of disputes between Christians, doctrine, discipline, and church membership.

In matters of disputes between Christians. In Matthew 18:15–17, Jesus tells of a dispute between brothers:

> If your brother sins against you, go and show him his fault, just between the two of you. If he listens to you, you have won your brother over. But if he will not listen, take one or two others along, so that "every matter may be established by the testimony of two or three witnesses." If he refuses to listen to them, tell it to the church; and if he refuses to listen even to the church, treat him as you would a pagan or a tax collector.

Notice to whom one finally appeals, what court is the final judicatory. It is not a bishop or a presbytery; it is not an assembly, a synod, a convention, or a conference. It is not a pastor, a board of elders, or a church committee. It is, we read, "the church," the whole local congregation, whose action must be the final court of appeal. In matters of disputes between Christians, the congregation as a whole is the final court held out in Scripture.

In matters of doctrine. Most of the letters of the New Testament were written to churches as a whole, instructing them as a whole on what their responsibilities were. Even in matters of fundamental understanding and definition of the gospel, the congregation seemed to be the court of final (earthly) appeal. So in Galatians 1, Paul calls on congregations of fairly young Christians to sit in judgment of angelic and apostolic preachers (even himself! Gal. 1:8) if they should preach any other gospel than the one the Galatians had accepted. Paul doesn't write merely to the pastors, to the presbytery, to the bishop or the conference, or to the convention or the seminary. He writes to the Christians who compose the churches, and he makes it quite clear that not only are they competent to sit in judgment on what is said to be the gospel, but that they must! They have an inescapable duty to judge even those who claim to be messengers of the good news of Jesus Christ by the consistency of the new claims with what these Galatian Christians have already known to be the gospel.

Paul makes this point again in 2 Timothy 4:3, where he counsels Timothy and the church in Ephesus on the best tack to take with false teachers. When he describes the coming tide of false teachers in the church, he particularly blames, we see in 4:3, those who, "to suit their own desires . . . gather around them a great number of teachers to say what their itching ears want to hear." Whether in selecting them, or paying them, or approving of their teaching, or in simply consenting to listen to them repeatedly, the congregation that Paul envisions here is culpable. They are held guilty for the teaching that they tolerate. In basic doctrinal definition, the congregation as a whole is the final court held out in Scripture.

In matters of discipline. In 1 Corinthians 5, Paul appeals to the whole Corinthian congregation (not just the elders) to act, in verses 5, 7, 11, and 13. This is not a matter merely or finally for Paul the apostle or for whatever elders the local Corinthian church may have had. This is a matter for the congregation as a whole. They have all accepted this one into their number. They are all now tolerating him. They are all now implicated in his sin. They must now either turn this man loose, or turn loose their claim to be Christ's disciples. In matters of church discipline, the congregation as a whole is the final court held out in Scripture.

In matters of church membership. Paul writes in 2 Corinthians 2:6–8, "The punishment inflicted on him *by the majority* is sufficient for him. Now instead, you ought to forgive and comfort him, so that he will not be overwhelmed by excessive sorrow. I urge you, therefore, to reaffirm your love for him." The church had acted to punish a particular man, it says here, "by the majority" (of church members who would have voted?), that is, by the greater part of the members consenting. The punishment seemed to have worked. It was "sufficient for him." Now Paul writes to the church as a whole calling for the repentant man's readmission into the church. But Paul can do no more than exhort, because in matters of church membership, the congregation as a whole must be the final court. So it is in Scripture.

So, we understand the Bible to teach us that we may have a senior pastor, and that we should have a plurality of elders normally leading the church, but that the church is finally congregational (which is one reason you must be very careful about whom you welcome into membership). Normally in a healthy church, a congregation will merely be able to understand and affirm what the elders recommend. But if push comes to shove, the congregation must be recognized as having the responsibility and therefore the final say.

Should We Ever Put Anyone Out of the Church?

In the Old Testament, God calls Abraham and his descendants to be his special people. However, God's holy presence with this people requires a special holiness on their part (Ex. 33:14–16). During the millennium between Moses and Ezra, Israel exists as a testimony of God's faithfulness to his promises to Abraham. It is an honor to belong to God's people, and membership has both obligations and privileges. Ultimately, the nation's sins become too great for God to tolerate, and so he judges the whole nation.

In the New Testament, we find that the church is to exercise discipline because God still expects his children to be holy. First Peter 1:14–16 (quoting Lev. 11:44–45; 19:2; 20:7) exhorted those early Christian communities, "As obedient children, do not conform to the evil desires you had when you lived in ignorance. But just as he who called you is holy, so be holy in all you do; for it is written, 'Be holy, because I am holy.'" The concept of church discipline, which can culminate in exclusion from the membership of the church, originates

101

in the teaching of Christ himself. In Matthew 18, Jesus teaches about what it means to follow him, about love that seeks the lost, and about mercifulness toward others. In the same context, Jesus also raised the matter of what should be done when one of his followers sins against another disciple and will not repent.

Discipline is inextricably bound up with the church Jesus envisions. Perhaps the most cited text on the practice of excommunication or church discipline is 1 Corinthians 5. The nature of the exclusion Paul enjoins is excommunication, which typically means excluding the parties in question from communion (the Lord's Supper) until there is sufficient evidence of their repentance. Church discipline should be practiced in order to bring sinners to repentance, to warn other church members, to encourage the health of the whole congregation, to promote a distinct corporate witness to the world, and ultimately to glorify God as his people display his character of holy love (Matt. 5:16; 1 Pet. 2:12). A true church is only for sinners, and only for repenting sinners.

What's the Church For? Why Have a Church?

Why questions pull the camera back and give us the big picture. Why is the church here? Why does it exist at all?

The church is here for you. We hope to serve non-Christians by at first confusing them, then provoking them, encouraging them, instructing them, informing them, exciting them, and loving them.

If you are a Christian who has been attending a church for a few years, or a few months, or even a few weeks, you should find spiritual nourishment at church and understand how your own biblical duties are left undone, your services unoffered, and your own life too unaccountable if you don't join some gospel-preaching church. If you refuse to commit yourself to any church, you put yourself in a dangerous position. You flout the provision God has made for your discipleship and ignore it to the impoverishment of a congregation and the imperilment of your own soul. By formally joining you help the local church as you let others know that you have committed yourself to their spiritual well-being.

If you are a member of a congregation, realize that you sit in the midst of one of God's most precious, most expensive provisions he's made for you. He bought the church, we read in Acts 20:28, with his own blood. Praise God that he has so richly provided for us in Christ!

What was it Jesus told his disciples, after they saw the rich young ruler refuse Jesus' call?

> I tell you the truth, . . . no one who has left home or brothers or sisters or mother or father or children or fields for me and the gospel will fail to receive a hundred times as much in this present age (homes, brothers, sisters, mothers, children and fields—and with them, persecutions) and in the age to come, eternal life. (Mark 10:29–30)

All the activity of every Christian congregation has the same purposes: the worship of God, the edification of the church, and the evangelization of the world.

Finally, though, the true church ultimately exists for God and his glory. Whether pursuing missions or evangelism, edifying one another through prayer and Bible study, encouraging growth in holiness, or assembling for public praise, prayer, and instruction, this one purpose prevails. The church is the unique instrument for bringing God glory. According to the Bible, God's "intent was that now, through the church, the manifold wisdom of God should be made known to the rulers and authorities in the heavenly realms, according to his eternal purpose which he accomplished in Christ Jesus our Lord" (Eph. 3:10–11). No lesser matters are at stake in the church than the promulgation of God's glory throughout his creation. As Charles Bridges expressed it, "The Church is the mirror that reflects the whole effulgence of the Divine character. It is the grand scene, in which the perfections of Jehovah are displayed to the universe."[8]

---

[8]Charles Bridges, *Christian Ministry* (London: Seeley & Burnside, 1830), 1.

4

Evangelical Self-Identity and the Doctrine of Biblical Inerrancy

JOHN D. WOODBRIDGE

Carl F. H. Henry—Fundamentalist?

One late afternoon in the early 1990s, Dr. Carl F. H. Henry shuffled along to his next appointment on the grounds of Trinity Evangelical Divinity School, Deerfield, Illinois.[1] He appeared deep in thought. I was walking toward my car and caught up with him on the sidewalk. I had known Dr. Henry since my boyhood days. My father and Dr. Henry had been colleagues at Fuller Theological Seminary in the 1950s.

Henry heard my footsteps and turned around and warmly greeted me. And yet he did not seem his normal buoyant self. Sensing something amiss, I asked him what was the matter. He replied that he had recently experienced an unpleasant conversation with an evangelical colleague from off campus. This person had accused Dr. Henry of being a "fundamentalist." Henry expressed how perplexed he was

---

[1] An earlier version of this chapter was delivered at Wheaton College on October 26, 2009, as the Armerding Lecture entitled "Wheaton College at 150: Faithful to the Church Doctrine of Biblical Inerrancy." The present version of the essay has been revised and expanded.

by the charge. He was apparently upset and saddened by the way the conversation had unfolded.

Upon first blush, the critic's charge did not make any sense to me. After all, Carl Henry was one of the prime architects of the post–World War II evangelical resurgence. He had penned the landmark book *The Uneasy Conscience of American Fundamentalism*. He had challenged the fundamentalist movement to reflect on "the social implications of its message for the non-Christian world." He wrote, "Today, Protestant Fundamentalism although heir-apparent to the supernaturalist gospel of the Biblical and Reformation minds, is a stranger, in its predominant spirit, to the vigorous social interest of its ideological forebears."[2] Although critical of aspects of American fundamentalism, Henry affirmed many of the same doctrinal "fundamentals" as those of fundamentalists. Nevertheless, in the 1940s and 1950s, he clearly began to identify himself more as an evangelical than as a fundamentalist. From 1947 until 1956, he taught at Fuller Theological Seminary, an evangelical school. From 1956 to 1968, Henry served as the editor of the flagship evangelical journal *Christianity Today*. Moreover, he had reflected seriously about defining traits of evangelical identity. In 1976, he had published the book *Evangelicals in Search of Identity*.[3] Consequently, when an evangelical scholar called Dr. Henry a fundamentalist, he had good reason to be nonplussed. Moreover, he apparently felt he had been wrongly labeled.

At the moment of our brief sidewalk encounter, I did not ask Henry what warrant his critic had proffered in making the charge. I later tried to surmise why the respected critic had described Dr. Henry, a man with impeccable "evangelical credentials," as a fundamentalist. Had the critic simply uttered the charge in anger? I really did not know. But as an admirer of the critic, I wanted to think the best. I concluded this person had apparently believed in good faith that Henry's commitment to the doctrine of biblical inerrancy rendered him a fundamentalist.

The Historic Doctrine of Biblical Inerrancy

By the early 1990s, a powerful historiography had emerged that portrayed the doctrine of biblical inerrancy as "fundamentalist" and not as an "evangelical" doctrine. With this historiography in mind, the critic

[2]Carl F. H. Henry, *The Uneasy Conscience of American Fundamentalism* (Grand Rapids: Eerdmans, 2003 [1947]), 39.
[3]Carl F. H. Henry, *Evangelicals in Search of Identity* (Waco, TX: Word, 1976).

may have felt fully justified in labeling Dr. Henry a fundamentalist. For the critic, Henry would have been simply mistaken in identifying himself as an evangelical.

Obviously, my reconstruction of what motivated the critic's labeling is speculative. What is not speculative, however, is the fact that the way historians recount the historical trajectories of various doctrines often affects our views of these same doctrines. If, for example, historians portray a doctrine as theologically innovative, a departure from what the Christian churches have consistently taught, we may suspect that the doctrine has departed from the "faith once delivered." Evangelicals have a vested interest in studying the history of doctrine.

Identifying and adhering to central church doctrines and confessions is a very important thing for us even if we uphold Scripture as our ultimate, final authority. The enterprise can provide us with a better understanding of our own evangelical theological self-identity. Do our beliefs about scriptural authority, for example, reside within identifiable central teachings of the historic Christian church? If they do not, we may have become doctrinal innovators regarding our views of Scripture despite our intentions to uphold orthodox Christian teaching.

Heeding and adhering to central church doctrines and confessions can also help steer us away from theological mishaps. In the volume *The Mark of Jesus*, Timothy George, Dean of Beeson Divinity School, describes well the value of statements of faith:

> How do such statements of faith serve the cause of evangelical unity? Perhaps they are best compared to the guardrails that help a driver especially in bad weather, to negotiate the treacherously narrow road and hairpin curves of a dangerous mountain highway. Such guardrails establish limits that protect us from the dangers of the gaping ravines to the right and to our left. Only a fool with suicidal tendencies would want to drive across a range of mountains such as the Alps in Switzerland without guardrails. It would be equally foolish, of course, to mistake the guardrails for the road, for when we start driving on the rails it is certain that catastrophe is imminent!
>
> For the Christian there is only one road. Jesus said, "I am the way [road] and the truth and the life" (John 14:6). Or, as Augustine put it, Christ is "both our native country and himself also the road to that country." This analogy is not a perfect one, of course; still, we might push it a little further to say that the Bible is our road map, a divinely given and indispensable resource that helps us to find the

road and keeps us on it while the Holy Spirit helps us to see both the road and the guardrails [statements of faith] and to keep both in proper perspective.[4]

In this essay, I will reiterate the thesis that biblical inerrancy has been a church doctrine or Augustinian central teaching of the Western Christian churches, including evangelical Protestant churches. Consequently, evangelicals who affirm the doctrine of biblical inerrancy are by no means doctrinal innovators. By biblical inerrancy, I mean in shorthand the doctrine that the Bible is infallible for faith and practice as well as for matters of history and science.[5] By the expression *church doctrine*, I am referring to a widespread shared belief of Christian churches that have had a historical existence in the West.[6]

The New View of Biblical Inerrancy

As already observed, not all theologians and church historians are agreed that biblical inerrancy has in point of fact been a central church teaching among Western churches. Indeed, during the past forty years an influential historiography has emerged arguing that biblical inerrancy is a doctrinal innovation—the provenance of which is American

---

[4]Timothy George and John Woodbridge, *The Mark of Jesus: Loving in a Way the World Can See* (Chicago: Moody Press, 2005), 82–83.

[5]The Chicago Statement on Inerrancy includes matters of faith and practice and history and "God's acts in creation" within its definition of inerrancy: "Being wholly and verbally God-given, Scripture is without error or fault in all its teaching, no less in what it states about God's acts in creation, about the events of world history, and about its own literary origins under God, than in its witness to God's saving grace in individual lives" (1.4). A. A. Hodge and B. B. Warfield provided a carefully nuanced definition of biblical inerrancy. The Bible provides us "a correct statement of facts or principles intended to be affirmed. . . . Every statement accurately corresponds to truth just as far forth as affirmed" (*Inspiration* [Grand Rapids: Baker, 1979 (1881)], 28–29). Moisés Silva points out that their definition assumed "that the Bible would be interpreted responsibly, and such a proper interpretation consists in determining what the original author meant, what he intended ("Old Princeton, Westminster, and Inerrancy," in *B. B. Warfield: Essays on His Life and Thought*, ed. Gary L. W. Johnson [Phillipsburg, NJ: P&R, 2007], 82).

[6]Cf. B. B. Warfield, "The Church Doctrine of Inspiration," in *The Inspiration and Authority of the Bible*, ed. Samuel G. Craig (Philadelphia: Presbyterian and Reformed, 1964), 105–28. The early church "rules of faith" and affirmations such as the Apostles', the Nicene, the Chalcedonian, and the Athanasian creeds were often perceived as summary statements of the apostolic faith and encapsulating doctrine of the church catholic. In his *Commonitorium* (AD 434), Vincent of Lerins wrote: "Now in the Catholic Church itself we take the greatest care to hold THAT WHICH HAS BEEN BELIEVED EVERYWHERE, ALWAYS AND BY ALL." He believed that reliance on the standards of universality, antiquity, and consent would help Christians to identify apostolically warranted interpretations of Scripture and eschew beliefs that were heretically innovative ("novel contagion"). See Henry Bettenson and Chris Maunder, *Documents of the Christian Church* (Oxford: Oxford University Press, 1999), 91–93.

fundamentalism, itself portrayed as a doctrinally innovative movement and thus suspect.

As late as the 1970s, most evangelicals assumed that biblical inerrancy was one of their nonnegotiable fundamental beliefs. For example, in 1975, in a book David Wells and I edited, *The Evangelicals: What They Believe, Who They Are, Where They Are Changing*, Martin Marty of the University of Chicago indicated that evangelicals and fundamentalists shared a belief in the doctrine of biblical inerrancy: "Both evangelicals and fundamentalists insist on the 'inerrancy of scripture' as being the most basic of all their fundamentals."[7] But under the influence of the new historiography, a good number of historians and theologians later balked at accepting the validity of Professor Marty's assessment. They claimed only fundamentalists uphold biblical inerrancy, not evangelicals. By the 1980s, Marty himself identified the doctrine of biblical inerrancy more as a fundamentalist doctrine than as a "most basic" doctrine of evangelicals.

This new historiography proposed that biblical inerrancy is supposedly neither an evangelical doctrine nor a central teaching of the Western Christian churches. Rather, it is a prototypic fundamentalist belief originating in the late nineteenth century. The actual expression *fundamentalist* did not gain widespread currency until 1920. In that year, Curtis Lee Laws (1868–1946) introduced the expression in an editorial of the *Watchman Examiner*: "We suggest that those who still cling to the great fundamentals and who mean to do battle royal for the fundamentals shall be called 'Fundamentalists.'"[8]

The new historiography that biblical inerrancy is a fundamentalist doctrine has shaped the thinking of a number of distinguished Protestant and Roman Catholic theologians and church historians.

In 1970, Ernest Sandeen, a historian, helped launch this influential historiography in a book entitled, *The Roots of Fundamentalism: British and American Millenarianism 1800–1930*.[9] He proposed the seminal thesis that the doctrine of biblical inerrancy in the original autographs was created by A. A. Hodge and B. B. Warfield in their

[7] David F. Wells and John D. Woodbridge, eds., *The Evangelicals: What They Believe, Who They Are, Where They Are Changing* (Grand Rapids: Baker, 1977), 200.
[8] Cited in David Beale, *In Pursuit of Purity: American Fundamentalism Since 1850* (Greenville, SC: Unusual Publications, 1986), 195.
[9] Ernest Sandeen, *The Roots of Fundamentalism: British and American Millenarianism 1800–1930* (Chicago: University of Chicago Press, 1970). The University of Chicago Press published a paperback edition of this book in 2008.

1881 article "Inspiration." According to Sandeen, these two Presbyterians, feeling hard-pressed by burgeoning higher critical studies in their day, crafted the doctrine supposedly as a means to escape the negative entailments of these critical studies for the Bible's authority. Professor Sandeen was emboldened to claim that the doctrine of inerrancy in the original autographs "did not exist in either Europe or America prior to its formulation in the last half of the nineteenth century."[10] He further charged that the Princeton doctrine of an inerrant Bible "was maintained only by recourse to completely useless original autographs."[11] He disputed the claim of Hodge and Warfield that their doctrine of Scripture reflected the Catholic teaching of the Christian churches since the Patristic era. For Sandeen, the doctrine of biblical inerrancy in the original autographs represented a nonheuristic doctrinal innovation. It strayed not only from the Calvinist Westminster Confession but also from the central teachings of the Western churches. Nevertheless, fundamentalists, assuming that the belief was biblically warranted, allegedly appropriated the doctrinal innovation and converted it into a nonnegotiable fundamental of their movement.

How might we respond to those who advocate Sandeen's interpretation, or ones similar to it—that is, who portray the belief not as an evangelical church doctrine but as a misleading formulation of late nineteenth-century Presbyterians, especially A. A. Hodge and B. B. Warfield? One obvious step to take is to assess the historical validity of Sandeen's thesis that the doctrine of inerrancy in the original autographs did not exist in Europe or America before 1881, or before 1850.

To this latter endeavor, I now turn. First, I will propose (citing initially particular Roman Catholics) that in fact a number of leading churchmen in the West affirmed the truthfulness of Scripture for matters of faith and practice as well as history and "science." They thereby contributed to an Augustinian tradition regarding biblical inerrancy. To demonstrate this point, I will offer a brief reception-history sketch of the way biblical inerrancy was perceived by these churchmen. By reception history, I mean the reconstruction of a history of the perceptions of individuals regarding a particular idea, an event, a

---

[10]Ernest Sandeen, *The Origins of Fundamentalism: Toward A Historical Interpretation* (Philadelphia: Fortress, 1968), 14.
[11]Sandeen, *Roots of Fundamentalism*, 128.

phenomenon, or material objects.[12] For example, Professor Sandeen provided his readers with a certain perception of the history of biblical authority. Our primary question would therefore be, Does Sandeen's perception or historical reconstruction correspond with the views of biblical authority evidenced by the churchmen we are bringing to the witness stand? If Sandeen's thesis is valid, we should expect to find no credible advocates of biblical inerrancy in the original autographs before 1850 or 1881.

Second, we will revisit the same history of biblical authority from the Patristic era until the late nineteenth century, but this time we will call to the witness stand an essentially different set of witnesses and authorities who will testify in the main about the views of Protestants. Some of these witnesses were not themselves partisans of the doctrine of biblical inerrancy. Nevertheless, they did acknowledge that such was a central church doctrine of the Western churches, both Roman Catholic and Protestant. Frequently, testimonies of nonpartisans are of special worth, issuing as they do from witnesses not suspected of making claims about biblical inerrancy owing to ecclesiastical or confessional loyalties.

Augustine on Inerrancy

Let us begin by bringing to the witness stand a number of persons who will help establish for us the premise that an Augustinian belief in the truthfulness of Scripture constituted a major church doctrine in the West (among Roman Catholics).

What better person to invite as our star witness to describe the Augustinian teaching about Scripture's truthfulness than St. Augustine (354–430) himself? After all, as we shall see in our brief reception history, Augustine's views on the Bible's infallibility were frequently cited by later theologians and perceived as tantamount to a central church doctrine or tradition for many Roman Catholics and Protestants. Hans Küng observed, "St. Augustine's influence in regard to

[12]Professor Harold Marcuse, University of California at Santa Barbara, defines reception history as "the history of the meanings that have been imputed to historical events. It traces the different ways in which participants, observers, historians and other retrospective interpreters have attempted to make sense of events both as they unfolded and over time since then, to make those events meaningful for the present in which they lived and live" (http://www.history.ucsb.edu/faculty/marcuse/receptionhist.htm, accessed Oct. 19, 2009). Jason Falck informed me of this reference.

inspiration and inerrancy prevailed throughout the Middle Ages and right into the modern age."[13]

Augustine clearly affirmed as a nonnegotiable church doctrine that there are no errors in sacred Scripture. Such was a working premise for him, an essential guardrail if you will. When St. Jerome in his commentary on Galatians 2:14 intimated that Paul had relied upon a "white lie," Augustine delivered a sharp if not alarmist rejoinder:

> It seems to me that the most disastrous consequences must follow upon our believing that anything false is found in the sacred books: that is to say that the men by whom the Scripture has been given to us, and committed to writing, did put down in these books anything false. . . . If you once admit into such a high sanctuary of authority one false statement . . . , there will not be left a single sentence of those books which, if appearing to any one difficult in practice or hard to believe, may not by the same fatal rule be explained away, as a statement in which, intentionally, . . . the author declared what was not true.[14]

Whatever we may think about Augustine's "all or nothing" logic regarding the significance of one error, it is clear the Bishop of Hippo believed the Bible is "true" through and through. It is without error, or, if you will, inerrant.

A number of Augustine's contemporaries had pointed to supposed errors in Scripture as the basis for their attacks on the Christian religion. In response to their charges, Augustine wrote *The Harmony of the Gospels*. He indicated that he felt obliged to confute unbelievers who denied the harmony of the four Gospels and affirmed the existence of errors in Scripture.

> And in order to carry out this design to a successful conclusion, we must prove that the writers in question do not stand in any antagonism to each other. For those adversaries are in the habit of adducing this as the primary allegation in all their vain objections, namely that the evangelists are not in harmony with each other.[15]

---

[13]Hans Küng, *Infallible? An Enquiry* (London: Collins, 1972), 174. For Augustine's views of Scripture, see A. D. R. Polman, *Word of God according to St. Augustine* (Grand Rapids: Eerdmans, 1961).

[14]Augustine, *Letters of St. Augustine* 28.3.

[15]Augustine, *Harmony of the Gospels* 1.7.10.

A further claim of Augustine became a salient component of a church doctrine about the truthfulness of Scripture. In his AD 405 letter to Faustus the Manichean, Augustine provided an explanation regarding the ways a reader may have supposed there are "errors" in the extant copies of Scripture. He wrote:

> I confess to your Charity that I have learned to yield this respect and honor only to the canonical books of Scripture: of these alone do I most firmly believe that the authors were completely free from error. And if in these writings I am perplexed by anything which appears to me opposed to truth, I do not hesitate to suppose that either the manuscript is faulty, or the translator has not caught the meaning of what was said, or I myself have failed to understand.[16]

In sum, Augustine proposed a threefold explanation of the provenance of supposed errors within Scripture. If you believed you had spotted one, it was because you had encountered a manuscript error, or the translator of your text had engaged in a faulty translation, or you had simply misunderstood what Scripture was saying. By Augustine's day, some Christian scholars were practicing a form of lower scriptural criticism, that is, attempting to remove copyists' errors from extant copies of the Scripture.

Augustine also argued that Scripture is written in a language accommodated to the weakness of our understanding.[17] This gracious divine accommodation helps us with our frail minds to understand Scripture. Some passages of Scripture are written in the language of appearance—how things appear to us. Scripture is not written in a way to render it as a "scientific" textbook. Rather, when it describes the natural world, it does so truthfully (without error) but not necessarily in exhaustive and overly precise terms.

Considerable confusion has recently emerged in evangelical circles regarding what the Augustinian doctrine of accommodation represents, some evangelical scholars portraying a Socinian doctrine of accommodation as if it were an Augustinian definition of accommodation.[18]

---

[16] Augustine, *Letters of St. Augustine* 82.3.

[17] For Augustine's view of accommodation, see Polman, *Word of God according to St. Augustine*; Stephen D. Benin, *The Footprints of God: Divine Accommodation in Jewish and Christian Thought* (Albany: State University of New York Press, 1993), 94–112.

[18] A notable example of the exchanging of a "Socinian" definition of accommodation for an Augustinian perspective is found in Jack Rogers and Donald McKim, *The Authority and Interpretation of the Bible: An Historical Approach* (New York: Harper & Row, 1979).

According to the Socinian definition, God accommodated Scripture to the faulty cosmologies of the biblical authors. The result: we have an errant Scripture owing to imported errors drawn from these faulty cosmologies that allegedly informed the writing of the biblical authors. By contrast, Augustine's view of accommodation did not have as an entailment that errors are found in Scripture. The Bible may describe the natural world simply, but truthfully as it is. Richard Muller clarifies further the differing meanings of a Socinian view of accommodation as opposed to an Augustinian view.[19] The Princetonian Charles Hodge argued that it was the dangerous advocacy of a Socinian view of accommodation that contributed to the undermining of a high view of Scripture at the turn of the nineteenth century in Germany among Protestants.[20]

Eck on Inerrancy

We will now invite our second witness to the stand, Johannes Eck (1496–1543), a Roman Catholic contemporary of Martin Luther.[21] In 1518, Eck became alarmed that Erasmus, the brilliant Roman Catholic classicist and competent biblical scholar, had indicated that Matthew had made a mistake in substituting one word for another. Erasmus was quite explicit about his point of view in a letter of response to Eck: "Nor, in my view, would the authority of the whole of Scripture be instantly imperiled, as you suggest, if an evangelist by a slip of memory did put one name for another, Isaiah for instance instead of Jeremiah, for this is not a point on which anything turns."[22] In the same passage, Erasmus, a skilled debater, tried to shelter himself from potential charges of heterodoxy by pointing out that he never had said

---

[19]Richard A. Muller, *Dictionary of Latin and Greek Theological Terms: Drawn Principally from Protestant Scholastic Theology* (Grand Rapids: Baker, 1996), 19, on *accommodatio*. See also Glenn Sunshine, "Accommodation in Calvin and Socinus: A Study in Contrasts" (MA thesis, Trinity Evangelical Divinity School, 1985); Zbigniew Ogonowski, "Faustus Socinus 1539–1604," in *Shapers of Religious Traditions in Germany, Switzerland, and Poland, 1560–1600,* ed. Jill Raitt (New Haven, CT: Yale University Press, 1981), 195–209.

[20]Charles Hodge had firsthand knowledge of theological developments in Germany owing to his studies there. He published Hugh Rose's "The State of the Protestant Church in Germany," *The Biblical Repertory and Theological Review* 2 (1826): 391–501. During the second half of the eighteenth century, some 31 volumes were published in Germany devoted to the subject of biblical accommodation. Many apparently advocated a Socinian definition.

[21]Concerning Luther's famous debate with Eck at Leipzig, see Heiko A. Oberman, *Luther: Man between God and the Devil* (New York: Image, 1992), 246–47, 262, 299–300.

[22]Letter 844, to Johann Maier von Eck, May 15, 1518, in *The Correspondence of Erasmus* (Toronto: University of Toronto Press, 1982), 6.28.

explicitly that an actual error existed in Scripture: "I would not wish to say this because I think the apostles ever did make mistakes, but because I deny that the presence of some mistake must needs shake the credit of the whole of Scripture."[23]

Now, Eck, respectful of Erasmus's reputation for scholarship ("most learned of men"), would have none of Erasmus's concession that an error existed as well in Matthew 2. For Eck, it was Augustine who had helped form his convictions regarding the church doctrine of Scripture. Wrote Eck:

> First of all then, to begin at this point, many people are offended at your having written in your notes on the second chapter of Matthew the words, "or because the evangelists themselves did not draw evidence of this kind from books, but trusted as men will to memory and made a mistake." For in these words you seem to suggest that the evangelists wrote like ordinary men, in that they wrote this in reliance on their memories and failed to inspect the sources, and so for this reason made a mistake.[24]

Then Eck cited what he deemed was the central church Augustinian doctrine of biblical inerrancy: "Listen, dear Erasmus: do you suppose any Christian will patiently endure to be told that the evangelists in their Gospel made mistakes?"[25] From Eck's point of view, no Christian would countenance Erasmus's alleged avowal of the errancy of Scripture. Then, Eck cited his Patristic authority or warrant for this stance—none other than St. Augustine's either-or teaching: "If the authority of Holy Scripture at this point is shaky, can any other passage be free from the suspicion of error? A conclusion drawn by St. Augustine from an elegant chain of reasoning."[26]

Please note what constituted an "error" for Eck—only one word substituted for another. Some critics of the doctrine of inerrancy have suggested that it was the Princetonians in the late nineteenth century who redefined the word *infallibility* by giving it a more demanding set of precisionist connotations for what constituted an error, a restriction not associated with earlier uses of the word *infallibility* in the history

---

[23]Ibid.
[24]Letter 769, from Johann Maier von Eck, February 2, 1518, in *The Correspondence of Erasmus* (Toronto: University of Toronto Press, 1979), 5.289.
[25]Ibid.
[26]Ibid., 289–90.

of the church.[27] The debate between Eck and Erasmus would suggest otherwise. Eck, at least, believed the Bible's infallibility could be placed in jeopardy by one misplaced word—a very small linguistic bit.

Simon on Inerrancy

Our third witness attesting to the powerful influence of the Augustinian church doctrine about the inerrancy of Scripture is Richard Simon (1638–1712).[28] An Oratorian priest, Simon is often hailed as the "Father of Higher Criticism." In the years spanned by Paul Hazard's famous "Crisis of the European Mind" (1680–1715), Simon was probably the most erudite biblical expert in all Europe.[29] He had a profound knowledge of Rabbinics as well as the theology and liturgies of the Eastern churches, gained in part while he served as the librarian at the Oratorian Order's House on Rue St. Honoré in Paris. He had read and cataloged precious manuscripts, both Western and Eastern. He became thoroughly familiar with the history of Bible translations and the worth of particular Bible commentaries. He had established principles of biblical interpretation. He drafted huge tomes in which he displayed uncommon knowledge of the history of exegesis and biblical versions.[30] For this reason, Simon's testimony regarding the

---

[27]See, e.g., George Marsden, *Fundamentalism and American Culture* (Oxford: Oxford University Press, 2006), 112–13: "The purpose of inspiration was to communicate a 'record of truth.' For such a record 'accuracy of statement' and an 'infallible correctness of the report' were essential. These would not be assured if the selection of words were left to humans, whose memories were faulty. Although the method of inspiration was not merely mechanical dictation, the Holy Spirit would guarantee the accuracy of the reports only by inspiring the authors to select correct words." Professor Marsden proposes that the alleged influence of Common Sense Realism and Baconianism upon the thought of the Princetonians prompted them to emphasize the accuracy of the words of Holy Scripture.

[28]Studies devoted to the life and thought of Richard Simon include Paul Auvray, *Richard Simon (1638–1712): Étude bio-bibliographique avec des textes inédits* (Paris: Presses Universitaires de France, 1974); August Bernus, *Richard Simon et son Histoire critique du Vieux Testament* (Genève: Slatkine Reprints, 1969 [1869]); Jacques Le Brun and John D. Woodbridge, eds., *Richard Simon: Additions aux Recherches curieuses sur la diversité des langues et religions d'Edward Brerewood* (Paris: Presses Universitaires de France, 1983); Henri Margival, *Essai sur Richard Simon et la critique biblique au XVIIe siècle* (Paris: Maillet, 1900); Jean Steinmann, *Richard Simon et les origines de l'éxègese biblique* (Paris: Desclèe De Brouwer, 1960).

[29]Paul Hazard, *The European Mind: The Critical Years 1680–1715* (New York: Fordham University Press, 1990). In 1935, Hazard's volume first appeared under the title *La crise de la conscience européenne*.

[30]See, e.g., Simon, *Histoire critique des versions du Nouveau Testament* (Rotterdam: Reinier Leers, 1690); Simon, *Histoire critique des principaux commentateurs du Nouveau Testament* (Rotterdam: Reinier Leers, 1693); Simon, *Nouvelles observations sur le texte et les versions du Nouveau Testament* (Paris: Jean Boudot, 1695).

beliefs of Europeans at the dawn of the European "Enlightenment" is significant indeed.

On the very first page of his epochal *Critical History of the Old Testament*, Simon generalized about the current belief of Christians and Jews concerning the Bible's infallibility in 1678:

> One is not able to doubt that the truths contained in Holy Scripture are infallible and of a divine authority, since they come immediately from God, who in doing this used the ministry of men as his interpreters. Is there anyone, either Jew or Christian, who does not recognize that this Scripture being the pure Word of God, is at the same time the first principle and the foundation of Religion. But in that men have been the depositories of Sacred Books, as well as all other books, and that the first Originals [*les premiers Originaux*] had been lost; it was in some measure impossible that a number of changes occurred, due as much to the length of time passing, as to the negligence of copyists. It is for this reason St. Augustine recommends before all things to those who wish to study Scripture to apply themselves to the Criticism of the Bible and to correct the mistakes [*fautes*] of their copies. *Codicibus emendandis primitus debet invigilare solertia eorum, qui Scripturas Divinas nosse desiderant* [Augustine, *On Christian Doctrine*, bk. 2].[31]

Simon believed he was the first scholar to apply the French word *critique* to the study of Scripture.[32]

In this passage, Richard Simon made the generalizing claim that all Jews and Christians in 1678 believed in the divine authority and infallibility of Scripture because it came from God. Simon recommended that critics needed to correct the mistakes in their copies because the *originaux* (originals) had been lost. What is more, Simon, Jesuit trained and quite anti-Augustinian, identified this program of "lower criticism" with none other than St. Augustine. Simon's contemporary J. A. Bengel, as well as some Protestant orthodox scholars, likewise advocated "lower criticism."[33] They used the Latin word *autographa* to identify biblical manuscripts that had perished and the word *apographa* for "original and authentic" extant texts in Greek

---

[31]Richard Simon, *Histoire critique du Vieux Testament* (Rotterdam: Reinier Leers, 1685), 1.
[32]Auvray, *Richard Simon (1638–1712)*, 42.
[33]Alan Thompson, "Pietist Critique of Inerrancy? J. A. Bengel's *Gnomon* as a Test Case," *JETS* 47 (2004): 71–88.

and Hebrew.[34] They viewed these latter texts as "infallible," any errors being those of copyists.[35]

Simon's generalization that all Jews and Christians in 1678 believed in the infallibility of Scripture *before* the so-called Enlightenment began renders less persuasive the historiography that proposes that infallibility or inerrancy constituted Enlightenment doctrines, logical entailments of a rationalistic "enlightenment religion."[36] In any case, we should perhaps exercise due care in using the English word *Enlightenment* if applying it to the eighteenth century. The English expression "Age of Enlightenment" did not come into parlance until the 1860s—although the word *enlightened* (Berkeley) did have some play in eighteenth-century speech.[37]

Leo XIII on Inerrancy

Our fourth witness attesting to the existence of an Augustinian tradition regarding biblical inerrancy is Pope Leo XIII, a contemporary of A. A. Hodge and B. B. Warfield. The pope sought to give counsel to Roman Catholic professors of sacred Scripture of his day, especially at "Seminaries and Academical institutions," regarding how they should study the Bible and interact with "higher criticism" and recent developments in science. The Rector of the Catholic Institute in Paris, Monseigneur d'Hulst, had written a piece (Jan. 25, 1893), in which he appeared open to limiting inspiration to matters of faith and practice.[38] In *Providentissimus Deus: Encyclical of Pope Leo XIII on the Study of Holy Scripture* (Nov. 18, 1893), Leo XIII indicated that the Roman Catholic Church affirmed that Holy Scripture is without error not only for matters of faith and practice but also for matters

---

[34]Richard A. Muller, *Post-Reformation Reformed Dogmatics: The Rise and Development of Reformed Orthodoxy, ca. 1520 to ca. 1725*, 2nd ed., 4 vols. (Grand Rapids: Baker, 2003), 2:413.

[35]Ibid., 413–14.

[36]See Marsden's chapter, "Presbyterians and the Truth," in *Fundamentalism and American Culture*, 109–18. For incisive critiques of Marsden's proposal, see Paul Helseth, *"Right Reason" and the Princeton Mind: An Unorthodox Proposal* (Phillipsburg, NJ: P&R, 2010); and David P. Smith's forthcoming volume *B. B. Warfield's Scientifically Constructive Theological Scholarship*.

[37]*The Oxford English Dictionary*, 2nd ed. (Oxford: Clarendon, 1989), 5:268: "1860 Froude Hist. Eng V. 3. He imagined that an age of enlightenment was at hand."

[38]Pope Leo XIII, *Providentissimus Deus: Encyclical of Pope Leo XIII on the Study of Holy Scripture, November 18, 1893*, sec. 20. Concerning Monseigneur d'Hulst's limitation on the extent of infallibility's purview, see James Tunstead Burtchaell, *Catholic Theories of Biblical Inspiration since 1810: A Review and Critique* (Cambridge: Cambridge University Press, 1969), 220.

of history and science (a core entailment of the doctrine of biblical inerrancy). He chastised those who limited the inerrancy of Scripture to matters of faith and morals.

> But it is absolutely wrong and forbidden, either to narrow inspiration to certain parts only of Holy Scripture, or to admit that the sacred writer has erred. For the system of those who, in order to rid themselves of these difficulties, do not hesitate to concede that divine inspiration regards the things of faith and morals, and nothing beyond, because (as they wrongly think) in a question of the truth or falsehood of a passage, we should consider not so much what God has said as the reason and purpose which He had in mind in saying it—this system cannot be tolerated.[39]

Concerning physical science, Pope Leo XIII wrote:

> We have to contend against those who, making an evil use of physical science, minutely scrutinize the Sacred Book in order to detect the writers in a mistake, and to take occasion to vilify its contents. Attacks of this kind, bearing as they do on matters of sensible experience, are peculiarly dangerous to the masses, and also to the young who are beginning literary studies.[40]

Leo XIII continued, "There can never, indeed, be any real discrepancy between the theologian and the physicist, as long as each confines himself with his own lines, and both are careful, as St. Augustine warns us." He cited Augustine's wise counsel:

> Whatever they can really demonstrate to be true of physical nature, we must show to be capable of reconciliation with our Scriptures; and whatever they assert in their treatises which is contrary to these Scriptures of ours, that is to Catholic faith, we must either prove it as well as we can to be entirely false, or at all events we must, without the smallest hesitation, believe it to be so.[41]

Pope Leo XIII acknowledged that the Vulgate was the "authentic" version of the Roman Catholic Church per the Council of Trent. At the same time, he quoted St. Augustine's counsel to the effect that the

---

[39]Pope Leo XIII, *Providentissimus Deus*, sec. 18.
[40]Ibid.
[41]Ibid.

"examination of older tongues" and manuscripts will be useful and advantageous to clear up the possible "ambiguity and want of clearness" in the Vulgate.[42]

Toward the end of his encyclical (sec. 21), Leo XIII summarized Catholic teaching regarding biblical inerrancy. He referred to a passage from Augustine we have already cited as the warrant for this church doctrine:

> It follows that those who maintain that an error is possible in any genuine passage of the sacred writings, either pervert the Catholic notion of inspiration, or make God the author of such error. And so emphatically were all the Fathers and Doctors agreed that the divine writings, as left by the hagiographers, are free from all error, that they laboured earnestly, with no less skill than reverence, to reconcile with each other those numerous passages which seem at variance— the very passages which in great measure have been taken up by the higher criticism. . . . The words of St. Augustine to St. Jerome may sum up what they taught: "On my part I confess to your charity that it is only to those Books of Scripture which are now called canonical that I have learned to pay such honor and reverence as to believe most firmly that none of their writers has fallen into any error. And if in these Books I meet anything which seems contrary to truth, I shall not hesitate to conclude either that the text is faulty, or that the translator has not expressed the meaning of the passage, or that I myself do not understand."[43]

Please note that Pope Leo XIII believed that the Patristic fathers had wrestled with a number of the same problem passages that had caught the attention of "higher critics" in his own day. Leo XIII apparently entertained the perception that what he meant by saying Holy Scripture is without error corresponded to what the church fathers believed about the truthfulness of Scripture. He did not think he was living in a different paradigm (our term) than their own so that he could not understand the textual problems they addressed. Moreover, Leo XIII confirmed the premise that in the Roman Catholic Church, Augustine's teaching about the Bible's inerrancy was tantamount to a central church doctrine.

---

[42]Ibid., sec. 13.
[43]Ibid., sec. 21.

Please note, too, that the claims of Hodge and Warfield in 1881 about the infallibility of the original autographs as constituting a church doctrine appear much less lonesome and doctrinally innovative in the context of Leo XIII's encyclical (1893). And should we be wondering whether Leo borrowed his thoughts about Scripture from Hodge and Warfield, who wrote a decade before him, we can safely surmise that he did not. Rather, the pope was reiterating an Augustinian church doctrine about inerrancy.

More Recent Catholic Developments

In 1910, the papacy tried to rein in the teachings of so-called "Catholic modernists" (a term first used in 1905) by stipulating that all members of the clergy must swear an antimodernist oath.[44] Catholic "modernists" such as Alfred Loisy at the Catholic Institute in Paris had earlier attempted to make teachings of higher criticism and evolution more acceptable within the Roman Catholic Church.[45] They denied the inerrancy of Scripture. The papacy categorically rejected the modernists' initiatives and continued to affirm the church doctrine of biblical inerrancy.[46]

Some years later, Pope Pius XII in his encyclical *Divino Afflante Spiritu* (1943) once again condemned the limited inerrancy position (that is, the exclusion of history and science from an inerrancy definition).[47] The pope wrote that when

> some Catholic writers, in spite of this solemn definition of Catholic doctrine [at Trent], by which such divine authority is claimed for the "entire books with all their parts" as to secure freedom from any error whatsoever, ventured to restrict the truth of Sacred Scripture solely to matters of faith and morals, and to regard other matters, whether in the domain of physical science or history, as "obiter dicta" and—as they contended—in no wise connected with faith,

---

[44]Burtchaell, *Catholic Theories of Biblical Inspiration*, 232.
[45]Ibid.
[46]Pope Pius XII, *Divino Afflante Spiritu on Promoting Biblical Studies, Commemorating the Fiftieth Anniversary of Providentissimus Deus.*
[47]Ibid., sec. 1. Citing Leo XIII and St. Augustine, Pius XII wrote: "Finally, it is absolutely wrong and forbidden either to narrow inspiration to certain passages of Holy Scripture, or to admit that the sacred writer has erred, since the divine inspiration not only is essentially incompatible with error but excludes and rejects it absolutely and necessarily as it is impossible that God Himself, the Supreme Truth, can utter that which is not true. This is the ancient and constant faith of the Church" (sec. 3).

Our Predecessor of immortal memory, Leo XIII in the Encyclical Letter "Providentissimus Deus" . . . justly and rightly condemned these errors.[48]

In the early 1960s, the drafters of the first edition of *Dei Verbum*, Vatican II's statement regarding Holy Scripture, continued to affirm the doctrine of biblical inerrancy for matters of faith and practice and history and science.[49] Nevertheless, in the final edition (Nov. 18, 1965) of *Dei Verbum* (the Constitution on Divine Revelation, art. 11), the Roman Catholic Church at Vatican II apparently broke with its own Augustinian definition of inerrancy and affirmed, "We must acknowledge that the books of Scripture firmly, faithfully, and without error teach that truth which God, for the sake of our salvation, wished to see confided to Sacred Scriptures."[50]

Thereafter, a number of Roman Catholic scholars began to identify the inerrancy position (including history and science) not with the longstanding Augustinian tradition of their church but, interestingly enough, with the viewpoint of Protestant fundamentalism and biblical literalism.[51] For example, the Most Rev. Charles J. Chaput, the archbishop of Denver, in addressing the US Conference of Catholic Bishops (2000), entitled his keynote address "*Dei Verbum* 35 Years Later: Understanding the Word of God." He declared:

> *Dei Verbum*, therefore, offers a middle way between Protestant fundamentalism and secular rationalism in interpreting the Bible. It clearly teaches the divine inspiration of the sacred authors and therefore, the inerrant quality of their writings. It says "that the books of Scripture, firmly, faithfully and without error, teach that truth which God, for the sake of our salvation, wished to be confided to the sacred Scriptures" (n. 11). In that qualifying phrase, "for the sake of our salvation," we hear the Catholic response to modern rationalism,

---

[48]Ibid., sec. 3.
[49]The first draft indicated that "the entire sacred Scripture is absolutely immune from error."
[50]*Dei Verbum* (Nov. 18, 1965).
[51]Consult "Pastoral Statement for Catholics on Biblical Fundamentalism" (National Conference of Catholic Bishops Ad Hoc Committee on Biblical Fundamentalism, Archbishop John Whealon of Hartford, Connecticut, chair, Mar. 26, 1987), 1: "A further characteristic of biblical fundamentalism is that it tends to interpret the Bible as being always without error or as literally true in a way quite different from the Catholic Church's teaching on the inerrancy of the Bible."

which denies the inerrancy of Scripture and even the need for salvation. But *Dei Verbum* also avoids a simple-minded literalism.[52]

On occasion, a few Roman Catholic scholars have dared to raise the objection that what some of their colleagues have disparaged as a fundamentalist view of Scripture actually represents what the Roman Catholic Church had essentially taught regarding Scripture from St. Augustine's day until the first draft of *Dei Verbum* of Vatican II.[53]

Protestant Viewpoints: James Kugel

In the preceding segment of our reception-history sketch we have proposed, contra Professor Sandeen's perception of the history of biblical authority, that the doctrine of biblical inerrancy constituted a central Augustinian church doctrine for the Roman Catholic Church until Vatican II. Certainly, there were biblical scholars and theologians in the Roman Catholic communion such as Erasmus, Lessius, Isaac de La Peyrère, Henry Holden, Richard Simon, Lammenais, and the Catholic "modernist" Alfred Loisy who dissented from the doctrine in one way or another.[54] But they constituted a distinct minority within the clergy.

But did the Augustinian church doctrine of Scripture's inerrancy also constitute a commonly held church belief for Protestants in the West? To address this question, we will again pursue a reception-history sketch of the doctrine of biblical inerrancy as it relates to Protestants.

Protestant Reformers from Martin Luther to Thomas Cranmer believed that the Christian church during the Patristic era and beyond, until 1200 or so, had remained basically orthodox and thus belonged

---

[52]Most Reverend Charles J. Chaput, Archbishop of Denver, "Dei Verbum 35 Years Later: Understanding the Word of God" (Scripture Conference 2000, US Conference of Catholic Bishops, Oct. 20, 2000).

[53]Cf. Collin Hansen, "Rome's Battle for the Bible, Synod of Bishops Revisits Inerrancy Compromise Reached at Vatican II" (blog), *Christianity Today*, October 20, 2008. The working document *Instrumentum Laboris*, drawn up for the Roman Synod of Bishops that met in Rome (Oct. 2008), appeared to limit the purview of the Bible's inerrancy to matters of saving truth (excluding history and science). A number of conservative bishops expressed reservations about the early drafts of this document.

[54]Cf. Burtchaell, *Catholic Theories of Biblical Inspiration*, 44–47 (Lessius), 59–60 (Henry Holden).

to them.[55] Cranmer, for example, postulated that the Catholic Church had upheld the true doctrine of the Lord's Supper until around AD 1000, but then the church's teaching was corrupted.[56] The Reformers believed they were recovering church doctrine, not inventing it. Our first witness is James L. Kugel, a specialist in the Hebrew Bible and its interpretation. His testimony provides further insights regarding the way in which the church fathers esteemed and revered Scripture. He helps us to understand that even if the church fathers did not treat the subject of inerrancy in a systematic fashion, they worked with the assumption of Scripture's inerrancy in doing their exegesis.

From 1982 to 2003, Professor Kugel, now living in Israel, served as the Starr Professor of Hebrew at Harvard. His class on the Bible attracted up to nine hundred students—one of the most popular classes at the university.

In his recent book *How to Read the Bible: A Guide to Scripture Then and Now*, Kugel argues that the church fathers believed Scripture is without error and engaged in harmonization efforts to demonstrate that such is the case.[57] Kugel writes, "It is a striking fact that all ancient interpreters seem to have shared very much the same set of expectations about the biblical text."[58] He continues,

> We can gain a rather clear picture of what their authors were assuming about the biblical text—and what emerges is that, despite the geographic and cultural distance separating some of these interpreters from others, they all seem to have assumed the same four basic things about *how* the Bible was to be read.[59]

Then Kugel outlines four assumptions held in common by ancient interpreters. According to the third assumption in his listing, the church fathers upheld the perfect truthfulness of Scripture. Assumption 3 reads: "Interpreters also assumed that the Bible contained no contradictions

---

[55]Luther was especially critical of the Roman Catholic Church's doctrine of transubstantiation. He believed it represented a doctrinal innovation based not on Scripture but particularly upon Aristotle's influence on the thinking of Thomas Aquinas and the Fourth Lateran Council.

[56]Graham Cole, *Cranmer's Views on the Bible and the Christian Prince: An Examination of His Writings and the Edwardian Formularies* (ThM thesis, University of Sydney, 1983), 132.

[57]James L. Kugel, *How to Read the Bible: A Guide to Scripture Then and Now* (New York: Free Press, 2007), 15.

[58]Ibid., 14.

[59]Ibid.

or mistakes. It is perfectly harmonious, despite its being an anthology. . . ."[60] Kugel further observes:

> And of course the Bible ought not to contradict itself or even seem to repeat itself needlessly, so that if it said "and the two of them walked together" twice, the second occurrence cannot be merely repetitive; it must mean something different from the first. In short, the Bible, they felt, is an utterly consistent, seamless, perfect book.[61]

Now, Professor Kugel is by no means an advocate of the doctrine of biblical inerrancy. His testimony, therefore, cannot be easily impugned as if it stems from a partisan spirit.

Luther, Calvin, and the Protestant Orthodox

On the eve of the Reformation, Johannes Eck, as we saw, claimed that "no Christian" would permit Erasmus to say that an actual error exists in Scripture. But did Martin Luther, Eck's Protestant contemporary and sometime disputant, likewise believe in biblical inerrancy? Much ink has been spilled regarding this controversial topic.[62]

Heimo Reinitzer, our second witness coming to the stand, may help us adjudicate the validity of competing interpretations of Luther's views of biblical authority. In 1983, Dr. Reinitzer published *Biblia deutsch: Luthers Bibelübersetzung und ihre Tradition* in celebration of Luther's five hundredth birthday.[63] In researching this book, Reinitzer, a historian, had studied the history of various editions of the Luther Bible (1534) and the Reformer's views of scriptural authority and interpretation. Reinitzer ranks among the leading experts in the world regarding Luther's view of biblical authority.[64]

In the early 1980s, I was a research fellow at the Herzog August Bibliothek in Wolfenbüttel, Germany, about the same time Professor Reinitzer's book was published under the library's auspices. Reinitzer was likewise doing research at the library on occasion. I had the oppor-

---

[60]Ibid., 15.
[61]Ibid.
[62]Mark D. Thompson, *A Sure Ground on Which to Stand: The Relation of Authority and Interpretive Method in Luther's Approach to Scripture* (Eugene, OR: Wipf & Stock, 2006 [2004]), 47–53.
[63]Heimo Reinitzer, *Biblia deutsch: Luthers Bibelübersetzung und ihre Tradition* (Wolfenbüttel: Herzog August Bibliothek, 1983).
[64]Professor Dr. Heimo Reinitzer became in time the president of the Akademie der Wissenschaften in Hamburg.

tunity of taking a few "coffee pauses" with him. The Germans love to talk over coffee, and Dr. Reinitzer, an Austrian by birth, was no exception.

Knowing that considerable controversy hovered over the issue of what Luther believed about Scripture, I asked Reinitzer what he thought Luther's view of biblical authority might be. Did Luther believe in biblical inerrancy, for example? Reinitzer's answer was straightforward: "Of course," he replied. He then proceeded to give me an unsolicited brief history lesson regarding how the idea had gained such currency that Luther did not believe in biblical inerrancy. From his perspective, it was in particular neoorthodox historians and theologians who created and promoted this misleading historiography. They often argued that a disjunction existed between Luther's view of biblical authority, with its christological focus, and views of later Lutherans called "Scholastics" or "Protestant Orthodox."[65]

Olivier Fatio of the University of Geneva has made the same case in reference to the existence of continuity of belief between John Calvin and the Reformed Orthodox. He and others, such as Jill Raitt, have specifically challenged the neoorthodox historiography of Ernst Bizer, who had claimed that Lambert Daneau was the first Reformed theologian to betray Calvin's views by introducing a rationalistic approach to doing theology and by including the natural world under the purview of the Bible's authority.[66]

Interestingly enough, Richard Muller also argues in agreement with Reinitzer and Fatio that a continuity of thought about the Bible's infallibility existed between Luther and Calvin and the Protestant orthodox

---

[65]Jill Raitt, ed., *Shapers of Religious Tradition in Germany, Switzerland, and Poland, 1560–1600* (New Haven, CT: Yale University Press, 1981), xix. Karl Barth provided this controversial assessment of seventeenth-century Protestant orthodox theologians: "All too confidently the heroes of orthodoxy, in their justifiable attempt to adopt Early and Medieval church tradition, overloaded it with presuppositions which were bound sooner or later to jeopardize Reformed knowledge of God and of salvation" (Foreword to Heinrich Heppe, *Reformed Dogmatics* [Grand Rapids: Baker, 1978], vi).

[66]Ernst Bizer, *Frühorthodoxie und Rationalismus*, Theologische Studien 71 (Zurich: EVZ-Verlag, 1963). Olivier Fatio wrote, "Why, then, should scholars [Bizer, note 38] criticize the rational framework to which he [Daneau] resorted as a corruption of the existential discoveries of the Reform," in *Shapers of Religious Tradition*, ed. Raitt, 111. Cf. Olivier Fatio, *Méthode et théologie: Lambert Daneau et les débuts de la scholastique réformée* (Genève: Droz, 1976). Ernst Bizer was a major proponent of a "neoorthodox" historiography. Other criticisms of a Barthian historiography regarding the Bible's authority are found in David Gibson and Daniel Strange, eds., *Engaging with Barth: Contemporary Evangelical Critiques* (New York: T&T Clark, 2009).

of the seventeenth century. Muller adds the further point that Catholic theologians before the Reformation also upheld the same doctrine. In his encyclopedic study *Post-Reformation Reformed Dogmatics: The Rise and Development of Reformed Orthodoxy, ca. 1520 to ca. 1720*, Muller writes:

> In a similar vein, the frequently heard characterization of the ortho-dox view of Scripture that Protestantism rejected an infallible Roman pope only to replace him with an infallible "paper pope" is, at best, a catchily worded misunderstanding of the history of the doctrine of Scripture. On the one hand, it ignores the continuity of Chris-tian doctrine on the point: catholic teaching before the Reformation assumed the infallibility of Scripture, as did the Reformers—the Protestant orthodox did not invent the concept. . . . The doctrine of the infallible authority of Scripture remained a constant while the framework of interpretation shifted away from a strong emphasis on churchly *magisterium* and tradition to an equally powerful emphasis on confessional norms and on a more closely defined tradition of interpretation. The central debate was not over the infallibility of Scripture—that was taken for granted by both sides—rather the debate was centered on the question of authority, specifically on the authority of interpretation.[67]

William Whitaker

Professor Muller's historical analysis is amply confirmed by one of the most significant polemical exchanges of the late sixteenth cen-tury, between the Protestant Cambridge professor William Whitaker and the renowned Roman Catholic theologian Robert Bellarmine.[68] In his *Disputation on Holy Scripture, against the Papists, especially Bellarmine and Stapleton* (1588), Whitaker indicated that Protestants upheld as church doctrine the inerrancy of Scripture:

> But, say they [Roman Catholics], the church never errs; the pope never errs. We shall shew both assertions to be false in the proper place. We say that scripture never errs, and therefore judge that interpreta-tion to be the truest which agrees with scripture. What have we to

---

[67]Muller, *Post-Reformation Reformed Dogmatics*, 2:101.
[68]Simon, *Histoire critique du Vieux Testament*, 471–73.

do with churches, or councils, or popes, unless they can show that what they define is in harmony with the scriptures?[69]

Like Catholics before him, the Protestant Whitaker claimed Augustine's teaching on Scripture as one essential warrant for his belief in inerrancy:

We cannot but wholly disapprove the opinion of those who think that the sacred writers have, in some places fallen into mistakes. That some of the ancients were of this opinion appears from the testimony of Augustine, who maintains, in opposition to them, "that the evangelists are free from all falsehood, both from that which proceeds from deliberate deceit, and that which is the result of forgetfulness" (De Cons. Ev. Lib. II. C.12). Consequently, Jerome judged wrong, if he really judged, as Erasmus supposes, "that the evangelists might have fallen into an error of memory."[70]

Like the Roman Catholic Eck, Whitaker specifically criticized Erasmus's concession that Matthew may have made a mistake. Wrote Whitaker, "But it does not become us to be so easy and indulgent as to concede that such a lapse could be incident to the sacred writers."[71]

In his *Critical History of the Old Testament* (1678), Richard Simon described Whitaker's *Disputation on Holy Scripture* as a "key" Protestant apologetic regarding biblical authority:

In addition, I have gone into more detail about the sentiments which Whitaker had of Bellarmine and other Jesuits, because that ought to serve as a key for understanding countless books which have been written thereafter by Protestants of France, England, and Germany against the books of Bellarmine.[72]

According to Simon, numerous Protestant theologians in Europe had recourse to Whitaker's *Disputation on Holy Scripture* when they needed arguments to use in disputes with Roman Catholic polemicists.

---

[69]William Whitaker, *A Disputation on Holy Scripture, against the Papists, Especially Bellarmine and Stapleton*, trans. and ed. William Fitzgerald (Morgan, PA: Soli Deo Gloria, n.d. [1588]), 476.
[70]Ibid., 36–37.
[71]Ibid., 37.
[72]Simon, *Histoire critique du Vieux Testament*, 472.

Simon was about the last major thinker in the West to ask, and not appear foolhardy, whether there is "anyone, either Jew or Christian, who does not recognize that this Scripture being the Word of God, is at the same time the first principle and the foundation of religion?" In other words, Simon indicated that as late as 1678, most self-identifying Christians and Jews affirmed, and I quote the priest, "The truths contained in Holy Scripture are infallible and of a divine authority, since they come immediately from God, who in doing this used the ministry of men as his interpreters."

Inerrancy Questioned and Defended

But during Paul Hazard's so-called "Crisis of the European Mind" (1680–1715), a good number of prominent participants in the Republic of Letters began to question the inerrancy position, as had some skeptics, deists, Socinians, and others before them.[73] These towering figures of European intellectual life included Pierre Bayle, Jean Le Clerc, and John Locke.[74] Already in the 1650s, Isaac de La Peyrère had proposed the pre-Adamite hypothesis, the view that there were pre-Adamites who lived before Adam and Eve. Evidence suggested that Greenland had possibly been inhabited fifty thousand years earlier.[75] This hypothesis challenged the calculations of numerous seventeenth-century biblical chronologists, whom Anthony Grafton of Princeton University is presently studying. James Ussher (1581–1656) was one of the most famous of the many chronologists.[76] Ussher had estimated the date of creation as 4004 BC. La Peyrère's hypothesis was perceived by orthodox Catholics and Protestants as directly challenging traditional views of biblical infallibility and the plain teaching of Genesis. Hauled before the Roman Catholic Inquisition, La Peyrère recanted his view, blaming his former Calvinist background for having led him astray.[77]

---

[73] Hazard, *The European Mind*, 80–98.

[74] Ibid., 99–115 (Pierre Bayle), 239–51 (John Locke). For the thought of Pierre Bayle, see also the extensive writings of Elisabeth Labrousse.

[75] Isaac de La Peyrère, *Prae-adamite* (1655); La Peyrère, *Relation de Groenland* (1647).

[76] In his lecture "Biblical Chronology: Legend or Science?," delivered at the Senate House, University of London, March 4, 1987, James Barr, a strong critic of the doctrine of biblical inerrancy, acknowledged that scholars such as Martin Luther, Joseph Justus Scaliger, James Ussher, and Isaac Newton, who drew up biblical chronologies, shared a belief that Scripture was "divinely inspired and equally infallible in matters of normal human history, as well as in theological matters" (p. 4).

[77] Richard Popkin, *Isaac La Peyrère (1596–1676): His Life, Work and Influence* (Leiden: Brill, 1987), 13.

Historian Richard Popkin has made a strong case that the La Peyrère affair, more than the Galileo controversy (Galileo indicated he believed in biblical infallibility), ignited an early round of the so-called war between science and religion.

Simon, a correspondent with La Peyrère, was likewise charged with overthrowing the doctrine of biblical infallibility—the very belief he had affirmed "all Christians and Jews" upheld. In the preface to the *Critical History of the Old Testament*, Simon proposed his controversial "public scribes hypothesis," that is, that the republic of Israel had public scribes who kept Israel's records.[78] These scribes, allegedly under the inspiration of the Holy Spirit and using Israel's records, added emendations to the Pentateuch. In consequence, said Simon, Moses did not write all of the Pentateuch. So dangerous was Simon's hypothesis thought to be that the French government, upon the urging of Bossuet, ordered the thirteen hundred copies of the first edition of Simon's *Critical History of the Old Testament* burned. Simon's Oratorian Order promptly expelled the priest.[79]

Ironically enough, in the preface to his controversial work, Simon had indicated he hoped his "public scribes hypothesis" would help answer serious objections Spinoza had raised about the Mosaic authorship of the Pentateuch in his *Tractatus Theologico-Politicus* (1670).[80] Some years later, Simon and the Remonstrant Jean Le Clerc locked horns in one of the most famous debates in European history (1685–1687), regarding the infallibility of Scripture and the authorship of the Pentateuch.[81] In this heated contest, Le Clerc penned two books, and Simon three. The two scholars pursued their debate in French rather than Latin—the normal language of choice when discussing sensitive theological matters. In many regards, the Simon–Le Clerc debate represented a turning point in European intellectual history. It constituted the last significant debate followed by major European intellectuals still seriously reflecting upon claims for the Bible's infallibility. In the

---

[78]Simon, *Histoire critique du Vieux Testament*, preface.

[79]Auvray, *Richard Simon (1638–1712)*, 45–53.

[80]Benedict de Spinoza, *A Theologico-Political Treatise* (New York: Dover, 1951). Regarding Richard Simon's assessment of Spinoza's views of Scripture, see John D. Woodbridge, "Richard Simon's Reaction to Spinoza's 'Tractatus Theologico-Politicus,'" in *Spinoza in der Frühzeit seiner religiösen Wirkung*, ed. Karlfried Gründer and Wilhelm Schmidt-Biggeman (Heidelberg: Lambert Schneider, 1984), 201–26.

[81]John D. Woodbridge, *Biblical Authority: A Critique of the Rogers/McKim Proposal* (Grand Rapids: Zondervan, 1982), 95–99.

mid-eighteenth century, scholars ranging from the biblical critic Jean Astruc to the *philosophe* Diderot, editor of the *Encyclopedia*, cited the Simon–Le Clerc debate as a very significant controversy over the Bible's authority.[82] For that matter, Johann Salomo Semler, the so-called "Father of Higher Criticism" in Halle, Germany, wrote in his diary that it was after reading the works of Simon and Le Clerc that he felt constrained to rethink his views of the Bible's authority.[83] Semler had been raised among German Pietists, many of whom not only had upheld the inerrancy of Scripture but, like his colleague John David Michaelis at the University of Halle, had even defended the infallibility of the Masoretic pointing (1739).[84]

In the 1720s, a good number of Pietist pastors and professors at Halle had likewise defended both the infallibility of the "vulgar text" and the infallibility of the Masoretic pointing. In the *Allgemeine Bibliothek*, Johann Gottfried Eichhorn, a renowned biblical critic, wrote:

> A Bible with various readings had been printed at Halle, in the year 1720, and notwithstanding the use of the whole noble apparatus, they adhered still pertinaciously to the infallibility of the vulgar text. . . . They had discovered upon investigation, and exposed to view in this edition of the Bible, the contradictions of the Masora—the most satisfactory evidence of their fallibility: and yet they had sworn, in as solemn a manner, to the absolute infallibility of the same, as they had sworn to their symbolical articles.[85]

The influential view that German Pietists generally did not embrace biblical inerrancy needs reexamination. In Lausanne, some Protestants fought it out in the streets over the Masoretic pointing, some in favor of the belief in its infallibility, others opposed.[86]

---

[82]Jean Astruc, *Conjectures sur les mémoires originaux dont il paroit que Moyse s'est servi pour composer le Libre de la Genèse* (Paris: 1753), 7, 9, 454, 476–77.

[83]John D. Woodbridge, "German Responses to the Biblical Critic Richard Simon: From Leibniz to J. S. Semler," in *Historische Kritik und biblischer Kanon in der deutschen Aufklärung*, ed. Henning Graf Reventlow, Walter Sparn, and John Woodbridge (Wiesbaden: Otto Harrassowitz, 1988), 80.

[84]Ibid., 78.

[85]"An Account of the Life and Writings of John David Michaelis from Eichhorn's *Allgemeine Bibliothek*," *The Biblical Repertory and Theological Review* 2 (1826): 261.

[86]Barthélemy Barnaud, *Mémoires pour servir à l'histoire des troubles arrivés en Suisse à l'occasion du Consensus* (Amsterdam: J. Frédéric Barnard, 1727). The influential claims of Professor Donald Dayton that German Pietists did not countenance the doctrine of biblical inerrancy appear

Coleridge, Sabatier, and Huxley

The testimony of our next witness, Samuel Taylor Coleridge, the famous English man of letters, will help us understand what were the beliefs of English Protestants not many decades before A. A. Hodge and B. B. Warfield penned their 1881 article "Inspiration." In his posthumous *Confessions of an Inquiring Spirit* (1841), Coleridge, who was intent upon overthrowing belief in the Bible's infallibility, quoted a skeptic's claim to the effect that most English Protestants, whether Methodist, Calvinist, Quaker, or other, believed in biblical infallibility:

> I have frequently attended meetings of the British and Foreign Bible Society, where I have heard speakers of every denomination, Calvinist and Arminian, Quaker and Methodist, Dissenting Ministers and Clergymen, nay dignitaries of the Established Church—and still have I heard the same doctrine,—that the Bible was not to be regarded or reasoned about in the way that other good books are or may be. . . . What is more, their principal arguments were grounded on the position that the Bible throughout was dictated by Omniscience, and therefore in all its parts infallibly true and obligatory, and that the men, whose names are prefixed to the several books or chapters, were in fact but as different pens in the hand of one and the same Writer, and the words the words of God himself.[87]

Coleridge responded, "What could I reply to this?—I could neither deny the fact, nor evade the conclusion—namely, that such is at present the popular belief."[88] According to Coleridge, a commitment to the Bible's infallibility remained an important church doctrine for most English Protestants until at least the 1830s.

Another pertinent witness is Louis Auguste Sabatier (1839–1901), one of Protestant liberalism's brilliant stars.[89] He helped establish the Protestant Faculty of Theology in Paris and served as the school's dean. His testimony will help us understand that despite the impact of the *siècle des Lumières* (Enlightenment) of the eighteenth century upon French culture, many French and Swiss Protestants in the nineteenth

---

less persuasive in light of Eichhorn's observation. Certainly some German Pietists upheld the infallibility not only of the vulgar text but also of the Masora.

[87]Samuel Taylor Coleridge, *Confessions of an Inquiring Spirit* (Boston: James Monroe and Company, 1841), 79–80.

[88]Ibid., 81.

[89]Alec R. Vidler, *The Church in an Age of Revolution: 1789 to the Present* (Baltimore: Penguin, 1971), 183.

century remained committed to the doctrine of the Bible's infallibility as late as the 1840s. A harsh critic of the doctrine, Sabatier in his posthumous *The Religions of Authority and the Religion of the Spirit* (1901) indicated that "Richard Simon, Jean Le Clerc, Lessing, Semler, and the German theologians of the nineteenth century" had sharply attacked the doctrine.[90] Sabatier averred that the "Final Crisis" for the doctrine in the French Protestant world took place between 1848 and 1860, precipitated in part when Professor Edmond Scherer of the Oratoire Theological School of Geneva resigned his position in 1849, no longer able to subscribe to the evangelical school's doctrine in good conscience.[91]

Professor Sabatier observed that some theologians in his own day (1870s to 1890s), unable to maintain "the absolute character of the infallibility of the bible, without which infallibility does not exist," were attempting to defend "a sort of indefinite and limited infallibility, a fallible infallibility which it is simply impossible to define." Their tactical efforts, he thought, were doomed to fail.[92]

Our final witness is Thomas Huxley (1825–1895), Darwin's well-known defender. Huxley argued that the most important intellectual trait of his day was the emergence of the authority of "natural knowledge" as a replacement for the authority of "revealed knowledge." He indicated that in 1869 he had "invented the word 'Agnostic' to denote people who, like myself, confess themselves to be hopelessly ignorant concerning a variety of matters about which metaphysicians and theologians, both orthodox and heterodox, dogmatise with utmost confidence." In 1893, Huxley, like Coleridge before him, acknowledged that the vast majority of the English people had believed in biblical infallibility in earlier decades:

> The doctrine of biblical infallibility was widely held by my countrymen within my recollection: I have reason to think many persons of unimpeachable piety, a few of learning, and even some of intelligence, yet uphold it. But I venture to entertain a doubt whether it can produce any champion whose competency and authority would

---

[90]Louis Auguste Sabatier, *The Religions of Authority and the Religion of the Spirit* (New York: McClure, Phillips & Company, 1904), 220.
[91]Ibid., 218–19.
[92]Ibid., 223.

be recognized beyond the limits of the sect, or theological coterie, to which he belongs.

Huxley noticed that, much like in Sabatier's France of the 1890s, an apologetic effort was underway in England devoted

> to the end of keeping the name of "Inspiration" to suggest the divine source, and consequently infallibility, of more or less of the biblical literature, while carefully emptying the term of any definite sense. For "plenary inspiration" we are asked to substitute a sort of "inspiration with limited liability," the limit being susceptible of indefinite fluctuation in correspondence with the demands of scientific criticism.[93]

Like Sabatier, Huxley believed this stratagem would fail.

Reflections: Evangelical Self-Identity and the Doctrine of Biblical Inerrancy

The doctrine of biblical inerrancy is no late imaginative creation of A. A. Hodge and B. B. Warfield in 1881 or of twentieth-century American fundamentalism. Rather, it is an essential evangelical belief based upon a biblical warrant. It resides squarely within the Augustinian tradition regarding the Bible's truthfulness. Both Roman Catholics and the Protestant Reformers affirmed the church doctrine.

Little wonder, then, that Hodge and Warfield, fully aware of the doctrine's historical provenance in the ante-Nicene Fathers, Roman Catholicism, and Protestantism, described it as the "great Catholic doctrine of Biblical Inspiration, i.e., that the Scriptures not only contain, but *are the Word of God*, and hence that all their elements and all their affirmations: are absolutely errorless, and binding the faith and obedience of men."[94] They called their view a church doctrine and observed:

> It is not questionable that the great historic churches have held these creed definitions in the sense of affirming the errorless infallibility of the Word. This is everywhere shown by the way in which all the great bodies of Protestant theologians have handled Scripture in their commentaries, systems of theology, catechisms and sermons. And this

---

[93]Cited in John C. Greene, "Darwin and Religion," in *European Intellectual History since Darwin and Marx*, ed. W. Warren Wagar (New York: Harper & Row, 1966), 15–16.
[94]Hodge and Warfield, *Inspiration*, 26–27.

has always been pre-eminently characteristic of epochs and agents of reformation and revival. All the great world-moving men, as Luther, Calvin, Knox, Wesley, Whitefield and Chalmers, and proportionately those most like them, have so handled the Divine Word.[95]

Among the confessions upholding "errorless infallibility," they cited the Roman Catholic Council of Trent, the Westminster Confession, and the Second Helvetic Confession.[96] Our reception histories lend credence to their claims.

By contrast, Ernest Sandeen's perception of the history of biblical inerrancy may stand in need of substantial revision. In the last decades of the nineteenth century, the doctrine of biblical inerrancy was not being created. Rather, as we saw, European Catholic modernists and Protestants such as the ones Sabatier and Huxley referenced were attempting to modify or jettison the doctrine. What's more, historian Clinton Ohlers has studied a number of American Protestant scholars who abandoned the doctrine of inerrancy at the turn of the twentieth century. It was often their perception that they were abandoning the old orthodox Protestant view of Scripture.[97] In addition, many used the words *infallibility* and *inerrancy* interchangeably. For example, Charles W. Pearson (1846–1905), an English literature professor at Northwestern University, whose attacks on biblical inerrancy in 1902 received extensive newspaper coverage, did just that. The president of Northwestern University asked him to step down from his post.[98]

As for the doctrine of infallibility in the original autographs, it was a common piece of theological furniture among nineteenth-century evangelical theologians, as historian Randall Balmer demonstrated in

---

[95]Ibid., 33.

[96]Ibid., 32–33.

[97]Clinton Ohlers, *The Roots of Inerrancy: A Comparison of Late Twentieth-century Anglo-American Protestant Perceptions of the Origins of the Doctrine of Biblical Inerrancy with Those of the Late 1800s* (MA thesis, Trinity Evangelical Divinity School, 1997).

[98]Professor Pearson's resignation was portrayed as voluntary in the newspapers. "Chicago: Feb. 12. Prof. Charles W. Pearson, whose recent utterances against the infallibility of certain portions of the Bible occasioned wide comment in the Methodist Episcopal Church circles, resigned today the professorship of English literature in the Northwestern University. The resignation, it is stated, was voluntary" (*The New York Times*, Feb. 13, 1902). The president of Northwestern had indicated to Professor Pearson that his stepping down would be salutary for the university. Professor Pearson had published an article "Open Inspiration versus a Closed Canon and Infallible Bible" (Northwestern University Archives, Evanston, IL; Description of Charles W. Pearson Family Papers, 1843–1968).

his master's thesis.[99] At Princeton Seminary itself, Charles Hodge, a predecessor of Warfield and editor of the *Biblical Repertory*, placed an article in the journal by German professor C. Beck in 1825. Beck clearly made a distinction between lost original autographs and extant copies of Scripture. He wrote, "The autographs appear to have perished early, and the copies which were taken, became more or less subject to those errors, which arise from the mistakes of transcribers, the false corrections of commentators and critics, from marginal notes, and from other sources."[100]

A. A. Hodge and Warfield were by no means theologically innovative in speaking about original autographs in their 1881 "Inspiration" article. Rather, they were reiterating a common assumption of lower biblical criticism that Richard Simon and others had articulated and associated with Augustine's program for correcting errors in extant copies of Scripture. Hodge and Warfield put the matter this way: Scripture is without error "when the *ipsissima verba* [very words] of the original autographs are ascertained and interpreted in their natural and intended sense."[101] The original autographs could be discerned through careful textual work. They are not "useless" as Sandeen had posited.

Before 1881, countless Roman Catholics and evangelical Protestants believed the Bible was infallible not only for matters of faith and practice but also for history and science. Augustine's teaching in this regard was tantamount to an essential church doctrine for many Roman Catholics and Protestants. Some claimed this belief flowed directly from the premise that God, the author of truth, is also the ultimate author of Holy Scripture. Thus Scripture is without error. Many believed the doctrine served as a strong guardrail against the possibility of slipping or plunging into heterodoxy or worse. Many assumed it was a non-negotiable belief of their evangelical theological identity.

Billy Graham and Carl F. H. Henry

Certainly two of America's leading post–World War II evangelicals, Billy Graham and Carl F. H. Henry, understood the doctrine's importance and its value as an essential guardrail. Just before Graham's

---

[99]Randall H. Balmer, *The Old Princeton Doctrine of Inspiration in the Context of Nineteenth-century Theology: A Reappraisal* (MA thesis, Trinity Evangelical Divinity School, 1981).

[100]Beck, "Monogrammata Hermeneutics N. T.," *The Biblical Repertory and Theological Review* 1 (1825): 27.

[101]Hodge and Warfield, *Inspiration*, 28.

famous Los Angeles Crusade in 1949, he experienced doubts about
the Bible's authority and truthfulness. Chuck Templeton, who had
been one of Youth for Christ's most talented fellow evangelists, had
apparently indicated that Billy would never amount to much given his
conservative views on Scripture. Chuck was overheard to have said,
"Poor Billy, I feel sorry for him. He and I are taking two different
roads." And indeed they did. Templeton ended up an agnostic, saying
with tears in his eyes not long before his death, "I miss Jesus."

Graham was seriously affected by Templeton's criticisms of the
Bible. In the very first fascicle of *Christianity Today* (1956), Graham
wrote a remarkable article entitled "Biblical Authority in Evangelism"—
a piece well worth reading even today. In the article (and in his autobiography, *Just As I Am*), he described how one evening, troubled by
his doubts about scriptural authority, he went out into the woods near
Forest Home camp up in the mountains around Los Angeles. Graham
placed his open Bible on a stump and he prayed.

> The exact wording of my prayer is beyond recall, but it must have
> echoed my thoughts: "O God! There are many things in this book I
> do not understand. . . . I can't answer some of the philosophical and
> psychological questions Chuck and others are raising."
>
> I was trying to be on the level with God, but something remained
> unspoken. At last the Holy Spirit freed me to say it: "Father, I am
> going to accept this as Thy Word—by *faith!*" . . .
>
> I sensed the presence and power of God as I had not sensed it
> in months. Not all my questions were answered, but a major bridge
> had been crossed. In my heart and mind, I knew a spiritual battle in
> my soul had been fought and won.[102]

Graham then indicated that this renewed commitment to the authority of Scripture constituted *the* "secret" of his ministry. He reminds us
that God's Holy Word has great power to transform people's lives. We
can sometimes study Scripture in an academic fashion and, paradoxically enough, lose our sense of its power as the very Word of God.

Graham recounted what he experienced once he began to depend
on the power of God's authoritative Word in preaching:

[102]Billy Graham, *Just As I Am: The Autobiography of Billy Graham* (San Francisco: Harper-
SanFrancisco, 1997), 139.

The people were not coming to hear great oratory, nor were they interested merely in my ideas. I found they were desperately hungry to hear what God had to say through His Holy Word. I felt as though I had a rapier in my hand, and through the power of the Bible was slashing deeply into men's consciences, leading them to surrender to God. Does not the Bible say of itself, "For the word of God is quick, and powerful, sharper than any two edged sword, piercing even to the dividing asunder of souls and spirit, and of the joints and marrow, and is a discerner of the thoughts and intents of the heart" (Heb. 4:12)? I found that the Bible became a flame in my hands. That flame melted away unbelief in the hearts of people and moved them to decide for Christ. The Word became a hammer breaking up stony hearts and shaping them into the likeness of God. Did not God say, "I will make my words in thy mouth fire" (Jer. 5:14) and "is not my word like as a fire? . . . and like a hammer that breaketh the rock in pieces?" (Jer. 23:29)?[103]

For Billy Graham, biblical authority and evangelism became beautifully wedded together. You may have noticed that in his messages, Dr. Graham repeatedly declared, "The Bible says." And during the last sixty plus years, millions of people throughout the world responded to Graham's gospel message and accepted Jesus Christ as Lord and Savior.

And finally, Carl F. H. Henry, one of the prime movers in the evangelical resurgence after World War II, wrote an elegant piece in 1991, in which he too encouraged evangelical Christians to uphold a high view of biblical authority. Dr. Henry reminds us that we do not serve any Christ but the Christ according to Holy Scripture.

In a moving fashion, Henry helps us to understand better the nature of our evangelical self-identity as it relates to the gospel, to the authority of Holy Scripture, and to Christ. Henry entitled his valedictory piece "If I Had to Do It Again." He wrote:

From the outset of my Christian walk I have treasured the Book that speaks of the God of ultimate beginnings and ends, and illumines all that falls between. . . . An evangelical Christian believes incomparable good news: that Christ died in the stead of sinners and arose the third day as living head of the church of the twice-born, the people of God, whose mission is mandated by the scripturally given Word of God. The term evangelical—whose core is the "evangel"—therefore embraces the best of all good tidings, that on the ground of the sub-

---

[103]Billy Graham, "Biblical Authority in Evangelism," *Christianity Today* 1, no. 1 (1956): 5–6.

stitutionary death of Christ Jesus, God forgives penitent sinners and he shelters their eternal destiny by the Risen Lord who triumphed over death and over all that would have destroyed him and his cause. That good news as the Apostle Paul makes clear, is validated and verified by the sacred Scriptures. Those who contrast the authority of Christ with the authority of Scripture do so at high risk. Scripture gives us the authentic teaching of Jesus and Jesus exhorted his apostles to approach Scripture as divinely authoritative. There is no confident road into the future for any theological cause that provides a fragmented Scriptural authority and—in consequence—an unstable Christology. Founded by the true and living Lord, and armed with the truthfulness of Scripture, the church of God is invincible. Whatever I might want to change in this pilgrim life, it would surely not be any of these high and holy commitments.[104]

Dr. Henry had given these valedictory remarks about evangelical self-identity only a few years before I encountered him walking on the sidewalk at Trinity Evangelical Divinity School in the early 1990s. After our brief conversation, Henry continued to shuffle along the way to his next appointment. I wish I had spoken to him about the patent weaknesses of the new historiography that portrayed biblical inerrancy not as an evangelical church doctrine but solely as a fundamentalist doctrinal innovation. But I did not do so. Hopefully, as he walked to his next appointment, he was comforted by remembering his own description of evangelical self-identity and his own "high and holy" commitments regarding Christ and Holy Scripture. After all, they had biblical warrant and resided squarely in the central teachings of the Western churches from the Patristic era through the Protestant Reformation until the late twentieth century. They remain some of the salient theological elements that make up a consistent evangelical self-identity in the early twenty-first century.[105]

---

[104]D. A. Carson and John D. Woodbridge, eds., *God and Culture: Essays in Honor of Carl F. H. Henry* (Grand Rapids: Eerdmans, 1993), 392–93.
[105]For theological elements of evangelical self-identity, see the historic Christian creeds and more recently Kenneth Kantzer and Carl F. H. Henry, eds., *Evangelical Affirmations* (Grand Rapids: Zondervan, 1990). Evangelicals have differed among themselves regarding how the believer comes to an understanding that Scripture is God's revealed written Word (witness of the Holy Spirit, historical evidence for its authority, the resurrected Christ's authority, etc.). For more sociologically oriented descriptions of evangelical self-identity, consult the insightful writings of Christian Smith and D. Michael Lindsay, among others.

PART
2

Special Topics
in New Testament Studies

5

Lifting Up the Son of Man and God's Love for the World

John 3:16 in Its Historical, Literary, and Theological Contexts

ANDREAS J. KÖSTENBERGER

John 3:16 is one of the most beloved verses in all of Scripture. Its declaration of God's love for the world, its depiction of Jesus' vicarious sacrifice, and its promise of eternal life for all who respond to God's offer of salvation in Christ through faith have brought hope and comfort to many. In addition, John 3:16 poignantly encapsulates the message of John's entire Gospel and provides a window into the heart of his theology. While John 3:16 is very widely known and loved, however, the verse is often quoted and preached with insufficient regard to its original historical setting and its place in the Johannine narrative.[1]

---

[1]The remark by D. A. Carson, "One Way (Matthew 7:13–27)," in *Only One Way? Reaffirming the Exclusive Truth Claims of Christianity*, ed. Richard D. Phillips (Wheaton, IL: Crossway,

This study will attempt to move beyond a "proof text" approach to John 3:16 and examine the verse in its historical, literary, and theological contexts.[2] The investigation of the historical context will focus on how several other Jewish works from the period between the destruction of Jerusalem in the year 70 and the Bar Kochba revolt cast the relationship between God's love and the world. The analysis of the literary context will examine how John 3:16 functions in the Johannine narrative. The study of the theological context will explore the passage's contribution to John's theology and to the theology of the New Testament.

As will become evident during the course of our investigation, the universal aspect of John 3:16 comes into sharper focus when the verse is understood in its historical, literary, and theological dimensions. John 3:16 commences the evangelist's commentary on the preceding narrative, which recounts the interchange between Jesus and Nicodemus and serves to draw out the universal implications of Jesus' words. This universalization, in turn, is part of John's emphasis on the unity of Jews and Gentiles in the one people of God, which is also affirmed elsewhere in the New Testament (e.g., Eph. 2:11–22).

I could not have written this essay without the seminal influence of the honoree of this volume, Don Carson, with whom I studied at Trinity Evangelical Divinity School during the years 1990–1993. Apart from many other kindnesses, Don allowed me to use his personal library during one of his Cambridge sabbaticals as I was writing my dissertation on the mission theme in John's Gospel. Contributing to this Festschrift is both a privilege and a tribute to Don Carson's shaping influence on many budding scholars all around the world, and I dedicate this essay to him as a small token of my gratitude and high esteem.

Historical Context
Introduction
The Gospel of John was most likely written, at least in part, in response to the destruction of Jerusalem by the Romans in the

---

2007), 133–34, is pertinent here: "Start with the structure of the sermon, and thus how it fits together. My father used to tell me that a text without a context becomes a pretext for a proof text, so when I was still quite young I learned to look at the context."
[2]See the discussion of the "hermeneutical triad" consisting of history, literature, and theology in Andreas J. Köstenberger and Richard D. Patterson, *Invitation to Biblical Interpretation: Exploring the Hermeneutical Triad of History, Literature, and Theology* (Grand Rapids: Kregel, 2011).

year 70.[3] Jesus is presented by John as the new temple, a new center of worship, in and through whom Jews and Gentiles could worship God in spirit and in truth (see esp. 1:14, 51; 2:14–22; 4:19–24; 9:38; 20:28).[4] This christological response to the destruction of the temple came at a time when Jews throughout Palestine and the Diaspora were attempting to cope with this momentous event and to grasp the significance of what had taken place.[5] The Jewish apocalyptic books *Apocalypse of Abraham*, *2 Baruch*, and *4 Ezra*, written within a few decades of John's Gospel, represent some of the manifold ways in which the Jewish people were coping with the loss of Jerusalem and the temple.[6] Each of these works provides relevant background material by which the distinctiveness of John's bold affirmation of God's love for the entire world in John 3:16 comes into sharper focus.[7]

---

[3]See Andreas J. Köstenberger, *A Theology of John's Gospel and Letters: The Word, the Christ, the Son of God*, Biblical Theology of the New Testament (Grand Rapids: Zondervan, 2009), 60–72, 422–35; and Alan R. Kerr, *The Temple of Jesus' Body: The Temple Theme in the Gospel of John*, JSNTSup 220 (Sheffield: Sheffield Academic Press, 2002), for detailed support of this thesis.

[4]See the discussion of these and other passages in Andreas J. Köstenberger, "The Destruction of the Second Temple and the Composition of the Fourth Gospel," in *Challenging Perspectives on the Gospel of John*, ed. John Lierman, WUNT 2/219 (Tübingen: Mohr Siebeck, 2006), 69–108 (including additional bibliographic references).

[5]Jacob Neusner, "Judaism in a Time of Crisis: Four Responses to the Destruction of the Second Temple," *Judaism* 21 (1972): 313–27, provides a basic survey of the primary responses to the temple's destruction.

[6]See Andreas J. Köstenberger, L. Scott Kellum, and Charles L. Quarles, *The Cradle, the Cross, and the Crown: An Introduction to the New Testament* (Nashville: B&H, 2009), 298–300, for a series of arguments that the Gospel of John should be dated to the mid-80s or early 90s AD. R. Rubinkiewicz, "Apocalypse of Abraham: A New Translation and Introduction," in *The Old Testament Pseudepigrapha*, ed. James H. Charlesworth, 2 vols. (New York: Doubleday, 1983, 1985), 1:683, dates the *Apocalypse of Abraham* between AD 70 and the middle of the second century and notes a broad scholarly consensus that the book was composed around the turn of the century. A. F. J. Klijn, "2 (Syriac Apocalypse of) Baruch: A New Translation and Introduction," in *Old Testament Pseudepigrapha*, ed. Charlesworth, 1:617, dates *2 Baruch* to the first or second decade of the second century. Michael E. Stone, *Fourth Ezra: A Commentary on the Book of Fourth Ezra*, Hermeneia (Minneapolis: Fortress, 1990), 9, dates *4 Ezra* during the reign of Domitian (AD 81–96) based on a widely agreed-upon identification of the third head in the eagle vision (chaps. 11–12) with Domitian.

[7]The appropriateness of choosing these three texts as a relevant background for John 3:16 rests on three factors: (1) each book functions, in one way or another, as a response to the destruction of Jerusalem and of the temple; (2) each book was probably written between the destruction of Jerusalem in the year 70 and the Bar Kochba revolt in AD 132–135; (3) John, as the probable author of the book of Revelation, would have been keenly aware of and sympathetic to the apocalyptic genre. See Köstenberger, Kellum, and Quarles, *Cradle, the Cross, and the Crown*, 810–14, for a discussion of the authorship of Revelation.

The Apocalypse of Abraham

The *Apocalypse of Abraham* presents a bleak picture of God's relationship to the Gentile world. The distinction between God's people—the Jews—and the Gentiles is built into the cosmic structure of the universe from the very beginning (21:1–22:5). From the beginning of creation, God has divided humanity into two groups: the descendants of Abraham on the right and the Gentiles on the left ("the people with Azazel," i.e., Satan, 22:4–5).

The destruction of Jerusalem and of the temple is seen in a vision of a crowd of heathens from the left side of the cosmos capturing and slaughtering those on the right (27:1–6). In the coming age, the Gentiles who ruled over the Jewish people in this age will be judged:

> Because I have prepared them [to be] food for the fire of Hades, and [to be] ceaseless soaring in the air of the underworld [regions] of the uttermost depths, [to be] the contents of a wormy belly. . . . For they shall putrefy in the belly of the crafty worm Azazel, and be burned by the fire of Azazel's tongue. (31:3, 5)[8]

The book ends with God addressing Abraham, making reference to a nation (Egypt) that will enslave and oppress Israel "for one hour of the impious age," and reassuring Abraham that he is the judge of "the nation whom they shall serve" (32:1–4). Clearly, God's love for the entire world—including Gentiles—is foreign to the worldview underlying the *Apocalypse of Abraham*.

2 Baruch

Even though *2 Baruch* does not ground the division between Israel and the nations of the world in the cosmological structure of the universe as the *Apocalypse of Abraham* does, there is no doubt as to where God's affections lie. Israel is described as those "whom you love" (5:1) and is called "a beloved people on account of your name" (21:21). In the attached letter to the twelve tribes in captivity, Baruch writes, "I remember, my brothers, the love of him who created me, who loved us from the beginning and who never hated us but, on the contrary, chastised us" (78:3). The special relationship between God and Israel is grounded in God's election: "For these are the people

---

[8]All quotations from the Old Testament Pseudepigrapha are from Charlesworth, *Old Testament Pseudepigrapha*. Unless otherwise noted, biblical quotations in this chapter are from the ESV.

whom you have elected, and this is the nation of which you found no equal" (48:20), who are blessed because "we did not mingle with the nations" (48:23).

In the future, "the nations will be thoroughly punished" (13:6). "But now, you nations and tribes, you are guilty, because you have trodden the earth all this time, and because you have used creation unrighteously" (13:11). While painting a rather dismal overall picture of the Gentiles' future, however, *2 Baruch* does offer some hope to the nations of the world who had no part in the subjugation of Israel:

> After the signs have come of which I have spoken to you before, when the nations are moved and the time of my Anointed One comes, he will call all nations, and some of them he will spare, and others he will kill. These things will befall the nations which will be spared by him. Every nation which has not known Israel and which has not trodden down the seed of Jacob will live. And this is because some from all the nations have been subjected to your people. All those, now, who have ruled over you or have known you, will be delivered up to the sword. (72:2–6)

This passing glimmer of hope for the nations who did not oppress Israel, however, does not represent the overall emphasis of *2 Baruch*. In the last black waters of the book, protection is said to be provided for those who are considered part of the holy land while all other nations and peoples of the world will be devoured: "The whole earth will devour its inhabitants. And the holy land will have mercy on its own and will protect its inhabitants at that time" (70:10–71:1). As in the case of the *Apocalypse of Abraham*, *2 Baruch* is far removed from the notion that God's love extends to the entire world, including Gentiles as well as Jews.

4 Ezra

Fourth Ezra presents a far more complicated picture of God's relationship to the world through the interplay of Ezra's probing questions concerning theodicy and the angel Uriel's responses. Ezra is deeply concerned with the problem of evil, which is traced back to Adam's sin at the beginning of time. Adam's original sin bequeathed an evil seed to all his descendants, both Jew and Gentile (*4 Ezra* 3:7, 20–22, 26; 7:118). This universal sin problem leads to Ezra's concern that very few, regardless of ethnicity, are righteous enough to receive salvation and that all will therefore experience judgment and punishment (7:17–18, 45–48, 62–69, 116–26). Ezra's love for the world seems to surpass even God's love for the world, for God seems unperturbed by the fact that the majority of the human race is doomed to destruction because of its unrighteousness (7:17–25, 45–74; 7:132–8:3, 37–62).[9]

Alden Thompson notes that one of the key interpretive decisions to be made regarding *4 Ezra* concerns the question of which perspective represents the "author's real concern, and therefore his purpose in writing": Ezra's universal compassion for all humankind or God's future deliverance of Israel and his destruction of the nations.[10] While space precludes a full treatment of this question, the revelatory emphasis of the apocalyptic genre itself strongly suggests that greater authority resides in the angel's pronouncements concerning God's will and ways than in humanity's questions.[11]

What is more, the fourth vision clearly signals a shift in Ezra's attitude by which he seems to be thoroughly converted to God's perspective.[12] The fifth and sixth visions are typical of other apocalyptic writings and portray the destruction of the Romans (12:10–34) and God's enemies, the nations (13:33–38), and the regathering of the ten lost tribes of Israel (13:39–50). In these final visions, the focus returns to the salvation of ethnic Israel in distinction from her enemies, the other nations of the world (13:48–50).

Ezra's concern for the impending damnation of the peoples of the world in the coming judgment clearly indicates that some Jews, even

---

[9]Despite God's declaration to Ezra that "you come far short of being able to love my creation more than I love it" (*4 Ezra* 8:47), he never responds positively to Ezra's prayers for mercy on the unrighteous but closes the third vision with the statement, "So let the multitude perish which has been born in vain, but let my grape and my plant be saved, because with much labor I have perfected them" (9:22).

[10]Alden L. Thompson, *Responsibility for Evil in the Theodicy of IV Ezra*, SBLDS 29 (Missoula, MT: Scholars Press, 1977), 288. Thompson argues that Ezra's concern over humanity's moral inability to live righteously represents the motivating force of the book. While this is certainly a primary concern of the third vision, it does not seem to account sufficiently for Ezra's "conversion" in the fourth vision and the focus on ethnic Israel in visions one, two, and five through seven. Stone, *Fourth Ezra*, 35–36, argues that the message of the book is tied to the destruction of Zion: "In an essential way, the response to the underlying issues is given in the vision of the heavenly Jerusalem which comforts Ezra for Jerusalem's present destruction and by the two dream visions which promise the destruction of Rome and the redemption and vindication of Israel" (36).

[11]See John J. Collins, "Introduction: Towards the Morphology of a Genre," *Semeia* 14 (1979): 1–20.

[12]Stone, *Fourth Ezra*, 31–32.

146

following the destruction of Jerusalem by the Romans, were deeply concerned for the salvation of those outside ethnic Israel. The problem remained, however, that this concern for humankind was not incorporated into the reigning paradigm, which emphasized God's exclusive love for, and election of, Israel and the future salvation of Israel and judgment of the Gentiles.[13]

The two concerns—that for the salvation of those outside ethnic Israel and that for the future salvation of Israel and the judgment of the Gentiles—sustain an uneasy coexistence, and Ezra, despite his compassion, comes out in full support of the reigning paradigm in the final four visions. The result is that even though *4 Ezra* evinces a spiritual concern for the nations of the world, it lacks the needed theological building blocks to translate this compassion into a concrete message of salvation for the nations.

Conclusion

The Jewish literature examined above, written in response to the destruction of Jerusalem by the Romans in the year 70, focuses on God's love and election of Israel with particular attention on Israel's final vindication and the judgment of her enemies.[14] The immediate difference, apart from genre, that surfaces when these responses to the destruction of Jerusalem are compared with John's Gospel is christological.[15] John was convinced that Jesus represented God's decisive intervention in the affairs of the world to bring salvation to *all* who believed, whether Jew or Gentile. John's christology provided him with the theological material necessary to bring together the apparently conflicting ideas found in documents such as *4 Ezra*, which speak of compassion for all the people of the world while maintaining God's special concern for national Israel.[16]

---

[13]Compare the emphasis on God's election of and exclusive love for Israel in *4 Ezra* 5:23–27, 33.

[14]Josephus represents an additional literary response to the destruction of Jerusalem, but because of his Roman sympathies and life in Rome he can hardly be considered representative of broader Judaism. Likewise, scholars debate whether or not Pseudo-Philo should be dated prior or subsequent to the year 70. Regardless of the date, Pseudo-Philo's narrative emphasizes the themes noted above of God's election and special relationship with Israel (*Liber Antiquitatum Biblicarum* 6, 7, 11). Cf. George W. E. Nickelsburg, *Jewish Literature between the Bible and the Mishnah*, 2nd ed. (Minneapolis: Fortress, 2005), 267; and D. R. Harrington, "Pseudo-Philo: A New Translation and Introduction," in *Old Testament Pseudepigrapha*, ed. Charlesworth, 2:299.

[15]Cf. Kerr, *Temple of Jesus' Body*, 66.

[16]In a certain sense, it could be said that John 3:16 provides an answer to the burning question of theodicy represented in Ezra's third vision, a question that is never adequately answered in

In John, the Jews are not given special privilege but are subsumed under all of humanity, without, however, losing their distinctiveness as a people.[17] The question of their salvation or judgment is dealt with in John's Gospel, but allegiance to Jesus replaces ethnicity as the determining factor.[18] The above survey of John's historical setting reveals the stark contrast between the worldview underlying John's Gospel and other Jewish perspectives from roughly the same time period. While, in response to the horrific Jewish war, many Jews in Palestine and throughout the Diaspora longed for revenge and divine vindication, which would consist in the destruction and punishment of the nations, John 3:16 rings forth loud and clear as an affirmation of God's love for the entire world, expressed in the sending of his Son for the salvation of all who believed.

Literary Context

Introduction

Now that we have investigated John 3:16 from a historical vantage point, we move on to an exploration of the passage's literary dimension. In so doing, it will at times be helpful, if not inevitable, to anticipate later findings in our study of the theological message conveyed by this verse. With regard to boundary markers, the spatial changes in geographical setting at 2:13 (from Capernaum to Jerusalem) and 3:22 (from Jerusalem to the Judean countryside) delimit the immediate narrative context for reading 3:16 to 2:13–3:21, the first recorded Passover in John.[19] This section is further subdivided into 2:13–22 (the temple clearing) and 2:23–3:21 (the Nicodemus narrative). Apart from the joint spatial and temporal setting of Jerusalem at the Passover, 2:13–22 sustains several links with 2:23–3:21. The "sign" of the temple clearing (cf. 2:18) is most likely included in the global references to Jesus' signs in 2:23 and 3:2, and Jesus' statement concerning the temple's destruction and the raising of

---

4 *Ezra*. God loves the entire world and has acted decisively in history in and through the Messiah to provide eternal life for all who believe in him.

[17]Kerr, *Temple of Jesus' Body*, 65, observes that "God is at work through Jesus' death and resurrection to bring in a new family to God (1.12; 20.17) through faith in Jesus Christ."

[18]See, e.g., 3:18, 36; 5:24–30; 6:40; 8:24; 11:25–26; 12:48–50; 20:31. For a fuller treatment, see Köstenberger, *Theology of John's Gospel and Letters*, chap. 10.

[19]This Jerusalem narrative (2:13–3:21), in turn, fits within the broader Cana cycle (2:1–4:54), which begins and ends with Cana as a geographical *inclusio*.

Jesus' body in 2:19 (cf. 2:20–22) anticipates the reference to the "lifting up" of the Son in 3:14.[20]

The Nicodemus Narrative

The Nicodemus narrative can be divided into three primary sections: an introduction (2:23–25); the interchange between Jesus and Nicodemus (3:1–15); and the evangelist's commentary (3:16–21).[21] The recurrence of the words "man" in 2:25 and 3:1 (γὰρ ἐγίνωσκεν τί ἦν ἐν τῷ ἀνθρώπῳ. Ἦν δὲ ἄνθρωπος ἐκ τῶν Φαρισαίων) and "signs" (τὰ σημεῖα) in 2:23 and 3:2, along with the fact that the antecedent for the pronouns in 3:2 (αὐτόν ... αὐτῷ) appears in 2:24 (Ἰησοῦς), clearly suggests that 2:23–25 is intended as the introduction to 3:1–15.[22] Nicodemus was one of the people who "believed" on account of Jesus' signs, but one to whom Jesus did not entrust himself because he knew what was in all people.[23] The introductory section also serves as a narrative link between the temple clearing and the Nicodemus narrative. The Jewish leadership responds with hostility to Jesus' ministry (2:18, 20); the general population reacts with a degree of superficial belief based on Jesus' signs (2:23); and Nicodemus, as a leader of the Jews (3:1; cf. 2:18, 20) and as a "believer" (cf. 2:23), represents a character who embodies elements from both responses. As the dialogue

---

[20]See Köstenberger, *Theology of John's Gospel and Letters*, 196–97, 323–35, for a detailed argument for the inclusion of the temple clearing among the Johannine signs.

[21]Opinions are divided as to where the Evangelist's commentary begins. Francis J. Moloney, *The Gospel of John*, SP (Collegeville, MN: Liturgical Press, 1998), 90, maintains that Jesus' words continue through 3:21. Ben Witherington, *John's Wisdom: A Commentary on the Fourth Gospel* (Louisville: Westminster John Knox, 1995), 99, contends that the Evangelist's comments begin in 3:12 or 3:16 at the latest. Rudolf Schnackenburg, *The Gospel according to St. John*, 3 vols. (New York: Crossroad, 1990), 1:360, argues for 3:13 as the transition to the Evangelist's reflections. Several points support 3:16 as the beginning of John's commentary: (1) Jesus alone uses the expression "Son of Man" (3:15) in the Gospel (12:34 is no real exception); (2) the introductory phrase of 3:16, οὕτως γάρ, signals a transition (cf. the use of γάρ to introduce the Evangelist's comments or clarification in 3:24; 4:8, 9, 44, 45; 6:64; 13:11, 29; 19:31, 36; 20:9; 21:7); (3) the cross is spoken of as a past event; (4) John alone uses μονογενής in the Gospel (1:14, 18; 3:16, 18); and (5) a similar transition occurs between 3:27–30 and 3:31–36. Cf. D. A. Carson, *The Gospel according to John*, PNTC (Grand Rapids: Eerdmans, 1991), 185, 203; Leon Morris, *The Gospel according to John*, rev. ed., NICNT (Grand Rapids: Eerdmans, 1995), 202; Gary M. Burge, *John*, NIVAC (Grand Rapids: Zondervan, 2000), 113, 117–18; and Gerald L. Borchert, *John 1–11*, NAC 25A (Nashville: Broadman & Holman, 1996), 180.

[22]See the analysis of the pericope by Peter Cotterell and Max Turner, *Linguistics and Biblical Interpretation* (Downers Grove, IL: InterVarsity, 1989), 278–87.

[23]I.e., the sinful condition of unbelief. This notion is conveyed by the play on words in the Greek original (ἐπίστευσαν ... ἐπίστευεν).

progresses, however, it becomes evident that Nicodemus functions in the narrative as a representative of the unbelieving world's inability to recognize Jesus' true identity.[24]

Jesus' interchange with Nicodemus centers on entrance requirements for the kingdom of God.[25] Nicodemus's comments steadily decrease as the conversation progresses and reveal a consistent lack of understanding. The double reference to the kingdom of God in 3:3 and 3:5 constitutes the only use of that phrase in John's Gospel (cf. "my kingdom" in 18:36) and serves as a strong indication of the historicity of the interchange between Jesus and Nicodemus.[26] It is quite possible that the scarcity of the phrase in John (in contrast to the Synoptics) reflects life between the destruction of Jerusalem and the Bar Kochba revolt, where retention of "kingdom" language could easily be interpreted in terms of political sedition (cf. the concern expressed in 11:48).[27] John most likely retains the use of "kingdom" language here because it represents the historical content of the conversation between Jesus and Nicodemus.

Theologically, the emphasis on the necessity of spiritual regeneration for entrance into God's kingdom in the Nicodemus pericope serves as an explanation for the antagonism of the Jewish leadership and

---

[24]Craig Blomberg, "The Globalization of Biblical Interpretation: A Test Case—John 3–4," *BBR* 5 (1995): 5–7, cogently argues in favor of seeing John's portrait of Nicodemus as "substantially more negative." See also the discussion in Andreas J. Köstenberger, *John*, BECNT (Grand Rapids: Eerdmans, 2004), 118–20.

[25]Cotterell and Turner, *Linguistics and Biblical Interpretation*, 284–85, draw attention to how Jesus sets the topic of conversation after rejecting the possible topics offered by Nicodemus.

[26]On the historical reliability of John's Gospel, see especially Richard Bauckham, *Jesus and the Eyewitnesses: The Gospels as Eyewitness Testimony* (Grand Rapids: Eerdmans, 2006); Craig L. Blomberg, *The Historical Reliability of John's Gospel* (Leicester, UK: Inter-Varsity, 2002); Samuel Byrskog, *Story as History—History as Story*, WUNT 123 (Tübingen: Mohr Siebeck, 2000); D. A. Carson, "Understanding Misunderstandings in the Fourth Gospel," *TynBul* 33 (1982): 59–91; Martin Hengel, "Das Johannesevangelium als Quelle für die Geschichte des antiken Judentums," in *Judaica, Hellenistica et Christiana: Kleine Schriften II*, WUNT 109 (Tübingen: Mohr Siebeck, 1999), 293–334; Köstenberger, *John*; Köstenberger, "John," in *Zondervan Illustrated Bible Backgrounds Commentary*, ed. Clinton E. Arnold, 4 vols. (Grand Rapids: Zondervan, 2002), 2:1–216; Eugene Lemcio, *The Past of Jesus in the Gospels*, SNTSMS 68 (Cambridge: Cambridge University Press, 2005); Andrew T. Lincoln, *Truth on Trial: The Lawsuit Motif in the Fourth Gospel* (Peabody, MA: Hendrickson, 2000); and Leon Morris, "History and Theology in John's Gospel," in *Studies in the Fourth Gospel* (Grand Rapids: Eerdmans, 1969), 65–138; contra Maurice Casey, *Is John's Gospel True?* (New York: Routledge, 1996).

[27]John 2:21–22, likewise, most likely indicates an intentional desire on John's part to differentiate between a historical account and post-Easter reflection.

the shallow belief of the people. Entrance into the kingdom of God is dependent not on ethnicity but on the new birth (3:3, 5–7). This confirms that old-style Judaism—represented preeminently by the temple that would soon be destroyed, but also by the half-hearted belief of the people and Nicodemus—was in desperate need of personal spiritual renewal. John 3:14–15 represents the climax of the Nicodemus narrative and Jesus' answer to the question as to how this new birth would be accomplished (cf. 3:9).

Jesus' answer concerning the *how* of the new birth in 3:14–15 centers on a typological comparison between himself and the bronze serpent in the wilderness, featured in the account of Numbers 21:8–9.[28] Upon Moses' intercession, God provided a way of salvation in the form of a raised bronze serpent, so that whoever was bitten and looked at the serpent survived. By way of typological fulfillment, Jesus prophesies his own "lifting up," so that whoever "looked" upon him by believing would in him have the life of the age to come (i.e., eternal life, ζωὴν αἰώνιον). Jesus here presents himself as the source of salvation, entrance into the kingdom of God, and bringer of the life of the coming age (cf. John 14:6).

John 3:16, as mentioned, most likely marks the opening words of the evangelist's commentary, taking on a function similar to that of a narrator who directly addresses the audience following a scene in a play. Specifically, John helps his readers understand the significance of Jesus' words to Nicodemus by pointing out their universal import (3:16). Because belief in Jesus is the sole requirement for entrance into eternal life, "whoever" believes—whether Jew *or Gentile*—will not perish but have eternal life. The universal scope of the gospel is grounded in God's love for the world (κόσμος), which led him to give his one and only (μονογενής) Son.

"World" (κόσμος) in John's Gospel typically refers to sinful humanity and only rarely to material creation.[29] It embraces all of

---

[28] For a detailed analysis, see Andreas J. Köstenberger, "John," in G. K. Beale and D. A. Carson, eds., *Commentary on the New Testament Use of the Old Testament* (Grand Rapids: Baker, 2007), 434–37.

[29] As Carson, *Gospel according to John*, 122–23, writes, "closer inspection shows that although a handful of passages preserve a neutral emphasis the vast majority are decidedly negative. There are no unambiguously positive occurrences. The 'world,' or frequently 'this world' (e.g., 8:23; 9:39; 11:9; 18:36), is not the universe, but the created order (especially of human beings and human affairs) in rebellion against its Maker (e.g., 1:10; 7:7; 14:17, 22, 27, 30; 15:18–19; 16:8, 20, 33; 17:6, 9, 14). Therefore when John tells us that God loves the world (3:16), far from

humanity, both Jew and Gentile, which sets itself in opposition to God.[30] "One and only" (NIV, μονογενής) accentuates the greatness of God's gift and, here as well as in its other instances in John's Gospel (1:14, 18; 3:18), recalls Abraham's similar sacrifice of his son Isaac (Genesis 22).[31] God's "giving" of his Son in 3:16 should be interpreted in light of the Passover theme and its fulfillment in Jesus, an important Johannine motif pervading the Gospel.[32] Jesus' fulfillment of Passover symbolism, in turn, is related to John's presentation of Jesus as the new temple.

Concerning the clearing of the temple, Porter writes, "Then, through a series of interchanges with the leaders who interrogate him, Jesus is depicted as transferring himself by reference to his own body into the equation as the substitute for the temple sacrificial system, that is, the temple system oriented toward the Passover sacrifice."[33] The setting of John's reference to God's giving of his Son (3:16) in the context of Jesus' first Passover in Jerusalem and clearing of the temple is significant. The significance of Jesus' Passover sacrifice, however, is extended beyond the borders of ethnic Israel. Jesus is the Lamb of God who will take away the sins of the entire world (1:29) and thus be the Savior of the world, reaching beyond the confines of Israel (4:42; cf. 3:17; 1 John 2:2; 4:14).

---

being an endorsement of the world, it is a testimony to the character of God. God's love is to be admired not because the world is so big but because the world is so bad."

[30]Carson (ibid., 205), states, "From this survey it is clear that it is atypical for John to speak of God's love for *the world*, but this truth is therefore made to stand out as all the more wonderful. Jews were familiar with the truth that God loved the children of Israel; here God's love is not restricted by race" (emphasis original).

[31]See Raymond E. Brown, *The Gospel according to John I–XII*, AB 29A (Garden City, NY: Doubleday, 1966), 147; and N. A. Dahl, "The Atonement—An Adequate Reward for the Akeda? (Ro 8:32)," in *Neotestamentica et Semitica: Studies in Honour of Matthew Black*, ed. E. Ellis and M. Wilcox (Edinburgh: T&T Clark, 1969), 28.

[32]For a detailed development of this theme, see Köstenberger, *Theology of John's Gospel and Letters*, 414–20. See also Gerald L. Borchert, "The Passover and the Narrative Cycles in John," in *Perspectives on John: Method and Interpretation in the Fourth Gospel*, ed. Robert B. Sloan and Mikeal C. Parsons (Lewiston, NY: Edwin Mellen, 1993), 303–16; Paul M. Hoskins, *That Scripture Might Be Fulfilled: Typology and the Death of Christ* (Longwood, FL: Xulon, 2009); Stanley E. Porter, "Can Traditional Exegesis Enlighten Literary Analysis of the Fourth Gospel? An Examination of the Old Testament Fulfillment Motif and the Passover Theme," in *The Gospels and the Scriptures of Israel*, ed. Craig A. Evans and William R. Stegner, JSNTSup 104 (Sheffield: Sheffield Academic Press, 1994), 396–428; and Mark W. G. Stibbe, *John* (Sheffield: Sheffield Academic Press, 1993).

[33]Porter, "Traditional Exegesis," 412. Porter discusses the following instances of Passover symbolism in John's Gospel: 1:19–36; 2:13–25; 6:1–14, 22–71; 11:47–12:8; 13:1–17:26; and 19:13–42 (esp. vv. 14, 29, 31, 36–37).

It is in light of the destruction of the temple that the universal significance of Jesus as the replacement of the temple and the fulfillment of the Passover can be seen. In the year 70, Judaism lost its ability to access God through the Jerusalem temple and through the Passover sacrifice. John presents Jesus as the answer. This new temple and final Passover sacrifice, not dependent on a particular geographical location (John 4:21–24), embodies God's love for the entire world. Allegiance to Jesus, demonstrated through believing in him, produces the new birth that enables entrance into the kingdom of God. This emphasis on Jesus alone, the fulfillment of the Passover and replacement of the temple, as the sole requirement for entrance into God's kingdom provides the theological rationale in John's Gospel for the universal proclamation of the gospel regardless of racial identity (20:31).

Conclusion

The universal significance of Jesus' words would not have been understood by Nicodemus in the original conversation. He would have understood the "kingdom of God" in nationalistic, ethnic terms. The typology presented by Jesus in 3:14–15 would have been limited to ethnic Israel. Just as the national people of Israel looked to the serpent for healing, so the national people of Israel would look at the exalted Son of Man for the life of the age to come.[34] Nicodemus would likewise not have thought of the "whoever" in 3:15 as extending beyond the borders of Israel. Yet a noticeable shift of perspective occurs from 3:15 to 3:16, where John's commentary on the preceding narrative functions to broaden the scope of the interchange between Jesus and Nicodemus to make it clear that "whoever" refers to the entire world, Jew as well as Gentile.

Theological Context

The exploration of the theological context surrounding John 3:16 will proceed by examining several important themes from the surrounding narrative (2:13–3:21) through the Gospel as a whole and briefly through the broader context of New Testament theology. The three themes that will be examined in John's Gospel are (1) the new birth, (2) the lifting up of the Son of Man, and (3) God's love for the world.

---

[34]"Lifting up" would not have been understood as crucifixion at this point in the narrative; see below.

The Johannine Context
The New Birth

John 1:11–13 foreshadows the emphasis in the Nicodemus pericope on the necessity and universality of a new birth.[35] The Word, the true light, came to his own (the Jews), who did not receive him (1:11). In contrast to his rejection by his own, whoever received him—that is, believed in him, whether Jew or Gentile—would become a child of God (1:12–13). This supernatural birth from God is contrasted with natural birth from blood or the will of man (1:12; cf. Nicodemus's confusion in 3:4). In 1:11–13, the prologue introduces both the necessity of a new birth and its universal availability (cf. 3:16).

This contrast between birth from God and natural birth resurfaces in the conflict between Jesus and the Jews in 8:31–59. Jesus emphasizes that the Jews' rejection of him proves that God is not their Father (8:42), despite their status as descendants of Abraham (8:37, 56). Their rejection of Jesus indicates that their true descent is from Satan, the prototypical liar and murderer (8:44). Although the language of new birth is not used, it is clear that being a child of God, that is, calling God "Father," is dependent on allegiance to Jesus and not physical descent or ethnicity.

The universal emphasis on the children of God is reiterated in John's commentary on Caiaphas's advice that it would be better for one man to die in place of the entire nation (11:50). John indicates that Caiaphas spoke better than he knew, for Jesus would indeed die for the Jewish nation, yet not for the Jews alone, but also for the scattered people of God, in order to make them one (11:51–52).[36] John here interprets the significance of Jesus' death primarily in terms of bringing unity between the Jewish nation and the Gentiles as the universal children of God.[37]

---

[35]On the new birth, see the discussion in Köstenberger, *Theology of John's Gospel and Letters*, chap. 12, sec. 28.

[36]The emphasis on the unity between the Jewish nation and the scattered people of God (Gentiles) in 11:52 likely informs Jesus' prayer for the unity of those who would believe in him through the message of his disciples (17:20–23). The unity he prayed for is the unity of Jews and Gentiles in the one people of God.

[37]See also Jesus' affirmation in 10:16, "I have other sheep that are not of this sheep pen. I must bring them also. They too will listen to my voice, and there shall be one flock and one shepherd," on which see Andreas J. Köstenberger, "Jesus the Good Shepherd Who Will Also Bring Other Sheep (John 10:16): The Old Testament Background of a Familiar Metaphor," *BBR* 12 (2002): 67–96.

The Lifting Up of the Son of Man

In addition to the emphasis on the new birth, the lifting up of the Son of Man (3:14) significantly conveys this universal message. It was noted above that Jesus presents himself as the typological fulfillment of the raised serpent of Numbers 21:8–9. The physical life of the Numbers account corresponds to eternal life,[38] while the lifted-up serpent corresponds to the lifted-up Son of Man. Jesus presents himself as the means to new spiritual life (cf. 1:12). "Lifted up" (ὑψωθῆναι) carries the double meaning of Jesus' exaltation and elevation in crucifixion on the cross (cf. 8:28; 12:32, 34). The phrase most likely draws on Isaiah's account of the suffering servant who would both suffer and be lifted up (ὑψωθήσεται) and exalted (Isa. 52:13–14).[39] Although Nicodemus would not have understood the "lifting up" to involve crucifixion, this double meaning becomes evident as the Johannine narrative progresses (see 8:28 and especially 12:33).

The reference to the lifting up of the Son of Man in 12:32 is particularly important for infusing the concept with universal significance. It is through being lifted up that Jesus will draw all people (πάντας) to himself. Similar to John's interpretation of Caiaphas's remarks, Jesus' crucifixion is presented as the indispensable prerequisite for him to draw all people, both Jew and Gentile, to himself. It was thus a salvation-historical necessity for the offer of salvation to go first to the Jews but then also to the Gentiles. The typological interpretation of Numbers 21:8–9 thus expands the boundaries of the people of God. In Numbers 21, it was *the Jewish people* who looked with faith upon the serpent for healing, while in John 3:16 it is *the entire world* that must look to Jesus in faith for salvation.

God's Love for the World

God's love for the world provides the third major theme that serves to universalize the interchange between Jesus and Nicodemus. John 15:13 well expresses the connection between love and sacrifice. Jesus, sent by God because of the greatness of his love for the world he has made, is the one who willingly laid down his life for his friends. The

---

[38] John 3:15 is the first reference to eternal life in the Gospel; see later 3:16, 36; 4:14, 36; 5:24, 39; 6:27, 40, 47, 54, 68; 10:28; 12:25, 50; 17:2–3.

[39] See Herman Ridderbos, *The Gospel of John: A Theological Commentary*, trans. John Vriend (Grand Rapids: Eerdmans, 1997), 136–37; and C. H. Dodd, *The Interpretation of the Fourth Gospel* (Cambridge: Cambridge University Press, 1953), 247.

limitation of Jesus' love to his "friends" stands in apparent tension with the universal scope of God's love in 3:16.[40] Does God love the entire world of sinful, hostile humanity or only his own people who are in the world? Don Carson is right to point out that "all believers have been chosen out of the world (15:19); they are not something other than 'world' when the gospel first comes to them. They would not have become true disciples apart from the love of God for the world."[41] There is thus a direct line of continuity extending from God's love for the world to his special love for the disciples and to those who believe in Jesus for salvation.

The world-encompassing extent of God's love in Jesus is practically expressed through John's Trinitarian mission theology.[42] Divine mission pervades the entire Gospel. God, in divine love, sent Jesus for the purpose that he might be "lifted up"—crucified and subsequently exalted—in order to bring salvation to all who believe. The Spirit witnesses with believers in Jesus the Messiah (15:26–27) and empowers the community's proclamation (20:22–23). Jesus' prayer in 17:20 foresees the spread of salvation to those who will believe through the message of the original followers. In 20:21, Jesus' mission to bring salvation to a hostile and lost world is explicitly extended to include his disciples. God's love for the world is concretely expressed through the Trinitarian mission to bring salvation to the entire world in which believers are made active participants.

Two historical events, in particular, shaped John's interpretation of Jesus' words in John 3:16. The first, as mentioned, was the destruction of Jerusalem and of the temple. With Jesus as the new temple and the center of worship, access to God was no longer limited by geography (4:21–24), ethnicity, or ritual ceremonies. The second significant historical event was the Gentile mission, which, by the time of John's writing, had already long been underway (cf. the book of Acts). The Gentile mission, for its part, represented the church's involvement in God's Trinitarian mission to the world. Since God himself was on a

---

[40]Cf. Carson, *Gospel according to John*, 204, for a discussion of the more typical restricted circle of love between the Father, the Son, and the disciples throughout the Gospel.
[41]Ibid., 205.
[42]See chap. 8 in Andreas J. Köstenberger and Peter T. O'Brien, *Salvation to the Ends of the Earth: A Biblical Theology of Mission*, NSBT 11 (Downers Grove, IL: InterVarsity, 2001); and Andreas J. Köstenberger, "John's Trinitarian Mission Theology," *SBJT* 9 (2005): 14–33.

mission to the entire world—not merely the Jews—the church must participate in that mission.

The New Testament Context

God's love for the world and his action in the giving of his Son to save sinful humanity is a central theme in New Testament theology.[43] Paul celebrates this love by proclaiming how "God shows his love for us in that while we were still sinners, Christ died for us" (Rom. 5:8; cf. Eph. 2:4–5; 2 Thess. 2:16). Both John 3:16 and Romans 5:8 emphasize how the death of Christ, as the supreme and all-sufficient manifestation of God's love, is directed toward sinners (the world). Even though Christ's death is directed toward sinners, those who respond by looking to the lifted-up Son of Man in faith experience new birth, that is, regeneration and new spiritual life (John 3:3, 5; Gal. 6:15; Titus 3:5; 1 Pet. 1:3, 23).

The universality of God's love and the resultant mission to the entire world, both Jew and Gentile, likewise constitute a primary theme of New Testament theology. The "Great Commission" provides a clear expression of the universal significance of Christ's coming: "Go therefore and make disciples *of all nations*" (Matt. 28:19; cf. Matt. 24:14; Luke 24:47). In Christ, the dividing wall, the barrier that separated Jews from Gentiles, has been broken down (Eph. 2:14–15), and the gospel of salvation through faith in Christ is being proclaimed to every nation (cf. Gal. 3:28–29; Col. 3:11).

The "Gentile mission," preeminently associated with Paul, receives different, but complementary, theological support in John and in Paul. Paul grounds his proclamation to the Gentiles particularly in his interpretation of the Abrahamic narrative (Rom. 4:1–25; Gal. 3:6–9, 14–18). He draws attention to the fact that Abraham was justified by faith (Gen. 15:6) before the law was given or circumcision commanded (Rom. 4:9–15), that God's original promise of blessing included the nations (Gen. 12:3; 18:18; 22:18; Gal. 3:8–9), and that the promises were spoken to Abraham and to his seed, Jesus Christ (Gen. 12:7; 13:15; 24:7; Gal. 3:16). Interpretation of specific texts in representative portions of the Hebrew Scriptures, whether in the Law or in the Prophets (primarily Gen. 15:6 and Hab. 2:4; cf. Rom.

---

[43]See D. A. Carson, *The Difficult Doctrine of the Love of God* (Wheaton, IL: Crossway, 2000).

1:1–2; 3:21) provides Paul with the theological justification for his proclamation to the Gentiles (see esp. Rom. 1:16–17).

John, on the other hand, does not derive the universal significance of Jesus' messianic mission from the Abraham narrative or a specific text from the Hebrew Scriptures. Instead, he portrays Jesus' mission more broadly against a wider salvation-historical backdrop, presenting Jesus as the fulfillment and replacement of the major Jewish festivals and institutions.[44] Salvation-historically, the Evangelist draws heavily from antecedent theology in the Hebrew Scriptures, including creation, the exodus, the revelation of God's glorious presence in the tabernacle and the temple, the exile, and Davidic typology.[45]

God's giving of his Son out of love for the world is connected with every major aspect of Israel's history and provides the fulfillment toward which that history pointed. Since the festivals and institutions had been fulfilled and replaced by Jesus, no ethnic or cultural barriers remained that hindered the universal proclamation of God's love and his provision of salvation in his Son. In this way, John 3:16 transformed the interchange between Jesus and Nicodemus over the question of entrance into the kingdom of God into a universal declaration of God's love for the world and the sufficiency of Jesus' "lifting up" to enable anyone who believed not to perish but to have the life of the age to come.

In his proclamation of the gospel to the Gentiles, Paul is careful not to deny or minimize the importance of the Jews as God's covenant people (e.g., Rom. 1:16; 9–11). Peter, in his sermon at Pentecost, movingly pleaded, "The promise is for you and for your children and for all who are far off, everyone whom the Lord our God calls to himself" (Acts 2:39). John, likewise, emphasizes Jesus' words that "salvation is from the Jews" (John 4:22), while at the same time refusing to limit the scope of salvation to ethnic Israel. Without denying that the Jews are God's chosen people, both Paul and John are emphatic that the message of salvation in God's Son, Jesus, extends to the entire world.

---

[44]For a thorough discussion of salvation history in John's Gospel, see Köstenberger, *Theology of John's Gospel and Letters*, 403–35. See also John W. Pryor, *John: Evangelist of the Covenant People* (Downers Grove, IL: InterVarsity, 1992). D. A. Carson, "John and the Johannine Epistles," in *It Is Written: Scripture Citing Scripture: Essays in Honor of Barnabas Lindars SSF*, ed. D. A. Carson and H. G. M. Williamson (Cambridge: Cambridge University Press, 1988), 254, rightly observes, "What is perhaps most noteworthy is not how many of the themes and institutions converge on Jesus, but how they are so presented as to make Jesus 'fulfill' them and actually *replace* them."

[45]See Köstenberger, *Theology of John's Gospel and Letters*, 403–12, for a fuller development of these themes.

Conclusion

The study of John 3:16 in its historical, literary, and theological contexts not merely confirms but even enhances the theological significance of this beloved verse in Scripture. As we have seen in the preceding study, the returns of a thorough exploration of this passage are rich indeed. The investigation of the historical context focused on how, in response to the destruction of Jerusalem and of the temple by the Romans, John 3:16 issues a universal proclamation of God's love for the entire world. This proclamation sets itself starkly apart from other Jewish responses to Jerusalem's destruction during the same period, which looked forward to the salvation of ethnic Israel and the destruction of her enemies, the Gentile nations.

The examination of the literary context drew attention to the function of John 3:16 as a commentary on the interchange between Jesus and Nicodemus. John's emphasis on Jesus' fulfillment of Passover symbolism in his replacement of the temple (cf. 2:13–22) finds deeper meaning in Jesus' discussion with Nicodemus concerning the new birth, entrance into the kingdom of God, and the typological fulfillment of Numbers 21:8–9. In Jesus as the new temple, there are no particular ethnic, cultural, or religious requirements for being granted access to God. God, in his love, gave Jesus as the final Passover Lamb to provide atonement for all the people of the world so that whoever believes in Jesus will not perish but have eternal life.

Finally, the investigation of the theological context traced several of the important themes surrounding John 3:16 through the Gospel and demonstrated the commonality it sustains with other voices in New Testament theology, particularly Paul. The Jewish nation was not set aside but is rather viewed as part of the larger people of God from every nation of the world. The atonement provided by Jesus' death carries universal significance and is not limited to one group of people. In his theological genius, John grounded this universal perspective in a salvation-historical understanding of Israel's history that is poignantly expressed in the message of John 3:16: "For God so loved the world, that he gave his only Son, that whoever believes in him should not perish but have eternal life."[46]

---

[46]I would like to acknowledge the help of my research assistant, Alex Stewart, in writing this chapter. In this, Alex went beyond the call of duty, and his competent work is greatly appreciated.

6

Justification in Galatians

DOUGLAS J. MOO

T hree contemporary developments have put justification toward the top of the list of current theological controversies. The reevaluation of the apostle Paul's appropriation of his Jewish heritage that has followed the "Sanders revolution" and is at the heart of the so-called New Perspective has inevitably turned scholarly attention to the Pauline teaching on justification, since it is so thoroughly interwoven with his response to Judaism. The strong current toward ecumenical rapprochement has stimulated both Protestant and Roman Catholic theologians to look afresh at their respective teachings on justification and to wonder quite seriously whether this historically divisive doctrine need any longer be a cause of separation between the two movements. And the perennial concern that "justification by faith alone" might be partly responsible for the widespread failure of Christians to take seriously the demands of discipleship has fostered a fresh batch of articles and books proposing various revisions to the traditional teaching.

These three powerful currents—the academic, the ecclesiological, and the practical—have flowed together to produce a flood of articles and books on justification. Surprising by its absence, however, has been any sustained attention to justification in Galatians—surprising because not only was Galatians historically the fountainhead of the distinctly Protestant teaching on justification (in the commentaries of Luther) but also because this letter has a much higher number, proportionally, of occurrences of the key verb δικαιόω than any other New Testament book. In this essay, accordingly, I will all too superficially survey and comment on justification in Galatians.

But what do we mean by "justification"? A failure to deal with the matter of definition (and sometimes even to raise it) has introduced unnecessary confusion into some of the recent discussions. At the extremes of the spectrum, justification can refer, on the one hand, to the entire Christian doctrine of salvation and, on the other, to the teaching of New Testament passages that use some form of the δικ-root. One can imagine how these conflicting definitions can bedevil discussions of the relative importance of justification in the Bible. The Lutheran systematic theologian who operates with the former definition, for instance, will have little difficulty showing that "justification" is immensely important in Scripture. The New Testament exegete who works with the latter definition, observing that δικ- language is common in only a few New Testament books, will, on the other hand, pretty easily show that justification is quite a minor and peripheral doctrine. Neither of these extreme definitions is satisfactory. The former, expansive, definition is questionable not only because it singles out one particular biblical portrayal of salvation and turns it into the whole but also because, in the process, it runs the risk of robbing justification of its own particular meaning. The latter, minimizing, definition errs in confusing lexicography with theology. Justification, whatever it is, is a theological concept. It is therefore both narrower and wider than the scope of δικ- language in the New Testament. Narrower because some occurrences of δικ- words in the New Testament have nothing to do with justification. While the matter is debated, for instance, we should probably exclude from our construct of the New Testament teaching about justification the many texts in which δικαιοσύνη occurs in its typical Old Testament sense of "what is right." But "justification" is also wider than the occurrences of δικ- language per se: other words may express the same *concept* that the relevant δικ- words are getting at.[1] Of course, this is to invite the question, which are the "relevant" δικ- words? It is because this question finds no easy answer that a simplistic lexical approach has its temptations, offering as it does an apparently objective basis for our definition. The matter deserves serious consideration, but I would have to stretch my own competencies and the scope of this essay to the breaking point even to start down this road. At the risk of determining my outcome by the way I set up the issue, then, I propose that the way forward is to start with those δικ- words, especially in Paul, that appropriate the imagery of the lawcourt to express the concept of the believer's vindication/deliverance. From this basis, one could then look for other words and phrases that express a similar idea.

In this essay, to keep it at a manageable size, I will focus on the first step: the significance of the δικ- words in Galatians.

Justification Language in Galatians

It is well known that Paul's use of δικ- language is hardly spread evenly throughout his letters, with the bulk of occurrences coming in Romans and Galatians. As I noted above, Paul uses the verb δικαιόω more often, proportionately, in Galatians than in any other of his letters, including Romans: it is found 8 times in Galatians (2230 words), 15 times in Romans (7111 words), and 4 times in other letters. In contrast, the noun δικαιοσύνη occurs much less frequently: only 4 occurrences in Galatians, in comparison with 33 in Romans (and 20 elsewhere in Paul). The only other δικ- word in Galatians is δίκαιος, which occurs once (7 in Romans; 10 elsewhere). How many of these words should we consider in our study of justification in Galatians? In what remains the most substantial lexical/theological study of the language of righteousness in Paul, John Ziesler argues that the verb δικαιόω has a narrow forensic sense but that the noun δικαιοσύνη refers to a combination of forensic and moral righteousness.[2] This

---

[1] Allen and Treier point out this methodological issue in their review of Peter Leithart's proposal about a broader meaning of *justification* (for which see below, note 5) (R. Michael Allen and Daniel J. Treier, "Dogmatic Theology and Biblical Perspectives on Justification: A Reply to Leithart," *WTJ* 70 [2008]: 105–10).

[2] J. A. Ziesler, *The Meaning of Righteousness in Paul: A Linguistic and Theological Enquiry*, SNTSMS 20 (Cambridge: University Press, 1972). This distinction has been followed by Richard N. Longenecker in his important commentary in the Word series, *Galatians*, WBC 41 (Waco, TX: Word, 1990), e.g., 95 (with ref. to 2:21).

neat distinction has, however, drawn few followers, and rightly so.[3] In Galatians, certainly, the verb and the noun overlap significantly. Every occurrence of the noun comes in close proximity to the verb (2:21 with 2:16; 3:6 with 3:8; 3:21 with 3:24; 5:5 with 5:4), and in each case the context strongly suggests that the verb and the noun occupy the same basic semantic space (for elaboration see the commentary on the relevant texts).

Of course, as is well known, Paul can use the noun, reflecting the common Old Testament use of צדקה/צדק (usually δικαιοσύνη in the LXX), to mean "the behavior that God deems to be right." But more often δικαιοσύνη in Paul echoes the basic semantic force of the verb, referring to the status of righteousness that the action, or verdict, of "justify" confers.[4] Thirty years ago, it could be taken almost as an assumption in Protestant—and particularly evangelical Protestant—circles that this verdict of justification is a purely forensic act. No longer, however, does this consensus hold, as a growing number of scholars from a variety of theological traditions argue for a transformative element within justification itself.[5] We will touch briefly on this issue below, although a thorough analysis of this matter would take us far beyond the scope of this chapter. In my view, however, every occurrence of δικ- language in Galatians relates to the doctrine of justification; and, in Galatians, justification is forensic. The issue in the letter is all about status before God.

---

[3]For brief critiques of Ziesler on this point, see Mark A. Seifrid, "Righteousness Language in the Hebrew Scriptures and Early Judaism," in *Justification and Variegated Nomism*, vol. 1, *The Complexities of Second Temple Judaism*, ed. D. A. Carson, Peter T. O'Brien, and Mark A. Seifrid (Tübingen: Mohr Siebeck, 2001), 442; John Reumann, *"Righteousness" in the New Testament* (Philadelphia: Fortress, 1982), 56–59.

[4]Westerholm perceptively notes that Paul's use of δικαιοσύνη is derived from his use of the verb δικαιόω and that it is the verb that stands in continuity with the Old Testament (Stephen Westerholm, *Perspectives Old and New on Paul: The "Lutheran" Paul and His Critics* [Grand Rapids: Eerdmans, 2004], 276–77).

[5]A certain element of transformation in justification is implied in the significant ecumenical agreement between the Roman Catholic Church and the Lutheran World Federation: *Joint Declaration on the Doctrine of Justification* (2000). Among those arguing for a transformative view are, e.g., the so-called "Finnish School" (e.g., Tuomo Mannermaa, *Christ Present in Faith: Luther's View of Justification* [Minneapolis: Fortress, 2005]); and cf. also Michael Gorman, *Inhabiting the Cruciform God: Kenosis, Justification, and Theosis in Paul's Narrative Soteriology* (Grand Rapids: Eerdmans, 2009); Don Garlington, "'Even We Have Believed': Galatians 2:15–16 Revisited," *Criswell Theological Review* 7 (2009): 9–15; Peter Leithart, "Justification as Verdict and Deliverance: A Biblical Perspective," *Pro Ecclesia* 16 (2007): 56–72; and especially Douglas A. Campbell, *The Deliverance of God: An Apocalyptic Reading of Justification in Paul* (Grand Rapids: Eerdmans, 2009); for a critical review, see Douglas J. Moo, "Review Article: *The Deliverance of God: An Apocalyptic Rereading of Justification in Paul*," *JETS* 53 (2010): 143–50.

The language of justification first occurs in 2:15–21, a transitional paragraph that uses Paul's theological rationale for his rebuke of Peter at Antioch (cf. 2:11–14) to put on the table the central matter in dispute between Paul and his opponents at Galatia: the means by which people, and especially Gentiles, can be justified before God. In this paragraph Paul introduces many of the key words that will dominate the central section of the letter:

Word	in 2:15–21	in 3:1–5:12	(in 1:1–2:14)	(in 5:13–6:18)
νόμος (nomos) "law"	6	22	0	5
ἔργα νόμου (erga nomou) "works of the law"	3	3	0	0
δικαιόω (dikaioō) "justify"	4	4	0	0
δικαιοσύνη (dikaiosynē) "righteousness"	1	3	0	0
δίκαιος (dikaios) "righteous"		(3:11 only)		
πίστις (pistis) "faith"	3	15	1	2
πιστεύω (pisteuō) "believe"	1	2	1	0
ζάω (zaō) "live"[6]	5	3	1	0

The heart of this paragraph is 2:15–16, where three occurrences of the verb δικαιόω are found. The rest of the paragraph elaborates the negative side of Paul's argument in verse 16: that a person is *not*

---

[6]See Frank J. Matera, *Galatians*, SP 9 (Collegeville, MN: Liturgical Press, 1992), 98. Most scholars think that the central argument of Galatians opens with Paul's address in 3:1. From a rhetorical point of view, they are probably right. But the close connections between 2:15–21 and the following argument (noted above) could also imply that the main line of division should be placed between 2:14 and 2:15 (F. F. Bruce, *The Epistle to the Galatians: A Commentary on the Greek Text*, NIGTC [Grand Rapids: Eerdmans, 1982], 135). The upshot is that most scholars, appropriately, recognize that 2:15–21 is a transitional paragraph. Paul continues, to some degree, his "speech" at Antioch (2:11–14); but he clearly has in view the Galatians, and more so as the speech progresses. As Betz puts it, "Paul addresses Cephas formally, and the Galatians materially" (Hans Dieter Betz, *Galatians*, Hermeneia [Philadelphia: Fortress, 1979], 114; see also, especially, Vincent M. Smiles, *The Gospel and the Law in Galatia: Paul's Response to Jewish-Christian Separatism and the Threat of Galatian Apostasy* [Collegeville, MN: Liturgical Press, 1998], 103–4; Heinrich Schlier, *Der Brief an die Galater*, 6th ed., KEK [Göttingen: Vandenhoeck & Ruprecht, 1989], 87–88).

justified by "works of the law."[7] Verses 17–18, though some of the most difficult in the letter, appear to be responding to an objection to the sharp antithesis that Paul draws in verse 16. If to be justified "in Christ" means that Jews must no longer seek that status through the law, are they not "sinners" just like the Gentiles (see v. 15)? Only, Paul responds, if Jewish Christians do what Peter's actions at Antioch implied and reestablish the law as their authority. Verses 19–20 look at this same point positively. Citing his own paradigmatic experience, Paul argues that he has "died to the law" so that he might identify fully with Christ and experience the life that he alone conveys. Verse 21, whether it responds to an objection or, more likely, is Paul's own climactic affirmation,[8] is important for two reasons. First, the continuity of Paul's argument in this paragraph requires that δικαιοσύνη in this verse must have the same basic sense as the verb δικαιόω in verses 16 and 17. "Righteousness" is the "right standing" with God that God's justifying verdict in Christ produces. Second, the mention of "grace" in this verse may hint at an underlying concern in the letter. "Grace" language does not appear often in Galatians, but it does crop up somewhat unexpectedly in some key texts, which feature grace as characteristic of Paul's gospel, in contrast to the "other gospel": "I am astonished that you are so quickly deserting the one who called you by the grace [ἐν χάριτι] of Christ and are turning to a different gospel" (1:6); "You who are trying to be justified by the law have been alienated from Christ; you have fallen away from grace" (5:4; cf. also 1:15; 2:8; 3:18). I will come back to this point.

As we have seen, justification language occurs exclusively in the central section of Galatians: (2:15) 3:1–5:12. But the language is not spread evenly through this section. A cluster of δικ- words occurs in 3:6–11, then two more in 3:21 and 3:24, and then again two in 5:4–5. The main argument within the central section is found in 3:1–4:20.[9]

---

[7]Unless otherwise indicated, Scripture quotations in this chapter are from the TNIV or are my own translations.

[8]For the former, see, e.g., Ernest de Witt Burton, *A Critical and Exegetical Commentary on the Epistle to the Galatians*, ICC (Edinburgh: T&T Clark, 1921), 140; for the latter, Scott Schauf, "Galatians 2.20 in Context," *NTS* 52 (2006): 96.

[9]Some interpreters, on the basis of the *inclusio* of personal rebukes in 3:1 and 4:11, and an alleged shift in rhetorical strategy (from "forensic" to "deliberative"), limit this argument to 3:1–4:12 (e.g., Longenecker, *Galatians*, 97; cf. also Walter G. Hansen, *Abraham in Galatians: Epistolary and Rhetorical Contexts*, JSNTSup 29 [Sheffield: JSOT, 1989], 78–79). But it makes better sense to attach the personal appeal of 4:12–20 to the rebuke of 4:9–11 than to see 4:12–20 as the beginning of a new stage of the argument (J. Louis Martyn, *Galatians: A New Translation with*

Paul frames this argument with appeals to the Galatians (3:1–5; 4:8–20) that focus on their own experience and Paul's relationship to them. The opening appeal, coming as it does at a pivotal point in the letter, is especially significant in setting the rhetorical direction for the whole argument. The strong contrast between faith and torah that was introduced in 2:16 as a fundamental principle surfaces here with respect to the Galatians' experience: they have entered into their Christian experience by "hearing characterized by faith" (ἀκοῆς πίστεως) and not by "works of the law" (ἔργα νόμου)(3:2, 5).[10] But Paul's real concern is not how they began but how they are to continue: "hearing characterized by faith" is the means by which they will sustain their Christian experience (see 3:3). Paul's appeal to Abraham's experience via Genesis 15:6 in Galatians 3:6 should probably be attached to this opening paragraph, as corroboration of the importance of faith in the Galatians' experience.[11] At the same time, however, the reference

---

Introduction and Commentary, AB 33A [New York: Doubleday, 1997], 409; François Vouga, *An die Galater* [Tübingen: Mohr, 1998], 113).

[10] The phrase ἐξ ἀκοῆς πίστεως is difficult to interpret, since the meaning of both nouns is disputed and their genitive relationship is ambiguous. Probably the majority opinion is that the phrase refers to the "message" (ἀκοή) that the Galatians believed; the NIV is here representative: "believing what you heard." A few have downplayed any focus on human response in the phrase, arguing that it can be reduced basically to "the proclamation of the gospel," "the faith message" (Richard B. Hays, *The Faith of Jesus Christ: The Narrative Substructure of Galatians 3:1–4:11*, rev. ed. [Grand Rapids: Eerdmans, 2002], 130–31; see also Martyn, *Galatians*, 284, 286–89). This interpretation is, of course, interwoven with the larger interpretive issue of the "faith of Christ" debate. Without entering that debate here, I simply note that the connection with Abraham's faith in 3:6 argues strongly for a focus on human believing (Debbie Hunn, "Πίστις Χριστοῦ in Galatians 2:16: Clarification from 3:1–6," *TynBul* 57 [2006]: 23–33). The meaning of ἀκοή is much more difficult to determine. The roughly parallel occurrences in Rom. 10:16 provide grounds for the sense "what is heard," e.g., "report" or "message" (see, e.g., Longenecker, *Galatians*, 103). But Paul usually uses the noun in an active sense (1 Cor. 12:17; 1 Thess. 2:13 [probably]; 2 Tim. 4:3, 4), and that makes better sense of the precedence given to ἀκοή here in Galatians 3. See James D. G. Dunn, *The Epistle to the Galatians* (Peabody, MA: Hendrickson, 1993), 154; Moisés Silva, "Faith versus Works of the Law in Galatians," in *Justification and Variegated Nomism*, vol. 2, *The Paradoxes of Paul*, ed. D. A. Carson, Peter T. O'Brien, and Mark A. Seifrid (Tübingen: Mohr Siebeck, 2004), 236. The "hearing" in the phrase perhaps conveys something of the connotation of the equivalent Hebrew word: faithful receptivity, an "attentiveness" to the Word of God that includes both trust in its content and giver and the disposition to obey. See, e.g., Ex. 15:26; 19:5; 23:22; Deut. 11:13, 22; 15:5; 28:1, 2; 2 Sam. 22:45; Jer. 17:24; 1 Sam. 15:22 ("To hear [ἀκοή] is better than sacrifice"). For this view of the phrase, see Oliver O'Donovan, *Resurrection and Moral Order: An Outline for Evangelical Ethics*, 2nd ed. (Grand Rapids: Eerdmans, 1994), 110; Don Garlington, *An Exposition of Galatians: A New Perspective/Reformational Reading* (Eugene, OR: Wipf & Stock, 2003), 134.

[11] So, e.g., ESV, NIV, and see Bruce, *Galatians*, 152–53; Moisés Silva, "Galatians" (unpublished essay, 2001), 253; Andrew H. Wakefield, *Where to Live: The Hermeneutical Significance of Paul's Citations from Scripture in Galatians 3:1–14*, SBL Academia Biblica 14 (Atlanta: SBL, 2003), 136; contra, e.g., NRSV, NLT; and see Burton, *Galatians*, 153; Longenecker, *Galatians*, 112.

to Abraham brings onto the stage of Paul's argument a figure whose place in salvation history is central to the argument through the end of the chapter (vv. 7, 8, 9, 14, 16, 18, 29; cf. 4:22).[12] The intricate, Old Testament–soaked, and controversial argument that follows is concerned especially to make two points: that Abraham's "family" was all along intended to include Gentiles; and that belonging to Abraham's family—for both Jews and Gentiles—comes only through faith (and not the law or the works it calls for). The brief but programmatic paragraph of Galatians 3:7–9 establishes both these points.[13] At the same time, it is important for our purposes to note that justification language surfaces here again, first with the substantive δικαιοσύνη in the quotation of Genesis 15:6 and then with the verb δικαιόω in Galatians 3:8. The basic semantic equivalence of the words is seen here again: the "righteousness" God granted Abraham is clearly the same as the "justifying verdict" promised to the Gentiles.

Having expounded the positive side of the principle of 2:16 in 3:7–9 (justified by faith), Paul turns in 3:10–14 to the negative side (*not* justified by works of the law). People who rely on works of the law suffer the curse (v. 10), the contrast, of course, to the blessing connected with Abraham. While of course contested, "as many as are 'out of' the works of the law" (ὅσοι ἐξ ἔργων νόμου) should be taken as referring to the Galatians. The verse therefore refers not to the historical curse that came on the people of Israel but to the curse that comes on anyone who tries to find blessing/righteousness via the works of the law (see below). Moreover, the connection between "doing" in this verse and "doing" in verse 12 suggests that *this* is the underlying issue in the failure of the law (again, more on this later). The torah, then, cannot be the means of justification because, by definition (for Paul), it involves "doing" rather than "believing." Justification language surfaces here in verse 11, where Paul quotes Habakkuk 2:4—"the person who is just will find life through faith"—as substantiation of the claim that "no one is justified before God through the law."[14] As

---

[12]Ronald Y. K. Fung, *The Epistle to the Galatians*, NICNT (Grand Rapids: Eerdmans, 1988), 137.
[13]James D. G. Dunn, *The Theology of Paul's Letter to the Galatians* (Cambridge: Cambridge University Press, 1993), 82–83.
[14]I assume here the usual reading of the sequence ὅτι . . . δῆλον ὅτι as "for it is clear that, because," rather than "because . . . it is clear that." See, e.g., Franz Mußner, *Der Galaterbrief*, 5th ed., HTKNT (Freiburg: Herder, 1988), 228; contra, e.g., Wakefield, *Where to Live*, 162–67, 201–14.

my paraphrase implies, I am tentatively associating the verb δικαιοῦται in Galatians 3:11a with ζήσεται in the quotation (largely on the basis of vv. 12 and 21).[15] If we follow this reading, then the substantival adjective δίκαιος in the quotation would have its standard Old Testament sense of "the person who is right before God" (often in a context showing that "doing right" is part of this "rightness"; see the contrast in the two other occurrences of צדיק/δίκαιος in Habakkuk with the "wicked": Hab. 1:4, 13). On this reading, this would be the only δικ-word in Galatians that does not refer to justification. Woven together in this paragraph, as in the preceding one, is the general principle that "faith" is the means of finding righteousness/blessing (Gal. 3:7, 9, 11, 14) *and* that faith also enables the inclusion of Gentiles within the people of God (vv. 8, 14).

The argument in this part of the letter unfolds via a series of linking words. "Faith" in 3:1–6 triggers Paul's focus on the faith of Abraham in 3:7–9. The "blessing" God promises to those who rely on faith (v. 9) becomes the climax of the next paragraph (v. 14) at the same time as that blessing brings up its opposite, the curse (vv. 10, 13). Mention of the "promise of the Spirit" at the end of verse 14 stimulates Paul's discussion of the contrast between promise and law in verses 15–18. And it is worth noting that Paul again appeals to the principle of grace at the end of this paragraph: "God gave it in grace to Abraham in the form of a promise" (τῷ δὲ Ἀβραὰμ δι' ἐπαγγελίας κεχάρισται ὁ θεός). Paul's depreciation of the law vis-à-vis the promise in salvation history leads him then to raise the obvious question: "What . . . was the purpose of the law?" (v. 19). Paul's answer is complicated and debated, but for our purposes it is sufficient to note that he insists on the compatibility of law and promise, and sustains this consonance by sharply distinguishing the purposes of each: the law acts as the guardian of the people of Israel during their "minority" and, because it issues demands that cannot be met (implied in v. 10, despite the many who doubt it),[16] locks everyone up under sin (v. 22). Or, to put

---

[15]While some interpreters attach ἐκ πίστεως to δίκαιος—"the one who is just by faith will live" (e.g., Bruce, *Galatians*, 161; Smiles, *The Gospel and the Law*, 204; Hans-Joachim Eckstein, *Verheissung und Gesetz: Eine exegetische Untersuchung zu Galater 2,15–4,7*, WUNT 2/86 [Tübingen: Mohr Siebeck, 1996], 143–44), most, following the connection in the Habakkuk text, attach it to ζήσεται (see, e.g., the arguments in Maureen W. Yeung, *Faith in Jesus and Paul: A Comparison with Special Reference to "Faith That Can Remove Mountains" and "Your Faith Has Healed/Saved You,"* WUNT 2/147 [Tübingen: Mohr Siebeck, 2002], 208–10).
[16]I elaborate this point later in the essay.

it negatively, the law cannot impart life/righteousness (v. 22). The logic of this verse suggests that Paul is basically identifying the "imparting of life" (ζωοποιῆσαι) with "righteousness" (δικαιοσύνη).[17] And, if this is the case, then δικαιοσύνη is forensic rather than moral. This imparting of life/righteousness, Paul implies, is the purpose of the promise first given to Abraham, which has Christ as its ultimate beneficiary. And promise operates in the sphere of faith (even as torah operates in the sphere of doing or works). After being absent for several verses, then, "faith" emerges again as a key point in verse 22 and is then identified in verses 23–25 as that which the era of torah has looked ahead to. And it is also specifically said once more to be the means of justification (ἵνα ἐκ πίστεως δικαιωθῶμεν, v. 24).[18]

Verses 26–29 circle back to the beginning of Paul's argument in verses 7–9, even as they gather up some of the key themes of verses 15–25. Whether "you all" (vv. 26, 28; see also ὅσοι in v. 27) refers to Gentiles or, as may be more likely, all believers,[19] there can be no doubt that the language (in contrast to the first-person plurals of vv. 23–25) alludes to the inclusion of Gentiles that was touched on in verse 8 (see also v. 14). Identifying these believers as "sons"/"children" (υἱοί) harks back to verse 7 ("sons/children of Abraham"). Key language from verses 15–25 is also integrated into this paragraph: "faith" (v. 26; see vv. 6, 7, 8, 9, 11, 12, 14, 22, 23, 24, 25), "seed" (v. 29; see vv. 16, 19), "heir"/"inheritance" (v. 29; see v. 18), "promise" (v. 29; see vv. 8, 16, 17, 18, 19, 21, 22). But the weight of these verses falls on the "in Christ" conception—a point to which we shall return.

We see again the linking-word mechanism at work, as the mention of "heirs" at the end of verse 29 leads Paul in 4:1–7 to use the metaphor of inheritance to illuminate the present juncture in salvation history. Justification language is absent in this paragraph, as it is in the appeal of 4:8–20 and the contrast between the two sons and their descendants in 4:21–30. This latter text has a somewhat secondary role in Paul's theological argument, perhaps being introduced as a response to the

---

[17]Burton, *Galatians*, 195; Bruce, *Galatians*, 180; contra Fung, *Galatians*, 163, who thinks that righteousness is the means to life.

[18]I deal with the salvation-historical focus on faith here in light of the "faith of Christ" controversy later in the essay.

[19]Bruce, *Galatians*, 183; contra, e.g., Dunn, *Galatians*, 201, and Brendan Byrne, *"Sons of God"—"Seed of Abraham,"* Analecta biblica 83 (Rome: Biblical Institute Press, 1979), 172–73, who think Gentiles are in view.

agitators' use of the argument from Abraham and Isaac.[20] In any case, it is best seen as an illustration designed to bolster the appeals that dominate the paragraph (4:21, 30; cf. 5:1).

The paragraph 5:2–6, with further support in verses 7–12, brings the theological argument of the letter to its paraenetic climax.[21] It begins with warning (vv. 2–4) and then turns to exhortation (vv. 5–6). Submitting to the agitators' insistence on torah obedience for justification will consign the Galatians again to their slavery under "the elements of the world" (see 4:3, 8–9) and mean nothing less than being cut off from Christ and from access to the grace found only in him. The first-person plural verb in 5:5—"we eagerly await" (ἀπεκδεχόμεθα)—includes the Galatians along with Paul[22] and signals a rhetorical shift. Paul is not just stating a truth; he is inviting the Galatians to join with him in taking ownership of that truth.[23] Returning to two of the key ideas in Galatians 2:16–4:31, Paul calls on the Galatians to wait through the

---

[20]See especially C. K. Barrett, "The Allegory of Abraham, Sarah, and Hagar in the Argument of Galatians," in *Rechtfertigung*, ed. J. Friedrich, W. Pöhlmann, and P. Stuhlmacher (Tübingen: Mohr Siebeck, 1976), 9–10.

[21]The place of 5:1 in the argument is debated: is it the concluding exhortation of the "allegory" (J. B. Lightfoot, *The Epistle of St. Paul to the Galatians* [repr., Grand Rapids: Zondervan, 1957], 185) or of the argument of the letter to this point (James L. Boyce, "The Poetry of the Spirit: Willing and Doing in Galatians 5 and 6," WW 20 [2000]: 293; Susan G. Eastman, *Recovering Paul's Mother Tongue: Language and Theology in Galatians* [Grand Rapids: Eerdmans, 2007], 133–34)? The literary marker ἴδε ἐγὼ Παῦλος in v. 2 suggests, in any case, that a new paragraph begins here (Richard B. Hays, "The Letter to the Galatians," in *The New Interpreter's Bible*, ed. Leander E. Keck, vol. 11 [Nashville: Abingdon, 2000], 302); 5:1 may be transitional.

[22]Galatians scholars debate the referent Paul intends in his first-person plural pronouns and verbs in the letter. On the basis of 2:15—ἡμεῖς φύσει Ἰουδαῖοι, "we who are by nature Jews"—and the nature of the argument in chap. 3, many interpreters think that Paul rather consistently uses "we" to denote himself and fellow Jews in the letter—including 5:5 (e.g., Longenecker, *Galatians*, 229; Ben Witherington III, *Grace in Galatia: A Commentary on St. Paul's Letter to the Galatians* [Grand Rapids: Eerdmans, 1998], 369; Garlington, *Galatians*, 221). But it is difficult to enforce this consistency throughout the letter; Paul's shift of pronouns appears at times to have more to do with rhetorical considerations. In 5:5, I think it likely that Paul uses the first-person plural to draw the Galatians into the conversation (see also Susanne Schewe, *Die Galater zurückgewinnen: Paulinische Strategien in Galater 5 und 6*, FRLANT 208 [Göttingen: Vandenhoeck & Ruprecht, 2004], 69–72; Dunn, *Galatians*, 269; Joachim Rohde, *Der Brief des Paulus an die Galater*, THKNT [Berlin: Evangelische Verlangsanstalt, 1989], 217; Gordon D. Fee, *God's Empowering Presence: The Holy Spirit in the Letters of Paul* [Peabody, MA: Hendrickson, 1994], 418).

[23]David G. Horrell notes that Paul's "indicative" often functions this way, providing a critical bridge to his imperatives: "The apparently paradoxical nature of the Pauline indicative-imperative formulations can, then, be resolved when the indicatives in question are seen not as statements which can be held to be either 'true' or not but as identity-descriptors and group norms which need to be constantly affirmed" (*Solidarity and Difference: A Contemporary Reading of Paul's Ethics* [London: T&T Clark, 2005], 94).

Spirit and through faith. Justification language appears in this paragraph for the last time in the letter, it again being clear that the verb in 5:4 must refer to the same thing as the noun in 5:5.[24]

The trend in recent Galatians scholarship has been away from the traditional (and therefore, in some quarters, automatically suspect) focus on justification and toward various other emphases, such as the Spirit or, particularly, inclusion in the people of God (expressed in the language of being Abraham's sons/children/seed (3:7 [9], 29; 4:28–31) or God's sons/children (3:26; 4:5–7). The Spirit is no doubt an important motif in the letter, one that has undoubtedly been neglected.[25] Yet the relative paucity of references in the central section of the letter (3:2, 3, 5, 14; 4:6, 29; 5:5) makes it difficult to put the Spirit at the center of the argument. Both justification and inclusion within the people of God are important and, we would argue, overlapping if not referentially equivalent concepts. But justification language, in comparison with "people of God" language, is more frequent and occurs at critical rhetorical points in the letter: it introduces the main argument (2:16) and climaxes Paul's appeal to the Galatians (5:5–6). Membership in God's people is basic to Paul's argument in 3:6–4:7, where being "sons of Abraham/God" brackets the argument (3:7 and 4:7).[26] We might conclude that the "seed of Abraham" argument is defensive, Paul responding to the agitators' own theological agenda, whereby his use of justification language is offensive, his own preferred way of putting the matter at issue. Of course, some interpreters would argue that justification language is in fact just another way of expressing the notion of membership within God's people or inclusion in the covenant; and so we now turn to the question of the breadth of the justification concept in Galatians.

Justification, Participation in Christ, and Inclusion in the People of God

Our survey of the central argument of Galatians suggests that δικαιόω and δικαιοσύνη have the same semantic force in this letter, denoting

---

[24]It is therefore unlikely that there is any reference to "moral" righteousness in Gal. 5:5 (contra, e.g., Burton, *Galatians*, 278; Ziesler, *Meaning of Righteousness*, 179).

[25]The centrality of the Spirit in Paul's argument is the basic thesis of Charles Cosgrove, *The Cross and the Spirit: A Study in the Argument and Theology of Galatians* (Mercer, GA: Mercer University Press, 1988).

[26]See, e.g., Fee, who sees 3:7—"those who have faith are the sons of Abraham"—as the thesis statement, with 3:29—"you are the seed of Abraham"—and 4:7—"you are sons of God"—as the double conclusion (*God's Empowering Presence*, 379).

the conveying of (in the case of the verb), or possession of (the noun), right standing with God. As is widely recognized, this application of the language picks up a particular strand in the usage of these words in the LXX: where δικαιόω, translating the hiphil of צדק, denotes a (forensic) declaration of "righteousness" (Gen. 38:26; 44:16; Ex. 23:7; Deut. 25:1; 1 Kings 8:32; 2 Chron. 6:23; Ps. 82:3; Isa. 5:23; 50:8; Jer. 3:11; Ezek. 16:51–52), and where δικαιοσύνη (צדקה/צדק) refers to the establishment of Israel's "righteousness" or "vindication," often with a distinctly eschatological focus.[27] Isaiah 40–55, a passage that has exercised considerable influence on Paul's theology, provides key instances of this language. In contrast to the idols, the living and powerful God will display his love and commitment to Israel by delivering them from their captivity and shame. This deliverance is expressed with the verb δικαιόω/צדק—"He who *vindicates* me is near" (50:8, alluded to in Rom. 8:33)—and with the noun δικαιοσύνη (צדקה/צדק), for example, "I am bringing my righteousness near" (also Isa. 51:6, 8; 54:14; this language is undoubtedly foundational to Paul's "righteousness of God" language in Rom. 1:17; 3:21–22; 10:3; 2 Cor. 5:21). Yahweh, by means of his Servant (Isa. 49:1–7; 52:13–53:12), will establish and display the "right standing" of Israel; he will "vindicate" his people. Along with the classic texts of Genesis 15:6 and Habakkuk 2:4, this seems to be the well from which Paul draws his distinctive language of "justification." To be sure, unlike Romans, where allusions to these texts are obvious, Galatians does not clearly ground the language in these Isaiah texts (though it may be no accident that Paul quotes from Isa. 54:1 in Gal. 4:27). We may, however, surmise that this use of "righteousness" language was common ground among Paul, the agitators, and the Galatians. Certainly Paul's claim in his first use of the language, that he and his fellow Jews "know" about the manner of justification (Gal. 2:15–16), suggests that the language was common currency in the early church (or at least the Pauline-influenced early church) before Paul wrote Galatians.

If one might describe the material in the last paragraph as a matter of general scholarly consensus, the same cannot be said of another matter: the degree to which, in Galatians, Paul "redefines" justification

---

[27]Ziesler provides a good survey of the linguistic data in the Old Testament (*Meaning of Righteousness*, 17–69); see also Seifrid, "Righteousness Language in the Hebrew Scriptures and Early Judaism," 415–42.

language to mean "to be declared to be members of God's people." N. T. Wright, while acknowledging that justification language functions in the metaphorical sphere of the lawcourt, insists that Paul, reflecting the strongly covenantal context of the language in the Old Testament, and in light of the immediate context (where the issue is, who can eat at the same table together? [2:11–14]), uses δικαιόω in its first programmatic occurrences in Galatians to mean "to be reckoned by God to be a true member of his family, and hence with the right to share table fellowship"—with particular emphasis on the inclusion of Gentiles (2:15–16).[28] This initial usage sets the tone for the letter as a whole, δικαιοσύνη, then, meaning, in turn, "membership in God's true family."[29] However, these apparently either/or propositions— forensic verdict of acquittal *or* membership in God's family—are later (within the same book) relativized with both/and language—forensic acquittal *and* membership in God's family (see esp. 133–34). So the real question is not whether, as Wright himself (too strongly) puts it, "The lawcourt metaphor behind the language of justification, and of the status 'righteous' which someone has when the court has found in their favor, has *given way to* the clear sense of 'membership in God's people'" (121, my emphasis); it is, rather, whether the notion of membership in the people of God should be *added to* the notion of forensic acquittal, and, indeed, to the extent that the latter becomes the dominant idea in the letter.

Wright (and others who follow a similar pattern of interpretation) is correct, of course, that Paul's first announcement of "justification by faith" comes in a dual context, both contexts being dominated by the issue of Gentile inclusion (the dispute at Antioch [2:11–14] and the crisis in Galatia). However, more precisely, the issue in both situations was not the inclusion of Gentiles in the new messianic community per se (which, as far as we can tell, no one was disputing) but the terms on which they should be recognized to be such. More importantly, Wright's claim that δικαιόω in 2:16 loses or sheds some of its forensic connotation because "Paul is not in a lawcourt, he is at a dinner table" (116) illegitimately privileges context over semantics. Only a few pages later, Wright claims that lawcourt imagery is "always there by implica-

[28]N. T. Wright, *Justification: God's Plan and Paul's Vision* (Downers Grove, IL: InterVarsity, 2009), 116.
[29]Ibid., 121.

tion in the language of 'justification'" (128); and he should observe this sound semantic observation in his interpretation of 2:16. In this text, and the paragraph of which it is a part, Paul is using the Antioch incident as a jumping-off place to address the central theological issue that lies behind that incident and the situation in Galatia as well. And in both situations, this issue is the terms on which people can expect to find right standing with God. Paul applies his teaching on justification to the issue of the means by which Gentiles can be included. But in this opening paragraph of his theological argument, he is establishing the broad framework of justification, with reference to Jews as much as (or more than) Gentiles. Paul stresses that Jews also "know" that this right standing comes by christologically oriented faith and not by "works of the law" (v. 16); if right standing with God could come by means of the torah, Christ need not have died at all (v. 21). This fundamental theological fact, "the truth of the gospel" for which Paul fought in Jerusalem (v. 5) and that Peter has called into question by his conduct at Antioch (v. 14), makes clear that it is wrong for Peter, by his withdrawal of table fellowship in Antioch, to force Gentiles to "Judaize" (v. 14) and equally wrong for the agitators to insist that the Gentile Galatians succumb to circumcision and a torah lifestyle (3:1–5; 5:2–6). There is no good contextual reason to insist that "justify" in 2:16 must be redefined to mean, or to include, the notion of membership in God's people. There is no need to collapse the two concepts into one. As Simon Gathercole insists, "The *content* of the doctrine of justification by faith should be distinguished from its *scope*."[30] The flow of the text makes perfect sense if Paul in 2:16 is using the δικαιόω language in its well-attested sense "declare righteous."

Moreover, while the issue cannot be explored adequately in this essay, it is also questionable whether "justification" language in the Old Testament ever takes on the sense of "membership in God's people." As we noted above, in Isaiah 40–55, "righteousness" denotes God's vindication of people already in covenant relationship with him. In other texts, justification language denotes God's initial acceptance of a person, an acceptance that at the same time normally implies that one "enters" the people of God. But that the language does not *denote* entrance into the people of God is clear, for instance, in the key text

---

[30]Simon J. Gathercole, "Justified by Faith, Justified by His Blood: The Evidence of Romans 3:21–4:25," in *The Paradoxes of Paul*, ed. Carson, O'Brien, and Seifrid, 156.

Genesis 15:6 (cf. Gal. 3:6): there is no "people of God" for Abraham to join at this point; his "justification" is foundational to the process by which that people is being created.[31]

Membership in God's people and justification are closely related; but they are not identical. Paul argues both points in Galatians: people by their faith in Christ are established as "righteous" in God's sight; and by that faith they are brought into the people of God. But in Galatians, as in Paul's letters in general, justification does not in itself include belonging to God's people; still less, how one *knows* a person belongs to God's people.[32]

One other definitional issue pertaining to justification in Galatians requires brief mention. Recent interpreters (echoing, to be sure, a minor strand in the Reformation theological heritage), sometimes out of an express concern to counteract the ethical indifference that they think tends to follow from a strictly forensic view of justification, want to expand the scope of justification to include a transformative element.[33]

---

[31]Wright tries to rescue his interpretation by suggesting that the text speaks of "membership in . . . the covenant family which God was creating" (*Justification*, 134). But this seems to be an attempt to force a text to fit a preordained mold. See, on this point, John Piper, *The Future of Justification: A Response to N. T. Wright* (Wheaton, IL: Crossway, 2007), 42–44.

[32]In Wright's earlier writing on justification, he separated justification from conversion, arguing that justification is a declaration of a relationship that has been previously established via conversion ("The Epistle to the Romans," in *The New Interpreter's Bible*, ed. Leander Keck, et al., vol. 10 [Nashville: Abingdon, 2002], 468; cf. also 466, 481; see also *What Saint Paul Really Said: Was Paul of Tarsus the Real Founder of Christianity?* [Grand Rapids: Eerdmans, 1997], 113–33; *Paul in Fresh Perspective* [Minneapolis: Fortress, 2005], 111–13). Of course this way of describing justification has considerable resonance with the Reformation tradition, which often conceptualizes the matter in just this general manner; justification is God's recognition of a person's "rightness" based on her identification with Christ and his righteousness. But in contrast to Wright, the tradition rightly notes that justification is closely tied to conversion itself; if not the actual point of "transfer"—Sanders's "getting in"—it is clearly bound up with it (see, e.g., Rom. 5:1, 9; 1 Cor. 6:11) (see on this point, e.g., Piper, *The Future of Justification*, 39–44; Simon Gathercole, "The Doctrine of Justification in Paul and Beyond: Some Proposals," in *Justification in Perspective: Historical Developments and Contemporary Challenges*, ed. Bruce McCormack [Grand Rapids: Baker, 2006], 228–31). This insistence on separating justification from conversion is not as evident in Wright's latest book on the subject (*Justification*). For a broader criticism of Wright's view on justification, see especially Gathercole, "The Doctrine of Justification," 219–41, 228–40; Michael F. Bird, "Justification as Forensic Declaration and Covenant Membership: A Via Media between Reformed and Revisionist Readings of Paul," *TynBul* 57 (2006): 109–30, 115–16; Bird, *The Saving Righteousness of God: Studies on Paul, Justification, and the New Perspective*, Paternoster Biblical Monographs (Waynesboro, GA: Paternoster, 2007), 113–54; Robert S. Smith, *Justification and Eschatology: A Dialogue with "The New Perspective on Paul"* (Doncaster, Australia: Reformed Theological Review, 2001), 89–92; Peter T. O'Brien, "Was Paul a Covenantal Nomist?," in *The Paradoxes of Paul*, ed. Carson, O'Brien, and Seifrid, 249–96, 286–95; Piper, *The Future of Justification*.

[33]The transformative power of justification is an important part of Ernst Käsemann's famous definition of "God's righteousness" in terms of both gift and power (see, e.g., "The Righteousness

Paul can certainly use the word δικαιοσύνη, in continuation with the
Old Testament and other New Testament authors, to refer to appropriate ethical behavior (e.g., Rom. 6:13, 16, 18, 19, 20; Eph. 5:9; 1 Tim.
6:11; cf. Matt. 5:20; Luke 1:75; Acts 10:35; James 1:20). But I am
not convinced that these occurrences should be incorporated into the
concept of Pauline "justification." We return here, of course, to the
methodological issue we raised at the beginning of the essay: which
occurrences of δικ- *language* in Paul should be the building blocks in
our construction of the *concept* of justification in Paul? I would argue,
simply, that at least two distinguishable semantic categories of δικ-
language—for the sake of brevity, the "moral" and the "forensic"—are
identifiable, on the basis of sound syntagmatic considerations, in both
the LXX and the New Testament, and that it is a mistake to merge
these categories. Certainly there is little reason to do so in Galatians.
The fact that Paul *associates* justification with transformation through
participation in Christ in texts such as Galatians 2:15–21 does not mean
that he *identifies* them.[34] Paul is concerned about the transformation of
character in Galatians, as the section 5:13–6:10 reveals most clearly. But
to argue that this concern must be *part of* justification tends to assume
that transformation can become part of what it necessarily means to
be a Christian only if it is folded into justification.

Following the lead of Calvin and many others in the Reformed
tradition, it does much better justice to Paul if we connect forensic
justification with transformation by viewing both as inevitable and
necessary products of our being "in Christ."[35] While not explicitly

---

of God in Paul," in *New Testament Questions of Today* [Philadelphia: Fortress, 1969], 168–82).
The transformative nature of justification was hinted at in the work of Adolf Schlatter (e.g.,
The Theology of the Apostles: The Development of New Testament Theology [Grand Rapids:
Baker, 1998 (1922)], 248–50) and has also been a hallmark of Peter Stuhlmacher's approach to
righteousness (see *Gerechtigkeit Gottes bei Paulus*, FRLANT 87 [Göttingen: Vandenhoeck &
Ruprecht, 1966]; *Revisiting Paul's Doctrine of Justification* [Downers Grove, IL: InterVarsity,
2001], 62–67; *Biblische Theologie des Neuen Testaments*, 3rd ed. [Göttingen: Vandenhoeck &
Ruprecht, 2005], 332–34). See also Eberhard Jüngel, *Justification: The Heart of the Christian
Faith: A Theological Study with Ecumenical Purpose* (Edinburgh: T&T Clark, 2001), 208–11;
Don B. Garlington, *Faith, Obedience, and Perseverance: Aspects of Paul's Letter to the Romans*,
WUNT 2/79 (Tübingen: Mohr Siebeck, 1994), 155–61; and, most recently, Michael J. Gorman,
Inhabiting the Cruciform God: Kenosis, Justification, and Theosis in Paul's Narrative Soteriology
(Grand Rapids: Eerdmans, 2009) and Campbell, *The Deliverance of God*.
[34]Contra, e.g., Gorman, *Inhabiting the Cruciform God*, 63–69.
[35]William B. Evans has recently surveyed some of the ways that union with Christ and justification are related in historical and contemporary Reformed theology ("Déjà Vu All Over Again?
The Contemporary Reformed Soteriological Controversy in Historical Perspective," *WTJ* 72
[2010]: 135–51).

taught in Galatians, the idea that our union with Christ produces these two inseparable but distinguishable benefits is clearly hinted. Being "in Christ" is foundational, as the important summarizing paragraph 3:26–29 makes clear. We should probably translate verse 26, as in the NIV, "So in Christ Jesus you are all children of God through faith."[36] And the union-with-Christ theme appears again in verse 27 ("clothed yourselves with Christ"), verse 28 ("all one in Christ Jesus"), and verse 29 ("belong to Christ"). Paul explicitly relates justification to participation in Christ in 2:17—"seeking to be justified *in Christ*"—and union with Christ appears at key points elsewhere in the letter (1:22; 2:4; 2:19–20; 5:6, 24; 6:14). Since Christ is *the* "seed of Abraham" (3:16), it can be only in and through Christ that a person can receive the promised "blessing of Abraham" and "the promise of the Spirit" (3:14). This verse reveals as clearly as any the underlying "theologic" of the letter. The "blessing of Abraham" is, in context, justification.[37] "The promise of the Spirit" looks back to 3:2 and 3:5; but, just as importantly yet often not recognized, this language also anticipates Paul's argument in 5:13–6:10. Paul's association of the blessing of Abraham and the promise of the Spirit depends on the prophetic anticipation of the fulfillment of God's promise to Abraham being accompanied by the transforming work of God's Spirit.[38] It is this transforming work of the Spirit, creating the conformity to God's will that the law was unable to accomplish, that is the theme of 5:13–6:10. In 3:13–14, then, Paul traces back to our association with Christ, who in his death took our curse on himself, the twin blessings of justification and transformation. As I would argue is the case throughout his letters, union with Christ, not justification, lies at the heart of Paul's theology.[39] But forensic justification is one of

---

[36]Taking διὰ τῆς πίστεως and ἐν Χριστῷ Ἰησοῦ as parallel rather than sequential. So, e.g., Longenecker, *Galatians*, 153–54; Karl Friedrich Ulrichs, *Christusglaube: Studien zum Syntagma Πίστις Χριστοῦ und zum paulinischen Verständnis on Glaube und Rechtfertigung*, WUNT 2/227 (Tübingen: Mohr Siebeck, 2007), 102; Mußner, *Der Galaterbrief*, 261.

[37]Chee-Chiew Lee, "The Blessing of Abraham and the Promise of the Spirit: The Influence of the Prophets on Paul in Galatians 3:1–14" (PhD diss., Wheaton College, 2009), 48–57.

[38]See ibid., esp. 312–13.

[39]This does not mean, however, that "justification" is a mere "subsidiary crater" or a "battle doctrine," as was famously alleged by Albert Schweitzer and Wilhelm Wrede (see Schweitzer, *The Mysticism of Paul the Apostle* [London: Black, 1931]; Wrede, *Paul* [Boston: American Unitarian Association, 1908]). Many contemporary scholars agree with Schweitzer and Wrede: E. P. Sanders also privileged the participationist category over the judicial (*Paul and Palestinian Judaism: A Comparison of Patterns of Religion* [Philadelphia: Fortress, 1977], 501–8); see also Philip Esler, *Galatians* (London: Routledge, 1998), 153–59; Gorman, *Inhabiting the Cruciform God*, and, in more polemical form, Douglas A. Campbell, *The Quest for Paul's Gospel* (London:

the primary and critical benefits that people who belong to Christ by faith receive. And in Galatians this forensic issue comes to the surface because the letter focuses resolutely on the question, Who, and how, will people experience God's vindicating judgment in their favor?

The Means of Justification

As we noted earlier, the "Gentile problem" in Galatians is not whether Gentiles should be included in the people of God. The issue is, rather, on what grounds they are included in the people of God. For the agitators, belonging to God's people and thereby enjoying God's eschatological vindication could come only by identifying with Abraham's descendants by the Old Testament–mandated and time-honored means of circumcision and torah piety. Central to Paul's disagreement with the agitators at this point is a more discontinuous reading of salvation history. For the agitators, the recognition of Jesus as Messiah was important but did not constitute any reason to shift the terms on which people could relate to God. For Paul, on the other hand, who experienced in his own life a fundamental paradigm shift (1:11–16), the coming of Christ meant a cataclysmic shift in the contours of salvation history. The "apocalyptic" significance of Christ's coming in Galatians, highlighted especially in the work of J. Louis Martyn, does not mean

---

T&T Clark, 2005); and *The Deliverance of God*. These critics have a point. Many of Paul's letters hardly refer to justification per se, and the texts in which the language is used (Galatians, Romans, Philippians 3) involve dialogue with Jewish viewpoints and disputes over torah. But Paul's teaching on justification is more than an occasional strategy to deal with Jewish opponents. The concept of "righteousness," and the juridical category to which it belongs, are important in the Old Testament, and Paul's explanation of the Christ event in these terms is therefore rooted in a central biblical concern. Udo Schnelle accuses Schweitzer and Wrede of confusing the origin of Paul's view with its importance (*Apostle Paul: His Life and Theology* [Grand Rapids: Baker, 2005], 471). Justification is not central in Paul's thought, but it is a critical and important means of explicating his gospel. Nor is there any need to set Paul's "juridical" and "participationist" categories in opposition to one another. The latter may be more fundamental for Paul, but it is also a very general category, comprising various other ways of thinking about the Christ event, including the juridical (see especially Richard B. Gaffin, Jr., *By Faith, Not by Sight: Paul and the Order of Salvation* [Waynesboro, GA: Paternoster, 2006], 35–41). The problem of positing a union with Christ that precedes the erasure of our legal condemnation before God (e.g., making justification the product of union with Christ; see, e.g., Michael S. Horton, *Covenant and Salvation: Union with Christ* [Louisville: Westminster John Knox, 2007], 147) can be answered if we posit, within the single work of God, two stages of "justification" (using the term here very broadly), one involving Christ's payment of our legal debt—the basis for our regeneration—and the second our actual justification—stemming from our union with Christ (see Henri Blocher, "Justification of the Ungodly (*Sola Fide*): Theological Reflections," in *The Paradoxes of Paul*, ed. Carson, O'Brien, and Seifrid, 497–98).

that Paul renounces salvation history (as Martyn has suggested);[40] it means, rather, that salvation history has within it a critical juncture, a decisive turning point.[41] And this turning point reveals that the issue confronted by the Galatians is an either/or one: if one tries to be justified "in the sphere of/through the law," one falls from grace and is separated from Christ (5:4). Justification "in Christ" (2:17) is set in stark contrast to the attempt to be justified "in the law." Why does Paul attach the kind of epochal significance to Christ's coming that the agitators did not? Galatians suggests that it was the implications of Christ's death on the cross that led Paul to such a radical interpretation. The argument of Galatians is remarkable for its focus on the cross and, of special significance for our point, believers' being caught up in that cross event (see esp. 2:19–20; 3:13–14; 5:24; 6:14).[42] The cross of Christ brings a "crisis" in human history and in the believer's own history and becomes the focal point around which everything must be reconfigured.

The christological κρίσις in salvation history is probably the explanation for Paul's distinctive claim in Galatians that belonging to God's people and justification come through faith and not through works of torah/torah. Paul uses the phrase "by faith" (ἐκ πίστεως) eight times in the letter, usually in direct or indirect connection with righteousness language (direct in 2:16; 3:8, 11, 24; indirect in 3:7, 9; see also 3:12, 22; two other texts use the verb to make the same point, 2:16; 3:6).[43] Paul and the agitators did not disagree, apparently, about the importance of faith. What they disagreed about was whether faith was to be followed by torah obedience; or, more precisely (and very importantly), whether torah obedience had to be added to faith for the purpose of securing one's relationship to God and his people.

---

[40]Martyn's seminal essay is "Apocalyptic Antinomies in Paul's Letter to the Galatians," *NTS* 31 (1985): 410–24.

[41]See, e.g., John M. G. Barclay, *Obeying the Truth: A Study of Paul's Ethics in Galatians* (Edinburgh: T&T Clark, 1988), 99–105.

[42]Frank J. Matera, "The Death of Christ and the Cross in Paul's Letter to the Galatians," *Louvain Studies* 18 (1993): 283–96.

[43]The use of ἐκ after πιστεύω is comparatively rare and probably expresses instrument (Charles H. Cosgrove, "Justification in Paul: A Linguistic and Theological Reflection," *JBL* 106 [1987]: 656–60); on the use of ἐκ to indicate instrument with this verb and the corresponding noun, see Murray J. Harris, "Appendix: Prepositions and Theology in the Greek New Testament," in *New International Dictionary of New Testament Theology*, ed. Colin Brown, vol. 3 (Grand Rapids: Zondervan, 1986), 1189.

The nature and significance of the contrast between faith and "works of the law" or "law" are deeply contested in Pauline scholarship—with quite significant consequences for one's overall soteriology. The Reformers understood the contrast that Paul draws in these texts to signal a fundamental distinction between human believing, on the one hand, and human "working" or "doing," on the other. Some contemporary interpreters want to revise both sides of the Pauline works-versus-faith polarity. On the one hand, the "works" that Paul excludes from justification are given a restricted sense—works "done in the flesh," as opposed to works done in the Spirit;[44] or, more often, "works of torah" intended to maintain a distinctly Jewish covenant identity as opposed to good works in general.[45] And on the other, faith is sometimes expanded to include works, at least of a certain kind. The literature on these matters is massive and the issues complex. I can here only state my own views with a very few arguments.

I turn first to the "works" side of the polarity. In Galatians, Paul contrasts faith with ἔργα νόμου ("works of the law") six times (2:16 three times; 3:2, 5, 10). Significantly, he abbreviates this phrase never with "works" but with "law" (as in 5:4). This suggests that Paul's chief concern in Galatians, as we might expect granted the situation being addressed, is with torah, not with works as such. The agitators were arguing not that people get right with God by doing good works but that people can have their right standing with God vindicated only by faithful observance of God's covenant stipulations. And it is just this argument that Paul contests with his strongly salvation-historical perspective: the era of torah has ended with the coming of Christ and any attempt now to require torah obedience for righteousness is to turn the clock back and, in effect, deny that Christ has come. This much is a matter of agreement among most contemporary Galatians scholars. The disagreement is over whether Paul's polemic against "works of the law" has any broader anthropological implications. New Perspective advocates tend to claim that it does not and that Galatians therefore provides no grounds for a principial contrast between faith and works.[46]

---

[44]See, e.g., Daniel P. Fuller, *The Unity of the Bible: Unfolding God's Plan for Humanity* (Grand Rapids: Zondervan, 1992), 310–16, 323; Paul A. Rainbow, *The Way of Salvation: The Role of Christian Obedience in Justification* (Waynesboro, GA: Paternoster, 2005), 79–96.

[45]James D. G. Dunn, "The New Perspective on Paul: Whence, What, Whither?," in *The New Perspective on Paul: Collected Essays*, rev. ed. (Grand Rapids: Eerdmans, 2008), 77.

[46]While distancing himself in several crucial ways from the New Perspective, Francis Watson has recently made this point quite vigorously: "The critique of Luther's essentially allegorical

James Dunn, for instance, argues that Paul can be rescued from inconsistency only if we distinguish between the "works of the law" that he argues against in 2:16 and those works that spring from faith that he commends later in the letter.[47] I have elsewhere defended the basic Reformation approach on this point, arguing that Paul's "works of the law," while obviously denoting works done in obedience to torah, can validly be seen ultimately as a subcategory of the broad human category "works."[48] This case is certainly more difficult to make in Galatians than in Romans, but I nevertheless think that it can be made.

The interpretation of 3:10 is pivotal to this issue and is one of the reasons the verse has received so much attention in recent years. A broadly "New Perspective" approach to the verse interprets the curse in purely salvation-historical terms: Israel, as the exile reveals, fell under God's curse, and anyone who now wants to identify with Israel by torah observance will fall under that same curse. This reading then becomes part of a broader approach to the letter according to which the only problem with the law is that it is outmoded (a new era in salvation history has dawned) and that it acts as a barrier to Gentile inclusion

---

interpretation of Paul's critique of works is presented here with all the emphasis I can muster" (*Paul, Judaism, and the Gentiles: Beyond the New Perspective*, rev. ed. [Grand Rapids: Eerdmans, 2007], 25; argument on 121–31). See also, for this general point of view, Barclay, *Obeying the Truth*, 235–41; Matera, *Galatians*, 242–43; James D. G. Dunn, *A Theology of Paul the Apostle* (Grand Rapids: Eerdmans, 1998), 354–66. New Perspective advocates are not always clear about whether Paul's polemic against "works of the law" has broader theological implications. For instance, in his commentary on Romans, Wright insists quite strongly in the "Commentary" section that "works of the law" are signs that one belongs to Israel and that any notions of legalism or "proto-Pelagianism" are simply not present (459–61). But in the "Reflections" section he acknowledges other "overtones" in Paul's teaching, including some that are compatible with traditional Reformation teaching (464). Wright is even clearer about these "old perspective" elements in Paul's teaching in his latest book. Note also Dunn's remarks in his latest essay on the matter ("The New Perspective," 27–28).

[47] James D. G. Dunn, "Noch Einmal 'Works of the Law': The Dialogue Continues," in *The New Perspective on Paul*, 427. An extreme form of this view is that of Michael Bachmann, who thinks the phrase (in keeping with his understanding of the phrase at Qumran) focuses on God's demand and not human doing in any form (see, e.g., "Keil oder Mikroskop? Zur jüngeren Diskussion um den Ausdruck 'Werke des Gesetzes,'" in *Lutherische und Neue Paulusperspektive: Beiträge zu einem Schlüsselproblem der Gegenwärtigen Exegetischen Diskussion,* ed. Michael Bachmann, WUNT 2.182 [Tübingen: Mohr Siebeck, 2005], 69–134). In response to Bachmann, see, e.g., Otfried Hofius, "Werke des Gesetzes": Untersuchungen zu der Paulinischen und Johanneischen Theologie und Literatur," in *Paulus and Johannes: Exegetische Studien zur Paulinischen und Johanneischen Theologie und Literatur,* ed. Dieter Sänger and Ulrich Mell, WUNT 2/198 (Tübingen: Mohr Siebeck, 2006), 273–85.

[48] Douglas J. Moo, "'Law,' 'Works of the Law,' and Legalism in Paul," *WTJ* 45 (1983): 73–100; see also Moo, *The Epistle to the Romans*, NICNT (Grand Rapids: Eerdmans, 1996), 211–17.

in the people of God.[49] The "traditional" reading, on the other hand, insists that the logic of the verse reveals that Paul is warning the Galatian Christians directly ("as many as") that reliance on "works of the law" will bring them under the curse because (implicitly) they will not be able to produce sufficient works to avoid the curse. This latter reading, while widely criticized, seems to be, in fact, the only way to make sense of the text.[50] And it finds confirmation in verse 12, where Paul identifies the law with the principle of *doing* (3:12; cf. also 5:3).[51] The point is, then, that Paul here views reliance on doing the law ("works of the law") as bringing people under the curse, not simply because the law belongs to a past stage of salvation history, but because the law is bound up with "doing," and "doing" or "works" in general are never able to justify a person before God. Paul's polemic against "works of the law" in Galatians, then, rests ultimately on a pessimistic anthropology. Stephen Westerholm puts the point well: "The fundamental question addressed by Galatians thus is not 'What is wrong with Judaism (or the Sinaitic law)?' but 'What is wrong with humanity that Judaism (and the Sinaitic law) cannot remedy?'"[52]

I turn now to the other side of the polarity, "faith." I have suggested above that the focus of Paul's argument in the central section of Galatians rests precisely on this word. "Believing" (πιστεύω) (2:16; 3:6, 22 [2:7 is different]) and "faith" (πίστις) (2:16 twice, 20; 3:2, 5, 7,

---

[49]For the "Israel in exile" view, see especially N. T. Wright, *The Climax of the Covenant: Christ and the Law in Pauline Theology* (Minneapolis: Fortress, 1993), 137–56; James M. Scott, "'For as Many as Are of Works of the Law Are under a Curse' (Galatians 3:10)," in *Paul and the Scriptures of Israel* (Sheffield: Sheffield Academic Press, 1993), 187–221. Dunn (*Galatians*, 170–74) takes a slightly different approach, viewing the curse in terms of exclusion of Gentiles.

[50]See especially Thomas R. Schreiner, "Is Perfect Obedience to the Law Possible: A Re-Examination of Galatians 3:10," *JETS* 27 (1984): 151–60; A. Andrew Das, *Paul and the Jews* (Peabody, MA: Hendrickson, 2003), 36–42; Seyoon Kim, *Paul and the New Perspective: Second Thoughts on the Origin of Paul's Gospel* (Grand Rapids: Eerdmans, 2002), 139–43; Westerholm, *Perspectives Old and New on Paul*, 375; Timo Laato, "Paul's Anthropological Considerations: Two Problems," in *The Paradoxes of Paul*, ed. Carson, O'Brien, and Seifrid, 354–59; Eckstein, *Verheissung und Gesetz*, 123.

[51]Preston M. Sprinkle, on the basis of a careful study of Lev. 18:5 in the Old Testament and Judaism and its place in Paul's argument, concludes that the text has clear soteriological implications: it refers to a way of salvation (*Law and Life: The Interpretation of Leviticus 18:5 in Early Judaism and in Paul*, WUNT 2/241 [Tübingen: Mohr Siebeck, 2008], cf. 136–42).

[52]Westerholm, *Perspectives Old and New on Paul*, 381; see his whole argument on 371–84; and see also, especially, Silva, "Faith versus Works of the Law in Galatians," 217–48; Robert H. Gundry, "Grace, Works, and Staying Saved in Paul," *Biblica* 66 (1985): 15–32; Kim, *Paul and the New Perspective*, 61–75; Bird, *Saving Righteousness*, 123; Bruce W. Longenecker, *The Triumph of Abraham's God: The Transformation of Identity in Galatians* (Edinburgh: T&T Clark, 1998), 76–77; Hofius, "Werke des Gesetzes," 299–301.

8, 9, 11, 12, 14, 22, 23 twice, 24, 25, 26; 5:5, 6; 6:10 [the occurrences in 1:23 and 5:22 may have a different sense]) dominate this part of the letter. This language has usually been interpreted anthropologically, as referring to human believing "in" Christ. But recent interpreters have drawn attention to the undeniably salvation-historical focus on this language in some texts in the letter; most notably 3:23, where Paul refers to "the coming of faith" in parallel to the coming of Christ (see v. 24). Since Paul attributes faith to Abraham earlier in the letter, it is argued that he must here, and in several other passages in the letter, be referring not to human believing but to Christ's faith or faithfulness.[53] On this point I remain stubbornly recalcitrant. I doubt that any reference to "faith" in Galatians refers to Christ's faith or faithfulness.[54] The significance of the verbal forms in both Galatians and elsewhere in Paul (with Christ as object and never as subject), along with the clear connections Paul draws between Abraham's faith and ours (3:1–9), among other arguments, convinces me that this is the correct reading of the letter.[55] Some of the more extreme proponents of the "faith of Christ" interpretation, claiming to want to avoid "anthropocentrism," are, in fact, in danger of eliminating any human element in Paul's soteriology at all.[56] Of course, much more could (and needs to) be said; but space limitations prevent me from pursuing the matter here.[57] In

---

[53]The view is, of course, widely held, but Hays's presentation of the case is classic. See Hays, *Faith of Jesus Christ*, 119–62; and see also the exchange between Dunn and Hays on this question (249–97). And see now, especially, Campbell, *The Quest for Paul's Gospel* and *The Deliverance of God*.

[54]See, e.g., Silva, "Faith versus Works of the Law in Galatians," 217–48.

[55]It is possible that the εἰς construction in 2:16 does not mean simply that Christ is the "object" of faith (see the careful linguistic work of Ulrichs, *Christusglaube*, 119–29). But nor does it mean, vaguely, as Campbell argues, that we believe "concerning" or "with respect to" Christ (*The Deliverance of God*, 840). Rather, as the linguistic evidence in the rest of the New Testament suggests (where almost all the relevant contemporary examples of the πιστεύω + εἰς combination appear), the idea seems be something like "we believe so as to join"; "we believe in order to enter into union with." Likewise, I am unconvinced that Abraham figures in Galatians 3 as a paradigm of Christ; this again flies in the face of the connections Paul makes back to the Galatians' own experience (3:1–5) and forward to "the people of faith" (v. 9). See also Gathercole, "Justified by Faith," 163–64, for this point in Romans 4.

[56]"Insofar as the argument [he is referring to Martyn's "faith of Christ" focus] turns on the perception that Paul wishes above all to emphasize God's initiative in justification, and therefore to have Paul assert that even human believing is God's (not human) work, such a view seems to be in danger of voiding the human reception of such salvific action of any substance at all" (John Riches, *Galatians through the Centuries*, Blackwell Bible Commentaries [Oxford: Blackwell, 2008], 133).

[57]The most extensive critique of the "faith/faithfulness of Jesus Christ" interpretation is Ulrichs, *Christusglaube*.

any case, most scholars who find "the faith of Christ" to be significant in the letter do not eliminate reference to human believing (although Douglas A. Campbell's massive and polemical reworking of justification in Paul virtually eliminates this element from the letter[58]).

The faith side of the Reformation works-versus-faith antithesis is eroded in another way also: by expanding the scope of faith to include, in some fashion, what we would call "good works."[59] The equivalent Hebrew word (אמונה), of course, includes the ideas of trust and faithfulness; and πίστις in Paul clearly has this sense at times. But any attempt to collapse works into faith in Paul founders on the same evidence that we have noted above: the polarity between faith, on the one hand, and "works of the law" or "works," on the other, includes a basic opposition between "believing" and "doing." Even in those texts where Paul appears to identify faith and obedience, he does not expand faith to include obedience, but he narrows down obedience to the one central requirement of faith. Believing in Paul is certainly more than an intellectual exercise; it involves the will and includes the disposition to trust and follow God. Paul and James on this point are in total agreement. True faith and works cannot be separated (Gal. 5:6); but they must be distinguished from one another also.[60] Faith is the disposition of the will necessary for works to be done in a way pleasing to God; but faith does not include in itself those works.[61]

With the two poles of the contrast now in place, we can consider a little more carefully the nature of this contrast. That Paul's argument in Galatians is characterized by a strongly salvation-historical framework that focuses on the extension of God's blessing to Gentiles in the new covenant era is, of course, quite clear. But some of the points we have made above suggest quite strongly that Paul also argues—at

---

[58]Campbell, *The Deliverance of God*, see esp. 833–95.

[59]Garlington is ultimately very unclear about the precise way he understands the relationship between faith, works, and obedience. He claims, on the one hand, that "*faith and works are two ways of saying the same thing*" (*Faith, Obedience, and Perseverance*, 146, emphasis his); and again, in the last sentence of the book: "In short, *faith, obedience, and perseverance are one and the same*" (163, emphasis his). But perhaps these are intended as generalizations (if so, they are very misleading ones!), since he also claims that faith, obedience, and perseverance are "three aspects of the same entity," and, "thus tested, 'faith' becomes the 'obedience' which is 'perseverance'" (163).

[60]James, then, who is probably responding to Pauline theology (though in garbled form), shows, by maintaining the distinction between faith and works, that this was probably Paul's view also (see Friedrich Avemarie, "Die Werke des Gesetzes im Spiegel des Jakobusbriefs: A Very Old Perspective on Paul," *ZTK* 98 [2001]: 282–309).

[61]See also, e.g., Gaffin, *By Faith, Not by Sight*, 102–3.

least implicitly—on another level also in Galatians. And this is to be expected. For the salvation-historical argument, in itself, does not explain *why* doing the torah cannot secure the promised Abrahamic blessing. Why couldn't the blessing of Abraham simply have been extended to Gentiles, as they were brought under the supervision of torah—as the agitators apparently argued? One clear indication that Paul's argument moves beyond (or behind) salvation history as such is his focus on Jews in his discussion of justification (the "we" who know about being justified by faith and not works of the law in 2:16 are clearly Jews [v. 15]; and the "we" who are "justified by faith" in 3:24 are also almost certainly Jews).[62] Justification by faith in Galatians does not focus only on providing a means to bring Gentiles into the people of God; it more fundamentally responds to a problem shared by Jews and Gentiles alike: sin.

Another indication along these same lines comes in the verse that best captures the essence of the issue in Galatia, 3:3. When Paul accuses the Galatians here of trying to "finish" their spiritual journey "by means of the flesh" (σαρκί, 3:3), the issue is not just salvation-historical (the "era of the flesh" versus "the era of the Spirit") but anthropological (cf. NIV, "After beginning with the Spirit, are you now trying to finish by *human effort*?").[63] Works are a problem in Galatians, therefore, not simply because they involve an outmoded torah; they are a problem also, and more fundamentally, because human inability renders them incapable of delivering people from sin. And, on the other side of the polarity, faith, Paul suggests, is the appropriate means of justification because it is the natural extension in the human sphere of God's grace. We noted earlier how Paul introduces the language of "grace"—somewhat unexpectedly—into his argument at several key points. Granted the significance of grace in Paul as a characteristic new covenant reality (see, e.g., Rom. 5:1), it is unlikely that Paul uses this language simply for defensive purposes.[64] It is more likely that he wants to tie the agitators' demand for torah obedience to the broader issue of human "achievement" as a contrast to the utterly gracious

---

[62]The first-person plurals in 3:23–25 probably refer to Paul and his fellow Jews (Dunn, *Galatians*, 198; Garlington, *Galatians*, 165; Longenecker, *Galatians*, 145; contra, e.g., Martyn, *Galatians*, 362; Bruce, *Galatians*, 182; Mußner, *Der Galaterbrief*, 256).

[63]See also Sprinkle, who thinks that the basic dichotomy reflected in Paul's use of Lev. 18:5 in Gal. 3:12 is divine versus human action (*Law and Life*, 150–63).

[64]As some commentators think he does in, e.g., Gal. 2:21 (Bruce, *Galatians*, 146; Burton, *Galatians*, 140; Schlier, *Brief an die Galater*, 103–4; Martyn, *Galatians*, 259).

character of God's justifying work in Christ. Again, the point is that this logic appears to move beyond (or behind!) salvation history to more fundamental theological issues, with anthropological and soteriological implications. Galatians is not a polemic against semi-Pelagianism (as N. T. Wright has often insisted); but Paul's argument suggests that he finds behind the agitators' views a reliance on human achievement that, indeed, has fundamental resemblances to semi-Pelagianism.

The Time of Justification

Perhaps the most interesting aspect of justification in Galatians is its time. Many traditional interpretations of the letter assume, or argue, that when Paul insists that people are "justified by faith," he is referring to entrance into Christian experience; to put it bluntly, "how you get saved." But a survey of Paul's justification language in the context of the letter's occasion and argument suggests that the matter is more complicated.

I begin with the last occurrence of justification language in the letter, 5:5: ἡμεῖς γὰρ πνεύματι ἐκ πίστεως ἐλπίδα δικαιοσύνης ἀπεκδεχόμεθα: "for we by the Spirit by faith await the hope of righteousness." The NIV translates the phrase ἐλπίδα δικαιοσύνης as "the righteousness for which we hope." This rendering reflects the majority scholarly opinion—that "righteousness" is the object of Christian hope (taking τῆς δικαιοσύνης as either an epexegetic or objective genitive). But a significant minority of interpreters argue that "righteousness" here is, in fact, the basis or source of our hope (a subjective genitive).[65] Ronald Fung thus translates "the hope to which the justification of believers points them forward."[66] Paul can certainly use a subjective genitive after "hope" as, for instance, he does in Colossians 1:23, where the translation of the NRSV, "the hope promised by the gospel," certainly captures Paul's intent.[67] But interpreters are usually driven to this view not by linguistics but by theology. They note that Paul associates justification with the believer's entrance into salvation in several

---

[65]No major English translation explicitly reflects the subjective genitive interpretation. But it receives support in the literature. See, in addition to Fung and George (see the notes below), Matera, *Galatians*, 182; Ziesler, *The Meaning of Righteousness*, 179; Eckstein, *Verheissung und Gesetz*, 142; Fee, *God's Empowering Presence*, 419.

[66]Fung, *Galatians*, 226.

[67]In addition to Gal. 5:5 and Col. 1:23, Paul uses a genitive after ἐλπίς eight other times. Two appear to be subjective (Eph. 1:18 and Eph. 4:4), while six appear to be objective/epexegetical (Rom. 5:2; Col. 1:27; 1 Thess. 1:3; 5:8; Titus 1:2; 3:7).

key texts, such as Romans 5:1 and 1 Corinthians 6:11, and that he accordingly argues *from* the past act of justification *to* future salvation from God's wrath (see esp. Rom. 5:9; and also 8:29–30). A reference to forensic righteousness as an object of hope for the believer would stand in tension with these texts.[68] (Of course, this argument assumes that "righteousness" in Gal. 5:5 and the justification language in these other texts refer to the same thing: the traditional notion of forensic righteousness, right standing before God. But, as we have seen, I think this assumption is justified.)

If, then, "righteousness" in Galatians 5:5 is forensic righteousness, those who think the reference must be to a present right standing as the basis for our hope would seem to have a pretty good case. Attaching justification firmly to the "already" side of Christian experience seems to be suggested by these texts in Paul's other letters and yields an attractively elegant consistency in Paul's soteriological terminology.[69] I have argued this view myself in the past. But I no longer think it is persuasive.

First, it does not seem likely that "righteousness" in Galatians 5:5 refers to the present status of righteousness as the basis for hope. If this is what was meant, Paul would in effect be saying that "we eagerly await hope," in the sense of "what we hope for." But after the verb ἀπεκδεχόμεθα ("eagerly await") we expect a more specific object than this.[70] "We are eagerly awaiting what we hope for" would make sense if Paul had defined this hope in the context. But he has not. This is the first reference to Christian hope in any form in Galatians.

---

[68]Timothy George summarizes the point: "Paul was not saying, of course, that we must wait until the second coming of Christ either to receive justification or to be assured of it. The whole burden of Paul's doctrine of justification is that divine righteousness is imparted here and now through faith in Jesus Christ" (*Galatians*, NAC [Nashville: Broadman & Holman, 1994], 361). S. M. Baugh explicitly grounds his opposition to a future element of justification in Paul on this consideration ("The New Perspective, Mediation, and Justification," in *Covenant, Justification, and Pastoral Ministry: Essays by the Faculty of Westminster Seminary California*, ed. R. Scott Clark [Phillipsburg, NJ: P&R, 2007], 150–56).

[69]See especially the way Karl Donfried puts the matter: "In short, the Christian life is a process which begins in justification, is actualized in sanctification and is consummated with salvation" ("Justification and Last Judgment in Paul," *ZNW* 67 [1976]: 90–110, here 100).

[70]Smith, *Justification and Eschatology*, 94–95. Paul uses the verb ἀπεχδέχομαι five other times, in each case referring to eschatological anticipation. In four cases the object of the verb has definite content: creation "waits in eager expectation for the children of God to be revealed" (Rom. 8:19); believers await "our adoption, the redemption of our bodies" (Rom. 8:23), "our Lord Jesus Christ to be revealed" (1 Cor. 1:7), and "a Savior" (Phil. 3:20). Only in Rom. 8:25 does Paul use a rather vague object (implicitly) after this verb; but "what we do not yet have" here has been elaborated in what precedes.

Second, the timing of justification in other texts in Galatians is surprisingly difficult to pin down. The verb occurs in the present indicative (2:16a; 3:8, 11; 5:4) and the future indicative (2:16c); with ἵνα in the aorist subjunctive (2:16b; 3:24); and in the aorist infinitive (completing the verb ζητοῦντες in 2:17). In none of these texts do we find a clear allusion to "initial" justification of the sort we find, for instance, in Romans 5. Two of these, in fact, might share with Galatians 5:5 a reference to future justification.[71] Paul's claim in 2:17 that he and other Jewish Christians are "seeking to be justified in Christ" might refer to their hope of ultimate vindication in the judgment.[72] And Paul's warning in 5:4 that the Galatians are "trying to be justified by the law" (I am taking the verb δικαιοῦσθε as a conative present, along with most scholars) is even more likely to have a future reference. The Galatians have already experienced new life in Christ. The problem is that they are in danger of being convinced that they can maintain their status of righteousness only by adding torah obedience to their faith in Christ. To be sure, some of these texts could well refer to, or at least include, reference to initial justification. But they seem rather simply not to be interested in the matter of time. Several of these verses have a gnomic force, Paul expressing the principle that "justification" is rendered (whenever that might be) in a certain way, on certain grounds. When we turn to the noun, the situation is a bit more complicated. If δικαιοσύνη in 5:5 refers to a future bestowal of righteousness, 3:6 pretty clearly has an "already" focus: Abraham, like the Galatians themselves (3:1–5), attained to a righteous status the moment he believed.[73] Galatians 2:21 and 3:21, on the other hand, fall pretty clearly in the gnomic or

---

[71]Moisés Silva argues that 2:16a is also a reference to future justification ("Galatians," in *Commentary on the New Testament Use of the Old Testament*, ed. G. K. Beale and D. A. Carson [Grand Rapids: Baker, 2007], 791).

[72]The issue is complicated by the contested nature of Paul's argument at this point. Much depends on how much temporal weight we give to the verb εὑρέθημεν. Most versions translate it with an English present tense (as in my paraphrase above), and in this case a reference to future justification is likely (see, e.g., Mark A. Seifrid, "Paul, Luther, and Justification in Gal 2:15–21," *WTJ* 65 [2003]: 218; Martyn, *Galatians*, 254; Garlington, *Galatians*, 117). But a past reference, to the time when Paul and his fellow Jewish Christians were seeking initial justification in Christ, is possible (see NRSV; and Fung, *Galatians*, 119; Michael Bachmann, *Sünder oder Übertreter: Studien zur Argumentation in Gal 2,15ff.*, WUNT 2.59 [Tübingen: Mohr Siebeck, 1992], 38–39).

[73]Dunn, "The New Perspective on Paul," 71–72.

principial category. Overall, justification language in Galatians has a timeless and, if anything, future-oriented focus.[74]

This focus makes good sense in light of the rhetorical situation of the letter. This situation is clearly revealed in 3:1–5, where Paul argues *from* the good start that the Galatians have made *to* the need to continue as they began. It is therefore not surprising that righteousness language in Galatians has a general, gnomic quality. A definitive act of justification at the beginning of the Christian life is presumed, as the parallel Paul draws between Abraham's experience and the Galatians' makes clear. And Romans, written in a different (and arguably less polemical) situation, affirms such a definitive initial justification unmistakably (Rom. 5:1, 9; cf. 8:30). But the situation in Galatia requires that Paul emphasize how the Galatians are to *maintain* their status of righteousness and, especially, how they can expect to be found to be in the "right" in the judgment. This last point deserves particular attention. Without denying that first-century Judaism viewed God's election as the ultimate basis for their place in the covenant, I think it is also the case that, in practice, many Jews operated with "a semi-tacit consciousness of having been born there, of always having been there," as Henri Blocher puts it.[75] In this scenario, the question becomes not simply how one "gets in" initially or how one "stays in" but how one can hope to "get in" the eternal kingdom on the day of judgment.[76] This seems to be exactly the issue that Galatians is addressing.[77]

---

[74]See also Gaffin, *By Faith, Not by Sight*, 98; A. Andrew Das, "Oneness in Christ: The *Nexus Indivulsus* between Justification and Sanctification in Paul's Letter to the Galatians," *Concordia Journal* 21 (1995): 173–86; C. K. Barrett, *Freedom and Obligation: A Study of the Epistle to the Galatians* (Philadelphia: Westminster, 1985), 63–65; Bernard H. Brinsmead, *Galatians: Dialogical Response to Opponents* (Chico, CA: Scholars Press, 1982), 201. Kwon, indeed, argues that justification in Galatians is exclusively future (Yon-Gyong Kwon, *Eschatology in Galatians: Rethinking Paul's Response to the Crisis in Galatia*, WUNT 183 [Tübingen: Mohr Siebeck, 2004], 51–76).

[75]Blocher, "Justification of the Ungodly," 488–89; see also Francis Watson, *Paul and the Hermeneutics of Faith* (Edinburgh: T&T Clark, 2004), 8–11.

[76]Simon Gathercole has drawn attention to the importance of this future "getting in" in Jewish literature and its comparative neglect in the debate (Simon J. Gathercole, *Where Is Boasting? Early Jewish Soteriology and Paul's Response in Romans 1–5* [Grand Rapids: Eerdmans, 2002], 113–19). On Galatians, see also Graham N. Stanton, "The Law of Moses and the Law of Christ: Galatians 3:1–6:2," in *Paul and the Mosaic Law*, ed. James D. G. Dunn (Tübingen: Mohr Siebeck, 1996), 99–116, 103–4.

[77] A reference to future justification in Galatians is at least consonant with two other phenomena. First, a good case can be made that Paul uses justification language to refer to a future time elsewhere. In contrast to the trend of recent interpretation (see especially Thomas R. Schreiner, "Did Paul Believe in Justification by Works? Another Look at Romans 2," *BBR* 3 [1993]: 131–58; Simon J. Gathercole, "A Law Unto Themselves: The Gentiles in Romans 2.14–15 Revisited,"

N. T. Wright is surely correct to stress that eschatology is one of the key lenses through which justification must be viewed. Indeed, it is traditional to assert that justification in Paul is a basically eschatological verdict, with his focus on the initial verdict then being seen in light of his typical "realized" perspective. I have no quarrel with this way of viewing the matter; and it does explain the bulk of occurrences in Romans quite well. However, our study of Galatians suggests that justification functions in Paul at both the "already" and "not yet" poles of his eschatology. A future element in justification does not fit entirely comfortably within my own Reformed tradition.[78] It is messy. But it appears to be biblical.

Conclusion

We will explore some implications of this conclusion in a moment. But I want first to summarize. Occurrences of δικ- language in Galatians (with the possible exception of δίκαιος in 3:11) all refer to one thing: the declaration of the forensic status of "right" before God (the verb) or that status itself (the noun). Paul probably draws this language especially from Old Testament passages such as Isaiah 46–55, where δικ-/צדק language occurs prominently to denote the vindicating deliverance that God will bring to his people. This background may be

---

JSNT 85 [2002]: 27–49; Bird, *The Saving Righteousness of God*, 155–78; Garlington, *Faith, Obedience, and Perseverance*, 56–71; Wright, "Romans," 440–42), I don't think Rom. 2:13 is one of these (see Moo, *Romans*, 139–42, 147–48). But Rom. 5:19 and 8:33 are at least possible references to a future aspect of justification. Dunn thinks that other texts may also refer to a future element in justification: Rom. 3:20, 30; Gal. 3:8, 11, 24 ("Jesus the Judge: Further Thoughts on Paul's Christology and Soteriology," in *The New Perspective on Paul*, 401–2). I doubt that Rom. 3:20, 30 or Gal. 3:8 have a future focus; Gal. 3:11 and 24 might. Some others who advocate a future focus in justification are Peter Stuhlmacher, "The Apostle Paul's View of Righteousness," in *Reconciliation, Law, and Righteousness: Essays in Biblical Theology* (Philadelphia: Fortress, 1986), 72 ("justification designates in Paul both the sharing in God's grace that has already been given by faith and acquittal before God in the last judgment"); Cosgrove, "Justification in Paul," 652–54; Peter T. O'Brien, "Justification in Paul and Some Crucial Issues of the Last Two Decades," in *Right with God: Justification in the Bible and the World*, ed. D. A. Carson (Grand Rapids: Baker, 1992), 90; Rainbow, *Way of Salvation*, 155–74. See also Gathercole, who argues that "salvation should be viewed as a unity, with justification referring to the whole while highlighting a certain aspect" ("Doctrine of Justification," 230). Contesting any future element to justification in Paul are, e.g., Fung, *Galatians*, 232–35; Chris VanLandingham, *Judgment and Justification in Early Judaism and the Apostle Paul* (Peabody, MA: Hendrickson, 2006), 317–18. The second phenomenon is the fact that justification language often has an eschatological significance in Judaism and elsewhere in the New Testament (e.g., Matt. 12:37; James 2:21–25). Of course, we must recognize that linguistic parallels do not necessarily translate into conceptual parallels. But I think that many of these texts are, indeed, conceptually parallel to Paul's justification teaching.

[78] Although, as Richard B. Gaffin Jr., notes, the view has been held by Reformed theologians in the past ("Justification and Eschatology," in *Justified in Christ: God's Plan for Us in Justification*, ed. K. Scott Oliphint [Fearn, Ross-shire: Mentor, 2007], 4–5).

one reason why Paul uses δικ- language in Galatians with a distinctly future orientation. Another reason, however, is the situation that Paul addresses. The agitators were not teaching the classic idea of "works righteousness," in the sense that one had to do works to "get in." Rather, they were insisting that the Galatians—already "in," in some sense—had to add to their faith in Christ torah obedience in order to maintain their "righteous" status and, especially, in order to be finally vindicated: declared to belong to God's righteous people in the day of judgment. Galatians is, therefore, in my view, not (mainly) about "sanctification," or "how to live,"[79] or even about "justification" in its usual sense of initial acceptance, but about justification broadly considered. In response to false teachers who claim that this vindication, since it is promised only to Israel, can be experienced only by those who identify with Israel by doing torah, Paul, reading salvation history in light of the epochal significance of the cross, insists that faith, and faith alone (accompanied, to be sure, by the transforming power of the Spirit), maintains one's relationship to Christ, in whose person the people of God are now constituted. Strikingly, in light of Romans, Paul puts no emphasis on an initial definitive act of justification.[80] This is not because he has no such notion as he writes Galatians (the logic of 3:6–9 suggests that he does) but because he addresses a situation that requires a focus on maintaining the status of righteousness in view of an ultimate declaration of vindication yet to come. By seeking to "supplement" their faith in Christ with torah observance, the Galatian Christians are in danger of forfeiting their (apparent) standing in Christ and therefore failing to achieve that final vindication. In Galatians, then, righteousness tends to have the idea of vindication, in continuity with the usage of this language that we noted earlier in Isaiah 46–55. In contrast to that latter passage, of course—and this is the nub of the issue in Galatia—the people of God who can expect to be vindicated are now defined not by their biological connection with Abraham and/or by torah observance but by their connection with Messiah Jesus, a connection maintained by faith alone.

---

[79] As, e.g., is argued by Wakefield, *Where to Live*; Das, "Oneness in Christ," 173; Esler, *Galatians*, 143.

[80] The contrast between Galatians and Romans on this point relates to their situations. In contrast to Galatians, where the agitators make it necessary for Paul to focus on warning about continuance in righteousness and ultimate vindication—the "not yet"—Romans focuses on the assurance promised to those who have been justified—the "already."

Paul's teaching on justification in Galatians strongly endorses the traditional Reformation emphasis on justification by faith alone. In contrast to some recent reconfigurations of this doctrine, the Reformers did not mean by this teaching that a person gains only initial entrance into the state of salvation by faith alone—the ultimate verdict being based on faith plus works.[81] They intended to assert that the eschatological gift of justification, at whatever "time" or in however many stages it might be manifested, came by faith alone. Paul seems to be saying just this in Galatians. Faith is the means not only of entering into relationship with God but also of maintaining that relationship and of confirming that relationship on the day of judgment.[82] Of course, it is not faith in itself that has this power; it is because faith connects the believer to Christ, in whose vindication (see 1 Tim. 3:16) the believer shares. My brief overview confirms those who find a monergism in Paul's teaching about salvation that stands in contrast to the synergism of covenant nomism.[83] Justification, not only in its initial phase, but in its totality, is *sola fide*—and, though it has not been a focus of this study, in light of Galatians 2:21 and 5:4, *sola gratia* also.

I conclude by suggesting two topics that require further reflection in light of this survey.[84]

---

[81] A well-known recent claim along these lines comes (again!) from N. T. Wright, who argues that God judges us on the basis of "the whole life lived" (e.g., *Paul in Fresh Perspective*, 111–13). His latest book, however, appears to back off from this way of putting matters. He suggests that works "demonstrate" membership in God's people (*Justification*, 146) and that from initial justification, "Paul sets out on a journey which, though its end is in fact secure, always *seems* like something that has to be struggled for" (153). On one reading of Wright's latest book, I believe he is arguing a view very close to what I am suggesting above. For others who suggest that works play some kind of instrumental role in ultimate justification, see Dunn, "The New Perspective on Paul," 80–89; Dunn, "Jesus the Judge," 407; Kent L. Yinger, *Paul, Judaism, and Judgment According to Deeds*, SNTSMS 105 (Cambridge: University Press, 1999), 288; Gathercole, "A Law Unto Themselves," 27–49; Daniel J. R. Kirk, *Unlocking Romans: Resurrection and the Justification of God* (Grand Rapids: Eerdmans, 2008), 223–27.

[82] Rainbow's claim, therefore, that Paul never suggests that the final judgment will be based on faith, while perhaps linguistically valid, is conceptually erroneous (see *Way of Salvation*, 194). Indeed, he seems to contradict his own claim two pages later, where he refers to "the sort of faith which is active will withstand the judgment" (196).

[83] See for this point especially Gundry, "Grace, Works, and Staying Saved," 1–38 ("For Paul, then, getting in and staying in are covered by the seamless robe of faith as opposed to works" [p. 12]); O'Brien, "Justification," 87; O'Brien, "Was Paul a Covenantal Nomist?," 265–66, 269–70; Watson, *Paul, Judaism, and the Gentiles*, 15–19; and Gathercole, who comments on Yinger's monograph, "If Yinger is correct to deny that 'the grace-works axis in Judaism generally is any more synergistic . . . than in Paul' then the Holy Spirit came at Pentecost for nothing (cf. Gal. 2:21!)" (*Where is Boasting?*, 134).

[84] Two consequences that do not follow might be mentioned. First, any future element in justification must not detract from the decisive nature of the declaration of righteousness that we receive

First, the focus on the future aspect of justification in Galatians raises difficult questions about the nature of this event, especially in its relationship to "initial" justification. Piper, reflecting the main line of Reformation teaching, argues that future justification is a declaration and not a "saving act."[85] Future justification declares publicly what initial justification has definitively settled in the divine lawcourt. This way of putting the matter would seem to be the inevitable logical deduction from a conviction that initial justification is a definitive act; and it may well be the best way of handling all the biblical data involved. Yet one has to wonder whether Paul would give the future aspect of justification the kind of prominence it has in Galatians if it was a matter simply of public declaration. The importance he attaches to the Galatians' continued reliance on faith and the Spirit—see especially Galatians 5:2–4—suggests that more may be involved. What is this "more"? I am not at all sure; but the evidence of Galatians (not to mention, e.g., James 2) should impel us to continue to think about how we might best formulate the relationship between an initial definitive declaration of justification and the final declaration.

---

when we first believe. To do so would be to rob initial justification of the decisive soteriological significance that it has in Romans 5, Romans 8, and 1 Corinthians 6. As long as the emphasis is on "unqualified" and "yet-to-be-determined," I therefore agree with Cornelis P. Venema: "An unqualified affirmation of a future, yet-to-be-determined justification based upon works would surely compromise in the most radical way Paul's teaching that there is now no condemnation for those who are in Christ Jesus" ("What Did Saint Paul Really Say? N. T. Wright and the New Perspective(s) on Paul," in *By Faith Alone: Answering the Challenges to the Doctrine of Justification*, ed. Gary L. W. Johnson and Guy P. Waters [Wheaton, IL: Crossway, 2006], 33–59, 58; see, e.g., O'Brien, "Justification," 94). These texts, and others, provide solid textual support for the traditional Reformed emphasis on the definitive nature of initial justification. Therefore, while I am happy to ascribe to justification an "already"/"not yet" quality, I am not comfortable with the language of "two justifications." Justification is a single, eschatological, act that we experience in two phases. Second, and for a similar reason, I would also prefer to avoid the language of "process" that some have applied to Paul's teaching on justification. See, e.g., Stuhlmacher: "*The justification of which he speaks is a process of becoming new that spans the earthly life of a believer, a path from faith's beginning to its end*" ("The Apostle Paul's View of Righteousness," 72 [emphasis his]; see also Stuhlmacher, *Revisiting Paul's Doctrine of Justification*, 62–63). Dunn does not use the language of "process," but suggests something like it: "Justification is not a once-for-all act of God. It is rather the initial acceptance by God into restored relationship. But thereafter the relationship could not be sustained without God continuing to exercise his justifying righteousness with a view to the final act of judgment and acquittal" (*The Theology of Paul*, 386). To be sure, the initial experience of justification brings us into a continuing state of justification, or "righteousness," a state that will be secured in the final phase of justification. But "process" suggests a continuing action, opening up the possibility of a "growing" in or into justification that inappropriately minimizes the eschatological character of justification as definitive verdict.

[85]*The Future of Justification*, 101–16.

Second, granted that "by faith alone" is, indeed, taught in Galatians, what of "works"? What role do they place in the believer's ultimate justification? In keeping with the balance that typifies all of Paul's letters, Galatians highlights, along with faith, the necessity of works for entrance into eternal life:

> Do not be deceived: God cannot be mocked. People reap what they sow. Those who sow to please their sinful nature, from that nature will reap destruction; those who sow to please the Spirit, from the Spirit will reap eternal life. Let us not become weary in doing good, for at the proper time we will reap a harvest if we do not give up. (6:7–9)

The issue we raise here is, of course, simply another way of putting the age-old question of the relationship between "justification by faith" and "judgment according to works"[86]—what Wright labels the "hardest point in the whole theology of justification."[87] The question becomes even more difficult if the "justification" in question, as we have argued, includes not just initial justification, but ultimate justification in all its forms. Any kind of temporal answer to the question—e.g., justified initially by faith, judged finally by faith plus works—is ruled out. Evangelicals in the broadly Reformed tradition have usually responded to this problem by arguing (1) that our works will have a bearing on the "reward" that we receive but not on salvation per se and/or (2) that works are the product or "evidence" of faith. I don't think the former is exegetically responsible. The latter has much more to be said for it and certainly captures an important aspect of biblical teaching. It is therefore usual to speak of works as the evidence of faith. And this way of approaching the matter has some grounding in Galatians. The "doing good" that will clear us in the judgment comes only by the influence of the Spirit. Christian "works," Paul suggests in texts such as Galatians 5:22–23, are the "fruit" of God's Spirit, dwelling within by faith. However, while surely not incorrect, labeling our Spirit-induced works *simply* as "evidence" may not finally do justice to the fact that

---

[86]For a recent survey of views on the relationship between justification by faith and judgment according to works, see Dane C. Ortlund, "Justified by Faith, Judged According to Works: Another Look at a Pauline Paradox," *JETS* 52 (2009): 323–39.
[87]Wright, *Justification*, 101–2.

this evidence is something we are commanded to produce.[88] Good works may be the fruit of the Spirit, yet they are also, Paul makes clear, fruit that can be produced only through the active and continuing commitment of the believer to "walk in the Spirit" (Gal. 5:16; cf. 25).

Paul, in keeping with the New Testament generally, stresses both the utter sufficiency of the righteousness that we have been given in Christ for our salvation and the significance of our righteous behavior for that same salvation. At its deepest level, the tension raised by these claims is an aspect of a much broader and more fundamental biblical tension: that between divine action and human action; or, as the man we honor in this volume might prefer to put it, divine sovereignty and human responsibility. D. A. Carson's first book-length work (his published dissertation) dealt with this matter,[89] and both the book and many conversations (and debates!) over the years have fundamentally shaped my own approach to this central biblical issue. I strongly suspect that the compatibilist view that Don has strongly endorsed is the framework within which we must think further about the tensions I have mentioned in the last several paragraphs. I am deeply grateful for Don's work on this matter and for the "fellowship in the gospel" that we have enjoyed over many years. As he would himself insist, *soli Deo gloria*.

---

[88]See also Mark Seifrid, who suggests that contenting ourselves with the language of "evidence" may sever the close tie between faith and obedience in Paul (*Christ, Our Righteousness: Paul's Theology of Justification*, New Studies in Biblical Theology 9 [Downers Grove, IL: InterVarsity, 2000], 148). Note also his comments on James 2: "Works therefore are not only evidence of faith; they are integral to it"; "James freely draws the conclusion that the justification of Abraham and Rahab was based upon works, as it is likewise for all others (2:21, 24, 25)"; "Justification must ultimately be by works, because works are faith's perfection" (180). And what Seifrid says of James he would apply also to Paul, since he concludes that they are in ultimate agreement: "Both understand that our justification at the last judgment will be based upon works. Both understand that these works belong to faith, and that they are God's works, not our own" (182).

[89]D. A. Carson, *Divine Sovereignty and Human Responsibility: Biblical Perspectives in Tension* (1981; repr., Eugene, OR: Wipf & Stock, 2002).

7

God as the Speaking God

"Theology" in the Letter to the Hebrews

PETER T. O'BRIEN

The opening words of the letter to the Hebrews provide us with one of the clearest statements in the New Testament about God's revelation in his Son. In a carefully crafted sentence that is basic to the whole argument of the discourse, as "indeed it is basic to Christian faith,"[1] the author affirms that God, whose revelation in the past to the Old Testament "fathers" was given "in fragmentary and varied fashion" (NEB), has "in these last days" spoken his definitive and climactic word in his Son (1:1–2).[2] Fundamental to the author's argument is the conviction that God has not remained silent but has taken the initiative and revealed himself.

God's speech and actions encompass Hebrews from this opening affirmation to the final benediction and doxology, which summarize what he has done in bringing back the Lord Jesus from the dead

---

[1] F. F. Bruce, *The Epistle to the Hebrews* (Grand Rapids: Eerdmans, 1990), 45.
[2] Unless otherwise indicated, Scripture quotations in this chapter are from the TNIV.

and what he continues to do in the lives of believers (13:20–21). God's mighty work of revelation and salvation frames the whole discourse.

This essay explores aspects of this magnificent theme, which is so fundamental to Christian faith, and provides an opportunity for me to honor my friend and colleague, Don Carson, to whom it is affectionately dedicated.

God as the Speaking God

The author of Hebrews emphatically stresses that God is the speaking God.[3] Throughout his discourse a wide range of terminology is used to represent what God says: he "speaks" (λαλέω, 1:1–2; 2:2–3; 3:5; 4:8; 5:5; 11:18; 12:25), "says" (λέγω, 1:5, 6, 7, [8], [10], 13; 2:12–13; 3:7, 15; 4:3, 4, 7; 5:6; 6:14; 7:13, 21; 8:8, 9, 10, 13; 10:5, 7, 8, 9, 15, 30; 12:26; 13:5), "testifies" (μαρτυρέω and cognates, 2:4; 7:17; 10:15; 11:4, 5, 39 [in Scripture; cf. 7:8]), "proclaims [good news]" (εὐαγγελίζομαι, 4:2, 6), "calls" (καλέω, 2:11; 11:8), "promises" (ἐπαγγέλλω, 6:13; 10:23; 11:11; 12:26), "swears [an oath]" (ὀμνύω, 3:11, 18; 4:3; 6:13; 7:28), "warns" (χρηματίζω, 8:5; 11:7; 12:25), "reproves" (ἐλέγχω, 12:5), and "declares" (δηλόω, 9:8; 12:27). In addition to these verbs, there are several related nouns: "word" (λόγος, 2:2; 4:2, 12; cf. 7:28; 13:7, 22), "promise" (ἐπαγγελία, 10:36), "oath" (ὅρκος, 6:17; ὁρκωμοσία, 7:20, 21), as well as terms such as "spoken word" (ῥῆμα, 1:3; 6:5; 11:3; 12:19), "voice" (φωνή, 3:7, 15; 4:7; 12:19, 26), and "word of encouragement" (παράκλησις, 12:5).

Hebrews begins and ends by stressing that the world is dependent on the *word* of God. He created the universe in the past (1:2; note v. 10, citing Ps. 102:25; Heb. 2:10) by his *word* (11:3; Gen. 1:3, "God

---

[3]So significant is this motif that William L. Lane, *Hebrews 1–8* (Dallas: Word, 1991), cxxvii, claims, "The central theme of Hebrews is the importance of listening to the voice of God in Scripture and in the act of Christian preaching." Note Gene R. Smillie, "Living and Active: The Word of God in the Book of Hebrews" (PhD thesis, Trinity Evangelical Divinity School, 2000); C. C. Newman, "God," in *Dictionary of the Later New Testament and Its Developments*, ed. Ralph P. Martin and Peter H. Davids (Downers Grove, IL: InterVarsity, 1997), 417–18; David Wider, *Theozentrik und Bekenntnis: Untersuchungen zur Theologie des Redens Gottes im Hebräerbrief* (Berlin: de Gruyter, 1997); William L. Vander Beek, "Hebrews: A 'Doxology' of the Word," *Mid-America Journal of Theology* 16 (2005): 13–28; Luke Timothy Johnson, *Hebrews: A Commentary* (Louisville: Westminster John Knox, 2006), 45–48; and more recently, Harold W. Attridge, "God in Hebrews," in *The Epistle to the Hebrews and Christian Theology*, ed. Richard Bauckham et al. (Grand Rapids: Eerdmans, 2009), 95–110, and Ken Schenck, "God Has Spoken: Hebrews' Theology of the Scriptures," in *The Epistle to the Hebrews and Christian Theology*, ed. Bauckham, 321–36.

said"), and established it (Heb. 3:4). What he declares he effects, for his word is performative.[4] This "work has been finished since the creation of the world" (4:3b; see 9:26). But God remains active in maintaining the world he has made since he continues to bless the fruitful earth (6:7). The universe is sustained by the *word* of the Son in the present (1:3), and it will be shaken by the *voice* of God in the future (12:25–27).

God's speech, which is so prominent throughout Hebrews, is of profound importance in relation to the Old Testament Scriptures that appear in the discourse, and it is to these that we now turn.

The God Who Speaks in the Scriptures

Hebrews is distinctive among the New Testament writings for the variety of ways in which it introduces its scriptural quotations. Unlike Paul, who shows a preference for "as it is written" (καθὼς γέγραπται), the author of Hebrews never introduces a citation with a form of the verb *write*.[5] Instead, Hebrews presents the reader with approximately thirty-seven Old Testament quotations[6] through which God continues to speak to his people in these days of eschatological fulfillment (1:5a, 5b, 6, 7, 8–9, etc.). These citations show that God is the ultimate authority of all Scripture. His Word is "living and active" (4:12)[7] like God himself (3:12; 9:14; 10:31; 12:22), and by it he speaks to his people now. This Word probes the inmost recesses of each person and discerns the thoughts and intentions of the heart (4:12b). The distinction between God and his "word"

---

[4]Note the recent discussion of speech-act theory in relation to the hermeneutics of Hebrews by Daniel J. Treier, "Speech Acts, Hearing Hearts, and Other Senses: The Doctrine of Scripture Practiced in Hebrews," in *The Epistle to the Hebrews and Christian Theology*, ed. Bauckham, 337–50, esp. 338–44.

[5]"It is written" stands *within* the citation from Ps. 40:8 (Heb. 10:7), but does not *introduce* it.

[6]There is difference of opinion as to the exact number of Old Testament references in Hebrews, with the figures ranging between thirty-one and forty. George H. Guthrie, "Hebrews," in *Commentary on the New Testament Use of the Old Testament*, ed. G. K. Beale and D. A. Carson (Grand Rapids: Baker, 2007), 919–95, esp. 919, suggests thirty-seven instances. Radu Gheorghita, *The Role of the Septuagint in Hebrews: An Investigation of Its Influence with Special Consideration to the Use of Hab 2:3–4 in Heb 10:37–38* (Tübingen: Mohr Siebeck, 2003), 32–33, considers that the lack of a precise definition of a quotation or the setting out of criteria to distinguish between citations and other types of Old Testament usage accounts for the variations in scholarly results.

[7]In its context this "word of God" refers particularly to Psalm 95. A strong case can be made theologically for claiming on the basis of our author's wide-ranging use of the Old Testament elsewhere in his discourse that he believed the whole of it was the Word of God, and therefore "living and active."

virtually disappears, for ultimately to stand before God's Word is to stand before him (4:13).

Consistent with its opening statement that God "*spoke* in the past to our fathers through the prophets" (1:1), Hebrews's series of expressions that introduce scriptural quotations is *oral*. With God as the subject the author introduces citations with verbs of saying (1:5, 6, 7, 13; 3:15; 4:3, 4; 5:5, 6; 7:21; 8:8; 10:15, 30; 13:5), promising (12:26), and swearing an oath (6:13–14). In fact, twenty-three of the quotations in Hebrews have God as the speaker, four passages put the words of the Old Testament on the lips of Christ (2:12–13; 10:5), and four others are attributed to the Holy Spirit (3:7; 10:15; see 9:8).

What is the significance of this manner of citing Scripture? In a discourse that emphasizes its own oral character (e.g., 2:1; 5:11; 6:9; 8:1) it might seem appropriate that Scripture be delivered orally rather than textually. But, as Luke Timothy Johnson rightly points out, there is more at work here than simply a "stylistic fit."[8] The prologue declares that God spoke through the prophets of old (1:1). By constantly citing passages from the Old Testament and introducing these with verbs of speaking, Hebrews is treating "*texts* as the voices of the 'prophets' through whom God spoke in the past." And because these verbs of introduction regularly signify a present activity, "the hearer experiences these voices as God's speech to the present and not simply to the past."[9]

Also, many of the quotations are direct speech, so that the text is not simply a record about something from the past, though it is no less than that. It is "a form of address, an expression of the living word of God (4:12–13)."[10] The scriptural texts address Christ as Son and priest (1:5–6; 5:5–6). The Holy Spirit bears witness through the text "to us" (10:15). Hebrews places David a long time after Joshua, but does so in order to assert the continuing pertinence of the admonition, "*Today*, if you hear his voice, do not harden your hearts" (4:7). The listeners are also urged to accept now the divine instruction from Proverbs that speaks to their present situation (12:5–6), while they are given promises that are directly applicable to them, such as the promise of a new covenant (Jer. 31:31–34; Heb. 8:8–12). In other

---

[8]Johnson, *Hebrews*, 22.
[9]Ibid., 23.
[10]Craig R. Koester, *Hebrews: A New Translation with Introduction and Commentary* (New York: Doubleday, 2001), 116.

words, "Scripture . . . is not a collection of ancient texts that can throw light on the present, through analogy. It is the voice of the living God" (4:12) that "speaks directly and urgently to people here and now."[11]

What God Said and Continues to Say

In order to find out what God has said and continues to say powerfully to his people, the following passages from this "word of exhortation" (13:22) have been examined. They include the programmatic introduction to the discourse (1:1–4), Old Testament citations that are introduced as God's speech, and statements about God's word or voice addressing the listeners of Hebrews.

Introduction: God's Final Word to Us in His Son (1:1–4)

Hebrews's magnificent opening sets the program for the whole discourse. The author moves from God's past revelation, his word to the Old Testament "fathers," to his definitive and final revelation in his Son, Jesus Christ. This revelation is presented by means of four parallel contrasts, relating to the eras, the recipients, the agents, and the ways in which God has spoken.[12] These contrasts, however, are not absolute. They draw attention to two stages of the divine revelation that correspond to the Old and New Testaments respectively. It is the same God who speaks in both, and the same message of salvation that he offers. What God has spoken in the Son is continuous with and the climax of his word uttered in earlier times. The author focuses first on the divine revelation, then the person, work, and status of the Son in whom that revelation is given.

Immediately following the mention of the *Son*, the author of Hebrews presents seven affirmations (vv. 2b–4) that describe the Son's attributes and achievements as God's final agent. Together they bring out his greatness and "show why the revelation given in him is the highest which God can give."[13] Jesus, the Son, has been invested as the messianic heir; he inherits not simply the nations (as in Gen. 17:5 and Ps. 2:8), but also the whole universe ("all things," Heb.

---

[11]Johnson, *Hebrews*, 23.
[12]The *eras*: "in the past" and "in these last days"; the *recipients*: "to our ancestors" and "to us"; the *agents*: "through the prophets" and "by his Son"; and the *ways*: "in various ways" and "in one way" (implied).
[13]Bruce, *Hebrews*, 46.

1:2), especially "the world to come" (2:5). Through the agency of the Son the Father has created the whole universe of time and space. As "the radiance of God's glory," that is, the manifestation of God's glorious presence, and "the exact representation of his being," the Son is the perfect embodiment of God as he really is (v. 3). God's being is made manifest in Christ, so that to see him is to see what God is like (v. 3a). The One who was the agent of creation also sustains the universe by his powerful word, and moves all things to their appointed goal (v. 3b).

He has effected God's saving work through the purification of sins, which Hebrews will later tell us occurred in his once-for-all death on the cross (7:27; 10:12; 12:2). The forgiveness he has won is permanent, and because the barrier between God and humanity has been removed, it enables men and women to enter into God's presence with confidence (cf. 4:16; 9:14). After completing the work of atonement, the Son was exalted and enthroned at the right hand of God on high (a clear allusion to Psalm 110). Christ's exaltation was God's mighty act of raising him to a position of unparalleled honor and universal authority. That Christ *sat down* as priest (after his definitive cleansing of sins) shows his work was finished, and his place at God's right hand means he shares the Father's throne (Rev. 3:21). Jesus' exaltation to this place of honor marks him out as superior to the angels, a superiority that is underscored by reference to the title he bears. His name, which is more excellent than the angels', is usually taken as that of "Son,"[14] because of the acclamation "my son" of Psalm 2:7, cited in Hebrews 1:5.

"Thus," says F. F. Bruce, "the greatness of the Son of God receives sevenfold confirmation, and it appears, without being expressly emphasized, that he possesses in himself all the qualifications to be the mediator between God and the human race."[15]

---

[14]After the first mention of Son in Heb. 1:2a the author used the term "heir," and the inclusion of "he inherited" implies that the "name" is that of "Son." Further, the movement of thought into the first citation also implies that the name is Son: note the scriptural explanation and grounding of v. 5 in the statement of v. 4, "*For* to which of the angels did he ever say, 'You are my Son'?" Note John P. Meier, "Structure and Theology in Heb 1,1–14," *Biblica* 66 (1985): 168–89, esp. 187. Guthrie, "Hebrews," 924–25, takes a different line. On the basis of 2 Sam. 7:14 and the broader context of the citations in Heb. 1:5–14, he claims that the name is the honor "conferred by God on the Messiah as the Davidic heir at the establishment of his throne in association with God himself" (925).

[15]Bruce, *Hebrews*, 50.

God's Speaking to the Son and to Angels (1:5–13)

The language of divine speaking appears again in the following theological section (vv. 5–13): there are seven proofs from Scripture[16] (framed by two rhetorical questions, vv. 5, 13: "To which of the angels did God ever say?") that undergird the seven affirmations about the Son in verses 1–4.

God is the one who speaks throughout (vv. 5, 6, 7, 8–9, 10–12, 13), and in the presence of angels he addresses the Son directly in the words of Scripture. Although there is some difference of opinion as to when this divine address occurred, most agree that the context points to Christ's enthronement (v. 6; see vv. 3, 5)—his entrance into the heavenly world at his ascension, following his sacrificial death. This was the time when God introduced his firstborn Son into that world, and thus the occasion when the angels were commanded to worship him.

God addresses the Son as "God," whose throne will last forever (v. 8), and as "Lord" (the name above every name), who laid the foundations of the earth and will remain for eternity, in contrast to the heavens and the earth (vv. 10–12). This same Son, God and Lord, is the priestly king of Psalm 110 who is now seated at the Father's right hand until all his enemies are subdued (Heb. 1:13).

The seven quotations from the Old Testament are presented as a succession of words spoken by God to the Son amid the company of angels in heaven, and the listeners on earth are now permitted to overhear what was said.[17] Those to whom this "word of exhortation" was read out in the congregation were privileged to hear God speaking to the Son in heaven. It was of profound importance for them to realize that in addressing the Son from his own Word, the Old Testament Scriptures, God himself was firmly endorsing the magnificent affirmations in the prologue about the Son's dignity and majesty.

God Announced and Confirmed the Gospel of Salvation so that Men and Women Heard and Believed (2:1–4)

Hebrews 2 picks up the introduction of 1:1–4, which affirms that God, whose earlier revelation of the law was communicated through

---

[16]Ps. 2:7; 2 Sam. 7:14 (Heb. 1:5); Ps. 97:7 (Heb. 1:6); Ps. 104:4 (Heb. 1:7); Ps. 45:6–7 (Heb. 1:8–9); Ps. 102:25–27 (Heb. 1:10–12); and Ps. 110:1 (Heb. 1:13).
[17]Lane, *Hebrews 1–8*, 32; and Koester, *Hebrews*, 208.

angelic messengers, has in these last days spoken his climactic word in no less a person than his Son. This revelation therefore demands even more serious attention than the message delivered by angels, that is, the Law. The author moves from exposition (1:5–14) to urgent exhortation, from lofty demonstration of the Son's superiority to angels to a pointed appeal designed to gain his listeners' attention and stop them drifting away from the gospel. The warning arises from the preceding theological exposition and presents a forceful statement of the consequences of rejecting the word spoken through God's Son.

The author reminds his listeners that God *announced* (λαλέω) the gospel of salvation "by the Lord"[18] (2:3). This declaration not only resumes the introduction of Hebrews that God has in these last days *spoken* (λαλέω) "by his Son" (1:2). It also affirms that the ministry of the Lord Jesus marked the first phase of God's final revelation. The apostles and other evangelists who heard Jesus' testimony confirmed it to the author of Hebrews and his listeners, and, as a result, they believed the gospel ("what we have heard," 2:1).

Moreover, the God who spoke his final revelation in his Son established beyond doubt the reliability of this saving message to the listeners. The unusual verb rendered "testified" (συνεπιμαρτυρέω, lit. to "bear witness together with"), which appears only here in the Greek Bible, speaks of God's corroboration of the testimony to his salvation. He powerfully bore witness to the truth of his authoritative word by confirmatory signs, wonders, and mighty works, together with gracious distributions of the Holy Spirit (v. 4).

What our author describes in Hebrews 1 and 2 points to a revelation at a time of climactic fulfillment in *salvation history* ("in these last days," 1:2; and "first announced," 2:3), and at a *personal level* in the lives of the congregation members ("to us," 1:2; 2:3). God is the speaking God who announces the gospel of salvation through the Lord Jesus and his evangelists, confirms it by signs and wonders, and summons men and women, including the author and his listeners, to be sharers in his heavenly calling (cf. 3:1). In consequence, they must pay the most careful attention to what they have heard and not drift away from this glorious message with its great salvation.

---

[18]Lit. "this salvation was announced [by God, λαλεῖσθαι—the passive implies his action] through the Lord."

The Crucified and Exalted Lord Directly Addresses His Brothers and Sisters (2:12–13)

For the first time in Hebrews the speaker (λέγων, "he says") is the crucified and exalted Lord Jesus. He is not ashamed to call God's family his "brothers and sisters"—because of their common origin in God (v. 11)—so now he addresses them directly through the Old Testament Scriptures (Ps. 22:22; Isa. 8:17, 18; cf. Heb. 10:5–7). All three citations are personal affirmations of Jesus, in whom these Scriptures are fulfilled: "I will declare . . . I will sing your praises," "I will put my trust . . . ," and "Here am I, and the children whom God has given me." Each quotation attests Jesus' solidarity with believers, and this is emphatically underscored in the exposition that follows (Heb. 2:14–18).

The ascended Lord speaks personally to the listeners of this "word of exhortation" and, by implication, to other Christians. The assembly in which he promises to declare God's name to his "brothers and sisters" is the eschatological congregation of God, which is already assembled around the exalted Christ, and to which they have already come (12:22–24). At the same time, as members of God's church ("Abraham's descendants," Jesus' "brothers and sisters," and "the people," 2:16, 17), they meet in Christ's name and under his authority here on earth.

As sons and daughters whom Jesus sanctifies (2:11), believers are in a continuous relationship with him. The assurance of their ongoing fellowship with their exalted Lord would have encouraged the hearers to remain faithful to him and other believers, even if they suffered the reproach of their wider society. Moreover, this affirmation by Christ anticipates the later declaration of 11:16, "God is *not ashamed* to be called their God," a covenantal promise first addressed to Abraham and his family, which now rings in the ears of these listeners.

Warning and Encouragement: The Power of God's Word and the Reality of Judgment (3:7–4:13)

Psalm 95:7–11 provides the basis of the exhortation in Hebrews 3:7–4:13, and it is introduced as an utterance of the Holy Spirit, whom Hebrews on occasion identifies as the ultimate source of the Scriptures (9:8; 10:15). Elsewhere the psalm is presented as what God says (3:15; 4:3).

The quotation of Psalm 95 in Hebrews 3:7–11 and the warning about the trenchant character of God's word (4:12–13) are bookends that provide the literary frame for interpreting 3:7–4:13. The section may be divided into three parts: (a) 3:7–19, a citation of Psalm 95, which is then expounded as a warning about the consequences of unfaithfulness; (b) 4:1–11, an exhortation to the listeners to persevere in faith and enter God's eternal Sabbath rest because his promise still remains open; and (c) 4:12–13, a clear statement about the trenchant power of God's word and the reality of judgment. In each of these paragraphs God's speech is highly significant.

(1) The focus of the introductory formula ("as the Holy Spirit says," 3:7) is on the Spirit continuing to address the present listeners through the text of the psalm, which according to 4:12–13 is called the living word of God. What God says is by way of warning, for the language of speaking (λέγω, 3:7) is conjoined with his swearing an oath (ὀμνύω, v. 11), the content of which warns of judgment. The admonition of the psalm, with its second-person plural, encounters the congregation directly, "Today, if *you* hear his voice, do not harden *your* hearts," while the *today* of the psalm does not refer to the time of David but stresses the immediacy of the word of God to the present generation ("as long as it is called 'Today,'" v. 13).

The lesson is reinforced by a fresh quotation of Psalm 95:7–8 (introduced by "when it [Scripture] or he [God] says," Heb. 3:15, author's trans.) and several pointed questions (vv. 16–18), which lead inexorably to the conclusion that the wilderness generation was excluded from God's promised rest because of rampant unbelief and faithlessness (v. 19). For the congregation to refuse to listen to God's voice and not to respond in obedience would result in the tragic loss of their inheritance. Hearing his voice is not simply listening to him audibly; it also involves paying attention to what is said and obeying him (Matt. 11:15; 13:9). When addressed by God, listeners have to respond one way or another. Clearly our author wants their response to be one of faith rather than disobedience or rejection.

(2) Three times in Hebrews 4, Psalm 95 (along with Gen. 2:2) is introduced as God's speech (vv. 3, 5, 7; cf. v. 4). The divine oath "They shall never enter my rest" (Ps. 95:11) does not so much rehearse the condemnation of the wilderness generation (as in Heb. 3:16–19) as remind the listeners of God's testimony in Scripture that a resting

place truly exists. He speaks of it as "my rest" (κατάπαυσις), that is, the rest that he himself enjoys and promises to share with his people. Despite Israel's unbelief and failure to enter God's rest, he did not annul his promise. Centuries after the exclusion of that generation from Canaan, God set (ὁρίζω) a new day of opportunity. In fact, the rest in Canaan was "a type or symbol of the complete rest that God intended for his people, which was prefigured in the Sabbath rest of God, according to Gen 2:2."[19]

In a concise and striking statement, Hebrews proclaims that a "Sabbath celebration" (σαββατισμός)—indeed, God's eternal, festive celebration—remains for the people of God (4:9). The psalmist's appeal to heed God's voice "Today," which does not signify an endless span of time, is now addressed to the listeners. The motive for their making every effort to enter God's rest is the fact that his promise remains open (4:1). Theirs is a privileged position: they now stand before God's word of promise, just as the wilderness generation did. Let them beware of the peril of being excluded from the divine rest because of unbelief.

(3) The author concludes the long exhortatory section of 3:1–4:11 with a short, compelling statement about the power of God's word[20] to scrutinize human hearts (4:12) and to render people helpless before his searching gaze (4:13). In the immediate context this *word of God* is his "voice" in Psalm 95,[21] the text of which has been cited extensively in Hebrews 3:7–4:11. It is the living, effective, and piercing word of God that "Today" addresses the author and his listeners, calling them to obedience and faithfulness. This dynamic understanding of the word of God is consistent with the introduction to Psalm 95, through which the Holy Spirit continues to address the listeners of Hebrews ("as the Holy Spirit says," 3:7). The God who speaks by his word (in this case Psalm 95) does so in and through his Holy Spirit.

---

[19]Lane, *Hebrews 1–8*, 101.
[20]Hebrews uses the expression "the word [*logos*] of God" for the message delivered to the listeners by their leaders (13:7). But *logos* by itself refers to the message that was brought by angels (2:2), and that which was heard by the desert generation (4:2). Later our author will speak of those who have partaken of the *logos* of righteousness (5:13), of the *logos* concerning the Messiah (6:1), of the *logos* of God's oath (7:28), and of the *logos* presented at Mount Sinai (12:19). In each instance, *logos* refers to a speech or message that takes its origin in God. See Johnson, *Hebrews*, 132.
[21]The majority Patristic and medieval view that the phrase refers to the Son (Rev. 19:15, 21) is not supported by this context or in Hebrews as a whole. The christological explanation has generally been abandoned since Calvin.

This word of God is first of all *alive and active*. Although the adjective *alive* here may indicate that God's word is not only living but also life-giving (Ps. 119:25), the context suggests that *alive* is used primarily in the sense of powerful to examine, discern, even judge. If taken with the following description, *active* or "effective,"[22] then it signifies that God's word, which powerfully examines and discerns, is able to effect the purpose for which he has uttered it (Isa. 55:11; also Jer. 23:29).

Using figurative and compelling imagery, the author conveys the idea that God's word is able to penetrate the deepest recesses of the human personality: it is sharper than the sharpest sword and is able to probe the inmost recesses of our being to bring the subconscious motives to light (note 1 Cor. 4:5). God's word sifts and judges the thoughts and intentions of the heart in a thoroughgoing and comprehensive manner. Every creature is totally exposed and defenseless in the presence of the God to whom all must render an account of their lives. And so close is the connection between God and his word that to be exposed to the word of Scripture is to be examined fully by God himself, and therefore to be answerable to him.

God Addresses the Messianic Son Directly and Appoints Him as High Priest in the Order of Melchizedek (5:5–6; 7:21)

In a context that speaks of the qualifications for the office of high priest (5:1–10), Hebrews asserts that Christ refused to take upon himself the dignity of this position. Instead, God designated him, the Son, as High Priest. In language that recalls the initial description of God as the speaking God (λαλέω, 1:1–2), our author affirms that the One who said (λαλέω), "You are my Son; today I have become your Father" (5:5; cf. Ps. 2:7), also says (λέγω), "You are a priest forever, in the order of Melchizedek" (Heb. 5:6; cf. Ps. 110:4). These expressions declare more than simply that Christ was called by God. The direct speech to Christ personally ("You are") and the linking of the two psalm texts show clearly that the incarnate and exalted messianic Son is the same person who has been divinely appointed to a new and unique high priesthood.[23]

---

[22]Johannes P. Louw and Eugene A. Nida, *Greek-English Lexicon of the New Testament Based on Semantic Domains*, 2 vols. (New York: United Bible Societies, 1988), 13.124; BDAG, 335.
[23]At Heb. 7:21 the language of "swearing an oath" and "saying" is used with reference to God speaking directly to the Son and appointing him as High Priest to an everlasting priesthood,

God Promises to Bless Abraham and Give Him Many Descendants (6:13–14)

Several of the key speaking terms are used in relation to God's promise to Abraham in 6:13, 14, that is, "promise" (v. 13; cf. vv. 15, 17), "swear" (v. 13 twice; cf. v. 16), "oath" (vv. 16, 17), and "saying" (v. 14), which introduces the words of Scripture, "I will surely bless you and give you many descendants" (v. 14).

The particular promise in view here is the one made by God to Abraham, after his offering up Isaac (known as the *Aqedah* or "binding" of Isaac), the supreme example of Abraham's faith: "I swear by myself, declares the LORD . . . I will surely bless you and make your descendants as numerous as the stars . . ." (Gen. 22:16–17). This oath was a repetition and expansion of God's earlier promise to Abraham that he would bless him and make him a great nation (Gen. 12:2–3). Every hope for the fulfillment of God's promises to Abraham regarding his descendants hung on Isaac (note Gen. 15:5). But Abraham believed God and received what was promised. His faithful obedience and patience are relevant to the listeners and other heirs of God's promise (Heb. 6:16–20). And God's faithfulness to his declarations affords the confidence that believers need in order to persevere and hold firmly to their hope.

God's Word of Promise of a New Covenant Is Fulfilled in the Hearts and Lives of His People (8:8–13; 10:15–17)

The language of divine speech is forcefully employed by the author of Hebrews in relation to the new covenant promise of Jeremiah 31. This key Old Testament passage is cited twice in Hebrews, first in full (8:8–13), then in a shorter form (10:15–17). The two quotations from Jeremiah are bookends that frame the whole section (8:7–10:18), and each is introduced by God's speaking: "he [i.e., God] says" (8:8), and "The Holy Spirit . . . testifies to us" (10:15).

God took the initiative in announcing his intention to establish a new covenant with Israel and Judah in the "coming" days. Throughout the oracle of Jeremiah 31, the dominant use of the first person

---

and then confirming it with an oath (so Ps. 110:4). There is no mention of a divine oath in the record of the appointment of the Aaronic priests. "This contrast expresses forcefully that the difference between Jesus and the Levitical priest is not one of degree (lesser and greater) but of kind, demonstrating that Jesus is the eschatological priest of the new age" (Lane, *Hebrews 1–8*, 187).

emphatically underlines the divine initiative: "I will make . . . I will put . . . I will write . . . I will be . . . I will forgive . . . I will remember" (Jer. 31:31–34; Heb. 8:8–12, ESV). Moreover, the prophecy itself is punctuated by the phrase, "oracle of Yahweh" (rendered as "declares the Lord," Heb. 8:8, 9).

According to the author of Hebrews, the "coming" days of Jeremiah 31 have arrived ("these last days," 1:2). The time anticipated by the prophet when God would "make a new covenant" has come. Jesus as mediator and guarantor has by his death inaugurated this covenant. Those who have come to him as this mediator know that God has fulfilled his new covenant promises in their lives. He has established a new relationship between himself and his people that involves: (a) the implanting of his law in their hearts, (b) the knowledge of God as a matter of personal experience, and (c) the definitive forgiveness of their sins, that is, the cleansing of the conscience, so that they may serve the living God. According to 10:15, the Holy Spirit "testifies" to both the author of Hebrews and his listeners directly ("us") that the promises of the new covenant are for their community (as well as for other believers). God's speaking by his Spirit effectively confirms that the word of promise concerning the new covenant has been fulfilled in the hearts and lives of his people.

As He Comes into the World, Christ Declares His Obedience to the Will of God (10:5–7)

Once more in Hebrews, Christ speaks (λέγω, vv. 5, 7; cf. 2:12–13), this time in the words of Psalm 40:6–8. Our author "overhears" the Son addressing the Father on the occasion of his entry into the world. The transcendent Son of God, who became man in order to fulfill the divine purposes for humanity (2:10, 14, 17), finds "his duty set out in Scripture . . . and [he sets] himself to carry it out with whole-hearted obedience."[24] On the occasion of his coming into the world,[25] he says, "I have come to do your will, my God" (10:7).

---

[24]David Peterson, *Hebrews and Perfection: An Examination of the Concept of Perfection in the "Epistle to the Hebrews"* (Cambridge: University Press, 1982), 147–48.

[25]If the preincarnate Christ's voice is being heard in the psalm, then presumably "his incarnation itself is viewed as an act of submission to God's will and, as such, an anticipation of his supreme submission to that will in death" (Bruce, *Hebrews*, 242; see William L. Lane, *Hebrews 9–13* (Dallas: Word, 1991), 262; Guthrie, "Hebrews," 977). Others, however, think that Christ's utterance, rendered as "I *have come* to do your will, my God" (10:7), describes "the

In this context of Hebrews 10, our author speaks of Christ's sacrifice and the ground of its efficacy. The Son's voice heard in the psalm shows: (1) that he "completely rejects . . . [all the Old Testament sacrifices] as the means of pleasing God or gaining access to his presence" (v. 8).[26] The animal sacrifices and everything associated with them, that is, the "first" system, were removed so that the "second" could be established permanently (v. 9). (2) His mission is his complete preoccupation with doing God's will. His obedience ("I have come to do your will, my God," v. 7) anticipates the important conclusion that the offering of Christ is the sacrifice that God desired. Christ's fulfilling of God's will is the reason that his sacrifice is effective and achieves what the animal sacrifices under the old covenant could not.

God Will Judge Severely Those Who Reject His New Covenant in Christ (10:30)

At the climax of the strong warning of 10:26–31, two brief citations from the Song of Moses (Deut. 32:35, 36) are used to speak of the inevitability of punishment awaiting apostate Christians. Through the mouth of Moses in this song, God says, "It is mine to avenge; I will repay" (Deut. 32:35a),[27] and "The Lord will judge his people" (v. 36a). In the first of these, the Lord assumes personal responsibility (note the emphatic "I") "for taking vengeance on those who have become his adversaries,"[28] while in the second, which is introduced by the words "and again," the main thought is that God's judgment on his enemies will result in the vindication of his people.

The divine words, which were originally addressed to Israel, are now spoken by God as he warns the listeners of Hebrews about rejecting his truth and the consequences of that rejection (note also 2:1–4; 3:7–4:11; 6:4–8). Those who persist in sin and utterly refuse God's Son cannot expect divine forgiveness, for no other sacrifice for sins is

---

attitude of one who has already come." Cf. Peterson, *Hebrews and Perfection*, 147; Koester, *Hebrews*, 432.

[26]Gareth L. Cockerill, "Structure and Interpretation in Hebrews 8:1–10:18: A Symphony in Three Movements," *BBR* 11 (2001): 179–201, esp. 195.

[27]Our author cites v. 35a in a version that differs from the MT and the LXX but is attested in the Targums and in Paul (Rom. 12:19). On the textual question, see Paul Ellingworth, *The Epistle to the Hebrews: A Commentary on the Greek Text* (Grand Rapids: Carlisle, 1993), 542; Koester, *Hebrews*, 453.

[28]Lane, *Hebrews 9–13*, 295.

left. Instead, there is a fearful expectation of judgment and fire that will consume God's enemies.[29]

God Addresses His Word of Exhortation to His Children Who Are Struggling (12:5–6)

The members of the community may have wondered why God's people suffer insult, rejection, and persecution. These experiences are enough to make them doubt God's love, and so lose heart. The author anticipates such questions with his firm but gentle rebuke, telling them that they have completely forgotten the exhortation in Scripture that speaks to them as God's children about discipline and suffering.

The citation from Proverbs 3:11–12 is called an "exhortation" (παράκλησις), the same term used of Hebrews as a whole (13:22). Like the discourse itself, the text from Proverbs contains both admonition and encouragement. It is Scripture itself that speaks, though for Hebrews this is tantamount to saying that God by his Spirit addresses them directly in Scripture, that is, in the exhortation of Proverbs 3.

God regards the community as his *children*. The listeners' relationship to him as sons and daughters is important not only for the argument in Heb. 12:7–11 but also for the whole epistle. Throughout, the author has emphasized the sonship of Jesus[30] and also has spoken of the parallel relationship of the listeners to God: they are his children (2:10–18). The choice of the verb "speaks" (διαλέγεται) underscores the relational dimension, for in the utterance of the scriptural text God is in conversation with his children.[31] The generic singular of the original ("my child") is applied to the particular circumstances of the community ("you . . . children"). Proverbs 3:11–12 is "God's personal word to those who enjoy sonship through the mediation of Jesus who inaugurated the new covenant."[32]

---

[29]On the appropriateness of these citations in Deuteronomy 32, which point to the judgment on Israel's enemies, see David M. Allen, *Deuteronomy and Exhortation in Hebrews: A Study in Narrative Re-presentation* (Tübingen: Mohr Siebeck, 2008), 59–60, and note the discussion in my *The Letter to the Hebrews* (Grand Rapids: Eerdmans, 2010).

[30]Heb. 1:2, 5, 8; 3:6; 4:14; 5:5, 8; 6:6; 7:3, 28; 10:29.

[31]BDAG, 232 [2], suggests the meaning of the verb here is to "inform" or "instruct." The addition of the personal pronoun "my" by Hebrews to the LXX text makes the citation more intimate.

[32]Lane, *Hebrews 9–13*, 421.

A Powerful Warning Not to Refuse the One Who Speaks to Them (12:25–26)

The language of divine speech occurs in the final warning of Hebrews, which is addressed to those who are in the privileged position of enjoying the blessings of the new covenant (12:22–24). "See to it that you do not refuse him who speaks." "Him who speaks" is not explicitly named, but the flow of the author's argument in verses 25–26 makes it clear that a single speaker is in view—God himself.

The ultimate seriousness of God's final revelation is highlighted by the contrast Hebrews draws between the shaking of the earth at Mount Sinai and the promise of an eschatological shaking of the heavens as well as the earth (vv. 25–26). When God spoke from Sinai, "the whole mountain trembled violently" (Ex. 19:18). Those who were warned "on earth" were held accountable to God. How much more, then, will members of the new covenant community be answerable to the Judge, the God of all, who *now* speaks to them and promises "I will once more shake" the foundations (Hag. 2:6)? Those who heed his speaking from heaven and hold fast to their confession during the final cataclysm show that they are true members of his kingdom, which will emerge unshakeable. For them the promise of God to fulfill his purposes, expressed through the citation of the biblical text, is a climactic and powerful message of assurance and encouragement (v. 28). But those who reject the new covenant revelation will "receive the same summary judgment as those who disregarded the revelation given at Sinai."[33]

None may presume upon the grace of God. The author brings this point home forcibly by including himself in the warning. He regarded himself as a believer. But consistent with his practice throughout the sermon, he applies his exposition to himself as well as to his listeners. He too must not reject the One who warns from heaven. It would be a total denial of all that he and they stand for.

God's Promise of His Unfailing Presence and Care Is the Ground for Being Content (13:5)

Within a series of practical exhortations indicating how the listeners should serve God faithfully (Heb. 13:1–6; cf. 12:28), they are admonished to live their lives free from the love of money and to be

---

[33]Ibid., 481.

content with what they have. The ground for such godly behavior is the climactic promise of Hebrews, in which God addresses the listeners for the last time through the words of the Old Testament Scripture (Josh. 1:5; cf. Deut. 31:6–8), and says,

> Never will I leave you;
> never will I forsake you.

God speaks in his own name[34] directly to them and assures them of his unfailing presence and care. The singular "you" in the address represents the whole people, but the promise is at the same time for each one of them. This affirmation of total commitment to them corporately and individually is all the more powerful because it comes from the God who has just been described as "a consuming fire" (Heb. 12:29). The assurance that God will never abandon them is intended to strengthen the listeners so that they will trust in the Lord's help. The divine promise is wide-ranging and can address all their needs, as the response of faith makes plain (v. 6). In fact, the Lord's constant presence in the midst of his people is ultimately the greatest of all his blessings to them.

His sure promise elicits the positive response of faith: "*So* we say with confidence, 'The Lord is my helper.'" The divine pledge is given in the first person ("Never will *I* leave you; never will *I* forsake you," v. 5), and this is echoed in the positive reply of the listeners, also in the first person ("so *we* say . . . 'the Lord is *my* helper'"). Their affirmation is tantamount to a confession of faith, especially as it is cast in the language of Scripture (Ps. 118 [LXX 117]:6). It is an example of "the fruit of lips that openly profess [God's] name" (Heb. 13:15).

Some Conclusions

The God who revealed himself to the fathers in the Old Testament has now spoken his definitive and final word in his Son at this time of climactic fulfillment ("in these last days," 1:1–2a). The seven affirmations that describe the attributes and achievements of the Son bring out his greatness and show why the revelation given in him is the highest God can give (vv. 2b–4). To see him is to see what God is like.

---

[34]In the original the redundant *autos* ("he") is emphatic, and the antecedent is "God" of v. 4.

The triune God speaks through the Old Testament Scriptures, of which he is both author and source. After Jesus' exaltation, God spoke to him amid the company of the angels in heaven, addressing him as Son, God, and Lord (1:5–13). The Father who said to Jesus, "You are my Son; today I have become your Father" (Ps. 2:7; Heb. 5:5), also says, "You are a priest forever, in the order of Melchizedek" (Ps. 110:4; Heb. 5:6; 7:21). On the occasion of his entry into the world, the Son addresses the Father in the words of Psalm 40:6–8: "I have come to do your will, my God" (Heb. 10:7). After his exaltation, the Lord Jesus declares God's name to his brothers and sisters, affirming his solidarity with them through the words of the Scriptures (Ps. 22:22; Isa. 8:17, 18; Heb. 2:12–13). Moreover, the Holy Spirit speaks words of warning to the listeners through Psalm 95:7–11 (Heb. 3:7–11) and testifies of promises concerning the new covenant that are for them (Jer. 31:31–34; Heb. 10:15).

God is the speaking God who announces the gospel of salvation through the Lord Jesus and his evangelists, confirms it by signs and wonders, and summons men and women to be sharers in a heavenly calling (Heb. 2:1–4; 3:1). God addresses his people corporately and individually, assuring them that the new covenant promise of long ago is now fulfilled in their hearts and lives. Through Jesus, the mediator of this new covenant, he implants his law in their hearts, brings them to a personal knowledge of himself, and definitively cleanses their consciences so that we may wholeheartedly serve him, the living God (8:8–12; 10:16–17).

Through promise, instruction, encouragement, warning, and oath God continues to address his living word, in this case the Old Testament Scriptures, directly and urgently to his people, exhorting them to fix their eyes on Jesus, the pioneer and perfecter of faith, to persevere in obedience and reach their heavenly rest. God's purpose for his many sons and daughters is to bring them to glory (2:10). He speaks encouragingly to them as a congregation and to each one of them personally when they suffer insult, rejection, and persecution, urging them neither to despise his discipline nor to lose heart since he disciplines each one of them as his beloved children (12:5–6). He is utterly committed to them for their ultimate good. God also addresses strong words of warning to them, urging them not to harden their hearts as Israel did in the wilderness. This word is urgent and the listeners must respond "Today." Those who persist in sin and utterly refuse God's Son cannot expect divine forgiveness, for no other sacrifice for sins is left. Instead, there is a fearful expectation of judgment and fire that will consume God's enemies. Because they are in the privileged position of enjoying his blessings of the new covenant, God finally urges them and us not to refuse him who speaks to them from heaven. He promises to shake the heavens and the earth in the final cataclysm (12:25, 26). Instead, they and we are to hold fast to their confession and show that they and we are true members of his kingdom, which will emerge unshakeable.

In light of these conclusions, we briefly note several characteristics of God's word that emerge from our short study.

First, God's word is *personal*. The living God himself addressed those who listened to Hebrews (both corporately and individually) when it was first read out in the congregation. He spoke directly and personally to his Son, to angels, and to the first hearers, and now speaks to us who "live in these last days" (1:2) and hear this same word. In Hebrews he addresses the Son through the Old Testament Scriptures and personally endorses the magnificent affirmations in the prologue about the Son's dignity and majesty. Moreover, God personally fulfills the promises he makes (e.g., the new covenant), he confirms the words of encouragement and carries out his warnings and judgments on his enemies. His word is *performative*; he effects what he *declares* he will do.

Second, the divine word is *living*, first, in the sense of being effective, because it powerfully examines and discerns human hearts, and is able to effect the purpose(s) for which God has uttered it (4:12–13). It is also living in that it is life-giving, as God himself is. He announced the gospel of salvation "through the Lord" Jesus (2:3), confirmed it through those who heard Jesus preach, and testified to it with signs and wonders so that the congregation came into existence. Men and women received new life through God's announcement to them by his Son and the first evangelists.

Third, God's address to his people is a word that is *clear* and wholly *trustworthy*. The living God who spoke to the first listeners expected them to hear his voice, understand what he said, believe it, and act upon it. God wanted them to grasp his gracious purposes of leading many sons and daughters to glory (2:10), to understand the place of his Son, the Lord Jesus, within those purposes, and to heed his words of promise, warning, and encouragement so that they and we might run with perseverance the race marked out for us, with our eyes fixed upon Jesus, the pioneer and perfecter of faith (12:2). God's word to the congregation was no garbled message, muted voice, or unintelligible sound; it was clear and trustworthy, addressing ultimate issues concerning their relationship to the living God.

Finally, for the author of Hebrews God's voice from the Scriptures was a *spoken* word to the congregation—it was oral. And yet, from the very first it was *written*—written in the Old Testament, and now written in Hebrews, the "word of exhortation" that was read out to the congregation and heard by them.

8

The Language of Baptism

The Meaning of Βαπτίζω in the New Testament

ECKHARD J. SCHNABEL

I n his short but important book *Exegetical Fallacies*, D. A. Carson specifies "false assumptions about technical meaning" as one of the categories of errors that "preachers and others" make when they describe the meaning of biblical terms. He writes that "in this fallacy, an interpreter falsely assumes that a word always or nearly always has a certain technical meaning—a meaning usually derived either from a subset of the evidence or from the interpreter's personal systematic theology."[1] One of the examples that he cites is the understanding of "baptism in the Spirit," a phrase, he argues, that should not be treated as a *terminus technicus* either in the sense of a post-conversion effusion of the Spirit or in terms of the effusion of the Spirit at conversion. He

---

[1] D. A. Carson, *Exegetical Fallacies*, 2nd ed. (Grand Rapids: Baker, 1996 [1984]), 45; for the reference to "preachers and others," see p. 28.

commends the Puritans for apparently not viewing the expression as having a consistent, technical meaning, taking it to mean "effusion in Spirit" or "inundation in Spirit."[2] What Professor Carson has left for other scholars to accomplish, I attempt here: to question the use of the English term *baptize* in Bible translations, commentaries, and other studies as "translation" for the Greek term βαπτίζω in all (or almost all) passages in which the term occurs in the New Testament.

Elsewhere, I have discussed the treatment of βαπτίζω in the standard Greek lexicons, argued for the necessity of revisiting the meaning of βαπτίζω, and surveyed the meaning of βαπτίζω (and of βάπτω: the two verbs have essentially identical meanings) in Greek and Jewish literary and documentary texts.[3] The result of this study was the following lexical entry for βαπτίζω, distinguishing the physical ("literal") and metaphorical meanings of the verb:

I. Physical uses
1. to put into a yielding substance (such as a liquid, e.g. water or dyes, or the body of an animal); glosses: "to plunge, to dip, to immerse";

    1a. to cleanse with water; gloss: "to wash" (extended meaning of 1: to remove dirt by immersion in water)

    1b. to make ceremonially clean; gloss: "to purify" or "to cleanse" (extended meaning of 1: to immerse in water symbolizing, or effecting, the removal of moral or spiritual defilement); gloss of (later) ecclesiastical language: "to baptize";

    1c. to take water or wine by dipping a drinking vessel (in a stream, a fountain, a well, a bowl); gloss: "to draw" (extended meaning of 1: to immerse a vessel in water or wine to obtain a drink);

    1d. to perish by submersion in water; gloss: "to drown" (extended meaning of 1: to suffer death by suffocation being immersed in water [of persons]; or to disappear by submersion in water, to sink [of ships]);

    1e. to put to death a living being; gloss: "to slaughter" or "to kill" (extended meaning of 1: to plunge a knife into the body of an animal or a human being);

---

[2]Ibid., 46.
[3]Cf. E. J. Schnabel, "The Meaning of βαπτίζειν in Greek, Jewish, and Patristic Literature" (forthcoming).

1f. to tinge fabric with a color; gloss: "to dye" (extended meaning of 1: to immerse fabric in liquid with color pigments); this meaning is frequently attested for βάπτειν, but not for βαπτίζειν.[4]

II. Figurative uses

2. to be overpowered by an abstract reality, such as debts or arguments or thoughts; gloss: "to be overwhelmed" or "to be immersed" (transferred meaning of 1: a person is "immersed" in intangible or abstract realities and consequently overwhelmed by their force);

3. to become intoxicated; gloss: "to be drunk" (transferred meaning of 1: a person is "submerged" in the effects of intoxicating liquids).

The following study seeks to clarify the meaning of the terms βάπτω and βαπτίζω, particularly the latter, with regard to two questions.[5] Can the New Testament use of the terms βάπτω and βαπτίζω be compared with the use of these verbs in earlier and contemporary Greek and Jewish sources? Is there a shift in meaning when New Testament authors use βαπτίζω, a shift toward a technical meaning that can be expressed in English only with the loan word "to baptize"? After a discussion of the four occurrences of the verb βάπτω, I will treat the New Testament passages in which βαπτίζω[6] is used in the sequence of the "senses" given in BDAG, starting with Jewish rites of purification, proceeding to John the Baptist, Jesus, and the early church, and ending with references in which βαπτίζω denotes, according to BDAG, some kind of experience akin to an initiatory water rite.[7]

---

[4]A related meaning is "to plate an object with silver or gold" with the gloss "to silver" or "to gild" (extended meaning of 1: to immerse an object in liquid silver or gold); this meaning is attested for βάπτειν, but not for βαπτίζειν; cf. Pseudo-Democritus, *Alchemista* 47B.

[5]The understanding (or "theology") of baptism/immersion in the New Testament is a different, albeit related, question that will not be discussed here.

[6]The verb βαπτίζειν occurs 77 times in the New Testament in 64 verses, with 43 occurrences in the four Gospels, 21 occurrences in the book of Acts, and 13 occurrences in Paul's letters.

[7]Walter Bauer, Frederick W. Danker, William F. Arndt, and F. Wilbur Gingrich, *A Greek-English Lexicon of the New Testament and Other Early Christian Literature*, 3rd ed., rev. and ed. F. W. Danker (Chicago: University of Chicago Press, 2000), 164–65. Note that Takamitsu Muraoka, *A Greek-English Lexicon of the Septuagint* (Leuven: Peeters, 2009), 106, lists the following meanings for βαπτίζω: "1. middle voice, *to immerse oneself*: so as to wash oneself (Judith 12:7); therapeutic (4 Kings 5:14); ritual (Sirach 31:30); 2. active voice and figuratively, *to affect thoroughly* (Isa. 21:4)."

The Use of βάπτω in Luke 16:24, John 13:26, and Revelation 19:13

Luke 16:24: πάτερ Ἀβραάμ, ἐλέησόν με καὶ πέμψον Λάζαρον ἵνα βάψῃ τὸ ἄκρον τοῦ δακτύλου αὐτοῦ ὕδατος καὶ καταψύξῃ τὴν γλῶσσάν μου, ὅτι ὀδυνῶμαι ἐν τῇ φλογὶ ταύτῃ. ("Father Abraham, have mercy on me, and send Lazarus to *dip* the tip of his finger in water and cool my tongue; for I am in agony in these flames.")[8]

Here βάπτειν has sense 1: the finger is put into water. As glosses, both "dip"[9] and "put into" can be used as translations, although "plunge" and "immerse" work as well.[10]

John 13:26: ἀποκρίνεται ὁ Ἰησοῦς, ἐκεῖνός ἐστιν ᾧ ἐγὼ βάψω τὸ ψωμίον καὶ δώσω αὐτῷ. βάψας οὖν τὸ ψωμίον λαμβάνει καὶ δίδωσιν Ἰούδᾳ Σίμωνος Ἰσκαριώτου. ("Jesus answered, 'It is the one to whom I give this piece of bread when I have *dipped* it in the dish.' So when he had *dipped* the piece of bread, he gave it to Judas son of Simon Iscariot.")

The meaning of βάπτω again corresponds to sense 1. The standard gloss used in translations is "dip."[11] The definition "put into" can be used as a substitute for "dip."

Rev. 19:13: καὶ περιβεβλημένος ἱμάτιον βεβαμμένον αἵματι, καὶ κέκληται τὸ ὄνομα αὐτοῦ ὁ λόγος τοῦ θεοῦ. ("He is clothed in a robe *dipped* in blood, and his name is called The Word of God.")

The verb βάπτειν again is used with sense 1. The standard translation is "dip,"[12] although "plunge" and "immerse" could be substituted.

---

[8]Unless otherwise indicated, Scripture quotations in this chapter are from the NRSV.

[9]ESV, GNB, NASB, NET, NIV, NLT, NRSV, RSV, TNIV all translate as "dip."

[10]Note the large number of examples that can be retrieved in Internet searches of "plunge your finger" and "immerse your finger."

[11]ESV, GNB, NASB, NET, NIV, NLT, NRSV, RSV, TNIV all translate as "dip." Internet searches do not yield many results for the collocation "to plunge a piece of bread," nor for "to immerse a piece of bread." For the former, Google produces the following reference: 56th Congress, *Hazing at the Military Academy: Testimony Taken by the Select Committee of the House of Representatives* (Report 2768 Part 3; Washington: US Government Printing Office, 1901), 936, which explains the "sammy straight" method as follows: "to make a man eat so much of that on bread [*sic*], take a soup plate and fill that with sammy, and then immerse a piece of bread in it and make him eat a certain number of slices of bread."

[12]ESV, NASB, NET, NIV, NLT, NRSV, RSV, TNIV; GNB has "the robe he wore was covered with blood." Eugene H. Peterson, *The Message: The Bible in Contemporary Language* (Colorado Springs: NavPress, 2002), has "soaked with blood."

It is not possible to formulate general conclusions regarding the use of a term from four occurrences in a large corpus. We note, however, that βάπτω is always used in the physical sense of "to put into a yielding substance" (dip, plunge, immerse). The fact that neither extended senses nor any of the two metaphorical senses occurs does not mean that the meaning of βάπτω has become more narrow—no New Testament text refers to the dyeing of textiles or to the plating of objects with silver or gold. When authors refer to the (potential) drowning of people (Matt. 14:30) or to the sinking of ships (Luke 5:7), other verbs are used.[13] The evidence from the later church fathers demonstrates that βάπτω retained its full range of extended and metaphorical senses.

The Use of βαπτίζω for Jewish Immersion Rites

Mark 7:3–4: οἱ γὰρ Φαρισαῖοι καὶ πάντες οἱ Ἰουδαῖοι ἐὰν μὴ πυγμῇ νίψωνται τὰς χεῖρας οὐκ ἐσθίουσιν, κρατοῦντες τὴν παράδοσιν τῶν πρεσβυτέρων, καὶ ἀπ' ἀγορᾶς ἐὰν μὴ βαπτίσωνται οὐκ ἐσθίουσιν, καὶ ἄλλα πολλά ἐστιν ἃ παρέλαβον κρατεῖν, βαπτισμοὺς ποτηρίων καὶ ξεστῶν καὶ χαλκίων καὶ κλινῶν. ("For the Pharisees, and all the Jews, do not eat unless they thoroughly wash their hands, thus observing the tradition of the elders; and they do not eat anything from the market unless they *wash* it; and there are also many other traditions that they observe, the *washing* of cups, pots, and bronze kettles.")

The passage expresses a progression from washing (νίψωνται) hands before meals[14] to immersion of the entire body after visiting the local marketplace, which, according to the tradition of (some?) Pharisees, required purification from defilement (potentially) contracted in the marketplace.[15] The verb βαπτίζω denotes more than merely washing (hands) for the purpose of hygiene: "traditions of the elders" refers to the

---

[13]In Matt. 14:30 καταποντίζω, and in Luke 5:7 βυθίζω.
[14]The meaning of πυγμῇ, translated by NRSV as "thoroughly," is unclear in connection with the washing of hands; it can mean "up to the fist or wrist" (implying immersion of the hands in water), "with a fistful of water," or "with a cupped hand." Cf. BDAG s.v. πυγμῇ; Robert A. Guelich, *Mark 1–8:26*, WBC 34A (Dallas: Word, 1989), 364–65; Joel Marcus, *Mark*, 2 vols., AB 27 (New York: Doubleday, 2000, 2009), 1:441. Regarding the Old Testament purity laws and the Jewish traditions concerning hand washing, cf. Roger P. Booth, *Jesus and the Laws of Purity: Tradition History and Legal History in Mark 7*, JSNTSup 13 (Sheffield: JSOT Press, 1986), 117–87.
[15]Guelich, *Mark*, 365.

Pharisaic interpretation of Old Testament laws concerning ritual purification. The verb thus means "to make ceremonially clean" (sense 1b) and can be translated with "cleanse" (NASB) or "purify" (RSV); the NLT interprets it in terms of "immerse their hands in water." Commentators argue that in the context of Second Temple Judaism and the context of what we know about the purity concerns of the Pharisees, "the washing in this case is not merely of the hands, but apparently involves immersion of the whole person."[16] The noun βαπτισμός is usually translated as "washing," a gloss that is easily (mis)understood in the hygienic sense of "removal of dirt." The Pharisaic traditions that Mark refers to concern the washing of containers and utensils that have contracted ritual impurity. This idea can be communicated in a translation either with the gloss "ceremonial washing" (NLT) or with "immersion."[17]

In Mark 1:44, Luke 2:22, 5:14, and John 2:6, Jewish rites of purification are described with the noun καθαρισμός, which emphasizes the purpose and result of ceremonial immersion in water.

Since the ceremonial washing of hands can be described with νίπτω, βαπτίζω, and καθαρίζω, the term βαπτίζω cannot be described as a "technical" term denoting "to make ceremonially clean." Rather, it is one of several terms that describes ceremonial cleansing, a term that focuses on the process of cleansing (hands or the entire body, immersed in water) while the other two terms focus on the purpose and result of the action.[18]

Luke 11:37–38: Ἐν δὲ τῷ λαλῆσαι ἐρωτᾷ αὐτὸν Φαρισαῖος ὅπως ἀριστήσῃ παρ' αὐτῷ· εἰσελθὼν δὲ ἀνέπεσεν. ὁ δὲ Φαρισαῖος ἰδὼν

---

[16]R. T. France, *The Gospel of Mark*, NIGTC (Eerdmans: Grand Rapids, 2002), 282; cf. Guelich, *Mark*, 365; Robert H. Gundry, *Mark: A Commentary on His Apology for the Cross* (Grand Rapids: Eerdmans, 1993), 360. The translation of JB ("sprinkling themselves") follows the reading ῥαντίσωνται (ℵ B pc sa), which is less likely to be original; cf. Bruce M. Metzger, *A Textual Commentary on the Greek New Testament*, 2nd ed. (Stuttgart: United Bible Societies, 1994), 80.

[17]Thus Marcus, *Mark*, 1:442.

[18]Cf. Louis H. Feldman, *Josephus: Judean Antiquities, Books XVIII–XIX*, LCL (Cambridge: Harvard University Press, 1981 [1965]), 81 note b, who asserts that Josephus may have used two different forms—βάπτισμός and βάπτισις in A. J. 1:117 (the latter term is attested in Greek literature only in A.J. 1.117)—"since there was no established Greek word for baptism" (evidently understanding "baptism" as used in the Christian tradition). Contra Robert L. Webb, "John the Baptist and His Relationship to Jesus," in *Studying the Historical Jesus: Evaluations of the State of Current Research*, ed. B. Chilton and C. A. Evans, NTTS 19 (Leiden: Brill, 1994), 179–230, 188n25, who claims that neither the verb βαπτίζω nor the nouns βάπτισμα and βαπτισμός are "the usual terms used for a Jewish ritual bath"; the fact that he mentions as "exceptions" Mark 7:4; Luke 11:38; Heb. 9:10 undercuts his case.

ἐθαύμασεν ὅτι οὐ πρῶτον ἐβαπτίσθη πρὸ τοῦ ἀρίστου. ("While he was speaking, a Pharisee invited him to dine with him; so he went in and took his place at the table. The Pharisee was amazed to see that he did not first *wash* before dinner.")

The context of the invitation of a Pharisee who comments on Jesus' behavior suggests that βαπτίζω denotes ceremonial cleansing (sense 1b), as in the parallel passage Mark 7:3–4. This is recognized by the NASB ("ceremonially washed") and the NLT ("performing the hand-washing ceremony").[19] Glosses such as "purify" and "cleanse" express the ceremonial aspect of βαπτίζω better than "wash." The term can refer to the ceremonial washing of hands or to total immersion.

The Use of βαπτίζω for the Immersion Practiced by John

The next set of passages listed by BDAG concerns the activity of John, son of Zechariah and Elizabeth (Luke 1:5), who is called ὁ βαπτιστής[20] or ὁ βαπτίζων,[21] which can be translated as "the Immerser."[22] Apart from verbs that denote proclaiming a message of judgment and renewal through the coming One and verbs that denote exhorting people, John's activity is described with the verb βαπτίζω.[23] The following

[19]Cf. I. Howard Marshall, *The Gospel of Luke*, NIGTC (Grand Rapids: Eerdmans, 1978), 494; Joseph A. Fitzmyer, *The Gospel According to Luke*, 2 vols., AB 28 (Garden City, NY: Doubleday, 1981, 1985), 2:947; John Nolland, *Luke*, 3 vols., WBC 35A–C (Dallas: Word, 1989–1993), 2:663. Fitzmyer recognizes that more than the ceremonial washing of hands may be involved, i.e., that the Pharisee may have expected Jesus to immerse himself in a *miqveh* before eating dinner (663).
[20]Matt. 3:1; 11:11, 12; 14:2, 8; 16:14; 17:13; Mark 6:25; 8:28; Luke 7:20, 33; 9:19; cf. Josephus, *A. J.* 18.116.
[21]Mark 1:4; 6:14, 24, 25; 8:28. The participle βαπτίζων explains the function of John, while the substantival term βαπτιστής is more formal; cf. France, *Mark*, 65.
[22]Joan E. Taylor, *The Immerser: John the Baptist within Second Temple Judaism* (Grand Rapids: Eerdmans, 1997), 49–50. Note James D. G. Dunn, *Jesus Remembered*, Christianity in the Making 1 (Grand Rapids: Eerdmans, 2003), 356, who argues that the term ὁ βαπτιστής was coined in Greek for John, probably as translation of the Aramaic term *tab°la* (טבלא) used in descriptions of John's ministry, which presumably was a fresh usage as well. Dunn suggests that the new term was coined in recognition of John's uniqueness, which carries over into the English term "the Baptist." It should be recognized, however, that the rendition of Aramaic *tab°la* (טבלא) into Greek as ὁ βαπτιστής cannot be explained in terms of drawing a foreign word into another language denoting "something for which there is no adequate native equivalent" (356)—ὁ βαπτιστής is a direct translation of the Aramaic term, not a transliteration; it is an expression that communicated, for native Greek speakers, precisely the same action that the Aramaic term described.
[23]Matt. 3:6, 11, 13, 14, 16; Mark 1:4, 5, 8, 9; 6:14, 24; Luke 3:7, 12, 16, 21; 7:29, 30; John 1:25, 26, 28, 31, 33; 3:23; 10:40; Acts 1:5; 11:16; the noun τὸ βάπτισμα is used in Matt. 3:7;

two passages are representative for the description of John's activity in the Gospels and in the book of Acts.

> Matt. 3:5–6: τότε ἐξεπορεύετο πρὸς αὐτὸν Ἱεροσόλυμα καὶ πᾶσα ἡ Ἰουδαία καὶ πᾶσα ἡ περίχωρος τοῦ Ἰορδάνου, καὶ ἐβαπτίζοντο ἐν τῷ Ἰορδάνῃ ποταμῷ ὑπ' αὐτοῦ ἐξομολογούμενοι τὰς ἁμαρτίας αὐτῶν. ("Then the people of Jerusalem and all Judea were going out to him, and all the region along the Jordan, and they were *baptized* by him in the river Jordan, confessing their sins.")

> Mark 1:4–5: ἐγένετο Ἰωάννης ὁ βαπτίζων ἐν τῇ ἐρήμῳ καὶ κηρύσσων βάπτισμα μετανοίας εἰς ἄφεσιν ἁμαρτιῶν. καὶ ἐξεπορεύετο πρὸς αὐτὸν πᾶσα ἡ Ἰουδαία χώρα καὶ οἱ Ἱεροσολυμῖται πάντες, καὶ ἐβαπτίζοντο ὑπ' αὐτοῦ ἐν τῷ Ἰορδάνῃ ποταμῷ ἐξομολογούμενοι τὰς ἁμαρτίας αὐτῶν. ("John *the baptizer* appeared in the wilderness, proclaiming a *baptism* of repentance for the forgiveness of sins. And people from the whole Judean countryside and all the people of Jerusalem were going out to him, and were *baptized* by him in the river Jordan, confessing their sins.")

The translation of βαπτίζω with "baptize" in the passages that describe John's ministry is both universal[24] and unfortunate, the latter because it presupposes that the verb is a (Christian) technical term, and because it artificially separates John's activity from Jewish purification rites involving immersion in water. The results are statements like the following:

> John's distinctive rite was a new phenomenon. Ritual *washing* was common enough, both in the OT and increasingly in later Judaism (see on 7:3–4). It was a prominent element in the religious life of Qumran, and its importance in mainstream Judaism is indicated by the increasing number of *miqwā'ōt* (ritual immersion baths) which archaeological discovery is revealing in Jerusalem and elsewhere in Palestine, as well as by a whole tractate entitled *Miqwā'ōt* in the

---

21:25; Mark 1:4; 11:30; Luke 3:3; 7:29; 20:4; Acts 1:22; 10:37; 13:24; 18:25; 19:3, 4.

[24]ESV, GNB, JB, NASB, NET, NIV, NLT, NRSV, RSV, TNIV; cf. Stanley E. Porter, "Mark 1.4, Baptism and Translation," in *Baptism, the New Testament and the Church: Historical and Contemporary Studies in Honour of R. E. O. White*, ed. S. E. Porter and A. R. Cross, JSNTSup 171 (Sheffield: Sheffield Academic Press, 1999), 81–98, who addresses various matters relevant for the translation of Mark 1:4, particularly the translation theory of Eugene A. Nida and Charles R. Taber, *The Theory and Practice of Translation* (Leiden: Brill, 1969), but never raises the issue of what βαπτίζω or βάπτισμα *means*.

Mishnah. But these were all regular, repeated *washings*, whereas John was calling for a single, initiatory *baptism*, indicating the beginning of a new commitment. For this many believe that the most likely Jewish precedent is the ritual *cleansing by immersion* of a Gentile on becoming a proselyte. But John's *baptism* was for Jews; to ask them to undergo *the same initiatory ritual* as was required of a Gentile convert was a powerful statement of John's theology of the people of God, one which is reminiscent of the "remnant" theology of the prophets.[25]

While I agree with R. T. France's historical and theological analysis,[26] the move from Jewish "washings" and "cleansing by immersion" to John's "baptism" is confusing, particularly as he insists that the "cleansing by immersion" required of a Gentile proselyte, that is, a person converting to Judaism, represents "the same initiatory ritual"— evidently the "cleansing by immersion (in water)." Commentators who reject parallels between John's activity at the river Jordan and practices in the Qumran community or in proselyte baptism seem to be, at first sight, more justified to use the word *baptism* as a technical term: they can claim that "John was called 'the Baptist' because the specific form and meaning of his baptism was his own 'original creation.'"[27] However, the authors of the Gospels use βαπτίζω and the derivative βάπτισμα to describe John's activity at the river, a word choice that was readily understood by Greek-speaking readers in the sense of "to immerse" (or, in the middle form, "to be immersed") and "immersion," with the additional extended meaning of an immersion resulting in cleansing from moral and spiritual defilement. The authors of the Gospels do not create a new "technical term" when they use either the verb βαπτίζω or the noun βάπτισμα.[28]

---

[25]France, *Mark*, 66, emphasis mine.

[26]Note, however, the continuing dispute concerning the historical questions connected with proselyte baptism in the first century; cf. Robert L. Webb, *John the Baptizer and Prophet: A Socio-Historical Study*, JSNTSup 62 (Sheffield: JSOT, 1991), 122–28; Shaye J. D. Cohen, "The Rabbinic Conversion Ceremony [1990]," in *The Beginnings of Jewishness: Boundaries, Varieties, Uncertainties*, Hellenistic Culture and Society 31 (Berkeley: University of California Press, 1999), 198–238, here 222–25.

[27]Guelich, *Mark*, 18, quoting Philipp Vielhauer, "Johannes, der Täufer," in *Religion in Geschichte und Gegenwart* (Tübingen: Mohr Siebeck, 1957–62), 3:804–8, here 806.

[28]Edward W. Burrows, "Baptism in Mark and Luke," in *Baptism, the New Testament and the Church*, ed. Porter and Cross, 99–115, esp. 110, speaks of "the action of baptism as John the Baptist practised it," suggesting that the following ideas are inherent in John's action: "(1) Total commitment: as symbolized by the submersion of the whole body. (2) Complete cleansing: as

J. Marcus speaks of "ritual washings" in the Old Testament period, of "immersion in a ritual bath" required of proselytes who "thereby purged themselves of the uncleanness of their pagan life," of the "ritual bathing" of the members of the Qumran community, which was "linked with the end-time cleansing" and renewal effected by God's Spirit just as in "John's baptism."[29] The sudden switch from "washing" and "immersion" to "baptism" may find its explanation in Marcus's assertion that John's "*baptism*, however, departed from the Qumran pattern by being a onetime rite performed by a second party, not a continually repeated *self-immersion*."[30] The statement that "before the NT, the word [i.e., βαπτίζω] does not have the technical sense of an act of water initiation"[31] is correct if the focus is on the act or process of "initiation," and if it is related to Christian water baptism. However, it is confusing when applied to John, unless one assumes that he "initiated" people into a particular movement (which Marcus does not seem to claim).

The (often undeclared) assumption that *baptism* is a technical term leads to curious formulations. For example, R. L. Webb asserts that "John's baptism involved bathing, that is, an immersion,"[32] which is tantamount to saying that "John's immersion involved immersion." Similarly, E. Ferguson asserts that like the Jewish washings, including the baths of the Essenes and proselyte baptism, "John's baptism was an immersion."[33] If βαπτίζω and βάπτισμα indeed mean "to immerse" and "immersion" respectively, which Ferguson argues in his chapter on the meaning of the words from the βαπτ- root,[34] this statement reads, "John's immersion was an immersion," a tautological statement triggered by the (sudden) shift from translating βαπτίζω as "to immerse, dip, plunge" to treating the term as a *terminus technicus* that is transliterated rather than translated.

---

symbolized by the ritual washing in water. (3) A new beginning: as symbolized by being raised from the water."

[29]Marcus, *Mark*, 154–55.

[30]Ibid., 155, emphasis mine.

[31]Ibid., 150.

[32]Webb, "John the Baptist," 188; cf. 188n25 for the meaning of βαπτίζειν.

[33]Everett Ferguson, *Baptism in the Early Church: History, Theology, and Liturgy in the First Five Centuries* (Grand Rapids: Eerdmans, 2008), 88; cf. 95: "John's baptism" was "an immersion."

[34]Ibid., 38–59.

While the number of ritual immersions and the presence of a person assisting in the process of immersion varies when Old Testament and Jewish immersion rites and the ministry of John are compared, the action itself—described by the same Greek verb—did not change: people who listened to and accepted John's message, who repented of their sins, and who were willing to receive the One who would bring to fulfillment God's promises that his Spirit would be poured out on all flesh, were immersed in water. Note that John 3:25–26 represents John and his practice of immersing people in the river Jordan as belonging to the Jewish tradition of purifications.[35] There does not seem to be any need to use a different English term (let alone a Greek loan word) when speaking of Jewish immersions in water for purification and of John's immersions in water for purification.

In the passages that describe John's message and activity, βαπτίζω is used with the extended meaning of "to make ceremonially clean" (1b); that is, in the sense of "to immerse in water symbolizing, or effecting, the removal of moral or spiritual defilement." There is no reason why one should not translate βαπτίζω in these passages in terms of the basic meaning "to immerse," since Matthew 3:6/Mark 1:5 specify that the action of βαπτίζειν took place "in the river Jordan" (ἐν τῷ Ἰορδάνῃ ποταμῷ). The translation "they were baptized by him in the river Jordan" invites readers to introduce their particular (ecclesial) understanding of the term *baptize* as a technical Christian term. The statement "they were immersed by him in the river Jordan" communicates clearly and unambiguously what happened.[36] Alternately, in order to highlight the extended meaning of ritual purification, one can translate "they were cleansed by him in the river Jordan."[37]

The Use of βαπτίζω for the Immersion Practiced by Jesus and His Disciples

The third group of passages that use βαπτίζω listed in BDAG, all in the Gospel of John, concern "cleansing performed by Jesus."

---

[35] Cf. C. K. Barrett, *The Gospel According to St. John*, 2nd ed. (London: SPCK; Philadelphia: Westminster, 1978), 219.

[36] Also note Mark 1:9, 10, which describe Jesus being "immersed by John in the Jordan" (ἐβαπτίσθη εἰς τὸν Ἰορδάνην) and "coming up out of the water" (ἀναβαίνων ἐκ τοῦ ὕδατος); cf. Matt. 3:16.

[37] On the meaning of John's practice of immersing people in the river Jordan, cf. Robert L. Webb, "Jesus' Baptism: Its Historicity and Implications," *BBR* 10 (2000): 261–309; Dunn, *Jesus Remembered*, 339–82; Ferguson, *Baptism*, 93–95.

John 3:22, 25–26: Μετὰ ταῦτα ἦλθεν ὁ Ἰησοῦς καὶ οἱ μαθηταὶ αὐτοῦ εἰς τὴν Ἰουδαίαν γῆν, καὶ ἐκεῖ διέτριβεν μετ' αὐτῶν καὶ ἐβάπτιζεν.... Ἐγένετο οὖν ζήτησις ἐκ τῶν μαθητῶν Ἰωάννου μετὰ Ἰουδαίου περὶ καθαρισμοῦ. καὶ ἦλθον πρὸς τὸν Ἰωάννην καὶ εἶπον αὐτῷ, Ῥαββί, ὃς ἦν μετὰ σοῦ πέραν τοῦ Ἰορδάνου, ᾧ σὺ μεμαρτύρηκας, ἴδε οὗτος βαπτίζει καὶ πάντες ἔρχονται πρὸς αὐτόν. ("After this Jesus and his disciples went into the Judean countryside, and he spent some time there with them and *baptized*. . . . Now a discussion about purification arose between John's disciples and a Jew. They came to John and said to him, 'Rabbi, the one who was with you across the Jordan, to whom you testified, here he is *baptizing*, and all are going to him.'")

The reference to a discussion about "purification" (καθαρισμός) between disciples of John and other Jews clarifies that Jesus' and his disciples' activity[38] involved immersion in water as a sign of repentance.[39] This demonstrates that both the basic meaning of βαπτίζω as "to immerse" (sense 1) and the extended sense "to cleanse, purify," which denotes ritual purification (sense 1b), are present. The assertion of A. Köstenberger that "the issue of ritual purification, while of significant interest to first-century Jews . . . clearly is peripheral to the ministries of Jesus and John the Baptist,"[40] makes sense only if "ritual" is understood in the context of the specific stipulations regarding purification in the Mosaic Law and in Jewish tradition. If the immersion in water administered by John and by Jesus (and his disciples) signaled removal of moral and spiritual defilement, most scholars would describe the use of βαπτίζω here also as "ritual." In a similarly unclear vein, E. Ferguson asserts on the one hand that, like the Jewish washings, including the baths of the Essenes and proselyte baptism,

---

[38]Cf. John 4:1; as regards the comment in 4:2 that "it was not Jesus himself but his disciples who baptized" (NRSV) note the explanation of D. A. Carson, *The Gospel According to John* (Grand Rapids: Eerdmans, 1991), 215: "Jesus himself did not baptize, but his disciples did—or, more pedantically, Jesus baptized only by using his disciples as the agents." Craig S. Keener, *The Gospel of John: A Commentary*, 2 vols. (Peabody, MA: Hendrickson, 2003), 1:578, suggests that 4:2 might help explain why the practice of baptism by Jesus and his disciples does not appear in the synoptic tradition.

[39]Cf. Keener, *John*, 578: "If John demanded immersion as a sign of repentance and Jesus regarded him as a prophet, presumably Jesus would have carried on the same tradition." See also Taylor, *The Immerser*, 299.

[40]Andreas J. Köstenberger, *John*, BECNT (Grand Rapids: Baker, 2004), 136.

John's baptism was an immersion. Unlike all of them, it was an administered rite and not a self-immersion. . . . John's baptism, moreover,
shared with all the Jewish practices the feature of purification or
cleansing. It differed from them, however, in being an eschatological
rather than a ceremonial or ritual purification.[41]

If John's purification was "an administered rite," there is no reason
why it cannot be called "ritual," a term that is not invalidated by the
eschatological dimension of John's message. There is again no need
to use the loan word "to baptize" in translating these texts: both the
gloss "to immerse" (sense 1) and the glosses "to cleanse, purify" (sense
1b) are translation options for βαπτίζω in these passages.

The Use of βαπτίζω Designating Christian Water Baptism

The fourth group of passages listed in BDAG concern "the Christian
sacrament of initiation after Jesus' death," with the suggested gloss
"baptize in or with respect to the name of someone."[42] As the reality
and the practice of what we call Christian water baptism involved
repentance and confession of faith in Jesus as Israel's Messiah and
Savior, the forgiveness of sins, and the bestowal of the Holy Spirit as
the Spirit of prophecy (cf. Acts 2:38),[43] the apostolic practice that is
described with the verb βαπτίζω and the nouns βάπτισμα and βαπτισμός
is a unique event. What we are concerned with in this section is not the
meaning of Christian water baptism in terms of its connection with the
death, resurrection, and exaltation of Jesus and with the requirement
of repentance and faith in Jesus as Israel's Messiah and Savior and
the bestowal of the Holy Spirit.[44] Our concern is the meaning of the
Greek term βαπτίζω and its translation into English. We will discuss
five passages that are either representative for other passages or "classical" passages for the understanding of Christian baptism.

---

[41]Ferguson, *Baptism*, 88.
[42]BDAG s.v. βαπτίζω 2c, with reference to Mark 16:16; Acts 2:41; 8:12–13, 36, 38; 9:18; 10:47;
16:15, 33; 18:8; 22:16; 1 Cor. 1:14–17; also Matt 28:19; Acts 8:16; 19:5; 1 Cor. 1:13, 15; also
Acts 2:38 (variant reading); 10:48; Rom. 6:3; 1 Cor. 12:13; 15:29; Gal. 3:27.
[43]Cf. Max M. B. Turner, *Power from on High: The Spirit in Israel's Restoration and Witness in
Luke-Acts*, Journal of Pentecostal Theology Supplement 9 (Sheffield: Sheffield Academic Press,
1996). On questions of authenticity regarding Luke's account of baptisms in Acts, cf. Friedrich
Avemarie, *Die Tauferzählungen der Apostelgeschichte: Theologie und Geschichte*, WUNT 139
(Tübingen: Mohr Siebeck, 2002).
[44]Ferguson, *Baptism*, 165, describes the understanding that Paul shared with the early church in
Jerusalem in terms of baptism being "a bath of cleansing, into the name of Jesus, and in unity
with the work of the Spirit."

Matt. 28:19: πορευθέντες οὖν μαθητεύσατε πάντα τὰ ἔθνη, βαπτίζοντες αὐτοὺς εἰς τὸ ὄνομα τοῦ πατρὸς καὶ τοῦ υἱοῦ καὶ τοῦ ἁγίου πνεύματος. ("Go therefore and make disciples of all nations, *baptizing* them in the name of the Father and of the Son and of the Holy Spirit.")

Jesus' post-resurrection commission in Matthew 28:19–20[45] focuses on the missionary work of taking the good news of God's sending of Jesus, Israel's Messiah and Savior, to all nations and of teaching new converts who have become followers of Jesus. Although theoretically possible, it is unlikely that βαπτίζω in verse 19 has the metaphorical meaning of "overpower" (sense 2).[46] In the context of Jewish washings and in the context of the activity of John and of Jesus and his disciples, who immersed people in water as a sign of repentance with a view to the forgiveness of sins and as an expression of preparation for the reception of God's Spirit as cleansing power, βαπτίζω most plausibly denotes "immerse" (in water) in the extended sense of "cleanse, purify" (sense 1b). This extended sense is confirmed by the following prepositional phrase, "in the name of the Father and of the Son and of the Holy Spirit." The phrase εἰς τὸ ὄνομα ("into the name")[47] can be taken as expressing transfer (as in commercial and legal documents), communicating the idea of "into the ownership of," or, in the context of the Hebrew and Aramaic expressions לשום/לשם, it can be taken as expressing a relationship, communicating the idea of "in order that they may enter into relationship with." While these two interpretations do not exclude each other and at the end lead to the same result,[48] the lack of a consensus suggests that it is wise to interpret the phrase

---

[45]In addition to the commentaries, cf. Eckhard J. Schnabel, *Early Christian Mission*, 2 vols. (Downers Grove, IL: InterVarsity, 2004), 1:348–67, for critical, grammatical, and missiological matters.

[46]This sense is also rendered unlikely in that the reality that overpowers a person is usually expressed with a dative, not with the preposition εἰς.

[47]Note other passages that construe the terms βαπτίζω and βαπτισμός with the preposition εἰς and a reference to the "name" (ὄνομα) of the Lord (Acts 8:16), the Lord Jesus (Acts 19:5), Christ Jesus (Rom. 6:3), Christ (Gal. 3:27). Other prepositions linked with βαπτίζω and βαπτισμός and with ὄνομα are ἐπί (Acts 2:38) and ἐν (Acts 10:48). Cf. Lars Hartman, *Into the Name of the Lord Jesus: Baptism in the Early Church* (Edinburgh: T&T Clark, 1997), 37–50; Hartman, Art. ὄνομα, in *Exegetical Dictionary of the New Testament*, ed. Horst Balz and Gerhard Schneider, 3 vols. (Grand Rapids: Eerdmans, 1990–1993), 2:519–22; Avemarie, *Tauferzählungen*, 26–43; Ferguson, *Baptism*, 182–83; see also H. Bietenhard, "ὄνομα," *TDNT* 5:242–81, who emphasizes the Semitic influence on the syntax (271).

[48]Hartman, *Into the Name of the Lord Jesus*, 41n23.

εἰς τὸ ὄνομα in terms of a semantic minimum denoting "with reference to." The expression "in the name of" names the one called on. In the LXX, the formulation "in the name of the Lord" (ἐν ὀνόματι κυρίου)[49] is used in connection with lifting up one's hand, praising or blessing Yahweh (κύριος).[50] In the narrative context of the Gospel of Matthew, where the βαπτ- word group was used only with reference to John son of Zechariah and his message and practice,[51] the phrase εἰς τὸ ὄνομα may serve mainly to distinguish the immersion that Jesus' followers are to administer from the immersion practiced by John.[52] The immersion in water to be practiced by Jesus' disciples receives its basic reference and meaning from the one divine name (note that ὄνομα is singular), which is shared by God the Father, by Jesus the Son, and by the Holy Spirit.[53] It relates the person who is immersed to God the Father, who revealed himself through Jesus, and to the Son who bestows the Holy Spirit. The verbal expression of the meaning and purpose of the immersion in water was presumably made by the person who was immersed, as a confession of faith. If translations continue to use the gloss "baptize" for βαπτίζω, the translators should at least include a note explaining that βαπτίζω denotes "to immerse" (here in water), signifying spiritual cleansing with reference to and on the basis of the new relationship to God, who revealed himself through Jesus, the messianic Son, through whom people receive the Holy Spirit.

Acts 2:37–41: Ἀκούσαντες δὲ κατενύγησαν τὴν καρδίαν εἶπόν τε πρὸς τὸν Πέτρον καὶ τοὺς λοιποὺς ἀποστόλους· τί ποιήσωμεν, ἄνδρες ἀδελφοί; Πέτρος δὲ πρὸς αὐτούς· μετανοήσατε, φησίν, καὶ βαπτισθήτω ἕκαστος ὑμῶν ἐπὶ τῷ ὀνόματι Ἰησοῦ Χριστοῦ εἰς ἄφεσιν τῶν ἁμαρτιῶν ὑμῶν καὶ λήμψεσθε τὴν δωρεὰν τοῦ ἁγίου πνεύματος. ὑμῖν γάρ ἐστιν ἡ ἐπαγγελία καὶ τοῖς τέκνοις ὑμῶν καὶ πᾶσιν τοῖς εἰς μακρὰν ὅσους ἂν προσκαλέσηται κύριος ὁ θεὸς ἡμῶν. ἑτέροις τε

[49]The LXX uses the prepositions ἐν and ἐπί in constructions with ὄνομα without a difference in meaning; Avemarie, *Tauferzählungen*, 36.
[50]Ps. 129:8 (LXX 128:8); cf. Ps. 63:5 (LXX 62:5); 105:3 (LXX 104:3). Cf. Adelheid Ruck-Schröder, *Der Name Gottes und der Name Jesu. Eine neutestamentliche Studie*, WMANT 80 (Neukirchen-Vluyn: Neukirchener, 1998), with a survey of scholarship, 11–63.
[51]Matt. 3:1, 6, 7, 11, 13, 14, 16; 11:11, 12; 14:2, 8; 16:14; 17:13; 21:25.
[52]Cf. Avemarie, *Tauferzählungen*, 34, with regard to the significance of the phrase εἰς τὸ ὄνομα in Acts. The people immersed by John were not immersed "in the name of John."
[53]Cf. William D. Davies and Dale C. Allison, *The Gospel According to Saint Matthew*, 3 vols., ICC (Edinburgh: T&T Clark, 1988–1997), 3:685–86, with reference to John 17:11 and Phil. 2:9, noting that there are no comparable texts regarding the Father giving his name to the Spirit.

λόγοις πλείοσιν διεμαρτύρατο καὶ παρεκάλει αὐτοὺς λέγων, σώθητε ἀπὸ τῆς γενεᾶς τῆς σκολιᾶς ταύτης. οἱ μὲν οὖν ἀποδεξάμενοι τὸν λόγον αὐτοῦ <u>ἐβαπτίσθησαν</u>, καὶ προσετέθησαν ἐν τῇ ἡμέρᾳ ἐκείνῃ ψυχαὶ ὡσεὶ τρισχίλιαι. ("Now when they heard this, they were cut to the heart and said to Peter and to the other apostles, 'Brothers, what should we do?' Peter said to them, 'Repent, and be *baptized* every one of you in the name of Jesus Christ so that your sins may be forgiven; and you will receive the gift of the Holy Spirit. For the promise is for you, for your children, and for all who are far away, everyone whom the Lord our God calls to him.' And he testified with many other arguments and exhorted them, saying, 'Save yourselves from this corrupt generation.' So those who welcomed his message were *baptized*, and that day about three thousand persons were added.")

In the context of Peter's sermon in Acts 2:14–36, the exhortation to repent means that the listeners regret their (active or passive) involvement in the crucifixion of Jesus, that they turn away from their former, negative attitude concerning Jesus, that they believe in Jesus as the promised Messiah and exalted Lord. The last emphasis is connected with the imperative βαπτισθήτω, which happens "in the name of Jesus the Messiah." In view of the fact that Peter's audience includes Diaspora Jews who were visiting Jerusalem as pilgrims attending the festival of Pentecost, they would have understood the term βαπτίζω—whether the Aramaic equivalent, or the Greek term—in the sense of "to be immersed in water," expressing cleansing from moral and spiritual defilement (sense 1b).[54]

Peter expects listeners who repent to go to an immersion pool and let themselves be immersed in water as a sign of their repentance, of being cleansed from their sin and guilt in the name of Jesus, and of the bestowal of the Holy Spirit. The importance of immersion for purification in Second Temple Judaism explains why numerous *miqvaot* have been discovered in Jerusalem throughout the city, as well as on and near the Temple Mount.[55] Among the six large pools were the Pool

---

[54]Cf. C. K. Barrett, *The Acts of the Apostles*, 2 vols., ICC (Edinburgh: T&T Clark, 1994, 1998), 2:717: "Baptism was a bath and could therefore be associated with cleansing" (commenting on Acts 15:9; in his comments on 2:38, 41, he does not explain the meaning of the term βαπτίζω).

[55]Cf. Eyal Regev, "The Ritual Baths Near the Temple Mount and Extra-Purification Before Entering the Temple Courts," *IEJ* 55 (2005): 194–204; Yonatan Adler, "The Ritual Baths Near the Temple Mount and Extra-Purification Before Entering the Temple Courts: A Reply to Eyal Regev," *IEJ* 56 (2006): 209–15; Shimon Gibson, "The Pool of Bethesda in Jerusalem and

of Siloam and the Pool of Bethesda. The Pool of Siloam, which was discovered in excavations in 2004 at the junction of the Tyropoeon Valley and the Kidron Valley, had a trapezoidal shape and measured 40 by 60 by 70 meters (ca. 130 by 195 by 230 feet). The Pool of Bethesda was located in the northeast section of the city in the area of the Sheep Gate (on the grounds of the Church of St. Anne); it had two large basins surrounded on four sides by colonnaded halls; the northern pool (53 by 40 meters, ca. 174 by 130 feet) served as the upper reservoir or *otzar*;[56] the southern pool (47 by 52 meters, ca. 154 by 170 feet) was used for immersion, as suggested by the series of steps extending down along the entire western side of the pool, with sets of steps connecting several landings.[57] These landings were capable of accommodating large numbers of people entering and leaving the water.[58] According to the stipulations recorded in the Mishnah, the persons who enter a *miqveh* disrobe and completely immerse themselves in the water.

The passive voice (βαπτισθήτω) indicates that the new converts would not be immersing themselves, as Jews were in the practice of doing, but would be immersed by one of the 120 followers of Jesus (1:15; 2:1). They would thereby confess their former rejection of Jesus and express their new faith in Jesus as Messiah and exalted Lord. Peter expected the Jews of Jerusalem and the visitors from the Jewish Diaspora communities—those who were prepared to repent and to

---

Jewish Purification Practices of the Second Temple Period," *Proche-Orient chrétien* 55 (2005): 270–93, 280–83, argues that the *miqvaot* proper on the Temple Mount, which were relatively small, must have been used "for the select immersion of Temple officials, dignitaries, or other people of special status" (281).

[56] An *otzar*, built adjacent to the *miqveh*, was a reserve pool filled with "living water" that could be transferred to the *miqveh* by opening a channel. For the archaeological evidence see Benjamin G. Wright, "Baths: Interpreting the Digs and the Texts: Some Issues in the Social History of Second Temple Judaism," in *The Archaeology of Israel: Constructing the Past, Interpreting the Present*, ed. N. A. Silberman and D. B. Small, JSOTSup 237 (Sheffield: Sheffield Academic Press, 1997), 190–214; Jodi Magness, *The Archaeology of Qumran and the Dead Sea Scrolls*, Studies in the Dead Sea Scrolls and Related Literature (Grand Rapids: Eerdmans, 2002), 134–62; Gibson, "Pool of Bethesda," 270–83; Jonathan D. Lawrence, *Washing in Water: Trajectories of Ritual Bathing in the Hebrew Bible and Second Temple Literature*, SBL Academia Biblica 23 (Atlanta: SBL, 2006), 155–83, 206–17.

[57] Cf. Gibson, "Pool of Bethesda," 283–88. Gibson argues that the Pool of Bethesda was a "well planned building initiative" probably built "before the construction of the new quarter on the Bezetha Hill and most likely at the time of Herod the Great, perhaps circa 25 BC, when the major building activities relating to the rebuilding of the Temple Mount were first initiated" (286).

[58] Cf. Urban C. von Wahlde, "Archaeology and John's Gospel," in *Jesus and Archaeology*, ed. J. H. Charlesworth (Grand Rapids: Eerdmans, 2006), 523–86, here 562–65.

accept Jesus as the promised Messiah and Savior—to be immersed in one of the immersion pools in Jerusalem: not for purification in preparation for participation in the temple cult, but for purification "in the name of Jesus the Messiah" (ἐπὶ τῷ ὀνόματι 'Ἰησοῦ). This was a new, unprecedented feature of immersion for the purpose of purification. Jews who immersed themselves may invoke the name of Yahweh, but they did not invoke the name of Moses, or the name of John son of Zechariah (the "Baptist"). In Acts 2:38, the preposition ἐπί may refer to pronouncing the name of Jesus in acknowledgment of Peter's proclamation that Jesus is the exalted Lord and Israel's promised Messiah (2:36).[59]

There is no reason why βαπτίζω in Acts 2:38, 41 should not be translated with the basic meaning of the verb (sense 1) "to immerse" ("Repent, and *be immersed* every one of you in the name of Jesus Christ so that your sins may be forgiven; and you will receive the gift of the Holy Spirit. . . . So those who welcomed his message *were immersed*"), or with the extended meaning (sense 1b) "to cleanse, purify" ("Repent, and *be cleansed* every one of you in the name of Jesus Christ so that your sins may be forgiven; and you will receive the gift of the Holy Spirit. . . . So those who welcomed his message *were cleansed*").

> Acts 8:36–39: ὡς δὲ ἐπορεύοντο κατὰ τὴν ὁδόν, ἦλθον ἐπί τι ὕδωρ, καί φησιν ὁ εὐνοῦχος· ἰδοὺ ὕδωρ· τί κωλύει με βαπτισθῆναι; καὶ ἐκέλευσεν στῆναι τὸ ἅρμα, καὶ κατέβησαν ἀμφότεροι εἰς τὸ ὕδωρ ὅ τε Φίλιππος καὶ ὁ εὐνοῦχος, καὶ ἐβάπτισεν αὐτόν. ὅτε δὲ ἀνέβησαν ἐκ τοῦ ὕδατος, πνεῦμα κυρίου ἥρπασεν τὸν Φίλιππον, καὶ οὐκ εἶδεν αὐτὸν οὐκέτι ὁ εὐνοῦχος· ἐπορεύετο γὰρ τὴν ὁδὸν αὐτοῦ χαίρων. ("As they were going along the road, they came to some water; and the eunuch said, 'Look, here is water! What is to prevent me from being *baptized*?' He commanded the chariot to stop, and both of them, Philip and the eunuch, went down into the water, and Philip *baptized* him. When they came up out of the water, the Spirit of the Lord snatched Philip away; the eunuch saw him no more, and went on his way rejoicing.")

The description of the Ethiopian's baptism provides more details about the manner in which the ritual was practiced than any other

---

[59] Cf. Ferguson, *Baptism*, 168–69.

passage in the New Testament. The medium in which the rite expressing conversion-initiation[60] takes places is water (ὕδωρ, v. 36). As the
carriage of the Ethiopian official travels on the road from Jerusalem
to Gaza, the reference to "some water" (τι ὕδωρ) could refer to a
stream[61] or a pool. Both the preacher who has proclaimed the good
news of Jesus and the convert who has accepted the message go down
into the water (κατέβησαν ἀμφότεροι εἰς τὸ ὕδωρ, v. 38). The preacher
immerses the convert in the water (ἐβάπτισεν αὐτόν, v. 38).[62] The
preacher and the convert come up out of the water (ἀνέβησαν ἐκ
τοῦ ὕδατος, v. 39). Luke's description shows that βαπτίζω means "to
immerse" (sense 1). In the context of the other references to βαπτίζω
in Acts, the extended meaning (sense 1b) denoting "to cleanse, purify"
may be present as well, although this is less clear here since βαπτίζω
is not linked explicitly with the name of Jesus.[63]

Rom. 6:3–5: ἢ ἀγνοεῖτε ὅτι ὅσοι ἐβαπτίσθημεν εἰς Χριστὸν Ἰησοῦν
εἰς τὸν θάνατον αὐτοῦ ἐβαπτίσθημεν; συνετάφημεν οὖν αὐτῷ διὰ
τοῦ βαπτίσματος εἰς τὸν θάνατον, ἵνα ὥσπερ ἠγέρθη Χριστὸς ἐκ
νεκρῶν διὰ τῆς δόξης τοῦ πατρός, οὕτως καὶ ἡμεῖς ἐν καινότητι
ζωῆς περιπατήσωμεν. εἰ γὰρ σύμφυτοι γεγόναμεν τῷ ὁμοιώματι τοῦ

[60]The term was coined by James D. G. Dunn, *Baptism in the Holy Spirit: A Re-examination
of the New Testament Teaching on the Gift of the Spirit in Relation to Pentecostalism Today*
(London: SCM, 1970), 5–7.

[61]There is sufficient precipitation on the coastal plain in winter and spring to produce intermittent streams of water; cf. Kirsopp Lake and Henry J. Cadbury, *The Acts of the Apostles:
English Translation and Commentary*, ed. F. J. Foakes-Jackson and K. Lake, The Beginnings
of Christianity 1/4 (London: Macmillan, 1933), 98. See Fred L. Horton and Jeffrey A. Blakely,
"'Behold, Water!' Tell el-Hesi and the Baptism of the Ethiopian Eunuch (Acts 8,26–40)," *RB*
107 (2000): 56–71, who suggest Wadi el-Hesi located north of Gaza. The older tradition
that localized a "well of Philip" in Beth Sur (En Dirweh) north of Hebron is geographically
implausible.

[62]It has been suggested that if the body of water was an intermittent stream resulting from
recent rains, there may not have been sufficient water for immersion, and baptism may have
been practiced by effusion (sprinkling), as allowed by the Didache in cases where running
water was not available (*Did.* 7:1–3); cf. I. Howard Marshall, "The Meaning of the Verb 'Baptize,'" in *Dimensions of Baptism: Biblical and Theological Studies*, ed. S. E. Porter and A. R.
Cross, JSNTSup 234 (London: Sheffield Academic Press, 2002), 8–24, esp. 18–23. Luke's vivid
description indicates that "a dipping administered by Philip is the most natural explanation"
(Ferguson, *Baptism*, 173).

[63]This is "remedied" by readings that insert a v. 37 into the text ("And Philip said, 'If you believe
with all your heart, you may.' And he replied, 'I believe that Jesus Christ is the Son of God'";
cf. Irenaeus, *Haer.* 3.12.8, and codices E 36. 323. 453. 945. 1739. 1891 *pc*). The verse is not
likely to be original; cf. Metzger, *Textual Commentary*, 315–16; see the recent discussion of
Friedrich W. Horn, "Apg 8,37, der Westliche Text und die frühchristliche Tauftheologie," in
The Book of Acts as Church History: Text, Textual Traditions and Ancient Interpretations, ed.
T. Nicklas and M. Tilly, BZNW 120 (Berlin: de Gruyter, 2003), 225–39.

θανάτου αὐτοῦ, ἀλλὰ καὶ τῆς ἀναστάσεως ἐσόμεθα. ("Do you not know that all of us who have been *baptized* into Christ Jesus were *baptized* into his death? Therefore we have been buried with him by *baptism* into death, so that, just as Christ was raised from the dead by the glory of the Father, so we too might walk in newness of life. For if we have been united with him in a death like his, we will certainly be united with him in a resurrection like his.")

Most English translations render βαπτίζω in verse 3 with the transliterated term *baptize*; an exception is the NLT, which translates it "joined with," and Wuest has "placed in."[64] C. E. B. Cranfield's comment on the phrase ὅσοι ἐβαπτίσθημεν εἰς Χριστὸν Ἰησοῦν is typical: "All that Paul wishes to convey in this clause is the simple fact that the persons concerned have received Christian baptism."[65] Similarly, D. J. Moo asserts that "by the date of Romans, 'baptize' had become almost a technical expression for the rite of Christian initiation by water, and this is surely the meaning the Roman Christians would have given the word."[66] He argues that since ten out of eleven occurrences of βαπτίζω denote Christian water baptism (with the exception of 1 Cor. 10:2), the same meaning should be assumed here. Now, if βαπτίζω was "almost" a technical expression, it should probably not be treated as such. Also, even if it could be established that Paul's use of βαπτίζω denotes without exception the rite of Christian water baptism, it does not follow that the term βαπτίζω has lost the basic meaning "to immerse" or the metaphorical meaning "to be overwhelmed" for Paul's readers, who would have regularly used the term in their everyday lives with the basic meaning "to immerse" and the various extended and metaphorical senses.

---

[64]NLT: "Or have you forgotten that when we were joined with Christ Jesus in baptism, we joined him in his death?" Kenneth S. Wuest, *The New Testament: An Expanded Translation* (Grand Rapids: Eerdmans, 1961 [1956–1959]): "Do you not know that all we who were placed in Christ Jesus, in His death were placed?" Peterson, *Message*, translates 6:3–5 as follows: "That's what baptism into the life of Jesus means. When we are lowered into the water, it is like the burial of Jesus; when we are raised up out of the water, it is like the resurrection of Jesus. Each of us is raised into a light-filled world by our Father so that we can see where we're going in our new grace-sovereign country."

[65]C. E. B. Cranfield, *The Epistle to the Romans*, 2 vols., ICC (Edinburgh: T&T Clark, 1975, 1979), 1:301.

[66]Douglas J. Moo, *The Epistle to the Romans*, NICNT (Grand Rapids: Eerdmans, 1996), 359; for the following observation see 359n38.

Many commentators explain Romans 6:3 without clarifying the meaning of the word βαπτίζω.[67] T. R. Schreiner does not specifically comment on the meaning of βαπτίζω, but speaks of "incorporation into Christ" and of being "plunged into his death, immersed together with him in it."[68] Similarly, K. Haacker asserts that Paul presents Jesus' death "as a space into which we enter."[69] While a few commentators show interest in the meaning of βαπτίζω, they often do not relate it to Paul's statement,[70] or if they do, give explanations that are one-sided or too narrow.[71]

In comments that seek to interpret Romans 6:3 in terms of the basic meaning of βαπτίζω, H. Lietzmann, O. Kuss, and U. Wilckens insist that ἐβαπτίσθημεν connotes, apart from the reference to the tradition of Christian water baptism, the concrete meaning "to immerse"[72]—the convert who is immersed in water is placed into the event of Jesus' death.[73] After asserting that "baptize" is not a translation but a trans-

---

[67]Recently Robert Jewett, *Romans*, Hermeneia (Minneapolis: Fortress, 2007), 396–98. When he asserts that "their baptism was some form of incorporation into Christ" (397), he could have pointed out that "incorporation" is an extension of the meaning "immersion" to a metaphorical sense of the Greek term.

[68]Thomas R. Schreiner, *Romans*, BECNT 6 (Grand Rapids: Baker, 1998), 307, 308.

[69]Klaus Haacker, *Der Brief des Paulus an die Römer*, THKNT 6 (Leipzig: Evangelische Verlagsanstalt, 1999), 128: "wie ein Raum, in den man hineinkommt."

[70]Cf. Joseph A. Fitzmyer, *Romans*, AB 33 (New York: Doubleday, 1993), 433, who defines βαπτίζω as "dip into, wash, plunge into" but relates this meaning only indirectly to Paul's statement when he asserts that the preposition εἰς connotes "the *initial* movement of introduction or incorporation by which one is born to life 'in Christ'" (emphasis Fitzmyer); "introduction" and "incorporation" could be taken as metaphorical meanings of βαπτίζω.

[71]Cf. Leon Morris, *The Epistle to the Romans* (Grand Rapids: Eerdmans; Leicester, UK: Inter-Varsity, 1988), 246–47, who comments on the meaning of βαπτίζω, but wants to distinguish between the meanings "immerse" and "dip" and asserts that the verb "evoked associations of violence," concluding that Paul uses the term to describe Christian initiation (baptism) as "death to a whole way of life." Some of the extended senses of βαπτίζω connote violence (senses 1d "drown, sink" and 1g "slaughter, kill"), but violence is not a general connotation of the Greek term. Joseph Shulam and Hilary Le Cornu, *A Commentary on the Jewish Roots of Romans* (Baltimore: Lederer/Messianic Jewish Publishers, 1997), 213, assert that "the primary meaning" of βαπτίζω is "to dye," concluding for Rom. 6:3 that as a cloth "takes on" the color of the dye, so "a person can be said to 'put on' Yeshua when they are 'dyed.'" The problem with this interpretation is that the connotation "to dye" is merely one of several extended senses of βάπτω (not of βαπτίζω).

[72]Hans Lietzmann, *An die Römer*, HNT (Tübingen: Mohr Siebeck, 1933 [1906]), 65; Otto Kuss, *Der Römerbrief übersetzt und erklärt*, 3 vols. (Regensburg: Pustet, 1957–1959), 1:298; Ulrich Wilckens, *Der Brief an die Römer*, EKK 6/1–3 (Neukirchen-Vluyn: Neukirchener; Einsiedeln: Benziger, 1978–1982), 2:11; also Peter Stuhlmacher, *Der Brief an die Römer*, NTD 6 (Göttingen: Vandenhoeck & Ruprecht, 1989), 85; Stuhlmacher, *Biblische Theologie des Neuen Testaments. Band 1: Grundlegung. Von Jesus zu Paulus*, 3rd ed. (Göttingen: Vandenhoeck & Ruprecht, 2005), 218–19.

[73]Wilckens, *Römer*, 2:11–12: "Die Übereignung des Täuflings an Christus bedeutet, daß er im Akt des Untertauchens hineingegeben wird in das Geschehen des Todes Christi." Cf. Ulrich

literation of βαπτίζω, K. S. Wuest defines the term as used by Paul in Romans 6:3, as "the introduction or placing of a person or thing into a new environment or into union with something else so as to alter its condition or its relationship to its previous environment or condition."[74] J. D. G. Dunn has made the case for understanding βαπτίζω in Romans 6:3 in a metaphorical sense, which he defines as "movement into in order to become involved with or part of."[75] He suggests that in the phrase ἐβαπτίσθημεν εἰς Χριστὸν Ἰησοῦν in verse 3, the verb βαπτίζω has a metaphorical meaning, stating that Paul "uses the imagery of immersion as a drowning to reinforce the point: their death by drowning was a sharing in Christ's death—as Jesus himself had hinted."[76] He thinks that it is the noun βάπτισμα in verse 4 that introduces the water rite that expresses the relationship between the metaphors (immersion/drowning and burial) and the rite itself (immersion in water).

For a proper understanding of Romans 6:1–11 it is important to recognize that Paul describes the spiritual reality of death to sin and life to God (v. 2) with a series of metaphors in verses 3–6:[77] "immersion" (βαπτίζω) into the Messiah Jesus (v. 3), signifying union with Jesus and with the reality of his death and resurrection; "fusion" (σύμφυτος) with the reality of Christ's death, which is effective in the present (v. 5), signifying union with the continuing growth and development that Jesus' death has made possible; "crucifixion" (συσταυροῦν) together

---

Wilckens, *Theologie des Neuen Testaments*, 4 vols. (Neukirchen-Vluyn: Neukirchener, 2002–2009), I/3:197: baptism in the name of Jesus the Messiah has resulted in the reality that "we have been immersed 'into his death'" (noting in note 76 the context of the immersion of the baptizand into water); see also II/2:19, 23.

[74] Kenneth S. Wuest, *Romans in the Greek New Testament for the English Reader*, Wuest's Word Studies in the Greek New Testament (Grand Rapids: Eerdmans, 1955), 96; he continues, "It refers to the act of God introducing a believing sinner into vital union with Jesus Christ, in order that that believer might have the power of his sinful nature broken and the divine nature implanted through his identification with Christ in His death, burial, and resurrection, thus altering the condition and relationship of that sinner with regard to his previous state and environment, bringing him into a new environment, the kingdom of God."

[75] James D. G. Dunn, *Romans*, 2 vols., WBC 38 (Dallas: Word, 1988), 1:311; cf. Dunn, *Baptism*, 140–41; Dunn, *The Theology of Paul the Apostle* (Grand Rapids: Eerdmans, 1998), 447–52. See now the discussion of Sorin Sabou, *Between Horror and Hope: Paul's Metaphorical Language of Death in Romans 6:1–11*, Paternoster Biblical Monographs (Milton Keynes: Paternoster, 2005), 95–109.

[76] James D. G. Dunn, "'Baptized' as Metaphor," in *Baptism, the New Testament and the Church*, ed. Porter and Cross, 294–310, 307, with reference to Mark 10:38. Dunn nevertheless "translates" ἐβαπτίσθημεν εἰς Χριστόν as "baptized into Christ." As long as such translations are used, it will be difficult for interpreters to recognize the force of the metaphorical sense of βαπτίζω in this passage, since "immerse" is not the default connotation of the English term *baptize*.

[77] Dunn, *Baptism*, 139–42.

with Jesus' death on the cross (v. 6), signifying the break with the past of the old creation. The subject of 6:1–11 is not Christian water baptism but the reality and power of God's grace granted through the death and resurrection of Jesus, who justifies sinners and thus deals effectively with the reality and power of sin introduced by Adam into the human condition (3:21–5:21). The question of 6:1 is given a basic answer in 6:2, which is further elaborated in 6:3–11 (and further developed in 6:12–8:30).

If indeed βαπτίζω in 6:3 is not merely a technical term for Christian water baptism but has a metaphorical meaning— βαπτίζω sense 2: to be immersed into an intangible reality and consequently being overpowered by the force of this reality—there is no reason why the phrase ἐβαπτίσθημεν εἰς Χριστὸν Ἰησοῦν cannot be translated as "we have been immersed into Jesus the Messiah,"[78] and the phrase εἰς τὸν θάνατον αὐτοῦ ἐβαπτίσθημεν as "we have been immersed into his death" (with a note explaining the meaning of the metaphor). If the metaphorical meaning is spelled out, one could translate, "we have been incorporated into Jesus the Messiah" and "we have been united with his death." Or, one could translate "we have been overwhelmed (by God) toward Christ Jesus" and "we have been overwhelmed (by God) toward Christ's death."[79] As regards βάπτισμα in verse 4, since *baptism* is the established term for the water rite expressing conversion-initiation, "we have been buried with him by baptism into death" is an acceptable translation (perhaps with a note explaining the English term *baptism* as denoting immersion in water); alternately, "we have been buried with him into death by (our) immersion" is a possible translation.

> 1 Cor. 12:13: καὶ γὰρ ἐν ἑνὶ πνεύματι ἡμεῖς πάντες εἰς ἓν σῶμα ἐβαπτίσθημεν, εἴτε Ἰουδαῖοι εἴτε Ἕλληνες, εἴτε δοῦλοι εἴτε ἐλεύθεροι, καὶ πάντες ἓν πνεῦμα ἐποτίσθημεν. ("For in the one Spirit we were all *baptized* into one body—Jews or Greeks, slaves or free—and we were all made to drink of one Spirit.")

---

[78]Cf. Frédéric Godet, *Commentaire sur l'épître aux Romains*, 3rd ed., 2 vols. (Geneva: Labor et Fides, 1968 [1879]), 2:17: "être plongé en lui, en sa mort"; Alphonse Maillot, *L'Épître aux Romains* (Paris: Centurion/Labor et Fides, 1984), 155: "nous tous qui avons été immergés dans le Christ-Jésus, nous avons aussi été immergés dans sa mort"; see also Dunn, *Romans*, 1:311, who uses "baptize" in his translation, however (304).
[79]Cf. Sabou, *Paul's Metaphorical Language of Death*, 101–9.

English translations nearly unanimously translate ἐβαπτίσθημεν as "we were baptized." An exception is Wuest, who translates the clause with "by means of one Spirit we all were placed into one body." BDAG suggests, apart from "baptize," the translation "plunged into one body."[80] While some commentators claim that since Paul never uses βαπτίζω in a metaphorical sense, the term ἐβαπτίσθημεν is a reference to Christian water baptism pure and simple,[81] many recognize that the verb has a metaphorical sense.[82] Since βαπτίζω is not a technical term in Hellenistic Greek, it does not automatically denote Christian water baptism. It can thus be argued that "the imagery of 'baptized in Spirit' is both coined as a metaphor from the rite of baptism and set in some distinction from or even antithesis to the rite of baptism."[83] The term βαπτίζω can serve as a metaphor independent from the Christian rite of immersion in water: all believers in Jesus have been "immersed" in (ἐν) the Spirit of God and into (εἰς) the reality of the community of God's people (described as "body," also a metaphor). When people come to faith in Jesus, they are "immersed" or "plunged" into the sphere of the Holy Spirit, with the goal or effect of being incorporated into the community of the followers of Jesus. The statement in verse 13b that "we were all made to drink of one Spirit" is another metaphor

---

[80]BDAG s.v. βαπτίζω 2c.

[81]Cf. Wolfgang Schrage, *Der erste Brief an die Korinther*, 4 vols., EKK 7 (Zürich: Benziger; Neukirchen-Vluyn: Neukirchener, 1991–2001), 3:216n607. Without stating such a postulate, Anthony C. Thiselton, *The First Epistle to the Corinthians*, NIGTC (Grand Rapids: Eerdmans, 2000), 997–98, does not explain βαπτίζω, which he interprets as reference to water-and-Spirit baptism. See also George R. Beasley-Murray, *Baptism in the New Testament* (1962; repr., Grand Rapids: Eerdmans, 1979), 167–71.

[82]Gordon D. Fee, *The First Epistle to the Corinthians*, NICNT (Grand Rapids: Eerdmans, 1987), 603–6; David E. Garland, *1 Corinthians*, BECNT (Grand Rapids: Baker, 2003), 591; Eckhard J. Schnabel, *Der erste Brief des Paulus an die Korinther*, Historisch-Theologische Auslegung (Wuppertal: R. Brockhaus, 2006), 728–29; Dunn, *Baptism*, 129–31; Dunn, *Theology of Paul*, 450–51; Thomas W. Gillespie, *The First Theologians: A Study in Early Christian Prophecy* (Grand Rapids: Eerdmans, 1994), 120. Also Joseph A. Fitzmyer, *First Corinthians* (New Haven, CT: Yale University Press, 2008), 477: "All Christians have been plunged into or immersed in 'one body,' i.e., into Christ"; however, Fitzmyer goes on to assert that "it is highly unlikely that Paul is referring to anything different from the well-known early Christian tradition about baptism by water and its effects." Similarly Raymond R. Collins, *First Corinthians*, Sacra Pagina (Collegeville, MN: Liturgical Press, 1999), 462–63: Paul refers to "Spirit-inspired ritual baptism as the act of incorporation into the one body."

[83]Dunn, *Theology of Paul*, 451. This is not to deny that Paul's readers *may* have thought of their past experience of water baptism; the point is that while the English term *baptize* as "translation" of βαπτίζω automatically connotes Christian water baptism, the Greek term βαπτίζω, as used in everyday life by Paul's readers, had a much larger pool of semantic options, both physical (literal) and metaphorical.

(ποτίζω means "to give to drink" and "to water, irrigate"): as a field or a garden is watered, so the believers in Jesus have experienced the "outpouring" of the Spirit of God.

There is thus no reason why the phrase ἐν ἑνὶ πνεύματι ἡμεῖς πάντες εἰς ἓν σῶμα ἐβαπτίσθημεν should not be translated as "we have all been immersed in the one Spirit into one body" (sense 2 of βαπτίζω); not impossible is the translation "we have all been over-whelmed by the Spirit with the goal of the body." The following statement may serve as a paraphrase of the expression: "we have all been given the one Spirit, and we have all been incorporated into the body."

The Use of βαπτίζω Designating Christian Experience

The fifth and final group of passages listed in BDAG for βαπτίζω are texts that, thus the suggestion, describe "an extraordinary experience akin to an initiatory water-rite."[84]

> 1 Cor. 10:1–2: οἱ πατέρες ἡμῶν πάντες ὑπὸ τὴν νεφέλην ἦσαν καὶ πάντες διὰ τῆς θαλάσσης διῆλθον, καὶ πάντες εἰς τὸν Μωϋσῆν ἐβαπτίσθησαν ἐν τῇ νεφέλῃ καὶ ἐν τῇ θαλάσσῃ. ("Our ancestors were all under the cloud, and all passed through the sea, and all were *baptized* into Moses in the cloud and in the sea.")

When scholars interpret Paul's statement as "the baptism of the Israelites in terms that recall Christian baptism,"[85] we again see the default reflex of Christian scholars who think that βαπτίζω actually *means* "to baptize" and always (or nearly always) describes Christian water baptism. Most English translations use "were baptized" as "translation" of ἐβαπτίσθησαν. Most scholars agree that the unique formulation in verse 2 was coined by Paul in the context of a comparison of Jesus Christ as Israel's eschatological Savior with Moses as Israel's first savior: Paul transferred the language of baptismal immersion from Jesus Christ to Moses.[86] Since Paul presents a typological interpretation of Israel's wilderness wanderings, a translation that preserves the clearly

---

[84]BDAG s.v. βαπτίζω 3.
[85]Collins, *First Corinthians*, 368; similarly, Schrage, *Korinther*, 2:389–92; Thiselton, *First Epistle to the Corinthians*, 724–25; Fitzmyer, *First Corinthians*, 381–82.
[86]Cf. Fee, *First Epistle to the Corinthians*, 445; Dunn, *Theology of Paul*, 448; Garland, *1 Corinthians*, 450.

metaphorical meaning of βαπτίζω is "all were immersed into Moses" or "all were incorporated in Moses" (sense 2).[87]

Several passages link βαπτίζω with fire and/or with the Holy Spirit in a context that describes the experience of Jesus' followers.

Matt. 3:11: ὁ δὲ ὀπίσω μου ἐρχόμενος ἰσχυρότερός μού ἐστιν, οὗ οὐκ εἰμὶ ἱκανὸς τὰ ὑποδήματα βαστάσαι· αὐτὸς ὑμᾶς βαπτίσει ἐν πνεύματι ἁγίῳ καὶ πυρί. ("One who is more powerful than I is coming after me; I am not worthy to carry his sandals. He will *baptize* you with the Holy Spirit and fire.") Cf. Luke 3:16.

Mark 1:8: αὐτὸς δὲ βαπτίσει ὑμᾶς ἐν πνεύματι ἁγίῳ. ("He [i.e., the One coming after John] will *baptize* you with the Holy Spirit.")

John 1:33: ἐφ᾿ ὃν ἂν ἴδῃς τὸ πνεῦμα καταβαῖνον καὶ μένον ἐπ᾿ αὐτόν, οὗτός ἐστιν ὁ βαπτίζων ἐν πνεύματι ἁγίῳ. ("He on whom you see the Spirit descend and remain is the one who *baptizes* with the Holy Spirit.")

Acts 1:5: ὑμεῖς δὲ ἐν πνεύματι βαπτισθήσεσθε ἁγίῳ οὐ μετὰ πολλὰς ταύτας ἡμέρας. ("You will be *baptized* with the Holy Spirit not many days from now.") Cf. Acts 11:16; also 1 Corinthians 12:13 (see above).

The connection between βαπτίζω and fire is not an oxymoron,[88] since the Greek term in and of itself does not connote water. The link between βαπτίζω and God's Spirit (and fire) is not an implied reference to Christian water baptism but a metaphorical reference to the fulfillment of the Old Testament promises concerning the Holy Spirit, which God will "pour out" (ἐκχεῶ) on all people (Joel 2:28; LXX 3:1) who are thus immersed into the reality of God's Spirit.

The verb βαπτίζω, as related to the Spirit (and fire) and thus used in a nonphysical, metaphorical sense, can be translated as "immerse" (sense 2; "he will immerse you in the Holy Spirit," and "you will be immersed in the Holy Spirit").[89] Another possibility is the mean-

---

[87]Less likely, but not impossible, is the translation "all were overwhelmed in the cloud and in the sea toward Moses," i.e., establishing Moses as their leader.

[88]Thus BDAG s.v. βαπτίζω 3b.

[89]The objection of Turner, *Power from on High*, 181, who acknowledges the possibility of such an understanding, that this is "simply unparalleled, and so improbable," is unconvincing: if the basic meaning of βαπτίζω is "to put into (a yielding substance)," the range of possibilities for

ing "to overwhelm" or "to be overwhelmed with" ("he will overwhelm you with the Holy Spirit" and "you will be overwhelmed by
the Holy Spirit").[90] A third possibility is the extended meaning "to
purify, cleanse" (sense 1b; "he will cleanse you with the Holy Spirit"
and "you will be cleansed by the Holy Spirit").[91]

> Mark 10:38: οὐκ οἴδατε τί αἰτεῖσθε. δύνασθε πιεῖν τὸ ποτήριον ὃ
> ἐγὼ πίνω, ἢ τὸ βάπτισμα ὃ ἐγὼ βαπτίζομαι βαπτισθῆναι. ("You do
> not know what you are asking. Are you able to drink the cup that
> I drink, or be *baptized* with the baptism that I am baptized with?")
> Cf. also Jesus' response to the disciple's answer in 10:39.

> Luke 12:50: βάπτισμα δὲ ἔχω βαπτισθῆναι, καὶ πῶς συνέχομαι ἕως
> ὅτου τελεσθῇ. ("I have a baptism with which to be *baptized*, and
> what stress I am under until it is completed!")

While most English translations use "baptize" and "baptism" for
Jesus' statement concerning his imminent death,[92] some translators
recognize that here βαπτίζω has a metaphorical meaning. The New
International Reader's Version (NIrV) translates Jesus' question, "Can
you go through the baptism of suffering I must go through?" rendering

---

substances into which somebody or something can be put is not predetermined, but potentially
endless.

[90]I. Howard Marshall, "The Meaning of the Verb 'to Baptize,'" *EQ* 45 (1973): 130–40; Max M. B.
Turner, "Spirit Endowment in Luke-Acts: Some Linguistic Considerations," *Vox Evangelica* 12
(1981): 45–63, 50–53; now rejected in Turner, *Power from on High*, 181–82, with arguments
that I do not find convincing; the best point is the objection that if Luke 3:16 (Matt. 3:11)
expressed a contrast between what John was doing (immersing people) and what the Messiah
would do, and if the Aramaic term used in both statements was טבל, the contrast does not
work because טבל does not mean "overwhelm." However, it is conceivable that John used
two different Aramaic words—טבל ("to dip, dive, plunge") and שטף ("to flood over," niphal
"to be overwhelmed, flooded away")—which were translated by the earliest Christians with a
single Greek word.

[91]Turner, *Power from on High*, 183–84; on Acts 1:5; 11:16, see pp. 301, 387: the Spirit is
explained as "the power of Israel's cleansing and restoration" as Jesus the Messiah "cleanses
and restores his Israel through the executive power of the Holy Spirit which he pours out." As
regards the suggestion of Marshall, "Meaning of the Verb 'Baptize,'" 8–24, who argues on the
basis of Jesus' promise that he would "baptize with the Holy Spirit," that the word *baptize*
focuses not primarily on "the mode of drenching" (by an act of immersion), but on "the fact
of the drenching and the cleansing which it conveys," note Ferguson, *Baptism*, 59n56: "This
conclusion emphasizing the result rather than the mode of the action neglects the basic resultant
characteristic that the person (or object) was covered, submerged, or overwhelmed." Also, the
basic meaning and the range of (extended and metaphorical) meanings of a Greek term should
not be determined on the basis of New Testament usage alone, since the readers of the New Testament texts encountered Greek not only in the writings of the apostles but in everyday life.

[92]ESV, GNB, NASB, NET, NIV, NLT, NRSV, RSV, TNIV.

βαπτίζω with "go through" and βάπτισμα with "baptism of suffering" (thus indicating that the Greek noun has a metaphorical meaning).[93] Wuest translates it, "Are you able to be drinking the cup which I am drinking, or with the immersion with which I am to be overwhelmed, are you able to be immersed?" Commentators who use "baptize" and "baptism" recognize the metaphorical sense of the Greek terms, usually without considering exchanging the baptismal language for terms such as "immerse" or "overwhelm."[94] The editors of BDAG suggest that "perhaps the stark metaphor of impending personal disaster is to be rendered, 'are you prepared to be drowned the way I'm going to be drowned?'"[95] This translation represents extended sense 1d, understood metaphorically. Since Jesus uses a metaphor in Mark 10:38a, the metaphorical sense "to overwhelm" for βαπτίζω (sense 2) is also possible ("are you able . . . to be overwhelmed by the submersion [or "flood"] by which I am overwhelmed?").[96]

Conclusions

The evidence for the use of βαπτίζω in the New Testament can be summarized as follows:

(1) The range of senses of βαπτίζω in the New Testament is much smaller than in Greek and Jewish texts. The senses "to wash,"

---

[93]Similarly Peterson, *Message*: "Are you capable of drinking the cup I drink, of being baptized in the baptism I'm about to be plunged into?" Here the second occurrence of βαπτίζω is translated with "plunged into."

[94]Cf. Rudolf Pesch, *Das Markusevangelium*, 2 vols., HTKNT 2 (Freiburg: Herder, 1976, 1977), 2:156–57; Gundry, *Mark*, 577, 584; also Marcus, *Mark*, 2:747–48, who asserts that "Jesus now speaks of being overwhelmed by the flood of death and of his disciples going down with him" (752, 754). France, *Mark*, 416–47, suggests that "Jesus has coined a remarkable new metaphor, drawing on his disciples' familiarity with the dramatical physical act of John's baptism, but using it (somewhere along the lines of the secular usage mentioned above [i.e., βαπτίζω used as a metaphor for being "overwhelmed" or "swamped" by misfortune, sorrow, etc.] to depict the suffering and death into which he was soon to be 'plunged'" (417). Such explanations fail to acknowledge that βαπτίζω in and of itself does not refer to water, nor to John's water baptism, nor to Christian water baptism. Craig A. Evans, *Mark 8:27–16:20*, WBC 34B (Nashville: Nelson, 2001), 117, does not comment on the meaning of βαπτίζω, which he translates as "baptize."

[95]BDAG s.v. βαπτίζω 3c. Cf. Ferguson, *Baptism*, 140, who writes that "'baptize' here draws on its usage for being drowned or overwhelmed . . . [Jesus] was submerged; he was completely overwhelmed in suffering and death."

[96]Cf. Marshall, *Gospel of Luke*, 547: βαπτίζω is used "in the metaphorical sense of being overwhelmed by catastrophe"; similarly Darrell L. Bock, *Luke*, 2 vols., BECNT (Grand Rapids: Baker, 1995, 1996), 2:1193–94; Turner, *Power from on High*, 182; M. Eugene Boring, *Mark: A Commentary*, The New Testament Library (Louisville: Westminster John Knox, 2006), 301 (who translates with "baptize" and "baptism," 298); Leland Ryken, James C. Wilhoit, and Tremper Longman, eds., *Dictionary of Biblical Imagery* (Downers Grove, IL: InterVarsity, 1998), 73.

"to drown," "to dye," "to slaughter," and "to be drunk" do not occur. Three senses of βαπτίζω are present in the New Testament: "to immerse" (basic meaning, sense 1), "to cleanse (from moral and spiritual defilement)" (extended sense 1b), "to be overwhelmed" (metaphorical meaning, sense 2). This means that there is not sufficient evidence to establish whether the early Christian use of βαπτίζω can be compared with the use of the verb in earlier and contemporary Greek and Jewish-Greek sources for the full scope of meanings. However, since the Greek church fathers use βαπτίζω with the same range of meanings as the non-Christian Greek texts, and since it is implausible to assume that the Christians of the first century used βαπτίζω in a completely unique sense, the available evidence warrants the conclusion that the use of βαπτίζω in the New Testament falls within the parameters of general Greek usage.

(2) Since the verb βαπτίζω in and of itself does not refer to water, nor to a particular rite or ceremony, the view that essentially all occurrences of βαπτίζω in the New Testament have a "ritual" meaning and should be "translated" as "to baptize" should be abandoned. Translators and commentators need to evaluate each occurrence of the verb in the context of the full range of meanings that βαπτίζω has in Greek.

(3) It is indeed correct, as often stated, that the majority of occurrences of βαπτίζω in the New Testament have a "ritual" sense, describing an immersion in water that symbolizes the removal of moral and spiritual defilement (extended sense 1b), that is, a rite of cleansing and purification—whether the referent is the ritual immersions of Jews, or the activity of John and of Jesus and his disciples, or the activity of the early Christians. However, there is no reason to treat the rites of purification by immersion practiced by Jews, by John, and by Jesus' disciples as separate "meanings" in the lexical entry for βαπτίζω.

(4) The editors of BDAG are certainly correct when they assert that "the transliteration 'baptize' signifies the ceremonial character that NT narratives accord such cleansing."[97] However, the fact that βαπτίζω is consistently used for what we call Christian water baptism does not mean that βαπτίζω has become a technical term.[98] The fact that

---

[97]BDAG s.v. βαπτίζω 2, as comment on sense 2, "to use water in a rite for purpose of renewing or establishing a relationship with God, *plunge, dip, wash, baptize.*"
[98]Cf. Joseph Ysebaert, *Greek Baptismal Terminology: Its Origins and Early Development,* Graecitas Christianorum Primaeva (Nijmegen: Dekker & Van de Vegt, 1962), 44, who concludes that when the meaning of βαπτίζω became more technical (as a reference to Christian water

the full range of physical (literal) and metaphorical senses of βαπτίζω continues to be present in all sources of the first century AD, as well as in the Greek church fathers, demonstrates that βαπτίζω retained the extended and metaphorical senses it had for centuries—meanings that would have been familiar to the readers of the New Testament.

(5) There is no linguistic necessity to translate, or rather transliterate, βαπτίζω with "baptize." The full and varied meaning of Christian baptism is not tied up with the English term *baptize* or *baptism*, nor is the significance of Christian baptism implicit in the Greek terms βαπτίζω or βάπτισμα. Rather, the "theology" of baptism is expressed in statements about what happens when people come to faith in Jesus as Israel's crucified and risen Messiah, when they are immersed in water in the name of Jesus, expressing commitment to him who forgives sins, and when they receive the promise of God's Spirit. The term *immerse* preserves the meaning of βαπτίζω quite satisfactorily, and the term *cleanse* adequately expresses the extended meaning "removal of moral and spiritual defilement," which God grants to those who believe in Jesus.

---

baptism), the meaning "to immerse" may have receded into the background; he asserts at the same time that the New Testament authors and readers were still aware of the meaning "to immerse" since "it is possible to play on it when using the verb in a metaphorical sense."

PART

3

New Testament Studies around the World

9

New Testament Studies in Africa

ROBERT W. YARBROUGH

T he purpose of this chapter, as part of a volume exploring New Testament studies in the early twenty-first century, is to characterize this discipline and activity in Africa. "The greatest surge in the history of Christianity occurred in Africa over the past one hundred years, and indeed continues its breathtaking trajectory into the twenty-first century."[1] This is having obvious ripple effects internationally, as seen for example in recent coalitions between African Anglicans and North American Episcopalians in response to moral and social issues.[2] Leading historian Andrew Walls notes that the twentieth century witnessed "Africa quietly slipping into the place in the Christian world once occupied by Europe."[3] Yet this continent "remains terra incognita, a blur on the margins of world Christianity's

---

[1] Jonathan J. Bonk, "Ecclesiastical Cartography and the Invisible Continent," *International Bulletin of Missionary Research* 28, no. 4 (Oct. 2004): 154.

[2] See, e.g., Miranda K. Hassett, *Anglican Communion in Crisis: How Episcopal Dissidents and Their African Allies Are Reshaping Anglicanism* (Princeton, NJ: Princeton University Press, 2007).

[3] Andrew Walls and Cathy Ross, eds., *Mission in the Twenty-first Century* (Maryknoll, NY: Orbis, 2008), 201. On Walls's key role in bringing African developments to light, see the

self-understanding."[4] It is a privilege to seek to honor my esteemed colleague D. A. Carson, whose work has served to encourage knowledge of the gospel throughout the world, including Africa, by calling much-needed attention to significant developments there related to formal study of the New Testament.

Limitations

Several limitations must be noted at the outset. First, the essay will center on publications in English, as this language is dominant in published works at present. There is another, albeit quantitatively smaller, world of printed discourse unfolding in Afrikaans, French, Arabic, and other languages. But canvassing and reporting on these conversations would require a lengthier study than can be pursued here.

Second, the essay will draw on some published works that are not limited to the field of New Testament studies proper (which in any case overlaps areas like Old Testament, history, hermeneutics, theology, church history, and the vast fields of religious studies and social-scientific investigation). African New Testament scholarship is not walled off to itself, and so a depiction of it needs to be broader in its purview than New Testament scholarship in a narrow sense.

Third, the essay will be limited in scope and validity. Much more is happening in Africa than can be noted here. As of 2004, Jan Botha determined that some 312 universities were to be found in 54 different African nations, with about 40 of these in 12 countries housing "research and/or teaching programmes in NT Studies."[5] A single essay cannot hope to do justice to such a broad range of sites—and there are many more nonuniversity colleges where the New Testament is studied, taught, and written about.[6] Moreover, development along any number of fronts is rapid and ongoing, so that any report completed in one year will already be dated by the time it sees the light of publication one or two years hence. And since any research report must be selective, this one will inevitably suffer from less-than-ideal

---

interview with Tim Stafford, accessed April 9, 2010, http://www.christianitytoday.com/ct/2007/february/34.87.html.

[4]Ibid.

[5]"The Study of the New Testament in African Universities," in *The New Testament Interpreted: Essays in Honor of Bernard C. Lategan*, ed. C. Breytenbach, J. C. Thom, and J. Punt (Boston: Brill, 2006), 248.

[6]Ibid., 249.

decisions regarding what to highlight, what to downplay, and what to leave to the side for now.

Fourth, I am neither African nor resident in Africa. My personal experience on that great continent is limited to a couple of dozen visits beginning in 1989 to countries where I have engaged in academic teaching, pastoral training, and discipleship instruction in Muslim-majority regions. This is probably better than no firsthand experience at all. But even many months spent in a few African locations may provide no more than an illusory appreciation of Africa's vast complexities and hermeneutical distinctives. I can only hope that my reading and reflections will prove free from the most egregious sorts of distortions and blind spots.

Challenges

Such inherent limitations pale, however, next to a number of challenges noted by African thinkers. Nigerian Jesuit Agbonkhianmeghe E. Orabator calls attention to *the complexity of the situation*: "Any reference to all things African would have to be partial, provisional, and contextualized."[7] He continues, "With fifty-three independent countries and 700 million people spread across an intricate linguistic, cultural, social, and geo-political landscape, the continent defies any facile attempt to sketch a homogeneous picture of its fortunes or misfortunes."[8] This includes fortunes and misfortunes in New Testament studies. Grant LeMarquand states, "Any label which attempts to describe all that happens when the Bible is read in Africa will be overly constraining."[9]

There is also *the elusiveness of the goal* of apprehending what one is looking at. Dirkie Smit writes from within the South African milieu, which in some ways has dominated African New Testament studies up till now. He notes that in Africa, "Worship mattered and still matters" for those who engage in biblical interpretation,[10] a claim that would not be true in anything like the same sense and degree for

---

[7]"Method and Context: How and Where Theology Works in Africa," in *Shaping a Global Theological Mind*, ed. Darren C. Marks (Burlington, VT: Ashgate, 2008), 122.
[8]Ibid.
[9]"'And the Rulers of the Nations Shall Bring Their Treasures into It': A Review of Biblical Exegesis in Africa," *Anglican Theological Review* 88, no. 2 (2006): 243.
[10]"On Belonging: Doing Theology Together," in *Shaping a Global Theological Mind*, ed. Marks, 154.

numerous interpreters in the post-Christian West. Smit reflects back to the years prior to the end of apartheid:

> We were to learn that lively worship is no guarantee of faithful worship, active and committed congregational and spiritual life, like flourishing religious activity and experience, not necessarily an indication of Christian discipleship. Learning to see that there may be a difference between religion, spirituality and even worship on the one hand, and Christian faith, life and obedience on the other, and then struggling how to discern between the two, became a crucial part of doing theology in the apartheid context—and it still remains a crucial challenge today.[11]

In other words, once the observer moves from merely chronicling publications to discerning evaluation of them and the living realities giving rise to them, one finds people using the same words about the same subject matter but connoting profoundly contrasting realities. New Testament studies both upheld and prohibited apartheid! This has analogies in current discussion elsewhere, where New Testament research by some claims to justify same-sex relations for those in the church and by others claims to prohibit it.[12] Some use theological means to deconstruct and decry the Western theological and ethical heritage, while others see betrayal of the Christian heritage in calls for radically "African" Christian expression. The point is that if we approach African New Testament scholarship with the expectation of arriving at a monolithic picture of its character and claims, we are pursuing a nonachievable goal. It is a variegated, dynamic, and at times seemingly self-contradictory enterprise.

Another writer asks perceptively whether anyone really cares about this subject. *Does Africa matter* for New Testament studies? Emmanuel Katongole, trained as a philosopher in Uganda and now teaching theology at Duke University, observes that "even though there is much

---

[11]Ibid.

[12]For a slice of the discussion in the South African setting see Jeremy Punt, "The Bible in the Gay-Debate in South Africa: Towards an Ethics of Interpretation," *Scriptura* 93 (2006): 419–31. Punt seems to affirm a hermeneutic that would make it difficult to see same-sex physical intimacy as immoral based on the Bible. But see N. Vorster, "Human Dignity and Sexual Behaviour—A Theological Perspective," *Verbum et Ecclesia* 26, no. 3 (2005): 891–911, who calls for sexual expression within monogamous marriage between a male and a female (909). See also Gerald West and Bongi Zengele, "The Medicine of God's Word: What People Living with HIV and AIDS Want (and Get) from the Bible," *Journal of Theology for Southern Africa* 125 (2006): 51–63.

talk about a Southern shift in World Christianity, and more specifically about the growth of the church in Africa, Africa has not become the subject of serious theological inquiry in the United States, or generally in the West."[13] He warns almost despairingly, "I have come to realize that without critical and sustained engagement with, as well as fresh theological scholarship on Africa, Western Christianity in general and Western theological reflection in particular degenerates into a kind of solipsistic self-importance or trivial preoccupation."[14] In the field of technical New Testament study, as will be seen below, Katongole's question is highly pertinent. The indifference, if not hostility, of many leading North American Episcopal clerics toward the reading of the Bible affirmed by their African colleagues on the homosexual issue illustrates his point.[15] Outside of Africa most sectors of New Testament study today proceed serenely oblivious to the explosion of the Christian population in Africa (and elsewhere), as far as its making any tangible difference to interpretive strategies or aims. The point here would be that practically speaking, whatever the results of an investigation of New Testament studies in Africa, for dominant players and schools of thought in the discipline in various quarters outside of Africa, the results of such investigation will be regarded as irrelevant for their own, largely self-referential, work.

This notion is echoed from another vantage point by Kenyan Nyambura J. Njoroge. Moving away from Africa to pursue a calling to a World Council of Churches position in Geneva, Switzerland, has led her to "raise issues with God about the enormous suffering in Africa. Why all this madness and destruction? For how long do we have to endure such indignity and misery? Do we indeed belong to the human race? Why this disproportionate suffering in one particular continent?"[16] Here the possible impediment to a focused analysis of "New Testament studies in Africa" would be *the question of whether there is any hope or promise* in this or any other religious enterprise, given the profundity of the problems that the African situation presents. Njoroge's hints at a solution—that we must learn to embrace "the

---

[13]"A Tale of Many Stories," in *Shaping a Global Theological Mind*, ed. Marks, 90.
[14]Ibid.
[15]There was analogous trampling of African sensibilities by Evangelical Lutheran Church in America (ELCA) leaders at the August 2009 national meeting, which voted to affirm ordination of practicing homosexuals, against pleas of African representatives.
[16]"Beyond Suffering and Lament: Theology of Hope and Life," in *Shaping a Global Theological Mind*, ed. Marks, 115.

divine within us" and find solutions in "engaged critical theology and faithful actions"[17]—will be felt by some as a counsel of despair implying a negative answer to this question. Africa needs more than what exists within humans and what can emerge from our reflection and good works alone. How should the brain-drain question (personified by Njoroge herself) be addressed, for example, whether of Africans to South Africa[18] or of Africans to other nations?[19] This phenomenon has inevitable implications for biblical scholarship and far beyond. Still, Njoroge raises pressing questions that are deserving of sustained reflection and response.

A note of caution is advised, however. In light of the 2004 Indian Ocean tsunami and the 2010 Haiti earthquake, it is not clear that Africa is as much the sole site of calamity as Njoroge implies. In fact, it is not clear that misery of imponderable magnitude is not the human lot on all inhabited continents over the course of time. It has been estimated that in the twentieth century, two hundred million people died from war and genocide. It is doubtful that Africa's loss was proportionately greater than that of all other continents, particularly Europe and Asia. Africa has certainly been the victim of great ills and evils in recent generations. But it is far from the only continent of which this could be said.

In any case, the cumulative effect of many African voices could discourage any attempt to characterize African New Testament scholarship at this point in its complex and rapidly changing character and in view of the enormity of issues interpreters face.

Approach to the Subject
The cautionary observations above, sobering though some are, should not rule out a hopeful approach to our subject. The fact that full-orbed Christian existence has roots in Africa going back to the faith's earliest days[20]

---

[17]Ibid., 120.

[18]J. Crush et al., eds., *States of Vulnerability: The Brain Drain of Future Talent to South Africa* (Cape Town: Institute for Democracy in South Africa, 2005).

[19]D. A. McDonald and J. Crush, eds., *Destinations Unknown: Perspectives on the Brain Drain in Southern Africa* (Pretoria: Africa Institute of South Africa, 2002), treats the issue from a South African perspective.

[20]Simon of Cyrene (Libya) carried Jesus' cross (Luke 23:26). Egypt and Libyan regions were represented at Pentecost (Acts 2:9–10). An Ethiopian was among the first to receive Christian baptism outside Judea (Acts 8:26–40). Africa's foundational status in the early Christian centuries is highlighted in Thomas Oden, *How Africa Shaped the Christian Mind: Recovering the African Seedbed of Christianity* (Downers Grove, IL: InterVarsity, 2008). See also K. A. Burton,

(to say nothing of links between Africa and the Old Testament world[21]), has long survived in quarters like Nubia (until Muslim conquests),[22] and still exists indigenously in the Nile basin (Coptic church) and Ethiopia[23] indicates that New Testament studies in Africa (at least in the sense of ecclesial interpretation and application) has a deep historical foundation.[24] Today it is undeniable that the study of the New Testament there is growing in volume, importance, and sophistication. Our hypothesis below is that there is merit, indeed empirical necessity, in taking the measure of African New Testament studies, if for no other reason than the burgeoning presence of Christians there and Africa's increasing importance as a center of world Christianity.[25] In addition, at least some African interpretation of the Bible underway constitutes a direct challenge to timeworn approaches in the West; as Kenyan archbishop Benjamin Nzimbi stated, "Our understanding of the Bible is different from them. We are two different churches."[26] No doubt Orabator is on to something in speaking of "an optimism that borders on hubris" when African church growth serves as a basis for declaring "the future of Christianity to be eternally

The Blessing of Africa: The Bible and African Christianity (Downers Grove, IL: InterVarsity, 2007). On Egypt in particular see Birger Pearson, "Earliest Christianity in Egypt," in *The World of Early Egyptian Christianity*, ed. J. E. Goehring and J. A. Timbie (Washington, DC: Catholic University Press of America, 2007), 97–112.

[21]Cf., e.g., E. Isaac, "The Question of Jewish Identity and Ethiopian Jewish Origins," *Mid-Stream* 51, no. 5 (2005): 29–34.

[22]See Calvin Shenk, "The Demise of the Church in North Africa and Nubia and Its Survival in Egypt and Ethiopia: A Question of Contextualization?," *Missiology: An International Review* 21, no. 2 (Apr. 1993): 131–54.

[23]Cf., e.g., Edward Ullendorf, *Ethiopia and the Bible* (Oxford: Oxford University Press, 1968). See also Philip Jenkins, "A Second Jerusalem," *Christian Century*, August 11, 2009, 45: "By 2050 Ethiopia may have 100 million Christians, making it home to one of the largest Christian communities" in the world.

[24]On Ethiopic roots in Patristic thought see Roger W. Cowley, *Ethiopian Biblical Interpretation: A Study in Exegetical Tradition and Hermeneutics* (Cambridge: Cambridge University Press, 1988).

[25]Amply documented, e.g., by various authors in Walls and Ross, eds., *Mission in the Twenty-first Century*. Note also the numerous works by Philip Jenkins: see, e.g., his "Reading the Bible in the Global South," in *Speaking about What We Have Seen and Heard: Evangelism in Global Perspective*, ed. J. J. Bonk et al. (New Haven, CT: OMSC, 2007), 79–90 (dealing with Asia, too); and the seminal *The Next Christendom* (New York: Oxford, 2002). See also www .worldreligiondatabase.org. For a succinct glimpse of numerous important aspects of African Christianity in global perspective see Todd Johnson, David Barrett, and Peter Crossing, "Christianity 2010: A View from the New Atlas of Global Christianity," *International Bulletin of Missionary Research* 34, no. 1 (2010): 29–36.

[26]Quoted in Philip Jenkins, *The New Faces of Christianity: Believing the Bible in the Global South* (New York: Oxford, 2006), 1, quoted slightly differently in Jenkins, "Reading the Bible in the Global South," in *Speaking about What We Have Seen and Heard*, ed. Bonk et al., 79: "Our understanding of the Bible is different from theirs."

willed to Africa."[27] But there may be offsetting considerations that will emerge as our investigation unfolds. It is not necessarily hubris to shine a spotlight on African biblical interpretation.

The formidable challenges facing Africa are not merely grounds for dismay; they also constitute a call for attention and respect. In many quarters African travail is related to Christian conviction and central claims surrounding Jesus, his death on the cross,[28] his resurrection, and his eternal reign. Unlike many Western theological enterprises (cf. Strauss, Harnack, Bultmann), which amount to grand "abstract theologizing,"[29] much African apprehension of the Bible is concrete. "The most prolific and vital period in the history of Dinka Christian music" in Sudan to date was the civil war period of 1983–1993.[30] Here "the narrative of scripture is continually interpreted and applied to contemporary experience" through song.[31] Scripture is real in many quarters of Africa in ways that it is not in the post-Christian and at times anti-Christian West, where, for example, the contributor to a recent symposium on life-of-Jesus studies denies that Jesus existed.[32] "In the experience of the church in Sudan, the cross, the community and hope have become concrete symbols of the life of faith in a time of war and suffering."[33] By no means does all African New Testament interpretation have direct ties to war and suffering. But geopolitical tensions, conflict, and acute human need are always relevant to understanding Scripture in this fallen world. This is no less true of Africa and is a fact to be borne in mind in any survey of biblical interpretation associated with its many regions and nations.

Negligible Presence?

One measure of New Testament scholarship internationally is the professional publication *New Testament Abstracts*. Each year it publishes

---

[27]"Method and Context: How and Where Theology Works in Africa," in *Shaping a Global Theological Mind*, ed. Marks, 122.

[28]Note African input into David Emmanuel Singh, ed., *Jesus and the Cross: Reflections of Christians from Islamic Contexts* (Eugene, OR: Wipf & Stock), including the foreword by Lamin Sanneh.

[29]Cf. Rollin C. Grams, "God, The Beneficent–the Merciful, and Jesus' Cross: From Abstract to Concrete Theologising," in *Jesus and the Cross*, ed. Singh, 157–61.

[30]Marc R. Nikkel, *Dinka Christianity* (Nairobi: Paulines Publications Africa, 2001), 303.

[31]Ibid., 304.

[32]See Robert M. Price, "Jesus at the Vanishing Point," in *The Historical Jesus: Five Views*, ed. J. K. Beilby and P. R. Eddy (Downers Grove, IL: InterVarsity, 2009), 55–83.

[33]Isaiah Majok Dau, *Suffering and God: A Theological Reflection on the War in Sudan* (Nairobi: Paulines Publications Africa, 2002), 243.

a list of journals containing New Testament research, along with summaries of articles (as well as books). Africa's periodical contribution to academic New Testament studies is comparatively slight, as table 1 makes clear. Figures come from a rough count of journals and their place of publication as listed in a recent edition of *New Testament Abstracts*.

Table 1. Geographical analysis of journals listed in *New Testament Abstracts*

Continent/Region	Total Number of Journals	Places of Publication and Number of Journals
Europe (Continent only)	178	Germany 44 Italy 32 France 24 Spain 21 Belgium 17 Netherlands 11 Switzerland 7 Austria 6 Poland 6 Norway 3 Sweden 2 Czech Republic 1 Denmark 1 Greece 1 Malta 1 Portugal 1
North America	120	United States 112 Canada 7 Mexico 1
United Kingdom, Ireland	55	Great Britain 50 Ireland 5
Africa	13	South Africa 8 Kenya 3 Congo 1 Tanzania 1
Asia	11	India 6 Philippines 2 Hong Kong 1 Indonesia 1 Japan 1
Middle East	9	Israel 8 Beirut 1
Australia, New Zealand	7	Australia 6 New Zealand 1
South America	5	Brazil 4 Argentina 1

Questions can be raised, of course, about this depiction of things. Numbers no doubt fluctuate from year to year. There are various ways of viewing nations and numbers—e.g., should the United Kingdom be included in Europe or not? Geographically, Mexico is part of North America, but does its biblical scholarship relate more naturally to Central and South America? But the point is the big picture, and in that picture just thirteen African journals out of a total of nearly four hundred internationally are regarded as regular contributors to New Testament scholarship. By this measure, Africa presently accounts for merely 3.25 percent of the world's New Testament academic periodical publication. The thirteen journals indexed in *New Testament Abstracts* are:

- *Acta Patristica et Byzantina* (Pretoria, South Africa)
- *Acta Theologica* (Bloemfontein, South Africa)
- *Africa Journal of Evangelical Theology* (Machakos, Kenya)
- *Africa Theological Journal* (Usa River, Tanzania)
- *African Ecclesial Review* (Eldoret, Kenya)
- *Hekima Review* (Nairobi, Kenya)
- *HTS Teologiese Studies/Theological Studies* (Pretoria)
- *Journal of Northwest Semitic Languages* (Stellenbosch, South Africa)
- *Journal of Theology for South Africa* (Pietermaritzburg, South Africa)
- *Neotestamentica* (Pretoria)
- *Scriptura* (Stellenbosch)
- *Telema* (Kinshasa-Gombe, Congo)
- *Verbum et Ecclesia* (Pretoria)

New Testament scholarship produced in Africa or by Africans is not limited, of course, to what appears in these thirteen journals (which contain much that is not focused on the New Testament). Certain African journals not found in the list above may still publish articles that are abstracted in *New Testament Abstracts*. An example would be Nigeria's *African Journal of Biblical Studies*.[34] Some percentage of the content of these African journals stems from authors who are not African. The situation is complex. Still, it is pointed out that "although

---

[34] According to http://www.nabis.8m.com/pub%20page.html (accessed Jan. 20, 2010), this journal is indexed by *New Testament Abstracts*. It does not, however, appear in the *New Testament Abstracts* list of journals.

African journals and scholarly books have a very limited readership, more and more are being produced, and the quality of this material is improving."[35] At the same time, this observer points to formidable obstacles to substantial change for the better in the form of political and trade barriers between African countries. Improvements are needed, for these and other factors hinder commerce, including the free flow of publications. "The movement of published work between African countries is quite difficult, and attempts made by African publishers to find distribution networks outside of Africa have proved futile up to this point."[36] This may be less true in some quarters than others but is by no means a total misrepresentation.

Growing Recognition of Africa's Church-Historical and Missiological Importance

A word is in order regarding the rapidly expanding and solidifying sphere in which assessment of African New Testament scholarship, along with other Bible-related phenomena there, may now proceed. Whereas "New Testament studies in Africa" might formerly have chronicled the way Western influences were playing out in Africa, today African voices play increasingly significant roles in and beyond their own traditional borders. Actually, in the growth of the African church there has always been an intricate interweaving of non-African and African persons and impulses,[37] a point underscored by Gerald West with respect to Isaiah Shembe[38] and by Tite Tiénou with respect to the indigenous, *African* nature of evangelical identity and the evangelistic enterprise (including missions) in Africa over the last two centuries.[39] Africans have until recent decades not figured prominently in scholarly, published New Testament interpretation in their lands, but they have

---

[35]LeMarquand, "And the Rulers of the Nations Shall Bring Their Treasures into It," 250.
[36]Ibid. Attempting to address the problem among Africa's sizable English-language population is Oasis International, Ltd.; see http://www.oasisint.net/index.php?menuTop=0&menuBottom=6, accessed April 9, 2010. New Testament scholar Matthew Elliott helps guide the organization.
[37]See Jehu J. Hanciles, "Missionaries and Revolutionaries: Elements of Transformation in the Emergence of Modern African Christianity," *International Bulletin of Missionary Research* 28, no. 4 (Oct. 2004): 146–52.
[38]"Reading Shembe 'Re-membering' the Bible: Isaiah Shembe's Instructions on Adultery," *Neotestamentica* 40, no. 1 (2006): 157–83. Calling for more African ownership of Bible translation is S. V. Coertze, "The African Agent Discovered: The Recognition and Involvement of the African Bible Interpreter in Bible Translation," *Verbum et Ecclesia* 29, no. 1 (2008): 77–90.
[39]Tiénou, "The Great Commission in Africa," in M. Klauber and S. Manetsch, eds., *The Great Commission: Evangelicals and the History of World Missions* (Nashville: B&H, 2008), 164–75.

never been mere passive recipients of a biblical message or interpretive methods, scholarly or practical, dictated to them. Appropriation of the Bible in Africa is not today, and in important respects never was, merely a function of outside and particularly "Western" influences.[40] Western missions in many quarters may have fostered initial dependency, but it sowed the seeds of its own obsolescence: "Despite their role as allies of the empire, missions also developed the vernacular that inspired sentiments of national identity and thus undercut Christianity's identification with colonial rule."[41]

However dependent Africa may have been on others in the past, it has now taken off on its own. Philip Jenkins followed up *The Next Christendom* (2002), which called attention to the explosive growth of Christianity in African regions, with *The New Faces of Christianity* (2006),[42] which painted a portrait and sketched much detail regarding the way the Bible is read and appropriated there (as well as in Asia). Jenkins includes ways in which the hermeneutics and practice of global South churches (like those in Africa) have much to teach the frequently shrinking and beleaguered ecclesial bodies of the global North.[43] More recently he has pointed out the pertinence of African Christian presence in Europe.[44] "New Testament studies in Africa" in the broad sense is by no means confined to locations and events in that geographical setting. African voices are increasingly prominent in missiological and biblical reflection and strategizing, whether in liberation theological mode,[45] in postcolonial criticism,[46] in feminist hermeneutics,[47] or along lines that connect more substantially with historic Christianity.[48] A Nigerian

---

[40]Cf. Lamin Sanneh, *Whose Religion Is Christianity? The Gospel beyond the West* (Grand Rapids: Eerdmans, 2003).

[41]Lamin Sanneh, *Disciples of All Nations: Pillars of World Christianity* (New York: Oxford University Press, 2008), 271.

[42]See note 26 above.

[43]See, e.g., *The New Faces of Christianity*, 189–93.

[44]*God's Continent: Christianity, Islam, and Europe's Religious Crisis* (Oxford: University Press, 2007), esp. chap. 4.

[45]See chapters by Musa Dube (Botswana) and Gerald O. West in *The Bible and the Hermeneutics of Liberation*, ed. Alejandro F. Botta and Pablo R. Andiñach (Atlanta: SBL, 2009).

[46]See, e.g., Humphrey Waweru, "Postcolonial and Contrapuntal Reading of Revelation 22:1–5," *Churchman* 121, no. 1 (2007): 23–38.

[47]Philomena Njeri Mwaura, "Feminist Biblical Interpretation and the Hermeneutics of Liberation: An African Woman's Perspective," in *Feminist Interpretation of the Bible and the Hermeneutics of Liberation*, ed. S. Schroer and S. Bietenhard (Sheffield: JSOT, 2003), 77–85.

[48]See, e.g., the innovative but recognizably Christian theological method ("generative contextualized method") set forth by Orobator, "Method and Context: How and Where Theology Works in Africa," in *Shaping a Global Theological Mind*, ed. Marks, 121–26.

heads up churches counting an adult membership of twenty thousand in Kiev, Ukraine, and over 90 percent of the members are indigenous Europeans.[49] The late Kwame Bediako wrote of the "crucial importance for any credible African Christian theological scholarship that one should appreciate the significance of the African evidence within the new Christian reality of the world."[50]

Scholars beyond Africa are recognizing the increasing significance of Africa for world Christianity and current understanding of Scripture. Keith Burton has written of "the Bible and African Christianity" through the centuries, going back all the way to peoples first mentioned in Genesis as background.[51] Lamin Sanneh's study of Christianity's role in world history refers repeatedly to Africa and offers new vistas of both world and missions history based on developments there.[52] None of this is insignificant for the enterprise of biblical studies. Timothy Tennent makes christology as understood in Africa a major component in his study of global Christianity.[53] Africa is no small part of Mark Noll's look at *The New Shape of World Christianity*.[54]

These and other studies are providing an unprecedented understanding of African realities and frame of reference for understanding Scripture. It is time, then, to sample particulars of what these new realities are producing by way of New Testament studies.

Recent Journal Literature

This section will comment on a range of articles published in recent years. A survey of this output will yield at least a glimpse of the current state of New Testament studies in Africa.

---

[49]J. Kwabena Asamoah-Gyadu, "African Initiated Christianity in Eastern Europe: Church of the 'Embassy of God' in Ukraine," *International Bulletin of Missionary Research* 30, no. 2 (Apr. 2006): 73.

[50]"'Whose Religion Is Christianity?' Reflections on Opportunities and Challenges in Christian Theological Scholarship: The African Dimension," in *Mission in the 21st Century: Exploring the Five Marks of Global Mission*, ed. Andrew Walls and Cathy Ross (Maryknoll, NY: Orbis, 2008), 108.

[51]Burton, *The Blessing of Africa*.

[52]Sanneh, *Disciples of All Nations*.

[53]See chap. 5 of Tennent's *Theology in the Context of World Christianity: How the Global Church Is Influencing the Way We Think about and Discuss Theology* (Grand Rapids: Zondervan, 2007).

[54](Downers Grove, IL: InterVarsity, 2009). See passim and esp. chap. 10.

South Africa, the Historic Center

In a pair of articles,[55] Pieter G. R. de Villiers has sketched the rise of New Testament study as a discipline in South Africa, which in many respects, due to its historic ties with Europe, has led the way. The New Testament Society of South Africa (NTSSA) was founded in 1965 and continues today.[56] Academic New Testament study in a modern sense goes back at least to 1866 at the University of Stellenbosch, which itself grew out of the Dutch Reformed Church seminary that had been founded there still earlier.[57] New Testament study in a practical vein was conducted before NTSSA was founded in various seminaries and training centers associated with Lutheran, Roman Catholic, Anglican, and other denominations across the nation.[58] Much New Testament study in South Africa has gone on outside the circles associated with NTSSA. Still, NTSSA has been a rallying point for important discussions and publications, like those surrounding discourse analysis under the leadership of J. P. Louw,[59] H. J. B. Combrink, and others.[60]

The oldest South African theological journal, *HTS Theological Studies*, was founded in 1943, although a few volumes of an attempted-but-abandoned theological journal published by the Greek Orthodox Patriarchate of Alexandria, Egypt, predate this.[61] Today there are some eighteen theological and related journals published in South Africa, with perhaps half of them containing items of interest to New Testament studies proper.[62] Of the thirteen African journals indexed by *New Testament Abstracts*, only five are not from South Africa (see list above).

---

[55]Pieter G. R. de Villiers, "Turbulent Times and Golden Years: The First Twenty Five Years of the New Testament Society of South Africa (1965–1990)—Part One," *Neotestamentica* 39, no. 1 (2005): 75–110; de Villiers, "Methodology and Hermeneutics in a Challenging Socio-Political Context: The First Twenty Five Years of the New Testament Society of South Africa (1965–1990)—Part Two," *Neotestamentica* 39, no. 2 (2005): 229–53.

[56]See http://newtestament.co.za/, accessed January 19, 2010. The home page offers the intriguing slogan "Innovative research changing yesterday."

[57]De Villiers, "Turbulent Times and Golden Years," 76.

[58]Ibid., 76–77.

[59]Called "perhaps the most influential figure in the first 25 years of the history of the" NTSSA in de Villiers, "Methodology and Hermeneutics," 237.

[60]See ibid., 231–37.

[61]Dirk Human and Andries van Aarde, "*HTS Theological Studies* and *Verbum et Ecclesia*—the Journals of the Faculty of Theology at the University of Pretoria: Historical Overview and Strategic Planning," *HTS Theological Studies* 64, no. 1 (2007): 12.

[62]Ibid., 15.

To say that South Africa is the center is not to say it is the sole significant location. A website gives information about the Nigerian Association for Biblical Studies.[63] It was founded in 1985. Its aim (in conjunction with its journal *African Journal of Biblical Studies*) is to relate biblical interpretation to issues in Africa. What this means is seen in the call for papers for the 2008 annual conference, devoted to "The Bible and Youth Development in Africa." Suggested topics for New Testament contributors were:

- The Virgin Mary's Relationship to Jesus: A Model in Youth Upbringing
- The Bravery of John the Baptist in Proclaiming His Message: A Challenge to Young Ministers in Africa
- The Place of Sunday School and the Youth-Church in the Total Development of Christian Youth
- The Role of the Young Saul of Tarsus in the Persecution of the Church: A Case of Misdirected Energy
- The Responsibility of the Church to Young Single Mothers in Africa
- The Role of the Church in the Care of Street Boys and Girls in Africa
- Jesus Christ, the Perfect Example for Christian Youths in Leadership Positions

A comparison of the topics above and New Testament publications by most South African scholars would show a disparity in focus, methods, and audience, with the South Africans more likely to be seeking to contribute to international academic discussion, in contrast with the church and practical focus of the Nigerian initiative. On the other hand, South African scholarship has been challenged (in this case by a systematician-ethicist) at the point of its insularity from practical issues and irrelevance to construction of a public theology.[64] A missiologist has lodged an analogous protest with respect to the aims and activities of his discipline.[65] It is hard to fault a local and practical focus

---

[63]http://www.nabis.8m.com/main.html, accessed January 20, 2010.
[64]Piet Naudé, "Can We Still Hear Paul on the Agora? An Outsider Perspective on South African New Testament Scholarship," *Neotestamentica* 39, no. 2 (2005): 339–58.
[65]Willem Saayman, "New Testament Studies and Missiology in South Africa: Uneasy Bedfellows?," *Missionalia* 33, no. 2 (2005): 205–13. But see the reply by Christian Stenschke, "New Testament Studies and Missiology in South Africa: Comfortable Bedfellows!," *Missionalia* 33, no. 22 (2005): 214–33.

in a setting when a New Testament scholar (in Jos, Nigeria) found it necessary to e-mail the following prayer request for his university's normal daily operation:

> Although there have been killings right outside the university gate, about a half mile from us and a pretty serious battle between the soldiers and militants in that same area, the fighting has not entered the university compound this time, for which we are grateful. We just learned about an hour ago that a man who has been my next door neighbor for the past 18 years was killed about three hours ago. He worked in my department at one time.[66]

Comparable notes were sounded thirteen months earlier in Bulus Y. Galadima's commencement speech at the evangelical theological seminary in Jos; such violence is recurrent and not necessarily decreasing.

De Villiers registers remorse that South African New Testament scholars were not more proactive in applying implications of biblical exegesis to current issues in the years leading up to the dismantling of apartheid.[67] This illustrates a central question for all African New Testament interpretation: What is its moral obligation to and interface with the broader societies in which it is carried out? M. Masoga, a researcher in Pretoria, is insistent on this point: "The biggest challenge facing biblical scholarship in South Africa is to find the right means by which the role and voice of the indigenous readers of the Bible can be acknowledged."[68] Among catalysts driving this challenge he cites globalization, HIV, unemployment, gay rights in the churches, and various security threats.[69] Others would no doubt cite the properly ecclesial concerns of evangelization, confirmation in the faith, church planting, and missions, or broader concerns like brain drain.[70]

Challenges and Trends
Some African New Testament scholarship follows dutifully in the train of developments elsewhere. J. Eugene Botha, for example, endorses

---

[66]Private e-mail message, January 19, 2010.
[67]"Methodology and Hermeneutics," 250–51.
[68]"How Indigenous Is the Bible? Challenges Facing 21st Century South African Biblical Scholarship," *Journal for Semitics* 13, no. 2 (2004): 152.
[69]Ibid., 141.
[70]See notes 18 and 19 above.

D. C. Parker's and Werner Kelber's views on the passé status of the last several centuries of New Testament textual criticism.[71] There never was a single stable form of the New Testament text to start with. The whole enterprise needs more or less to start over.

Other studies work hard to plot out a more productive future. Peter Nyende, writing from the Nairobi Evangelical Graduate School of Theology, Kenya, observes that there needs to be closer cooperation between academic and popular interpretation of the Bible in Africa, much of which has traditionally been oral.[72] But there is insufficient data to talk meaningfully about the principles that inform popular interpretation. Biblical scholarship ought therefore to make part of its research mandate a better grasp and systematization of these principles or practices.[73] Paul Gifford concurs.[74] He furnishes a full, fascinating, and not altogether complimentary account of Pentecostal hermeneutics in certain African churches. He calls this "the fastest growing sector of African Christianity" and a zone that is "almost totally ignored in academic discussions."[75] These churches preach "a theology of success, power, victory, and prosperity."[76] Among them would be the World Harvest Church,[77] the Jesus Manifestation Church,[78] and the Winners' Chapel,[79] all in Nairobi. Preaching often becomes a form of fundraising for pastors, despite impoverished parishioners. Hope is engendered through the impassioned proclamations of the ministers.

> An exclusive and relentless message of hope, assurance, uplift, aspiration, perseverance, with all the accompanying histrionics, rhetorical flourishes, participation, the whole performance supported by superb soloists and choirs, is the distinguishing feature of these churches. Obviously to be told that you matter, you belong at the top, God

---

[71]"New Testament Textual Criticism Is Dead! Long Live New Testament Textual Criticism," *HTS Theological Studies* 63, no. 2 (2007): 561–73.

[72]John Mbiti long ago called attention to this: "'Cattle Are Born with Ears, Their Horns Grow Later': Towards an Appreciation of African Oral Theology," *Africa Theological Journal* 8, no. 1 (1979): 15–25.

[73]"Institutional and Popular Interpretations of the Bible in Africa: Towards an Integration," *Expository Times* 119, no. 2 (2007): 59–66.

[74]"The Bible in Africa: A Novel Usage in Africa's Churches," *Bulletin of the School of Oriental and African Studies* 71, no. 2 (2008): 203–19.

[75]Ibid., 205.

[76]Ibid., 206.

[77]Ibid., 207.

[78]Ibid., 208.

[79]Ibid.

wants to bring you there, must provide incentives in conditions where it is all too easy to give up. That is the function of this preaching—which, it must be said, it is not very different from the function of the original Hebrew prophets at the time of the exile. This Pentecostal preaching is not expository, nor doctrinal (to illustrate classical Christian doctrines), nor even ethical in the traditional sense. Despite the undeniable tensions inherent in this declarative preaching, it is proving a winning formula and constitutes the most interesting use of the Bible in Africa today.[80]

John Mbiti, a Kenyan who is emeritus professor at the University of Bern, Switzerland, has made a start in surveying other types of indigenous interpretation in various settings and forms.[81]

The challenge here is not only scholarly ignorance of indigenous knowledge, underscored also by Masoga.[82] There is the corresponding reluctance of scholars to acknowledge the relevance of that knowledge in the first place. A North American scholar observes that for Western scholars "the most difficult step" toward positive interface with and understanding of African scholarship will be "openness to those who are more conservative than many scholars have become."[83] Western scholarship in many quarters has helped midwife the demise of Christian populations in former centers like Europe.[84] In other words, scholarship is openly destructive of Christian faith as understood by many who practice it. African interpretive communities may well incorporate and encourage populations seeing meteoric conversion to Christian faith and church growth. These developments may seem unimportant or even undesirable to secularized Western scholars "because the lens through which the religious academy peers are opaque, rendering Africa barely visible."[85]

---

[80]Ibid., 219. From another angle see Madipoane Masenya, "The Bible and Prophecy in African–South African Pentecostal Churches," *Missionalia* 33, no. 1 (2005): 35–45. The call here is for prophetic preaching that deals with society's culpable structures and not just personal sins.
[81]John Mbiti, "Do You Understand What You Are Reading? The Bible in African Homes, Schools and Churches," *Missionalia* 33, no. 2 (2005): 234–48.
[82]"How Indigenous Is the Bible?," 143.
[83]Everertt Huffard, "When Scholarship Goes South: Biblical Scholarship and Global Trends," *Restoration Quarterly* 48, no. 2 (2006): 69.
[84]See, e.g., Roger Schroeder, "Catholic Church Growing Everywhere—Except in Europe," *International Bulletin of Missionary Research* 30, no. 3 (2006): 142–43. Skeptical biblical scholarship in Europe is not the sole responsible party for this, but it can also hardly be irrelevant to it.
[85]Bonk, "Ecclesiastical Cartography," 154.

They will be less opaque if studies like Ernest van Eck's and Grant LeMarquand's are heeded. The former surveys the history of biblical interpretation in Africa, analyzes current African theologies and hermeneutics, calls for interpretation that is biblical and not merely anti-Western, and plots ways forward.[86] At critical points, he draws on African theologian Tite Tiénou, a Burkina Faso native who is impacting international theological education as dean of one of the world's largest seminaries, Trinity Evangelical Divinity School near Chicago. Van Eck concludes, "If African theology wants to be Christian, it should be Biblical and contextual. The first and foremost resource for African theology, as in any other theology that purports to be Christian, should be the word of God," by which he means the Bible.[87] By contextual he means that "the results of African theology should make a difference in all walks of life" in Africa.[88] Van Eck furnishes an unusually wide-ranging, perceptive, and, where needed, iconoclastic synthesis of the complexities of current biblical interpretation, especially in the African academy.

LeMarquand surveys a range of biblical scholarship in a primarily descriptive fashion.[89] He calls attention to a valuable tool he compiled some years ago: "A Bibliography of the Bible in Africa."[90] He reviews four important doctoral dissertations in the area of New Testament studies written by Africans in recent generations: Kenyan John Mbiti's 1963 Cambridge thesis published as *New Testament Eschatology in an African Background*,[91] Ghanaian John Pobee's Cambridge thesis published in 1985 as *Persecution and Martyrdom in the Theology of Paul*,[92] and Nigerian Teresa Okure's *The Johannine Approach to Mission: A Contextual Study of John 4:1–42*.[93] Okure illustrates LeMarquand's point that "in Africa . . . there is no rift between biblical scholarship and a believing scholar. Faith and exegesis go hand in hand."[94] Part of the dedication of her doctoral dissertation included

---

[86]"The Word Is Life: African Theology as Biblical and Contextual Theology," *HTS Theological Studies* 62, no. 2 (2006): 679–701.
[87]Ibid., 698.
[88]Ibid.
[89]"And the Rulers of the Nations Shall Bring Their Treasures into It," 243–55.
[90]In Gerald O. West and Musa W. Dube, eds., *The Bible in Africa: Transactions, Trajectories, and Trends* (Leiden: Brill, 2000), 633–800.
[91]London: Oxford University Press, 1971.
[92]Sheffield: JSOT, 1985.
[93]WUNT 2/31 (Tübingen: Mohr Siebeck, 1988).
[94]"And the Rulers of the Nations Shall Bring Their Treasures into It," 248.

an acknowledgment LeMarquand says is "unlike any I have seen in a thesis written by a Western scholar":[95]

> This litany of acknowledgements would be incomplete without the special mention of Jesus. The statement of the Psalmist applies most aptly in my case: "If the Lord had not been my help," this work would never have seen the light of day (Psalm 94:17). Jesus' unfailing help sustained me most tangibly throughout my entire course of study in ways that might be described as miraculous. . . . For the schooling in trust which he provided for me through these trying circumstances, I am deeply grateful to him.[96]

In contrast, a fourth dissertation, done at Vanderbilt by Botswanan Musa Dube, strikes LeMarquand as perhaps "anti-biblical and even anti-Christian"[97]: *Postcolonial Feminist Interpretation of the Bible.*[98] Musa argues that the Bible is simply a colonialist book used to subjugate people; most of it is both patriarchal and imperial in culpable ways.

LeMarquand also surveys a number of articles that illustrate how "biblical scholars in Africa are also theologians who are concerned about the life of the church."[99] He refers to research organizations like the Pan-African Association of Biblical Exegetes and the Nigerian Association for Biblical Studies, as well as key enterprises like Acton Publishers in Nairobi. African biblical interpretation proceeds under conditions often adverse to life in general, let alone the cultured activity of research and writing. Sometimes what is produced seems to fall short of standards elsewhere in the world. Yet he concludes:

> It may be that the most significant readings, at least in the eyes of the Creator, are not those of the detached, objective scholarship of the rich Western world, but rather the interpretations of committed and engaged scholars, church leaders, and lay people seeking to be faithful in and to their own context. We have much to learn from them.[100]

---

[95]Ibid.
[96]Okure, *The Johannine Approach to Mission*, vii.
[97]"And the Rulers of the Nations Shall Bring Their Treasures into It," 250.
[98]St. Louis: Chalice, 2000.
[99]"And the Rulers of the Nations Shall Bring Their Treasures into It," 251.
[100]Ibid., 255.

Hermeneutical Perspectives

As might be expected in a setting characterized by rapid developments and flux, a wide range of proposals vie for the attention of anyone seeking to understand the dynamics of New Testament interpretation as it unfolds in various African locales.

J. Muthengi makes a plea for integration of evangelism and social concern. Evangelism calls for careful attention to the message that is derived from the New Testament text in light of the acute need for it to be shared in conjunction with "holistic ministry" as "the only missions approach with a promise" in Africa.[101] Much New Testament scholarship, of course, in the West and elsewhere, relegates matters of evangelism and social outreach to domains outside of the interpretive guild. One scholar who has attempted to incorporate the outlook of the marginalized poor is Gerald West. But Godwin Akper questions the extent to which a white, middle-class scholar like West can really succeed at speaking for the "ordinary reader" in marginalized populations through whose eyes West wishes to view biblical texts.[102] Akper wants to check the spectacle of "socially engaged biblical scholars" like West "simply reading through the 'ordinary reader'" of their own projection. Instead, he feels it is vital that "the 'ordinary readers' are actually doing their own reading" so that scholars like West can benefit from the validly "critical" readings of the nonprivileged.[103]

The fact is that there are frequently tensions between "readings" conditioned by post-Christian Western assumptions, on the one hand, and the readings favored by indigenous "ordinary" Africans, on the other. At the University of Pretoria, for example, there have occasionally been "major tensions between faculty and Church" and even "accusations regarding theological heresy during the last decade."[104] New Testament scholar Andries van Aarde felt constrained to pen words of self-defense.[105] Another illustration of hermeneutics in conflict: North American scholar Glenna Jackson gamely persevered in urging Jesus

---

[101] "Integral Missions as a Church Mandate: The Current State of the Church in Africa," *Evangelical Journal* 26, no. 1 (2008): 41.

[102] "The Role of the 'Ordinary Reader' in Gerald O. West's Hermeneutics," *Scriptura* 88 (2005): 1–13.

[103] Ibid., 11.

[104] P. R. Du Toit, "The Dutch Reformed Church and the Faculty of Theology at the University of Pretoria," *Verbum et Ecclesia* 30, no. 3 (2009): 1; accessed April 9, 2010, http://www.ve.org .za/index.php/VE/article/viewFile/263/313.

[105] Ibid., 15–16.

Seminar convictions on African students who came to college bearing quite different theological convictions about God and Scripture. Apparently this went smoothly enough for her at Otterbein College in Ohio and among various Methodist constituencies near there.[106] But in Zimbabwe, one student, she recalls, "has yet to forgive me for the fact that Mary was not a virgin."[107] This is a fact for Jackson, presumably, because of her privileged vantage point as a Western biblical scholar committed to Jesus Seminar teachings. But rather than wonder whether she might need to rethink, Jackson concludes that her students' "understanding of early Christianity comes as the result of fundamentalist, white, western missionaries who, in many cases, unloaded a white, male god on them."[108]

Wilhelm Meyer observes a similar reluctance among African students to embrace historical-critical readings that are inimical to their understandings of Scripture and theological realities.[109] He notes Daniel Patte's insight that "critical exegetes have committed the same mistakes as fundamentalists, universalizing their own experience and denying the legitimacy of other interpretations."[110] Observing the turmoil that Western "critical" approaches to Gospels texts inflicted on students brought up believing in the historicity of the Gospels (in contrast to Western scholars like Jackson above, who view at least portions of the Gospels as contrived myths), Meyer perceptively asks, "Could issues of sources, authorship and inspiration of the biblical texts be raised by a method that does less to estrange students from their faith and their family and church discourse communities?"[111] Still more pointedly, "Do we really recognize that the problems faced by the students often arise as the result of our [i.e., Western "critical"] discourses and our teaching practices rather than as the result of any inherent weaknesses in the students?"[112]

Reflection on hermeneutics in Africa is extensive and wide-ranging. "Intercultural exegesis" is proposed, understood as "a constructive dialogue between an original biblical culture and the culture of a receptive audience, taking into account cultures of Christian tradi-

[106]Glenna Jackson, "The Jesus Seminar in Africa," *Forum* 6, no. 1 (2003): 85.
[107]Ibid., 93.
[108]Ibid., 92.
[109]"Histories of Reading and Readings of 'History,'" *Neotestamentica* 39, no. 1 (2005): 141–62.
[110]Ibid., 145.
[111]Ibid., 160.
[112]Ibid.

tions as well."[113] "From this perspective, African context and people are not used just as a field of applying 'exegetical' conclusions, but they stand as the subject of interpretation, equipped with genuine epistemological privilege."[114] Humphrey Mwangi Waweru offers a contrasting tripartite scheme, drawing heavily on Edward Said's concept of contrapuntalism.[115] J. Eugene Botha observes the differences between Western and African social values, particularly when viewed alongside the values present in Scripture. The similarities and differences pose major challenges for biblical interpretation.[116] Richard Rohrbaugh makes the important point that culture (particularly the interpreter's own) must not be allowed to become canon.[117] The role of the Bible and its message for political and social life is part of ongoing African hermeneutical discussion, particularly in South Africa.[118] There are plenty of quarters in Africa, of course, where writers would need to be circumspect in publishing ideas too critical of persons in power.

Outside the field of hermeneutics proper but illustrative of the interpretive task, a number of studies seek to bring clarity to understanding of such topics as spirituality,[119] witchcraft,[120] God in his relation to

---

[113] Jean-Claude Loba-Mkole, "The New Testament and Intercultural Exegesis in Africa," *Journal for the Study of the New Testament* 30, no. 1 (2007): 20. There appears to be substantial overlap between this article and two others by the same author: "Rise of Intercultural Biblical Exegesis in Africa," *Hekima Review* 35 (2006): 9–22; and "Rise of Intercultural Biblical Exegesis in Africa," *HTS Theological Studies* 64, no. 3 (2008): 1347–64.

[114] Loba-Mkole, "The New Testament and Intercultural Exegesis in Africa," 24.

[115] "Reading the Bible Contrapuntally: A Theory and Methodology for a Contextual Bible Interpretation in Africa," *Swedish Missiological Themes/Svensk missionstidskrift* 94, no. 3 (2006): 333–48.

[116] "Exploring Issues around Biblical, Western, and African Social Values," *HTS Theological Studies* 63, no. 1 (2007): 147–69.

[117] "Hermeneutics as Cross-Cultural Encounter: Obstacles to Understanding," *HTS Theological Studies* 62, no. 2 (2006): 559–76.

[118] See, e.g., Jeremy Punt, "Popularising the Prophet in Parliament: The Bible in Post-Apartheid, South African Public Discourse," *Religion and Theology* 14, no. 3–4 (2007): 206–23; Gerrie Snyman, "Social Identity and South African Biblical Hermeneutics: A Struggle against Prejudice?," *Journal of Theology for Southern Africa* 121 (2005): 34–55; Benno van den Toren, "The Political Significance of Jesus: Christian Involvement for the Democratisation of Africa," *Africa Journal of Evangelical Theology* 26, no. 1 (2007): 65–88.

[119] Christo Lombardo, "Four South Africans' Proposals for a Central Theme to 'Scriptural Spirituality,'" *Scriptura* 88 (2005): 139–50.

[120] Esther J. Kibor, "Witchcraft and Sorcery: A Biblical Perspective with Implications for Church Ministry," *Africa Journal of Evangelical Theology* 25, no. 2 (2006): 151–61. The author urges readers not to give in to the syncretism that fosters faith in/fear of witchcraft. She gives five steps for dealing with the problem.

the problem of evil in people—including "Christians" (who too often don't live what they profess)[121]—and reconciliation.[122]

Patterns and Prospects

Specialists tend to regard the history of African interpretation through an established template. I have delayed describing it until now so that the reader could wrestle inductively with current ideas and approaches without resorting immediately to a taxonomy that might contribute to facile categorization. Justin Ukpong outlines major phases and thematics as follows.[123]

Patristic interpretation centered in Alexandria, Egypt, and associated with Origen favored allegorical methods. This approach never died out and continues today in the Coptic Orthodox Church. In the nineteenth and twentieth centuries Western impulses introduced new ecclesial bodies and interpretive outlooks, including historical-critical and literary-critical methods. (Largely overlooked in the academic template are the evangelical theological readings of Scripture that were integral to the evangelization of much of sub-Saharan Africa.[124]) These methods are "practiced in sub-Saharan Africa and particularly by the whites in South Africa."[125] Many of the articles cited above are to be located in this methodological sphere.

Black African scholars have preferred some form of what is called a contextual method. At its core is serious engagement with the African context. Ukpong divides this method into two exegetical paradigms. The first is rooted in the indigenous religious culture and is called "inculturation." The second is the "liberation" paradigm and is "rooted in the secular culture."[126] There are four models in the "inculturation" paradigm (1–4 below) and three in the liberation paradigm (5–7 below).

1. *Comparative approach.* African writers dating into the nineteenth century have sought to vindicate African culture and religion

---

[121]J. Enuwosa, "Exploring the Nature of God in the New Testament for Meaningful Development in Nigeria," *Bible Bhashyam* 31, no. 2 (2005): 106–22.

[122]A. M. Meiring, "From Christianity to African Religion and Back Again," *Verbum et Ecclesia* 26, no. 3 (2005): 718–39.

[123]"African Interpretation," in *The New Interpreter's Dictionary of the Bible*, ed. Katharine Doob Sakenfeld, 5 vols. (Nashville: Abingdon, 2006–2009), 1:62–63.

[124]For a suggestive overview of historical developments in which these readings unfolded, see Burton, *The Blessing of Africa*, chap. 18.

[125]Ukpong, "African Interpretation," 1:62.

[126]Ibid.

in comparison with Christianity, given that the missionary message called for a turn to something allegedly superior to anything inherent in African (or any other) culture. Continuities and discontinuities were discovered. The approach enabled articulation of African convictions and values. But it sometimes overvalued African traditions and undervalued Christian claims. "It also demonstrated little concern for hermeneutical or secular application."[127] Ukpong sees as one of its major results the realization that traditional African religion served as effective preparation for the gospel. From within a comparative framework J. N. K. Mugambi perceptively calls for renewed and discerning appreciation for African religion, culture, and heritage, not to displace or attenuate the gospel message but to prevent its captivity to Western interests.[128]

2. *Africa-in-the-Bible approach.* With little interest in social or theological application, this method has raised awareness of ties between the African continent and biblical history. For example, Jesus spent time in Egypt as an infant; Cush is significant in Old Testament and Ethiopia in New Testament accounts. More comprehensively, the descendants of Abraham become subsumed under the "African" rubric: "African nations consist of more than just Cush; they include Egypt, Canaan, Edom, Libya, Arabia, Midian, and even Israel and Judah."[129] The land conquered by Joshua is attached to the African continent: "Those who exegete the Bible should recognize that the Promised Land itself is a prime piece of African real estate, at the very heart of the biblical story."[130]

3. *Evaluative approach.* The Bible is brought into dialogue with the African context. Some typical questions are: What does Scripture say about this or that element of African life? How does a biblical text appear when viewed from the standpoint of a given African cultural conviction? How does a biblical teaching apply to an African setting? This approach is classical in that it understands "exegesis as the recovery of text meaning, and hermeneutics as the application"[131] (though hermeneutics in many definitions does not pertain to application). A

---

[127]Ibid.

[128]"A Fresh Look at Evangelism in Africa," *International Review of Mission* 87, no. 346 (1998): 342–60.

[129]Rodney Sadler Jr., "Africa, African," in *The New Interpreter's Dictionary of the Bible*, ed. Sakenfeld, 1:62.

[130]Ibid.

[131]Ukpong, "African Interpretation," 1:62.

major contribution of this approach (adopted, for example, by John Mbiti) has been a highlighting of the ways that African culture and religion bring positive elements to the interpretive enterprise.

4. *"Inculturation" approach.* The theory here is that "the *meaning of a text is a function of the interaction between the text in its social-historical context, and a community of readers in their contemporary contexts.*"[132] The idea is to combine religious and secular aspects of culture as interconnected; it is a holistic approach. Academic insights are integrated with what are taken to be ordinary readings. We noted earlier the questions raised by Godwin Akper regarding how "ordinary" the readings of trained academicians affecting to speak for the downtrodden masses can actually be.[133]

5. *Liberation-theology approach.* The Bible is a resource for overcoming oppression, understood as economic and political victimization. As God liberated Israel from Egypt, the Bible's message calls people out of bondage. The Bible's prophets call for social justice in ways that pave the way for similar outcries now. Jesus, like the prophets, is concerned above all for the poor. In many ways concern for the poor is a historic Christian concern, firmly rooted in both the Old Testament and the New. At a more fundamental level, however, at work here is the attempt to wed Marxist theory with aspects of Christian thought and practice. Mario Aguilar argues that liberation theology holds the key for transformational justice in a place like Rwanda.[134] There are also approaches exploring social justice without overt appeal to liberation theology, however.[135]

6. *Feminist-theology approach.* Some interpreters stress recovery of women's muted voice in and beneath Scripture.[136] Others critique the androcentrism and patriarchy of the Bible and its historic interpretation, calling many biblical passages into question and highlighting women's oppression as a theological concern and social scourge. In

---

[132]Ibid., 1:63, Ukpong's emphasis.

[133]"The Role of the 'Ordinary Reader,'" 1–13.

[134]*Reclaiming Liberation Theology: Theology, Liberation and Genocide* (London: SCM, 2009). For historical and sociological insight see Timothy Longman, *Christianity and Genocide in Rwanda* (Cambridge: Cambridge University Press, 2010).

[135]See, e.g., Piet J. Naudé, "Cultural Justice under Conditions of Globalisation," in *The New Testament Interpreted*, ed. Breytenbach, Thom, and Punt, 267–87.

[136]See, e.g., with appeal to Lategan, Elna Mouton, "Interpreting the New Testament in Africa: Bernard Lategan on the Threshold of Diverse Theological Discourses," in *The New Testament Interpreted*, ed. Breytenbach, Thom, and Punt, 177–98.

general this is an importation of Western social and political debate into the segment of (especially academic) African society that is sufficiently privileged through education and employment to take part in it.

7. *Black-theology approach*. Pioneered by Desmond Tutu, among others, this approach challenged the racism of apartheid, which in South Africa held sway officially until 1994. "African Christians have examined the same book the oppressors used to justify their conquest, and have discovered encouraging words of freedom."[137] It was "the Bible's teaching on 'the brotherhood of man' that inspired Protestant and Catholic leaders in South Africa to put heady theological differences aside and develop the *Kairos* document in 1985."[138] This was foundational to international support for the antiapartheid movement, which was influential in helping bring it to an end.[139] Black theology understood in this way plays a continuing role wherever racism rears its head.

These are major, academically recognized categories of New Testament (and Old Testament) interpretation in Africa. What lies ahead? Saayman states that "a new model of African Bible reading or a truly African hermeneutic is of immense importance for both New Testament scholars as well as missiologists."[140] One can certainly hope for such a breakthrough.[141] Given the diversity of the continent's history, languages, peoples, cultures, heritage, governments, religions, forms of Christianity, and much else, a single "new model" that would make a fundamental widespread difference seems unlikely. It seems rather the case that African New Testament interpretation in coming years, like the unpredicted expansion of Christian belief among Africans there and around the world in recent generations, will continue to hold surprises that defy current projections, where these even exist.[142]

---

[137]Burton, *The Blessing of Africa*, 239.

[138]Ibid., 241.

[139]Cf. Ukpong, "African Interpretation," 1:63.

[140]"New Testament Studies and Missiology in South Africa," 211.

[141]A commendable attempt at a comprehensive indigenous rendering of the Bible is Tokunboh Adeyemo, ed., *Africa Bible Commentary* (Grand Rapids: Zondervan, 2006). Reviewers have not tended to see it as constituting a hermeneutical breakthrough though it may mark forward strides. For a discerning discussion see Christopher Peppler, *Journal of the South African Theological Society* 3 (2007): 111–16. For a less welcoming assessment see Chad Pollock, *ATLA Newsletter* 54, no. 3 (2007): 14–15.

[142]Probing the past and making suggestions for the future, albeit primarily for South Africa, is Botha, "The Study of the New Testament in African Universities," 247–65.

It is true that Africa, like all parts of today's world, faces acute challenges. Yet the continent's potential in terms of not only natural but also human resources is staggering. Moreover, among the masses are tens of millions who seem to be calling on the God of Abraham, the God of the Lord Jesus Christ, who "opposes the proud, but gives grace to the humble" (James 4:6, ESV; cf. Prov. 3:34). Unless the faith of these millions, and the many who have preceded them in history, is delusional, this introduces a living and active divine factor into the equation. Combine that with the vigor of African discussion, the rapidity of ecclesial expansion, and the significance of Africa's geopolitical positioning, and it would not be surprising if distinctively African elements assumed unprecedented hermeneutical significance in coming generations for New Testament studies at the international level.[143]

[143]My thanks to colleagues in the Deerfield Dialogue Group (sponsored by the Carl F. H. Henry Center for Theological Understanding) and to my assistant Craig Long for critical comments. For all things Ethiopic, the gracious analysis and bibliographic assistance of Tekletsadik Belachew Nigru was invaluable.

10

New Testament Studies in North America

CRAIG L. BLOMBERG

Years ago at a Tyndale Fellowship New Testament study group in Cambridge, I recall Don Carson initially reluctant to give his opinion on a vexing exegetical question in Matthew 23. He likened it to being asked his views on creation and evolution, which he was equally reluctant to formulate without numerous introductory remarks, cautions, and caveats. Finally, David Wenham blurted out something like, "Oh come on, Don, just tell us what you think!" After blushing, he responded very cogently and concisely despite his previous protestations.

It feels like I am in at least as precarious a position with a topic as broad and multifaceted as the one assigned to me here, and I have even less hope of responding either as succinctly or as persuasively.

This section of our Festschrift surveys the state of the discipline of New Testament studies in several large parts of the world. Presumably, our mandate is to focus on the distinctives of each continent, but in a global village there are inevitable overlaps. Particularly given the linguistic affinities and cross-pollination of scholarship between North America and the United Kingdom, there will be emphases that link Britain more with North America than with the Continent and thus not loom large in Robert Yarbrough's chapter on Europe (see below).[1] Given that "North America" usually includes Mexico and the Caribbean, and sometimes denotes Central America as well, there will also be trends noted here that have more in common with Majority World scholarship elsewhere than with dominant features of the West.

The other obvious introductory caveat has to do with the amount of material to review. North America remains one of the two most prolific continents by far when it comes to New Testament scholarship, at least as traditionally conceived. Any article-length survey of the most dominant distinctives of so enormous a body of literature must be highly selective. One can barely get started, or so it feels. Still, Don Carson himself has excelled at producing precisely such wide-ranging yet manageably sized surveys,[2] so his colleagues and former students ought certainly to "give it a go." With a strong sense of inadequacy for the task, then, I plunge ahead.

The Historical Jesus and the Synoptic Gospels

The decade after the majority of the Jesus Seminar's work (a distinctively North American phenomenon), the perspectives of its former cochairs, Marcus Borg and Dominic Crossan, remain highly influential. If there has been any shift in their thinking, it has been somewhat away from the Jesus as "Cynic sage" or "Spirit person" of their works from the 1980s and '90s toward Jesus' implicit, and at times explicit,

---

[1] In speaking of North American trends, then, I have tried to limit myself to works by writers teaching or living in North America and produced and published in North America, even if also copublished overseas. This, by definition, excludes works written by North Americans as part of European doctorates published in European monograph series, of which there are many good ones. I have, however, included items in the Journal for the Study of the New Testament: Supplement Series/Library of New Testament Studies from North American seminaries or universities, once Sheffield Academic Press began publishing in New York and then was quickly bought out by Continuum and actually based in New York (while still copublishing in London).

[2] One thinks, e.g., of his "Hermeneutics: A Brief Assessment of Some Recent Trends," *Themelios* 5, no. 2 (1980): 12–20; "Recent Literature on the Fourth Gospel: Some Reflections," *Themelios* 9, no. 1 (1983): 8–18; "Current Issues in Biblical Theology: A New Testament Perspective," *BBR* 5 (1995): 17–41; "The Challenge of the Balkanization of Johannine Studies," in *John, Jesus and History*, vol. 1, ed. Paul N. Anderson, Felix Just, and Tom Thatcher (Atlanta: SBL, 2007), 133–64; and "Ongoing Imperative for World Mission," in *The Great Commission: Evangelicals and the History of World Missions*, ed. Martin I. Klauber and Scott M. Manetsch (Nashville: B&H, 2008), 176–95.

countercultural threat to Rome. Their jointly authored work, *The Last Week: A Day-by-Day Account of Jesus's Final Week in Jerusalem,* encapsulates this perspective as clearly as any, as they narrate:

> Two processions entered Jerusalem on a spring day in the year 30. It was the beginning of the week of Passover, the most sacred week of the Jewish year. . . .
>
> One was a peasant procession, the other an imperial procession. From the east, Jesus rode a donkey down the Mount of Olives, cheered by his followers. . . .
>
> On the opposite side of the city, from the west, Pontius Pilate, the Roman governor of Idumea, Judea, and Samaria, entered Jerusalem at the head of a column of imperial cavalry and soldiers. Jesus's procession proclaimed the kingdom of God; Pilate's proclaimed the power of empire. The two processions embody the central conflict of the week that led to Jesus's crucifixion.[3]

At least Borg and Crossan still think a fair amount of information can be known about the historical Jesus, noticeably more than the 18 percent of the sayings and 16 percent of the deeds of Jesus that were colored red or pink in the two major volumes on the *five* Gospels that the Jesus Seminar produced.[4] At least they agree with most evangelical researchers that historical inquiry is an appropriate form of investigation into Jesus' identity and that its results can prove fruitful. So, too, does John Meier, whose laudable experiment simulating the results of a quartet of Protestant, Catholic, Jewish, and atheist scholars secluded in the Harvard Divinity School library until they produce a consensus statement, has led to volumes 3 and 4 of *A Marginal Jew: Rethinking the Historical Jesus* over the last decade, with no end to the project clearly in sight, despite promises in each volume that the next one would be the last. Meier's recent works show that "Jesus, even more than John, was not so charismatic that he totally neglected the question of how to structure his movement and give it a distinct

---

[3]Marcus J. Borg and John Dominic Crossan, *The Last Week: A Day-by-Day Account of Jesus's Final Week in Jerusalem* (San Francisco: HarperSanFrancisco, 2006), 2.

[4]Robert W. Funk, Robert W. Hoover, and the Jesus Seminar, *The Five Gospels: The Search for the Authentic Words of Jesus* (New York: Macmillan, 1993); and Robert W. Funk and the Jesus Seminar, *The Acts of Jesus: The Search for the Authentic Deeds of Jesus* (San Francisco: HarperSanFrancisco, 1996).

identity within Palestinian Judaism" and that the historical Jesus was a halakhic Jesus.

> As the Elijah-like prophet of the end time who seeks to regather all Israel and prepare it for God's kingdom (imminent and yet somehow present), he and he alone can tell Israel how to interpret and practice God's Law as befits members of the kingdom. Nothing more and nothing less explains what seems to us to be a patchwork approach to the Law on Jesus' part.[5]

Just when Robert van Voorst had thoroughly surveyed the evidence for Jesus outside the New Testament, seemingly hammering the final nails in the coffin of the view that Jesus never existed,[6] an extreme skepticism about what we can know of him or whether there was such a figure at all has begun to reemerge. The appearance of the so-called new atheism and a proliferation of online writers not accountable to the traditional constraints of scholarly peer review have abetted this resurgence. Hector Avalos, for example, can declare:

> The quest for the historical Jesus is an abject failure. After hundreds of years and probably millions of person-hours, reconstructions of Jesus are no better than the one of Reimarus in the eighteenth century. Reimarus had nearly exhausted the critical search for any historicity, and he found mostly a myth.[7]

Indeed, so damaging an influence has the Bible been, in Avalos's opinion, that he believes the sole remaining task for biblical scholarship is to redefine its purpose "so that it is tasked with eliminating completely the influence of the Bible in the modern world"![8]

Such calls are extreme and will not generally be heeded. More damaging are the relentless crusades of those like Bart Ehrman, who appeal to "lost Scriptures" and "lost Christianities," to all the supposed contradictions in the Scripture, and to textual variants in the Gospels

---

[5]Vol. 3, *Companions and Competitors* (New York: Doubleday, 2001), 626; and vol. 4, *Law and Love* (New Haven, CT: Yale University Press, 2009), 415, respectively. In vol. 4 Meier adds a hypothetical Muslim scholar into the mix.

[6]Robert E. van Voorst, *Jesus outside the New Testament: An Introduction to the Ancient Evidence* (Grand Rapids: Eerdmans, 2000).

[7]Hector Avalos, *The End of Biblical Studies* (Amherst, NY: Prometheus, 2007), 212.

[8]Ibid., 341.

as if they were "misquoting Jesus."[9] Ehrman, along with Paula Fredriksen, has revived the old refuted Schweitzerian hypothesis of Jesus as a failed apocalyptic prophet, without giving it any new support;[10] but Ehrman's charisma as a speaker, his clarity and candor as a writer, and his aggressiveness in marketing his views by all available media have given his perspectives an influence all out of proportion to their merit. Like Elaine Pagels and Karen King, known primarily for their selective appeals to the Gnostic Gospels (and related works) to support a kind of feminism supposedly found there and a create-your-own religion from the god(dess) within yourself, which *is* genuinely found there,[11] Ehrman has tapped into a significant contemporary North American impulse to cast off traditional Christianity and remake Jesus in any way that suits one. Indeed, although it is not a work of historical Jesus research per se, Stephen Prothero's *American Jesus: How the Son of God Became a National Icon* well captures the current spectrum of populist portrayals of the famous Nazarene with its chapter titles: "Enlightened Sage," "Sweet Savior," "Manly Redeemer," "Superstar," "Black Moses," "Rabbi," and "Oriental Christ."[12] And not all of these inadequate interpretations of Jesus are found merely in "liberal" circles!

Fortunately North American evangelical scholarship on all of these issues is likewise flourishing; if only it could become as well known in the public square as some of the more avant-garde work just noted! Craig Evans, Darrell Bock, and Ben Witherington, in particular, have published widely and also sought out the necessary media attention to spread their views to those who don't read (or at least who don't read *their* works).[13] Bock's debunking of the *Da*

---

[9]See, respectively, Bart D. Ehrman, *Lost Scriptures: Books That Did Not Make It into the New Testament* (New York: Oxford University Press, 2003); Ehrman, *Lost Christianities: The Battles for Scripture and the Faiths We Never Knew* (New York: Oxford University Press, 2003); Ehrman, *Jesus, Interrupted: Revealing the Hidden Contradictions in the Bible (and Why We Don't Know about Them)* (New York: HarperCollins, 2009); Ehrman, *Misquoting Jesus: The Story Behind Who Changed the Bible and Why* (San Francisco: HarperSanFrancisco, 2006).

[10]Bart D. Ehrman, *Jesus: Apocalyptic Prophet of the New Millennium* (New York: Oxford University Press, 1999); Paula Fredriksen, *Jesus of Nazareth, King of the Jews: A Jewish Life and the Emergence of Christianity* (New York: Alfred Knopf, 2000).

[11]Most recently, see Elaine Pagels, *Beyond Belief: The Secret Gospel of Thomas* (New York: Random House, 2003); and Karen L. King, *The Secret Revelation of John* (Cambridge, MA: Harvard University Press, 2006).

[12](New York: Farrar, Straus, and Giroux, 2003).

[13]See especially Craig A. Evans, *Fabricating Jesus: How Modern Scholars Distort the Gospels* (Downers Grove, IL: InterVarsity, 2006); Darrell L. Bock, *The Missing Gospels: Unearthing the*

Vinci Code fiction about Christian origins[14] has sold more than all of his other books put together. Dan Wallace and several coauthors have repeatedly set Ehrman's textual criticism and other claims in their proper, larger contexts,[15] while Paul Eddy and Greg Boyd, Rob Bowman and Ed Komoszewski, Wayne House, Mark Roberts, and the immensely successful popularizer Lee Strobel have all offered important, accessible rebuttals to the misinformation widely circulating on the formation of the canon, the reliability of the Gospels, and the nature of Jesus.[16] I have continued to pursue my interests in several of these areas as well.[17] Pride of place must now, however, go to two large volumes that appeared in late 2009. The fruit of a decade of work by the IBR Historical Jesus Study Group, *Key Events in the Life of the Historical Jesus: A Collaborative Exploration of Context and Coherence*[18] takes a dozen core themes or events from Jesus' life and ministry and details the case for their authenticity via all the standard historical criteria, as well as assessing their significance. The results show significant correlation between what historians can demonstrate and what evangelical theology has classically asserted about the life of Christ. Even more impressive inasmuch as it has

---

Truth Behind Alternative Christianities (Nashville: Nelson, 2006); and Ben Witherington III, *What Have They Done with Jesus? Beyond Strange Theories and Bad History—Why We Can Trust the Bible* (San Francisco: HarperSanFrancisco, 2006). And for those who read only online publications, see Craig L. Blomberg, "Jesus of Nazareth: How Historians Can Know Him and Why It Matters" (2008) accessible at http://www.henrycenter.org/files/blomberg.pdf.

[14]Darrell L. Bock, *Breaking the Da Vinci Code: Answers to the Questions Everyone's Asking* (Nashville: Nelson, 2004).

[15]See especially Daniel B. Wallace, "The Gospel according to Bart: A Review Article of *Misquoting Jesus* by Bart Ehrman," *JETS* 49 (2006): 327–49; J. Ed Komoszewski, M. James Sawyer, and Daniel B. Wallace, *Reinventing Jesus: What* The Da Vinci Code *and Other Novel Speculations Don't Tell You* (Grand Rapids: Kregel, 2006); and Darrell L. Bock and Daniel B. Wallace, *Dethroning Jesus: Exposing Popular Culture's Quest to Unseat the Biblical Christ* (Nashville: Nelson, 2007).

[16]Paul Rhodes Eddy and Gregory A. Boyd, *The Jesus Legend: A Case for the Historical Reliability of the Synoptic Jesus Tradition* (Grand Rapids: Baker, 2007); Boyd and Eddy, *Lord or Legend? Wrestling with the Jesus Dilemma* (Grand Rapids: Baker, 2007); Robert M. Bowman Jr. and J. Ed Komoszewski, *Putting Jesus in His Place: The Case for the Deity of Christ* (Grand Rapids: Kregel, 2007); H. Wayne House, *The Jesus Who Never Lived: Exposing False Christs and Finding the Real Jesus* (Eugene, OR: Harvest House, 2008); Mark D. Roberts, *Can We Trust the Gospels? Investigating the Reliability of Matthew, Mark, Luke, and John* (Wheaton, IL: Crossway, 2007); and Lee Strobel, *The Case for the Real Jesus* (Grand Rapids: Zondervan, 2007).

[17]See especially Craig L. Blomberg, *The Historical Reliability of the Gospels*, rev. ed. (Downers Grove, IL: InterVarsity, 2007).

[18]Ed. Darrell L. Bock and Robert L. Webb (Tübingen: Mohr Siebeck, 2009; Grand Rapids: Eerdmans, forthcoming).

a single author is Craig Keener's latest tome.[19] As is characteristic of his scholarship, Keener furnishes the fullest compilation of and interaction with both primary historical sources and contemporary secondary literature in defending the plausibility of an even larger amount of every main segment of Jesus' words and deeds by conventional criteria and reasoning.

Meanwhile, the Third Quest of the Historical Jesus continues with largely less well-known contributors working painstakingly on individual portions of the Gospels and Jesus' life and occupying less "exciting" but more centrist positions on countless issues. For an excellent overall anthology of perspectives, with excerpts of relevant primary literature from antiquity, see the work coedited by Amy-Jill Levine, Dale Allison, and Dominic Crossan, *The Historical Jesus in Context*.[20] For one expert's succinct summary of what the majority of the well-hidden middle-of-the-road scholarship is concluding, consult James H. Charlesworth's *The Historical Jesus: An Essential Guide*.[21] For perhaps the most interesting individual scholar's reconstructions, which defy simple categorization as either conservative or liberal, follow Dale Allison's ongoing work.[22]

Excellent front-line scholarly commentaries on individual Synoptic Gospels have also come out of North America since the turn of the millennium. One thinks especially of David Turner and Craig Keener on Matthew;[23] Joel Marcus, Ben Witherington, James Edwards, Eugene Boring, Adela Yarbro Collins, and Robert Stein, all on Mark;[24] and François Bovon on Luke.[25] While the majority of these have been

---

[19]Craig S. Keener, *The Historical Jesus of the Gospels* (Grand Rapids: Eerdmans, 2009).

[20]Princeton, NJ: Princeton University Press, 2006.

[21]Nashville: Abingdon, 2008.

[22]See, already, Dale C. Allison Jr., *Jesus of Nazareth: Millenarian Prophet* (Minneapolis: Fortress, 1998). Cf. also especially Allison, *Resurrecting Jesus: The Earliest Christian Tradition and Its Interpreters* (New York: T&T Clark, 2005); Allison, *The Historical Christ and the Theological Jesus* (Grand Rapids: Eerdmans, 2009); Allison, *Constructing Jesus: Memory, Imagination, and History* (Grand Rapids: Baker, 2010).

[23]David L. Turner, *Matthew* (Grand Rapids: Baker, 2008); Craig S. Keener, *The Gospel of Matthew: A Socio-Rhetorical Commentary*, rev. ed. (Grand Rapids: Eerdmans, 2009).

[24]Joel Marcus, *Mark*, 2 vols. (New York: Doubleday, 2000; New Haven, CT: Yale University Press, 2009); Ben Witherington III, *The Gospel of Mark: A Socio-Rhetorical Commentary* (Grand Rapids: Eerdmans, 2001); James B. Edwards, *The Gospel according to Mark* (Grand Rapids: Eerdmans, 2002); M. Eugene Boring, *Mark: A Commentary* (Louisville: Westminster John Knox, 2006); Adela Yarbro Collins, *Mark* (Minneapolis: Fortress, 2007); Robert H. Stein, *Mark* (Grand Rapids: Baker, 2008).

[25]François Bovon, *Luke 1* (Minneapolis: Fortress, 2002).

on Mark,[26] valuable monographs and multiauthor collections have appeared on all three Synoptics. David Aune's *The Gospel of Matthew in Current Study* offers a wide-ranging collection of essays with good textbook value, Charles Talbert treats important dimensions of the Sermon on the Mount for spiritual formation, and Glenna Jackson provides an excellent *Forschungsbericht* for the Matthean account of the Syrophoenician woman's encounter with Jesus (even while suggesting a fairly far-fetched exegesis of her own).[27] For Markan studies, particularly useful are Douglas Geyer's analysis of fear and silence on the part of Jesus' followers, Marion Moeser's form-critical comparisons involving the *chreia*, and Kelly Iverson's study of Gentiles in the Gospel.[28] Key Lukan works include Guy Nave's dissertation on repentance as change of mind and action available to all, James Resseguie's study of the journey of spiritual formation, and Dwayne Adams's ETS monograph on the sinner as the morally, but not necessarily notoriously, evil person.[29]

Specialized corpora spanning all of the Synoptics have also seen important advances. Arland Hultgren's and Klyne Snodgrass's large compendia of materials on the parables have put researchers into their debt for years to come.[30] Mary Ann Beavis has opened up new vistas of the kingdom by comparing it with Greco-Roman thinking about utopia.[31] Dennis Smith has gathered together his numerous studies on

---

[26]Two additional volumes on Matthew are Grant R. Osborne, *Matthew* (Grand Rapids: Zondervan, 2010); and D. A. Carson, "Matthew," in *Expositor's Bible Commentary*, vol. 9, *Matthew and Mark*, rev. ed., ed. Tremper Longman III and David E. Garland (Grand Rapids: Zondervan, 2010). Not too long after Osborne in the ZECNT should be David E. Garland, *Luke* (Grand Rapids: Zondervan).

[27]*The Gospel of Matthew in Current Study*, ed. David E. Aune (Grand Rapids: Eerdmans, 2001); C. H. Talbert, *Reading the Sermon on the Mount: Character Formation and Decision Making in Matthew 5–7* (Columbia: University of South Carolina Press, 2004); Glenna S. Jackson, *"Have Mercy on Me": The Story of the Canaanite Woman in Matthew 15.21–28* (New York: Sheffield Academic Press, 2002).

[28]Douglas W. Geyer, *Fear, Anomaly, and Uncertainty in the Gospel of Mark* (Lanham, MD: Scarecrow, 2000); Marion C. Moeser, *The Anecdote in Mark, the Classical World and the Rabbis* (New York: Sheffield Academic Press, 2002); Kelly R. Iverson, *Gentiles in the Gospel of Mark: "Even the Dogs under the Table Eat the Children's Crumbs"* (New York: T&T Clark, 2007).

[29]Guy D. Nave, *The Role and Function of Repentance in Luke-Acts* (Atlanta: SBL, 2002); James L. Resseguie, *Spiritual Landscape: Images of Scriptural Life in the Gospel of Luke* (Peabody, MA: Hendrickson, 2004); Dwayne H. Adams, *The Sinner in Luke* (Eugene, OR: Pickwick, 2008).

[30]Arland J. Hultgren, *The Parables of Jesus: A Commentary* (Grand Rapids: Eerdmans, 2000); Klyne R. Snodgrass, *Stories with Intent: A Comprehensive Guide to the Parables of Jesus* (Grand Rapids: Eerdmans, 2008).

[31]Mary Ann Beavis, *Jesus and Utopia: Looking for the Kingdom of God in the Roman World* (Minneapolis: Fortress, 2006).

Greco-Roman symposia, making an influential, if not entirely convincing case for reading the Lord's Supper against their backdrop.[32] Greg Carey overstates his case for labeling Jesus and his earliest disciples "sinners," but does show how ambiguous their behavior would have been by the conventional cultural standards of their day, not least in the arenas of masculinity and family values.[33] John and Adela Yarbro Collins amass an impressive case for reading the title "Son of God" in the Gospels as both regal and messianic.[34] Scot McKnight thoroughly examines questions of authenticity and meaning surrounding numerous details of the Passion Narrative,[35] while Gary Habermas and Michael Licona nicely summarize all the major lines of evidence for the historicity of the resurrection.[36] Alan Stanley convincingly shows that Jesus taught the necessity of good works flowing from salvation, assessed on judgment day as a demonstration of faith, not the means by which one earns rewards above and beyond the perfections of the eternal state itself (as if such were even conceptually possible).[37] James Charlesworth edits a large and comprehensive collection of essays on archaeological foundations for historical Jesus research.[38] Craig A. Evans, finally, has edited the first ever *Encyclopedia of the Historical Jesus*, with concise and generally helpful contributions on a wide swath of relevant entries.[39]

The Gospel of John and the Acts of the Apostles
Flurries of activity continue to surround the Gospel of John, but my subheadings in this essay and the categorizations they reflect also show what has *not* happened. The Fourth Gospel has yet to be taken seriously enough for it to be used to any significant extent in scholarly

---

[32]Dennis E. Smith, *From Symposium to Eucharist: The Banquet in the Early Christian World* (Minneapolis: Fortress, 2003).

[33]Greg Carey, *Sinners: Jesus and His Earliest Followers* (Waco, TX: Baylor University Press, 2009).

[34]Adela Yarbro Collins and John J. Collins, *King and Messiah as Son of God: Divine, Human, and Angelic Messianic Figures in Biblical and Related Literature* (Grand Rapids: Eerdmans, 2008).

[35]Scot McKnight, *Jesus and His Death: Historiography, the Historical Jesus, and Atonement Theory* (Waco, TX: Baylor University Press, 2005).

[36]Gary R. Habermas and Michael R. Licona, *The Case for the Resurrection of Jesus* (Grand Rapids: Kregel, 2004).

[37]Alan P. Stanley, *Did Jesus Teach Salvation by Works? The Role of Works in Salvation in the Synoptic Gospels* (Eugene, OR: Pickwick, 2006).

[38]*Jesus and Archaeology*, ed. James H. Charlesworth (Grand Rapids: Eerdmans, 2006).

[39]New York: Routledge, 2008.

historical Jesus portraits. North American Johannine scholars use this Gospel as a test case for each new scholarly method or critical tool that comes down the pike. Several recent, wide-ranging anthologies reflect this diversity (including two to which Carson himself has contributed), particularly owing to the editorial efforts of Tom Thatcher.[40] But most of these surveys show little interest in John's theology and even less in integrating his theology with biblical or systematic theologies (contrast the published papers from a recent Scottish conference).[41] Nor are they nearly as interested in reviving questions of historicity as either British or Continental counterparts.[42] Part of this mirrors trends that are consistent across all of New Testament studies in the various regions of the world, while part represents a distinctively Johannine "club" subculture in North America that seems noticeably less interested in theology and dramatically less interested in history than even their North American counterparts in synoptic studies.

Paul Anderson seems almost alone on this continent in his repeated and sophisticated calls for a bi-optic reading of the Gospels and for formulation of historical Jesus portraits that utilize both John and the Synoptics.[43] Anderson's coedited second volume in *John, Jesus, and History* offers a multiauthor work that assesses "aspects of historicity" for each major section of the Fourth Gospel,[44] affording the one North American collection of exegetical essays to supplement my decade-old monograph[45] and heed his own call. What John Robinson

---

[40]*John, Jesus, and History*, vol. 1, ed. Anderson, Just, and Thatcher; and *What We Have Heard from the Beginning: The Past, Present, and Future of Johannine Studies*, ed. Tom Thatcher (Waco, TX: Baylor University Press, 2007). Carson's article in the latter volume is "Reflections upon a Johannine Pilgrimage," 87–104. See also *New Currents through John: A Global Perspective*, ed. Francisco Lozada Jr. and Tom Thatcher (Atlanta: SBL, 2006); and *Anatomies of Narrative Criticism: The Past, Present, and Future of the Fourth Gospel as Literature*, ed. Tom Thatcher and Stephen D. Moore (Atlanta: SBL, 2008). From the beginning of the decade and somewhat more balanced in dealing with theology and with historicity is *Jesus in Johannine Tradition*, ed. Robert T. Fortna and Tom Thatcher (Louisville: Westminster John Knox, 2001).

[41]*The Gospel of John and Christian Theology*, ed. Richard Bauckham and Carl Mosser (Grand Rapids: Eerdmans, 2008).

[42]See especially *Challenging Perspectives on the Gospel of John*, ed. John Lierman (Tübingen: Mohr Siebeck, 2006); and Richard Bauckham, *The Testimony of the Beloved Disciple: Narrative, History, and Theology in the Gospel of John* (Grand Rapids: Baker, 2007).

[43]See especially Paul N. Anderson, *The Fourth Gospel and the Quest for Jesus: Modern Foundations Reconsidered* (New York: T&T Clark, 2006).

[44]Paul N. Anderson, Felix Just, and Tom Thatcher, eds., *John, Jesus, and History*, vol. 2, *Aspects of Historicity in the Fourth Gospel* (Atlanta: SBL, 2009).

[45]Craig L. Blomberg, *The Historical Reliability of John's Gospel* (Downers Grove, IL: InterVarsity, 2001).

in the UK dubbed the "new look on John" way back in the late 1950s, has gone a long way, especially in Europe (with Richard Bauckham in the UK and Martin Hengel in Germany as the two towering figures in the movement), to rehabilitate John for historical Jesus research,[46] but North American universities have paid little notice. One might have expected the distinctively evangelical wing of North American scholarship to have fared better, but it has not. Excellent studies on John's history and/or theology have appeared on their own,[47] but, presumably to avoid being perceived as even more out of sync with the rest of academia, evangelicals have, for the most part, intentionally avoided integrating this material into their historical Jesus work.[48]

Literary and sociological study of the Fourth Gospel, nevertheless, continues to blossom. Wayne Brouwer has developed a plausible chiastic outline for the Farewell Discourse, which supports its unity, so conceived from the outset.[49] Scott Kellum has come to similar conclusions looking at other narrative and stylistic features of this passage.[50] Mary Spaulding shows how John has utilized social memories to reconfigure Jewish traditions concerning *Sukkoth* to highlight Jesus as the fulfillment of this festival.[51] In terms of recent commentaries, Andreas Köstenberger's one-volume and Craig Keener's two-volume offerings deserve highest marks.[52]

North American study of Acts in the twenty-first century seems even more lacking. On the one hand, there has been an encouraging

---

[46]See ibid., for detailed documentation.

[47]See especially, on history (from varying angles), Charles E. Hill, *The Johannine Corpus in the Early Church* (New York: Oxford University Press, 2004); Tom Thatcher, *Why John Wrote a Gospel: Jesus—Memory—History* (Louisville: Westminster John Knox, 2006); and Allen D. Callahan, *A Love Supreme: A History of the Johannine Tradition* (Minneapolis: Fortress, 2005); on theology, Marianne Meye Thompson, *The God of the Gospel of John* (Grand Rapids: Eerdmans, 2001); Craig R. Koester, *The Word of Life: A Theology of John's Gospel* (Grand Rapids: Eerdmans, 2008); and Andreas J. Köstenberger and Scott R. Swain, *Father, Son and Spirit: The Trinity and John's Gospel* (Downers Grove, IL: InterVarsity, 2008).

[48]I have made one initial attempt at this in "The Historical Jesus from the Synoptics and the Fourth Gospel: Jesus the Purifier," in a forthcoming monograph of essays on the historical Jesus from the Greer-Heard forum at New Orleans Baptist Seminary, February 2010, ed. Robert B. Stewart (Minneapolis: Fortress).

[49]Wayne Brouwer, *The Literary Development of John 13–17: A Chiastic Reading* (Atlanta: SBL, 2000).

[50]L. Scott Kellum, *The Unity of the Farewell Discourse: The Literary Integrity of John 13.31–16.33* (New York: T&T Clark, 2004).

[51]Mary B. Spaulding, *Commemorative Identities: Jewish Social Memory and the Johannine Feast of Booths* (New York: T&T Clark, 2009).

[52]Andreas Köstenberger, *John* (Grand Rapids: Baker, 2004); Craig S. Keener, *The Gospel of John: A Commentary*, 2 vols. (Peabody, MA: Hendrickson, 2003).

cluster of excellent commentaries appearing in just the last decade, more so than for any single Gospel. Justo González has incorporated Latin American themes, including missiological and charismatic emphases.[53] Scott Spencer has excelled in literary criticism, Jaroslav Pelikan in the history of interpretation, and Bruce Malina and John Pilch in social-scientific backgrounds.[54] More general commentaries, among the best in their respective series to date, have appeared from Darrell Bock, Beverly Gaventa, Bradley Chance, and Mikeal Parsons.[55] But little cutting-edge scholarship of great merit has emerged since the late 1980s–late 1990s, UK-based productions of the highly significant five-volume set, *The Book of Acts in Its First Century Setting*,[56] and the individual tomes on historicity by Colin Hemer and on theology edited by Howard Marshall and David Peterson.[57] What has continued to appear in the twenty-first century of greatest substance on Acts has also tended to come from outside the North American orbit of scholarship.[58] This includes now James Dunn's magisterial second volume of his Christianity in the Making series, even though it is much broader than just a study of Acts and much of it is a summary of the best of others' work.[59]

The major exception to these trends involves the painstakingly detailed works of Richard I. Pervo, culminating in his Hermeneia

---

[53]Justo L. González, *Acts: The Gospel of the Spirit* (Maryknoll, NY: Orbis, 2001).

[54]F. Scott Spencer, *Journeying through Acts: A Literary-Cultural Reading* (Peabody, MA: Hendrickson, 2004); Jaroslav Pelikan, *Acts* (Grand Rapids: Brazos, 2005); *Social-Science Commentary on the Book of Acts*, ed. Bruce J. Malina and John J. Pilch (Minneapolis: Fortress, 2008).

[55]Darrell L. Bock, *Acts*, BECNT (Grand Rapids: Baker, 2007); Beverly R. Gaventa, *The Acts of the Apostles*, Abingdon New Testament Commentary (Nashville: Abingdon, 2003); J. Bradley Chance, *Acts*, Smyth and Helwys Bible Commentary (Macon, GA: Smyth & Helwys, 2007); and Mikeal C. Parsons, *Acts*, Paideia Commentary on the New Testament (Grand Rapids: Baker, 2008).

[56]Ed. Bruce W. Winter (Grand Rapids: Eerdmans, 1993–1996).

[57]Colin J. Hemer, *The Book of Acts in the Setting of Hellenistic History*, ed. Conrad W. Gempf (Tübingen: Mohr, 1989); I. Howard Marshall and David Peterson, eds., *Witness to the Gospel: The Theology of Acts* (Grand Rapids: Eerdmans, 1998).

[58]One thinks especially of Andrew C. Clark, *Parallel Lives: The Relation of Paul to the Apostles in the Lucan Perspective* (Carlisle: Paternoster, 2001); Daniel Marguerat, *The First Christian Historian: Writing the "Acts of the Apostles"* (Cambridge: Cambridge University Press, 2002); Rick Strelan, *Strange Acts: Studies in the Cultural World of the Acts of the Apostles* (Berlin: de Gruyter, 2004); Loveday C. A. Alexander, *Acts in Its Ancient Literary Context: A Classicist Looks at the Acts of the Apostles* (London: T&T Clark, 2005); and the outstanding commentary by David G. Peterson, *The Acts of the Apostles* (Grand Rapids: Eerdmans, 2009). One important exception to this trend is David W. Pao, *Acts and the Isaianic New Exodus* (Grand Rapids: Baker, 2002).

[59]James D. G. Dunn, *Beginning from Jerusalem* (Grand Rapids: Eerdmans, 2009).

commentary on Acts.[60] Unfortunately, Pervo's literary interests, while providing a wealth of comparative material from the Greco-Roman world, have led him to conclude that Acts is the product of a mid-second-century author writing a mostly fictional novel. It is disheartening to observe how the critical establishment can dismiss innumerable examples of historical verisimilitude by claiming an author was wanting simply to produce *historical* fiction, and yet not allow for the option that such details, combined with literary artistry reminiscent of the novella, could suggest the presence of artistic *history*.[61] Put another way, we are told that there are few if any features of literary genre that enable one to distinguish historiography from fiction when a case for historicity has been made. But that important caution is then disregarded when a case for fiction is being made. At any rate, a detailed assessment of the strengths and weaknesses of Pervo's case should become a key agenda item for twenty-first-century Acts scholarship.

Pauline Studies

The respective roles of the law and the gospel in Pauline theology continue to spawn far more debate than any other single issue in the study of this always fascinating but often frustrating apostle. The debate is scarcely unique to North American scholarship; indeed N. T. Wright, until recently bishop of Durham, has emerged as the key, magnetic figure in the debate, who noticeably either attracts or repels.[62] But whereas the rest of the world still seems focused on "the New Perspective" on Paul, Magnus Zetterholm observes that a much more "radical new perspective" has been growing particularly among North American scholars. Zetterholm singles out Lloyd Gaston, Peter Tomson, Stanley Stowers, Mark Nanos, and Caroline Johnson Hodge for extended treatment; all but Tomson are (or were) North Americans teaching in North American institutions.[63]

---

[60]*Acts* (Minneapolis: Fortress, 2009).

[61]Cf. Bock, *Acts*, 1–15, and the literature there surveyed. For the full range of proposals concerning the genre of Acts, see Todd Penner, "Madness in the Method? The Acts of the Apostles in Current Study," *CBR* 2 (2004): 223–93, esp. 233–41. There is a reasonable consensus that the combination of historical, theological, and literary elements makes the book somewhat *sui generis*.

[62]Most recently, see his *Justification: God's Plan and Paul's Vision* (Downers Grove, IL: InterVarsity, 2009).

[63]Magnus Zetterholm, *Approaches to Paul: A Student's Guide to Recent Scholarship* (Minneapolis: Fortress, 2009), 127–63.

Despite otherwise diverse perspectives, what all these scholars share is that, even more consistently than the New Perspective, they have located Paul as thoroughly at home in first-century Judaism, whether by adopting a two-covenants theory in which Jesus is Messiah only for the Gentiles (Gaston), by stressing Paul's teaching as halakhic (Tomson), by seeing treatment usually taken as critical of existing Judaism (e.g., in Romans 2) as actually addressed to Gentiles (Stowers), by seeing entire epistles usually viewed as directed to a mixed audience (like Romans) as exclusively addressing Gentiles (Nanos), or by seeing Gentiles related to Jews in Christ via a fictive aggregative kinship network (Johnson Hodge).[64] When most of these theories first emerged in the 1990s, they were the exclusive purview of nonevangelical scholars. In the past decade, however, they have made increasing inroads into evangelicalism, especially as the Messianic Jewish movement has been split by the frustration of not reaching more of their unsaved Jewish friends and relatives for Christ. If one could just declare them to be right with God through faithfulness to the Mosaic covenant, how much easier life would be! If one could just follow *non-Christian* Jewish scholars like Nanos and see Paul's key letters as addressed merely to Gentiles, one wouldn't have to come to grips in the same ways as before with the main texts in which Paul proclaims freedom from the law in Christ (at face value for *Jew* as well as Gentile).[65] But the exegesis required to defend these options is extremely contorted; Christ and him crucified in fact remains a scandal to Jew and Gentile alike (1 Cor. 1:18–2:4).[66]

As for the *original* "New Perspective," North American scholars have contributed significantly to its critique and to toning down some

---

[64]See, respectively, Lloyd Gaston, *Paul and the Torah* (Vancouver: University of British Columbia Press, 1990); Peter J. Tomson, *Paul and the Jewish Law: Halakha in the Letters of the Apostle to the Gentiles* (Assen: Van Gorcum, 1990); Stanley K. Stowers, *A Rereading of Romans: Justice, Jews, and Gentiles* (New Haven, CT: Yale University Press, 1994); Mark D. Nanos, *The Mystery of Romans: The Jewish Context of Paul's Letter* (Minneapolis: Fortress, 1996); and Caroline Johnson Hodge, *If Sons, Then Heirs: A Study of Kinship and Ethnicity in the Letters of Paul* (New York: Oxford University Press, 2007).

[65]No one has defended this shift in approach in more detail and with greater passion than Mark S. Kinzer in his *Post-Missionary Messianic Judaism: Redefining Christian Engagement with the Jewish People* (Grand Rapids: Brazos, 2005).

[66]See further Craig L. Blomberg, "Freedom from the Law Only for Gentiles? A Non-Supersessionist Alternative to Mark Kinzer's 'Postmissionary Messianic Judaism,'" in *Jesus Christ, Lord and Savior: New Testament Theology in the Light of the Church's Mission*, ed. Grant R. Osborne, Ray van Neste, and Jon Laansma (Colorado Springs: Paternoster; Eugene, OR: Wipf & Stock, forthcoming).

of its more sweeping claims. In just the past decade alone, Mark Seifrid, Andrew Das, Seyoon Kim, Stephen Westerholm, and Chris VanLandingham have all corrected important portions either of the New Perspective's portrait of first-century Judaism or of its reading of Paul.[67] Pride of place, in this undertaking, however, must go to the two-volume international anthology of essays edited by Carson, Seifrid, and O'Brien, *Justification and Variegated Nomism*.[68] At the same time, there is growing acknowledgment that we cannot simply return to a pre–New Perspective era. If the above critiques have demonstrated that classic legalism was by no means absent from first-century Judaism as the New Perspective has at times seemed to claim, then they also largely agree that covenantal nomism and ethnocentrism were present, too, to a degree not regularly recognized before E. P. Sanders and J. D. G. Dunn. Similarly, if the New Perspective has given the appearance at times of jettisoning the role of imputed righteousness in Paul's thought (the recurring complaint made especially by John Piper[69]), then many American evangelicals are increasingly recognizing that they have not always done a good job of proclaiming the whole gospel either. Paul clearly teaches that it is not just about the need for individual humans to become right with God by means of faith in Jesus, but also about God's plans for Israel being fulfilled in Christ, assuring us that his promises of restoration and renewal for the whole cosmos will one day likewise come to fruition. One North American evangelical teaching in an ecumenically Roman Catholic context, Michael Gorman, has produced a number of very balanced treatments of Pauline theology, reflecting much of the best of the "old" and "new" perspectives combined.[70]

---

[67]Mark A. Seifrid, *Christ Our Righteousness: Paul's Theology of Justification* (Downers Grove, IL: InterVarsity, 2001); A. Andrew Das, *Paul, the Law, and the Covenant* (Peabody, MA: Hendrickson, 2001); Seyoon Kim, *Paul and the New Perspective: Second Thoughts on the Origin of Paul's Gospel* (Tübingen: Mohr Siebeck, 2002); Stephen Westerholm, *Perspectives Old and New on Paul: The "Lutheran" Paul and His Critics* (Grand Rapids: Eerdmans, 2004); and Chris VanLandingham, *Judgment and Justification in Early Judaism and the Apostle Paul* (Peabody, MA: Hendrickson, 2006).

[68]*Justification and Variegated Nomism*, ed. D. A. Carson, Mark A. Seifrid, and Peter T. O'Brien, 2 vols. (Tübingen: Mohr Siebeck, 2001, 2004).

[69]See especially John Piper, *The Future of Justification: A Response to N. T. Wright* (Wheaton, IL: Crossway, 2007).

[70]Michael J. Gorman, *Apostle of the Crucified Lord: A Theological Introduction to Paul and His Letters* (Grand Rapids: Eerdmans, 2004); Gorman, *Reading Paul* (Eugene, OR: Cascade, 2008); and Gorman, *Inhabiting the Cruciform God: Kenosis, Justification, and Theosis in Paul's Narrative Soteriology* (Grand Rapids: Eerdmans, 2009).

Other particularly useful North American Pauline studies in this new millennium fit less well into any discernible patterns. But we have seen excellent thematic treatments, especially by David Pao on thanksgiving, Eckhard Schnabel on missionary work, Jim Howard on the importance of the community for sanctification, and Ann Jervis on suffering;[71] background material, especially by Paul Sampley and Walter Wilson;[72] essays reconnecting Jesus and Paul;[73] and analyses of Paul's use of Scripture, particularly involving Chris Stanley.[74] More generally, good introductions to Paul's life and thought have appeared, most notably by John McRay and by David Capes, Rodney Reeves, and Randy Richards;[75] and excellent theologies, with Tom Schreiner's and Gordon Fee's (which is specifically on christology) standing head and shoulders above the rest from this continent.[76] Richards also has distilled his doctoral thesis into a very useful introduction to letter writing in Paul's world.[77] Brevard Childs's last major work before his death was a major canon-critical study of Paul, while an important ecumenical collection of essays on the apostle's thought in light of classic Protestant-Catholic debates is edited by David Aune.[78] Charles

[71]David W. Pao, *Thanksgiving: An Investigation of a Pauline Theme* (Downers Grove, IL: InterVarsity, 2002); Eckhard J. Schnabel, *Paul the Missionary: Realities, Strategies and Methods* (Downers Grove, IL: InterVarsity, 2008); James M. Howard, *Paul, the Community, and Progressive Sanctification: An Exploration into Community-Based Transformation within Pauline Theology* (New York: Peter Lang, 2007); L. Ann Jervis, *At the Heart of the Gospel: Suffering in the Earliest Christian Message* (Grand Rapids: Eerdmans, 2007). Schnabel's work is a spinoff of his two-volume *magnum opus*, *Early Christian Mission* (Downers Grove, IL: InterVarsity, 2004), which must be mentioned in an article of this nature, too.
[72]J. Paul Sampley, *Paul in the Greco-Roman World: A Handbook* (Harrisburg, PA: Trinity Press International, 2003); Walter T. Wilson, *Pauline Parallels: A Comprehensive Guide* (Louisville: Westminster John Knox, 2009).
[73]*Jesus and Paul Reconnected: Fresh Pathways into an Old Debate*, ed. Todd D. Still (Grand Rapids: Eerdmans, 2007).
[74]Christopher D. Stanley, *Arguing with Scripture: The Rhetoric of Quotations in the Letters of Paul* (New York: T&T Clark, 2004); *As It Is Written: Studying Paul's Use of Scripture*, ed. Stanley E. Porter and Christopher D. Stanley (Atlanta: SBL, 2008).
[75]John McRay, *Paul: His Life and Teaching* (Grand Rapids: Baker, 2003); David B. Capes, Rodney Reeves, and E. Randolph Richards, *Rediscovering Paul: An Introduction to His World, Letters, and Theology* (Downers Grove, IL: InterVarsity, 2007).
[76]Thomas R. Schreiner, *Apostle of God's Glory in Christ* (Downers Grove, IL: InterVarsity, 2001); Gordon D. Fee, *Pauline Christology: An Exegetical-Theological Study* (Peabody, MA: Hendrickson, 2007).
[77]E. Randolph Richards, *Paul and First-Century Letter Writing: Secretaries, Composition and Collection* (Downers Grove, IL: InterVarsity, 2004).
[78]Brevard S. Childs, *The Church's Guide for Reading Paul: The Canonical Shaping of the Pauline Corpus* (Grand Rapids: Eerdmans, 2008); *Rereading Paul Together: Protestant and Catholic Perspectives on Justification*, ed. David E. Aune (Grand Rapids: Baker, 2006).

Cosgrove, Herold Weiss, and K. K. Yeo, finally, have collaborated to produce a unique and uniquely valuable set of studies on applying Paul cross-culturally in our modern world.[79]

As for commentaries, an all-star list (across all theological perspectives) should include at least Robert Jewett and Ben Witherington on Romans,[80] David Garland and Joseph Fitzmyer on 1 Corinthians,[81] and Frank Matera on 2 Corinthians.[82] Brad Braxton has a short but important African American reading of Galatians that those not of his ethnic tradition need particularly to understand.[83] Harold Hoehner's monumental volume on Ephesians finally saw the light of day, while Ben Witherington and Charles Talbert both completed shorter but more user-friendly analyses that included Colossians and/or Philemon as well.[84] The other Prison Epistles were likewise blessed with good, new commentaries. Philippians was well treated by Stephen Fowl's integration with systematic theology, Walter Hansen's Pillar Commentary offering, and John Reumann's expansive, revised Anchor Bible volume.[85] In addition to the works already noted in conjunction with Ephesians above, Colossians and/or Philemon received excellent illumination from Fitzmyer, Douglas Moo, Jerry Sumney, and Marianne Meye Thompson.[86] Four outstanding commentaries for the Thessalonian letters fall within the purview of this survey—by Abraham Malherbe, Gene Green, Gordon Fee, and Witherington;[87]

[79]Charles H. Cosgrove, Herold Weiss, and Khiok-Khng Yeo, *Cross-Cultural Paul: Journeys to Others, Journeys to Ourselves* (Grand Rapids: Eerdmans, 2005).
[80]Robert Jewett, *Romans* (Minneapolis: Fortress, 2007); Ben Witherington III, with Darlene Hyatt, *Paul's Letter to the Romans: A Socio-Rhetorical Commentary* (Grand Rapids: Eerdmans, 2004).
[81]David E. Garland, *1 Corinthians* (Grand Rapids: Baker, 2003; Joseph A. Fitzmyer, *First Corinthians* (New Haven, CT: Yale University Press, 2008).
[82]Frank J. Matera, *II Corinthians* (Louisville: Westminster John Knox, 2003).
[83]Brad R. Braxton, *No Longer Slaves: Galatians and African American Experience* (Collegeville, MN: Liturgical Press, 2002).
[84]Harold Hoehner, *Ephesians: An Exegetical Commentary* (Grand Rapids: Baker, 2002); Ben Witherington III, *The Letters to Philemon, the Colossians, and the Ephesians: A Socio-Rhetorical Commentary on the Captivity Epistles* (Grand Rapids: Eerdmans, 2007); C. H. Talbert, *Ephesians and Colossians* (Grand Rapids: Baker, 2007).
[85]Stephen E. Fowl, *Philippians* (Grand Rapids: Eerdmans, 2005); John Reumann, *Philippians* (New Haven, CT: Yale University Press, 2008); G. Walter Hansen, *The Letter to the Philippians* (Grand Rapids: Eerdmans, 2009).
[86]Joseph A. Fitzmyer, *The Letter to Philemon* (New York: Doubleday, 2000); Douglas J. Moo, *The Letters to the Colossians and to Philemon* (Grand Rapids: Eerdmans, 2008); Jerry L. Sumney, *Colossians* (Louisville: Westminster John Knox, 2008); Marianne Meye Thompson, *Colossians and Philemon* (Grand Rapids: Eerdmans, 2005).
[87]Abraham J. Malherbe, *The Letters to the Thessalonians* (New York: Doubleday, 2000); Gene L. Green, *The Letters to the Thessalonians* (Grand Rapids: Eerdmans, 2002); Gordon D. Fee, *The*

and for the Pastorals, three excellent volumes have emerged from the keyboards of Bill Mounce, Luke Johnson, and Phil Towner.[88] Part commentary, part paraphrase, part introduction, and part sociologically based advocacy, Brian J. Walsh's and Sylvia C. Keesmaat's *Colossians Remixed: Subverting the Empire*, which deals also with Philemon, is delightfully readable and eminently provocative.[89]

Hebrews, the General Epistles, and Revelation

Apart from various commentaries on Hebrews and the General Epistles, some of them quite good,[90] these New Testament works remain comparatively underserved by North American scholarship. Cynthia Long Westfall has produced one of the most creative and intriguing applications to date of the discourse analysis of an entire New Testament document, arguing for literary peaking at the clusters of hortatory subjunctives in Hebrews 4:11–16 and 10:19–25.[91] Mark Taylor has thoroughly surveyed past proposals for the structure of James and employs a text-linguistic approach to suggest his own.[92] John Elliott nicely summarizes his social-scientific approach to 1 Peter, developed in several previous publications,[93] while Christopher Bass offers a

---

First and Second Letters to the Thessalonians (Grand Rapids: Eerdmans, 2009); Ben Witherington III, *1 and 2 Thessalonians: A Socio-Rhetorical Commentary* (Grand Rapids: Eerdmans, 2006).

[88]William D. Mounce, *Pastoral Epistles* (Nashville: Nelson, 2000); Luke T. Johnson, *The First and Second Letters to Timothy* (New York: Doubleday, 2001); Philip H. Towner, *The Letters to Timothy and Titus* (Grand Rapids: Eerdmans, 2006).

[89]Downers Grove, IL: InterVarsity, 2004.

[90]From North America, on Hebrews, see especially David A. de Silva, *Perseverance in Gratitude: A Socio-Rhetorical Commentary on the Epistle to the Hebrews* (Grand Rapids: Eerdmans, 2000); and Craig A. Koester, *Hebrews* (New York: Doubleday, 2001); on James, see Craig L. Blomberg and Mariam J. Kamell, *James* (Grand Rapids: Zondervan, 2008); Douglas J. Moo, *The Letter of James* (Grand Rapids: Eerdmans, 2000); and Dan G. McCartney, *James* (Grand Rapids: Baker, 2009); on 1 Peter, see John H. Elliott, *1 Peter* (New York: Doubleday, 2000); and Karen H. Jobes, *1 Peter* (Grand Rapids: Baker, 2005); on 2 Peter and Jude, see Gene L. Green, *Jude and 2 Peter* (Grand Rapids: Baker, 2008); and Peter H. Davids, *The Letters of Second Peter and Jude* (Grand Rapids: Eerdmans, 2006); on the three letters together, see Thomas R. Schreiner, *1, 2 Peter, Jude* (Nashville: Broadman & Holman, 2003); and on the Epistles of John, see Robert Yarbrough, *1–3 John* (Grand Rapids: Baker, 2008); and Daniel L. Akin, *1, 2, 3 John* (Nashville: Broadman & Holman, 2001).

[91]Cynthia Long Westfall, *A Discourse Analysis of the Letter to the Hebrews: The Relationship between Form and Meaning* (New York: T&T Clark, 2005).

[92]Mark E. Taylor, *A Text-Linguistic Investigation into the Discourse Structure of James* (New York: T&T Clark, 2006).

[93]John H. Elliott, *Conflict, Community, and Honor: 1 Peter in Social-Scientific Perspective* (Eugene, OR: Cascade, 2007).

thorough and balanced study on the theme of assurance in 1 John.[94] SBL study groups, spearheaded by Bob Webb, have produced a quartet of volumes applying new methods to the catholic letters, sometimes with significant results.[95]

The political theology inherent in the book of Revelation has finally started to be mined properly. Beyond the endless debates over futurism versus preterism, amillennialism versus premillennialism, and the like,[96] what difference does the one canonical book-length apocalypse make for Christian living now? Far from intending to encourage believers merely to save as many souls as they can as quickly as possible from the sinking ship of this world, it suggests, in largely unexplained ways, some continuity between this world and the world to come. Even into the new heavens and new earth, the kings of the earth will bring their splendor (Rev. 21:24). And if either premillennialism or postmillennialism is right that a literal period of time still in the future will bring the golden age of this earth's history, then believers' work and stewardship of the world in this present age takes on *much* greater meaning. At last, evangelicals in recognizable numbers are explicating these truths,[97] while nonevangelicals today are less likely to tie them in with Marxist or other ideological agendas that completely swamp sane exegesis.[98] Paul Rainbow captures the message well: "To serve God and Christ faithfully in the midst of a pagan society that exalts power, wealth,

---

[94]Christopher D. Bass, *That You May Know: Assurance of Salvation in 1 John* (Nashville: B&H, 2008).

[95]Robert L. Webb and John S. Kloppenborg, eds., *Reading James with New Eyes: Methodological Reassessments of the Letter of James* (New York: T&T Clark, 2007); Robert L. Webb and Betsy Bauman-Martin, eds., *Reading First Peter with New Eyes: Methodological Reassessments of the Letter of First Peter* (New York: T&T Clark, 2007); Robert L. Webb and Peter H. Davids, *Reading Jude with New Eyes: Methodological Reassessments of the Letter of Jude* (New York: T&T Clark, 2009); Robert L. Webb and Duane F. Watson, *Reading Second Peter with New Eyes: Methodological Reassessments of the Letter of Second Peter* (New York: T&T Clark, 2010).

[96]Though less well served in these debates in recent years has been historic or classic premillennialism; hence, Craig L. Blomberg and Sung Wook Chung, eds., *The Case for Historic Premillennialism* (Grand Rapids: Baker, 2009).

[97]See especially throughout the commentaries by Craig S. Keener (*Revelation* [Grand Rapids: Zondervan, 2000]) and Grant R. Osborne (*Revelation* [Grand Rapids: Baker, 2003]).

[98]See especially Steven H. Friesen, *Imperial Cults and the Apocalypse of John: Reading Revelation in the Ruins* (New York: Oxford University Press, 2001); Brian K. Blount, *Can I Get a Witness? Reading Revelation through African American Culture* (Louisville: Westminster John Knox, 2005); and David Rhoads, ed., *From Every People and Nation: The Book of Revelation in Intercultural Perspective* (Minneapolis: Fortress, 2005).

and pleasure is the tenor of the prophetic summons to the church in the book of Revelation."[99]

Hermeneutical Methods and Approaches

Indeed, one of the very noticeable North American trends, already mentioned in conjunction with historical Jesus research, is to read virtually every part of the New Testament in light of the background of Roman imperial activity. There are some books for which this makes better sense than others—Mark, among the Gospels, given its probable Roman audience, and, for the same reasons, Romans and Hebrews among the letters. Important correctives have been offered to more traditional readings in commentaries like Witherington's and Jewett's on Romans.[100] Letters like 1 and 2 Thessalonians can be enlightened by this approach, too, given their plethora of key terms regularly reserved in paganism for the various Roman emperors—*Kyrios, Sōtēr, parousia, epiphania, apantēsis, katechon*, and the like.[101] Whether Neronic or Domitianic in provenance, Revelation obviously qualifies for anti-imperial readings as well.[102] But it is not as clear that writers like Matthew, John, or Paul, overall, are as appropriately viewed as combating the empire(s).[103]

Closely related to anti-imperial readings of Scripture are postcolonial ones. With the demise of most of the classically Marxist governments worldwide by at least the mid-1990s, traditional liberationist exegesis almost disappeared. But in some respects, it has simply mutated into various forms of cultural criticism. The dominant form to have emerged has been dubbed "postcolonialism."[104] The term itself suggests primary application to countries that were

[99]Paul A. Rainbow, *The Pith of the Apocalypse: Essential Message and Principles for Interpretation* (Eugene, OR: Wipf & Stock, 2008), 169.

[100]See throughout Jewett, *Romans*; and Witherington with Hyatt, *Romans*.

[101]See throughout Witherington, *1 and 2 Thessalonians*; and Abraham Smith, "The First and Second Letters to the Thessalonians," in *A Postcolonial Commentary on the New Testament Writings*, ed. Fernando F. Segovia and R. S. Sugirtharajah (New York: T&T Clark, 2007), 304–22.

[102]See Rhoads, *From Every People and Nation*; David L. Barr, ed., *The Reality of Apocalypse: Rhetoric and Politics in the Book of Revelation* (Atlanta: SBL, 2006).

[103]Contra, e.g., Warren Carter, *Matthew and Empire: Initial Explorations* (Harrisburg, PA: Trinity Press International, 2001); Carter, *John and Empire: Initial Explorations* (New York: T&T Clark, 2008); and John Dominic Crossan and Jonathan L. Reed, *In Search of Paul: How Jesus's Apostle Opposed Rome's Empire with God's Kingdom: A New Vision of Paul's Words and World* (San Francisco: HarperSanFrancisco, 2004). For a more balanced perspective, see especially Seyoon Kim, *Christ and Caesar: The Gospel and the Roman Empire in the Writings of Paul and Luke* (Grand Rapids: Eerdmans, 2008).

[104]See especially *Postcolonial Commentary on the New Testament Writings*, ed. Segovia and

once colonies of the major European empires, including most all of Latin *America*. In addition, and somewhat paradoxically, much of the more theoretically rigorous postcolonial criticism emerges from North American (and to a lesser extent European) contexts, where scholars, including some with no actual prolonged experience of living in Majority World contexts, have the liberty and luxury of reflecting in the abstract on more avant-garde readings of Scripture much more so than they would elsewhere. Moreover, if it was often the case that liberation theology opted for the poor, but the poor opted for Pentecostal Christianity, the same remains the case with much of postcolonialism. Nevertheless, for those who have never seriously reflected on the potential parallels between the first-century church's subjugation to Rome (and, in Israel, to Jewish leaders complicit with Rome) and the ongoing colonial mentalities and relationships still displayed in many parts of the world even in politically independent nations, postcolonialism offers important challenges not to be ignored.

Slightly less novel, if for no other reason than that they have been around a little longer, are ongoing feminist approaches to biblical texts and themes. In terms of current North American trends, they show no signs of slowing down. We now have full-fledged feminist commentaries or anthologies of studies on every part of the New Testament, mostly from outside evangelical circles, in which full egalitarianism, at least in theory, has long since triumphed.[105] The same appears increasingly to be the case within evangelicalism outside distinctively American or American-influenced contexts. Meanwhile, the debate rages in the States, with the pendulum having swung in some places to positions more conservative than those held *before* the feminist challenge.[106] In

---

Sugirtharajah. More broadly, cf. Miguel de la Torre, *Reading the Bible from the Margins* (Maryknoll, NY: Orbis, 2002).

[105]See especially the series of "Feminist Companions" to each part of the New Testament edited by Amy-Jill Levine, sometimes jointly with either Marianne Blickenstaff or Maria Mayo Robbins (New York: T&T Clark, 2003–2009).

[106]Margaret Kim Peterson ("Identity and Ministry in Light of the Gospel: A View from the Kitchen," in *Women, Ministry and the Gospel: Exploring New Paradigms*, ed. Mark Husbands and Timothy Larsen [Downers Grove, IL: InterVarsity, 2007], 161–62) observes that her students at Eastern University blame egalitarianism for the culture of divorce and therefore find a very traditional form of complementarianism attractive both because they think that is what the Bible teaches and because they think it will keep their marriages from breaking up. Peterson observes that neither traditionalist nor egalitarian "constructions of gender relationships tend, either logically or practically, to issue in [healthy] mutuality," because they, "as commonly construed, are much more about the distribution of power than they are about cooperation"

some circles, evangelical egalitarianism winds up being doubly marginal-ized—by the critical establishment because it is evangelical and by large wings of the *evangelical* church and academy because it is egalitarian![107] In terms of exegetical acumen, an important new egalitarian treatment is Philip B. Payne, *Man and Woman, One in Christ*, dealing primarily with the key Pauline texts.[108] More wide ranging and still slightly more persuasive, from the complementarian side is Robert L. Saucy and Judith K. TenElshof's *Women and Men in Ministry*.[109]

Methodological fragmentation, in fact, characterizes much of the North American academic guild. We have scarcely mentioned the whole array of literary criticisms, though now these seem noticeably more popular in the UK than in the US.[110] Although not as prominent as anti-imperial, postcolonial, or feminist studies, GLBT (gay-lesbian-bisexual-transgendered) readings, publications, and professional organizations compete for attention with still other newly minted methods and their supporters, like "performance criticism" or "reception theory."[111]

Spanning the bridge between a critical method and a hermeneu-tical interest is a healthy, ongoing cottage industry of studies of the use of the Old Testament in the New. Greg Beale's and Don Carson's coedited *Commentary on the New Testament Use of the Old Testa-ment* overshadows all other recent efforts in this arena.[112] Increas-ingly useful reference works are appearing in the burgeoning areas of sociological or social-scientific criticism, too, and leading to globalized commentaries on one or both Testaments of various kinds.[113] The

(163). The same is often the case with institutional battles played out under the supposed ban-ner of faithfulness to Scripture.

[107]See especially *Living on the Boundaries: Evangelical Women, Feminism and the Theological Academy*, ed. Nicola Hoggard Creegan and Christine D. Pohl (Downers Grove, IL: InterVarsity, 2005).

[108]Grand Rapids: Zondervan, 2009.

[109]Chicago: Moody Press, 2001.

[110]See especially James L. Resseguie, *Narrative Criticism of the New Testament: An Introduction* (Grand Rapids: Baker, 2005).

[111]See, respectively, Thomas D. Hanks, *The Subversive Gospel: A New Testament Commentary of Liberation* (Cleveland: Pilgrim, 2000); David Rhoads, "Performance Criticism: An Emerging Methodology in Biblical Studies," *BTB* 36 (2006): 118–33, 164–84; David P. Parris, *Reception Theory and Biblical Hermeneutics* (Eugene, OR: Pickwick, 2009).

[112]Grand Rapids: Baker, 2007.

[113]See especially David A. de Silva, *Honor, Patronage, Kinship and Purity: Unlocking New Testa-ment Culture* (Downers Grove, IL: InterVarsity, 2000); *Social-Scientific Models for Interpreting the Bible*, ed. John J. Pilch (Boston: Brill, 2001); and *The Social World of the New Testament: Insights and Models*, ed. Jerome H. Neyrey and Eric C. Stewart (Peabody, MA: Hendrickson, 2008). Commentaries include *Africa Bible Commentary*, ed. Tokunboh Adeyemo (Grand Rapids:

never-ending succession of new commentary series, not all of which are actually needed, is at times helpfully focusing more on application and contextualization.[114] Interest in the first five hundred years of Christian interpretation of texts has led to the remarkably popular Ancient Christian Commentary series and is spawning shadow series of various sorts.[115] And William Webb's proposals concerning redemptive trajectories are among the more influential (and controversial) of new twenty-first-century North American hermeneutical methods to emerge.[116]

Conclusion

As anticipated, I have barely begun to unfold the menu of North American offerings. But hopefully I have at least sampled the flavor of current scholarly cuisine and served a few tasty exegetical and critical morsels along the way. It is no coincidence that Don Carson's name appears as often as it does en route. When one adds the countless numbers of students and others around the world he has addressed and taught over the years, one quickly recognizes how much of the current face of New Testament studies he has influenced. As one of those former students, I count it a deep privilege to have been invited to participate in this Festschrift and a great blessing to have learned so much from Don's scholarship, exposition, tutelage, support, and friendship for over thirty years. May that ministry continue to flourish *ad multos annos*!

Zondervan, 2006); *True to Our Native Land: An African American New Testament Commentary*, ed. Brian K. Blount (Minneapolis: Fortress, 2007); *The International Bible Commentary*, ed. William R. Farmer (Collegeville, MN: Liturgical Press, 1998); *The IVP Women's Bible Commentary*, ed. Catherine C. Kroeger and Mary J. Evans (Downers Grove, IL: InterVarsity, 2002); *Women's Bible Commentary: Expanded Edition.*, ed. Carol A. Newsom and Sharon H. Ringe (Louisville: Westminster John Knox, 1998); *Global Bible Commentary*, ed. Daniel Patte (Nashville: Abingdon, 2004).

[114]See especially the Zondervan Exegetical Commentary; the New International Version Application Commentary, also from Zondervan; and the Two Horizons New Testament Commentary from Eerdmans.

[115]*New Testament*, ed. Thomas C. Oden, 12 vols. (Downers Grove, IL: InterVarsity, 1998–2007).

[116]William J. Webb, *Slaves, Women and Homosexuals: Exploring the Hermeneutics of Cultural Analysis* (Downers Grove, IL: InterVarsity, 2001). Arguably, Webb is correct in encouraging the church to continue a growing trajectory of liberation already existing in Old and New Testaments beyond what the Bible explicitly commands, and correct in his assessment that such a trajectory exists for the liberation of slaves, whereas no such trajectory exists with respect to homosexual practice. More disputed is whether such a trajectory can be identified with respect to gender roles.

11

New Testament Studies in Asia

DAVID W. PAO

In a collection of essays on contextual hermeneutics, Walter Dietrich provides readers with a parable that serves as the concluding remarks for the volume.[1] In this parable, one finds Western theologians compared to scientists who conduct research in a "huge astronomical research laboratory, which is subdivided into various segments." One day, the laboratory invites "three star scholars from far away." In their own contexts, they "are highly respected star scholars, even though, unlike us, they do not have well-equipped 'think tanks,' computers, servers, but rather very modest telescopes and a comparatively limited amount of books." Impressed by their ability to introduce new findings in the field, the Western astronomers ask them how they were able to do so without comparable resources. In response, they assert that they brought their research to places that had not been considered worthy of the visit of notable scientists.

---

[1]Walter Dietrich, "Instead of a Conclusion: Theological Astronomy—A Parable," in *The Bible in a World Context: An Experiment in Contextual Hermeneutics*, ed. Walter Dietrich and Ulrich Luz (Grand Rapids: Eerdmans, 2002), 77–80.

We ask the people we encounter what they see. And we try to provide them with equipment that they can handle. We neither do it all by ourselves, nor do we explicitly show them how to do it, but we observe these ordinary people, we use their tools, and—above all: we are out there in the open and look up together. And, believe us, there are stars out there!

Despite protests by some who see this parable as further consolidating the divide between those of the privileged "center" and those on the "margin,"[2] this parable does highlight issues involved in any discussion of biblical scholarship in the non-Western world. These issues include resources, methodology, and political and social locations. Moreover, in such discussions, one is expected to focus on the foreign and the exotic. What remains unclear, however, is whether something foreign and exotic is to be expected in the area of biblical scholarship, and whether biblical scholarship done in a different context will necessarily yield a different set of results.

In any discussion of "New Testament Studies in Asia," the expectation of that which is foreign and exotic naturally leads many to focus on the various Asian christologies that have developed in the past decades. Scholars who are involved in such projects readily admit to the constraints of their resources, but they are nevertheless bold in affirming the contextual necessity that gives rise to these constructs. Notably, many of these christologies are not products of self-professed New Testament scholars; instead, theologians who work with such christologies often consciously distance themselves from New Testament scholarship.

In this essay, I will first provide a brief introduction of these christologies. This will be followed by a general discussion concerning their stance on the relationship between contextual theology and New Testament studies. After this survey, some general critiques will be provided in relation to the entire enterprise of ethnochristologies. Finally, selected issues raised by Asian New Testament scholars will be highlighted, insofar as they relate to Asian christological projects. While less glamorous and less eager to claim to have produced that which is foreign and exotic, these scholars, it will be suggested, do

---

[2]See, e.g., R. S. Sugirtharajah, "Muddling Along at the Margins," in *Still at the Margins: Biblical Scholarship Fifteen Years after Voices from the Margin*, ed. R. S. Sugirtharajah (New York: T&T Clark, 2008), 8–21.

make a meaningful contribution to both New Testament scholarship and the lives of the churches in both the East and the West.[3]

Asian Christologies

No generalizations are without risks when discussing issues across the vast continent of Asia, one that includes various people groups, language families, thought patterns, religious systems, and histories of interaction with Western powers. Even when one focuses on the area of ethnochristologies, broad generalizations are often misleading. In this section, four theologians from different geographical regions will be discussed. Instead of focusing on their personal journeys or distinct contributions, I will draw attention to elements in their writings that they share with other, similar constructs. Even though these general comments may not apply to every local christology constructed on the Asian soil, they do reflect a pattern common to such christologies.

Kosuke Koyama

Kosuke Koyama (1929–2009) is considered one of the leading Japanese theologians of the previous century. After receiving his doctorate from Princeton Theological Seminary, he served in various institutions in Asia and New Zealand before moving to Union Theological Seminary (New York), where he retired in 1996 as John D. Rockefeller Jr. Professor Emeritus of Ecumenical Studies. Author of numerous works, he is perhaps best known for his *Water Buffalo Theology*,[4] a book that represents an early attempt to ground christology in the context of Asian villages. Affirming the uniqueness of the Christian gospel, Koyama seeks to present a gospel that is understandable and relevant to those who live within a Buddhist worldview.

Reflecting on the cross, Koyama sees suffering as the center of Jesus' experience. To be identified with Christ, therefore, is to be identified with the suffering Christ: "We are called to share the *pathos* of God, God's *pathos* toward all scattered things which are

---

[3]This essay is dedicated to Don Carson, who has tirelessly pointed not only to the urgency of the task of contextualization, but also to the dangers of carrying out such tasks apart from a clear biblical-theological framework; see, e.g., his *The Gagging of God: Christianity Confronts Pluralism* (Grand Rapids: Zondervan, 1996), 537–53; and "A Sketch of the Factors Determining Current Hermeneutical Debate in Cross-Cultural Contexts," in *Biblical Interpretation and the Church: Text and Context*, ed. D. A. Carson (Grand Rapids: Baker, 1984), 11–29.
[4]Kosuke Koyama, *Water Buffalo Theology* (Maryknoll, NY: Orbis, 1974).

held together in the *glory* of the *crucified* Lord."[5] The gospel is therefore not an abstract idea, but one that is in touch with human experience: "The biblical truth is not an *intact* truth but a *suffered* truth. The truth suffers because it is deeply in *contact* with man."[6] To Koyama, as to others, suffering is the common experience of Asians, and this suffering is often considered to be related to the sociopolitical contexts in which they find themselves.[7] To follow Christ, therefore, is to move from the center of power and take on the role of the oppressed: "Over against such destructive centrism in the world of religion and politics, the crucified Christ affirms his centrality by giving it up for the sake of the periphery. This is his way to *shalom*. Jesus Christ is not 'imperial.'"[8] This focus on suffering and the liberation from the center of power lies at the heart of various types of Asian christologies.

Choan-Seng Song

Choan-Seng Song (1929–), a contemporary of Koyama, is arguably one of the most prolific Chinese theologians. He has authored volumes promoting Asian theology,[9] with a distinct focus on christology.[10] After receiving his doctorate from Union Theological Seminary, he served for a number of years in Asia and is now retired as the distinguished professor emeritus of theology and Asian Cultures at the Pacific School of Religion.

---

[5]Ibid., 238.
[6]Kosuke Koyama, *No Handle on the Cross: An Asian Meditation on the Crucified Mind* (Maryknoll, NY: Orbis, 1977), 86.
[7]Others have explicitly identified this suffering as the direct result of the oppression of the Western colonial powers. To preach the "Western" gospel is, therefore, to continue to commit this oppressive act: "The 'Colonial Christ[s]' we received from many of the western missionaries have been mainly poisonous. They were not the seeds of life which would bring out the fullness of life, the seeds which came from historical Jesus in the Jesus movement. Rather they were heavily deformed, diseased, bad seeds which came from western, middle class, patriarchal, white, capitalist, elite, homophobic, colonial, power hungry Christ. They were indeed environmental hazards for many Asian people" (Hyun Kyung, "Asian Christologies and People's Religions," *Voices from the Third World* 19 [1996]: 218).
[8]Kosuke Koyama, "The Crucified Christ Challenges Human Power," in *Asian Faces of Jesus*, ed. R. S. Sugirtharajah (Maryknoll, NY: Orbis, 1993), 155.
[9]See, e.g., his *Third-Eye Theology: Theology in Formation in Asian Settings* (Maryknoll, NY: Orbis, 1979); and *Tell Us Our Names: Story Theology from an Asian Perspective* (Maryknoll, NY: Orbis, 1984).
[10]See his trio: *Jesus, The Crucified People* (Minneapolis: Fortress, 1990); *Jesus and the Reign of God* (Minneapolis: Fortress, 1993); and *Jesus in the Power of the Spirit* (Minneapolis: Fortress, 1994).

For Song, suffering is considered the common predicament for many Asians: "Asians do not have to look for suffering; it comes to them. They do not have to wait for it; it strikes them out of the blue. They cannot choose one kind of suffering as against another kind of suffering; suffering chooses them. In short, for them, to be is to suffer."[11] This suffering includes the fate of Asia in the hands of the Western powers, as well as the inner conflict among Asian people groups.[12]

Sharing the same concerns with Koyama, Song also argues that to follow Christ is to share in his suffering. Song makes it explicit, however, that the significance of the death of Christ lies in his identification with the suffering people, and not with the fact that he is the atonement for the sins of humanity.

> The God who is crucified on the cross is not so much the God who vicariously suffers and dies *for* the world as the God who suffers and dies *with* the world. Here vicariousness is replaced by identification. The crucified God is the God who identifies all the way with us in our suffering and death. He suffers with us and dies with us.[13]

In this emphasis on identification, the historical and ontological status of Jesus as the Son of God is no longer important. Jesus is therefore not the unique agent that brings about the kingdom of God: "Strictly speaking, Jesus did not bring God's reign into the world, for it is already there. What he did was to engage people in the manifestation of it, to enable them to know it is there, to open their minds' eye to see it."[14] Stripping Jesus of his unique status, Song also reduces the eschatological kingdom into the struggle for liberation in the present era. As Jesus' death is merely an example to be followed, his resurrection is also reduced to an "affirmation that even though Jesus fell

---

[11]C. S. Song, *The Compassionate God* (Maryknoll, NY: Orbis, 1982), 163.

[12]Many would also consider poverty, another common denominator among many Asian regions, as the result of such political conflicts. See, e.g., the discussion in Peter C. Phan, "Jesus the Christ with an Asian Face," *TS* 57 (1996): 401.

[13]Song, *Third-Eye Theology*, 165 (emphasis his). Others echo Song in emphasizing the need to follow Jesus rather than worship him: "We are called Christians, not because we worship Christ Jesus but we are the followers of Jesus, the Christ" (Israel Selvanayagam, "Who Is This Jesus? A Biblical Outline for Clearer Self-Understanding and Communication in a Multi-Faith Context," *Asia Journal of Theology* 7 [1993]: 243).

[14]Song, *Jesus and the Reign of God*, 162.

victim to the evil forces in the world, his vision of God's reign will remain in the memory of humanity."[15]

This understanding of the death and resurrection of Jesus paves the way for a pluralism that refuses to affirm the unique power of the Christian gospel. When people suffer "evil" from which they must be delivered, "compassion" becomes "the heart of religion. . . . And religion without compassion, religion that ceases to love and suffer together with its believers within and nonbelievers without, is no longer religion."[16] Apart from this criterion, one cannot claim to be "unique and absolute" as a religion.[17]

Jung Young Lee

In Jung Young Lee (1935–1996) one finds a Korean theologian who interacts with Taoism and Confucianism in formulating his theology. He was born in North Korea and received his doctorate at Drew University, where he served as professor of systematic theology until his death. Reflecting on his own social location, Lee writes consciously as an Asian American. Author and editor of twenty volumes, Lee emerges as one of the significant voices that challenge the dominance of Western theology.

Lee's interest in an Asian christology is prompted by the shift of the center of Christianity.

As the demographical picture of Christianity shifts from the First World to the Third World countries, Christianity is no longer exclusively identified as a Western religion. In fact, Christianity is already not only a world religion but also a world Christianity. This means Christianity cannot be understood exclusively from a Western perspective: Our understanding of Christianity requires a world perspective.[18]

In creating space for other manifestations of the divine, Lee emphasizes the subordination of Christ the Savior to God the Creator.

God as the creator is the source of creativity and the source of all that is and will be, while Christ is only what is manifested of God.

---

[15]Song, Jesus in the Power of the Spirit, 63.
[16]Song, Theology from the Womb of Asia (Maryknoll, NY: Orbis, 1986), 141.
[17]Ibid., 152.
[18]Jung Young Lee, The Trinity in Asian Perspective (Nashville: Abingdon, 1996), 11.

> To identify the creator with the revealer, the Christ, is to deny the inexhaustible nature of the divine creativity. God as creator is more than what is manifested, and his mystery is not and will not be exhausted. He is more than the One revealed in Christ.[19]

This kind of distinction between God the Father and Christ the Son further provides justification for Lee to draw from other religious traditions in understanding the role of Jesus Christ himself. Drawing from one of the Chinese classics, *I Ching* (literally, *Book of Changes*), Lee is therefore able to suggest that "Jesus' crucifixion and resurrection are unique, not because they happened to him, but because they became the primordial symbol of all changing."[20]

Consistent with other forms of Asian christology, Lee theologizes from the margin and sees love as the ultimate instrument through which the center can be displaced: "Marginality is overcome through marginality, and all are marginal to God manifest in Jesus-Christ. When all of us are marginal, love becomes the norm of our lives, and service becomes the highest aspiration of our creativity. We then become servants to one another in love."[21] In keeping with the Eastern philosophy from which Lee draws, he emphasizes the ethical impulse more than ontology; thus, the community instead of the individual becomes the focus of any religious discourse.

Rasiah S. Sugirtharajah

This survey, though brief, would not be complete without mentioning the influence of Rasiah S. Sugirtharajah, a notable player in postcolonial criticism especially in relation to the Asian context.[22] A Sri

---

[19]Jung Young Lee, *The Theology of Change: A Christian Concept of God from an Eastern Perspective* (Minneapolis: Fortress, 1995), 88.

[20]Jung Young Lee, "The Perfect Realization of Change: Jesus Christ," in *Asian Faces of Jesus*, ed. Sugirtharajah, 73.

[21]Jung Young Lee, *Marginality: The Key to Multicultural Theology* (Minneapolis: Fortress, 1995), 170. Elsewhere, Lee identifies Christ as "the margin of all marginalities" (*The Trinity in Asian Perspective*, 91).

[22]See, e.g., his *Asian Biblical Hermeneutics and Postcolonialism: Contesting the Interpretations* (Maryknoll, NY: Orbis, 1998); *The Bible and the Third World: Precolonial, Colonial and Postcolonial Encounters* (Cambridge: Cambridge University Press, 2001); *Postcolonial Criticism and Biblical Interpretation* (Oxford: Oxford University Press, 2002); *Postcolonial Reconfigurations: An Alternative Way of Reading the Bible and Doing Theology* (London: SCM, 2003); *The Bible and Empire: Postcolonial Explorations* (Cambridge: Cambridge University Press, 2005); and *Troublesome Texts: The Bible in Colonial and Contemporary Culture* (Sheffield: Phoenix, 2008).

Lankan scholar who has taught in West Bengal, Sugirtharajah is currently serving as professor of biblical hermeneutics at the University of Birmingham, where he received his doctorate, in addition to being an adjunct professor at Tamilnadu Theological Seminary in Madurai, South India.

Sugirtharajah shares many of the concerns of the previous three scholars, and the basis for this theologizing lies in the significance of the context of people: "Christological discourse is not only about the explication of preconceived notions about Jesus or an exercise in the application of time-tested truths, but also about their experience of struggle and survival."[23] To him, creative christological constructs are possible because one finds the same diversity in the canonical Gospels: "It is possible from gospel records, depending on what text one chooses, to reconstruct almost any picture of Jesus one wishes."[24] The criteria for any valid or useful christology is not, therefore, its adherence to the Gospel records, but its utility in a postcolonial context: "Any christological formulations that tend to alienate people from their own cultural heritage should be discouraged."[25] In such a context, the biggest sin is to affirm "that the Christian manifestation is final and unique."[26]

In considering the various images of Jesus, Sugirtharajah affirms the power of seeing Jesus as the wisdom teacher. To Sugirtharajah, this image not only downplays the uniqueness and superiority of one individual, but it also is relatively more palatable to an audience that has suffered under various types of oppressive powers: "Jesus as sage is open and less imperialistic than some alternative portraits, and at the same time committed to the uplifting of the poor, women, children and the dispossessed."[27]

---

[23]R. S. Sugirtharajah, "Prologue and Perspective," in *Asian Faces of Jesus*, ed. Sugirtharajah, ix.

[24]R. S. Sugirtharajah, "Reconceiving Jesus: Some Continuing Concerns," in *Asian Faces of Jesus*, ed. Sugirtharajah (Maryknoll, NY: Orbis, 1993), 259.

[25]Ibid., 260.

[26]R. S. Sugirtharajah, "Introduction," in *Frontiers in Asian Christian Theology: Emerging Trends*, ed. R. S. Sugirtharajah (Maryknoll, NY: Orbis, 1994), 4.

[27]Sugirtharajah, "Reconceiving Jesus," 264. Seeing Jesus as a sage is one theme that can be found among many Asian christologies. See, in particular, the recent discussions in Jonathan Yun-ka Tan, "Jesus, the Crucified and Risen Sage: Towards a Confucian Christology," in *Asian Faces of Christ* (Bangalore: Asian Trading Corporation, 2005), 49–87; Michael Amaladoss, *The Asian Jesus* (Maryknoll, NY: Orbis, 2006), 29–50; and Paul S. Chung, "The Mystery of God and Tao in Jewish-Christian-Taoist Context," in *Asian Contextual Theology for the Third Millennium:*

For our purposes, the significance of Sugirtharajah lies in his explicit rejection of New Testament scholarship, at least as it is practiced in many quarters in the West. It is to this topic that we shall now turn.

Asian Christologies and New Testament Scholarship
In the West, many significant works in christology are produced by New Testament scholars.[28] For those working on Asian christologies, however, not only does one rarely encounter a New Testament scholar working in this area,[29] but one actually finds in their works a conscious distancing from the field of New Testament studies. The four scholars noted above, each in their own way, provide justification for their lack of interaction with New Testament scholarship.

For Koyama, New Testament scholarship in general is considered a colonial instrument, and one cannot rely on the scientific study of the Bible or theology in the preaching of the gospel. Any such act is an act of crusading: "Christian faith does not and cannot be spread by crusading. It will spread without money, without bishops, without theologians, without plannings, if people see a crucified mind, not a crusading mind, in Christians."[30] For Koyama, to be involved in New Testament studies, as defined in the Western world, is to be identified with the center rather than the margin. To perpetuate such scholarship is to be involved in the sin of idolatry.

Far too many students from the world outside of the West come to the West to receive their theological education. But the majority of

---

Theology of Minjung in Fourth-Eye Formation, ed. Paul S. Chung, Veli-Matti Kärkkäinen, and Kim Kyoung-Jae (Eugene, OR: Pickwick, 2007), 256–60.

[28]Recent examples include James D. G. Dunn, *Christology in the Making: A New Testament Inquiry into the Origins of the Doctrine of the Incarnation*, 2nd ed. (Grand Rapids: Eerdmans, 1996); Marinus de Jonge, *God's Final Envoy: Early Christology and Jesus' Own View of His Mission* (Grand Rapids: Eerdmans, 1998); Christopher M. Tuckett, *Christology and the New Testament: Jesus and His Earliest Followers* (Louisville: Westminster John Knox, 2001); Larry W. Hurtado, *Lord Jesus Christ: Devotion to Jesus in Earliest Christianity* (Grand Rapids: Eerdmans, 2005); Richard N. Longenecker, ed., *Contours of Christology in the New Testament* (Grand Rapids: Eerdmans, 2005); Martin Hengel, *Studien zur Christologie: Kleine Schriften IV*, WUNT 201 (Tübingen: Mohr Siebeck, 2006); and Richard Bauckham, *Jesus and the God of Israel* (Grand Rapids: Eerdmans, 2008).

[29]A notable exception can be found in one of the founders of the Korean *Minjung* ("People") Theology, Byung-Mu Ahn (1921–1996). See his Heidelberg dissertation, *Draußen vor dem Tor. Kirche und Minjung in Korea* (Göttingen: Vandenhoeck & Ruprecht, 1986), and "Jesus and Ochlos in the Context of His Galilean Ministry," in *Asian Contextual Theology for the Third Millennium*, ed. Chung, Kärkkäinen, and Kyoung-Jae (Eugene, OR: Pickwick, 2007), 33–50.

[30]Kosuke Koyama, *Three Mile an Hour God* (Maryknoll, NY: Orbis, 1980), 54.

theological schools in the West are still dreaming a happy dream of center-complex. Such a dream is not innocent. It is harmful to the living reality of the Church Universal. It is idolatrous because it is elevating the tribal to the universal. The crucified Lord is as much present in Jakarta as in Jerusalem, in Rangoon as in London. The dynamism of the periphery judges our center-complex.[31]

This sentiment is echoed in the work of Song, who argues for a people hermeneutic that focuses on those in the margin. To Song, this involves not simply applying a new set of tools in the reading of the New Testament. He suggests that the starting point in this hermeneutical process is the suffering people and not any sacred text: "People are now clues to who the real Jesus is—people who are poor, outcast, and socially and politically oppressed."[32] This is possible because Jesus is present in those who are oppressed and exploited. "Jesus, in short, is the crucified people!"[33]

To Song, the message of Jesus is clear, and it is a message of liberation. Therefore, "to know who Jesus is for us today, one cannot begin with a historical reconstruction of a 'biography' of Jesus, nor can one begin with the metaphysical reflections on his divine and human natures."[34] Instead, one should begin with the message of Jesus that is already at work among the oppressed.

Affirming the significance of the people, Lee posits that one need not validate one's work by the criteria of those working in the West. To do so is to submit oneself to the same imperial forces that plagued much of Asian history: "This means that I have avoided as much as possible citing the work of Western theologies to support or validate my work. I have spent more time in meditation than in library research and more time in rereading the Bible than reinterpreting existing theological works."[35]

The most explicit discussion of the danger of relying on New Testament scholarship in the construction of one's christology can be found in the works of Sugirtharajah. While Lee focuses on "meditation," Sugirtharajah emphasizes the significance of "intuition" in light of the

[31]Koyama, "The Crucified Christ Challenges Human Power," 156.
[32]Song, *Jesus, The Crucified People*, 12.
[33]Ibid., 215–16.
[34]Song, *Jesus and the Reign of God*, xi.
[35]Lee, *Trinity in Asian Perspective*, 12.

context in which these christologies are to be developed, and because of the difference between Eastern and Western thought processes. Commenting on the works of his fellow Asian theologians, he writes:

> Whereas Euro-American christological reflections insist on logic, internal coherence, and precise theories of knowledge, they prefer to discover Jesus in the pages of the written text, and place him in a social, political and religious environment, Asian understandings of Jesus rely on impulses and assortments of ideas and contextual needs; they take him out of his milieu and place him with the peoples of Asia and with other venerated sages like Buddha, Krishna of Asia and let him mingle with other seers and savior figures.[36]

Elsewhere, Sugirtharajah provides a more pragmatic reason for the proclamation of Jesus "intuitively and imaginatively without benefit of the technical skill or sophisticated knowledge": "The enormous cost and the time needed to undertake such research is often prohibitive for Third World exegetes."[37]

Theologically, Sugirtharajah argues that "one need not necessarily appeal to precedents or paradigms enshrined in the gospels or in other early Christian works, nor have these constructions based on or legitimated by canonical writings."[38] This provides further justification to downplay the fruits of New Testament research.

Finally, Sugirtharajah even argues against the translation practices of missionaries who seek to provide the indigenous people with an accurate and authoritative text. Calling such practices "textual cleansing," he argues for a definitive departure from the Bible of the missionaries.

> Translation in a postcolonial context is not merely seeking for dynamic equivalence or aiming for linguistic exactness but is desiring

---

[36]Sugirtharajah, "Prologue and Perspective," x. On the Eastern way of knowing, see also K. P. Aleaz, "An Indian Understanding of Jesus—Findings of a Research," *Asia Journal of Theology* 12 [1998]: 119: "Knowledge of anything is an immediate existential knowledge formulated in the very knowing-process. In our knowing-process there exists nothing externally ready-made that can be adapted, indigenized, incultured or contextualized. Our hermeneutical context decides the content of our knowledge."

[37]R. S. Sugirtharajah, "'What Do Men Say Remains of Me?' Current Jesus Research and Third World Christologies," *Asia Journal of Theology* 5 (1991): 33.

[38]Sugirtharajah, "Prologue and Perspective," ix. Many working on Asian christologies also see the New Testament portrayals of Jesus merely as "experiments providing insights" (Selvanayagam, "Who Is This Jesus?," 243).

to rewrite and re-translate the texts as well as the concepts against the grain. Rewriting and retranslating are not a simple dependence upon the past, but a radical remoulding of the text to meet new situations and demands.[39]

To Sugirtharajah, without the Bible of the missionaries, one is finally free to encounter God in one's own context and through one's own medium.

Good News for the Global East?
Many of those working on Asian christologies are firmly committed to planting the Christian gospel in their own homeland. Taking into full consideration the sociopolitical and economic contexts of various Asian regions, they have successfully highlighted often-neglected aspects of the gospel message. Moreover, in attempting to bring the gospel to the "people," they have also rightly drawn attention to the need to preach the good news to those outside the centers of power, whether these "centers" represent the colonizing powers or the local elite who consider themselves to be "more equal than others."[40]

Many criticisms that have been launched against liberation theology in general apply to the problems behind the Asian christologies surveyed above,[41] but our focus in this section is to draw attention to two of the distinct elements in these christologies that in turn strip away their power for the people in Asia.

For the People, or Of the People
The first and immediately notable element of the Asian christologies we have surveyed is that they are purportedly "for the people," but are actually rejected by the theology *of* the people. While most Asian

---

[39]R. S. Sugirtharajah, "Textual Cleansing: A Move from the Colonial to the Postcolonial Version," *Semeia* 76 (1996): 16. Sugirtharajah also argues that "the Bible translations in the colonial period introduced such virtues as accuracy, authenticity, and being true to original texts—virtues to which Indian translators paid less attention. Indians were more interested in aesthetic flavour than literal accuracy."

[40]Borrowing the phrase from George Orwell, *Animal Farm* (New York: Harcourt, Brace and Company, 1946), 112.

[41]See the useful surveys in Carl E. Armerding, ed., *Evangelicals and Liberation* (Nutley, NJ: Presbyterian and Reformed, 1977); J. Andrew Kirk, *Liberation Theology: An Evangelical View from the Third World* (Atlanta: John Knox, 1979); Daniel S. Schipani, ed., *Freedom and Discipleship: Liberation Theology in an Anabaptist Perspective* (Maryknoll, NY: Orbis, 1989); and Priscilla Pope-Levison and John R. Levison, *Jesus in Global Contexts* (Louisville: Westminster John Knox, 1992).

theologians, like Lee, recognize that "the demographical picture of Christianity shifts from the First World to the Third World countries,"[42] many of these Asian theologians refuse to recognize the authenticity of the faith of many of these Christians as Asian Christians. To them, these "ordinary Asian Christians"[43] are still under the deceptive influence of Western missionaries. Song labels this theological "indigestion," and urges immediate procedures to deal with such ailment: "Our chief concern must be how to cure its indigestion, reduce its weight, and regain its agility and dynamic to win the hand of theology authentic to the Asian mind."[44] Others have even called for "theological exorcism."

> The western missionaries who came to Asia taught us about the uniqueness, exclusiveness, formativeness and finality of the Christian Bible. This kind of view is still very common among Christian churches in Asia and is haunting the minds of some biblical scholars who approach the Christian canon from a different perspective. The task of doing theology in Asia is primarily one of performing theological exorcism.[45]

In response to such ignorance imposed by the West, Asian christologies are constructed. Those who construct such christologies become the elite theologians whose job is to educate the ignorant—the naïve and simplistic who have accepted the Christian gospel, which has already proved to be a powerful gospel in other contexts.

A striking example of the manifestation of the powerful gospel can be found in mainland China. After the departure of the Western missionaries in 1949, the Christian population grew from seven hundred thousand[46] to seventy million[47] today. Many of these Chinese Christians

---

[42]Lee, *The Trinity in Asian Perspective*, 11.

[43]See Hyun Kyung Chung, "Asian Christologies and People's Religions," *Voices from the Third World* 19 (1996): 79, who admits that these Christians often hold a christocentric faith, but even this christocentrism has to be understood within a "multicentric" worldview. Many others have used the term *fundamentalists* in describing these Christians, thus dismissing them in any consideration of authentic and self-reflective Christianity in Asia.

[44]Song, *Theology from the Womb of Asia*, 3.

[45]Archie C. C. Lee, "Biblical Interpretation in Asian Perspectives," *Asia Journal of Theology* 7 (1993): 35.

[46]This figure is widely accepted, and is affirmed by the official website of the Embassy of the People's Republic of China in the United States of America, accessed June 6, 2009, http://www.china-embassy.org/eng/zt/zjxy/t36493.htm.

[47]Some have provided a much higher estimate (one hundred million) while others consider fifty million a conservative estimate. Cf. Philip Jenkins, *The Next Christendom: The Coming of Global Christianity* (New York: Oxford University Press, 2002), 70.

still stand with one of their admired elders, Wang Mingdao, when he accepts the scriptural witnesses that point to Jesus as the fulfillment of God's promises to his people, as the one who is the unique Son of God, and as the only one who is able to provide redemption for those who believe in him through his death and resurrection. Quite conscious in his arguments against the "modernists," Wang argues against seeing Jesus simply as a great teacher and minimizing the significance of his atoning death and resurrection.[48] Such examples can be multiplied *ad infinitum*, but the point is clear: the majority of ordinary Christians affirm the gospel as presented in the New Testament, and this gospel has proved to be powerful in the lives of these indigenous believers. Philip Jenkins's description of the challenge posed by the Christians in the global South against their Western counterparts may apply here as well, in that the christology espoused by many "ordinary" Asian Christians challenges the christological constructs of their theologians:

> Numbers are not everything; but at the same time, overwhelming numerical majorities surely carry some weight. Let us imagine a (probable) near-future world in which Christian numbers are strongly concentrated in the global South, where the clergy and scholars of the world's most populous churches accept interpretations of the Bible more conservative than those normally prevailing in American mainline denominations. In such a world, then surely, Southern traditions of Bible reading must be seen as the Christian norm.[49]

For christologies that consider the people as the starting point, one wonders whether the voice of these self-professed followers of Christ is being heard.

Beyond the East-West Divide

In many of the Asian christologies we have surveyed, one often encounters dichotomies evoked to justify constructs that move beyond the christological framework of the historic church councils and even that of the New Testament apostles. These include the dichotomies

---

[48]Cf. C. C. Wong, ed., *Wang Mingdao Wenku (Treasures of Wang Mingdao)*, vol. 7 (Taiwan: Conservative Baptist, 1984), 136–62. See the succinct discussion of Wang's understanding of Jesus in Poling J. Sun, "Jesus in the Writings of Wang Mingdao," in *The Chinese Face of Jesus Christ, v. 3a.*, ed. Roman Malek (Sankt Augustin, Germany: Institut Monumenta Serica, 2005), 1137–48.
[49]Philip Jenkins, *The New Faces of Christianity: Believing the Bible in the Global South* (Oxford: Oxford University Press, 2006), 2.

between Jesus' words and deeds, historical events and texts, dogma and practice, community and the individual, and the political and the spiritual. These divisions often lead to various forms of reductionism that produce a gospel that is foreign to the New Testament text. Some Asian christologies turn out to be more Asian than christological. The Sri Lankan scholar Aloysius Pieris, another major figure in the field of Asian christologies,[50] rightly notes that for many of those who are involved in such projects "the mission to Christianize Asia was somewhat deemphasized in favour of the mission to Asianize Christianity."[51]

Pieris's insight leads us to the discussion of perhaps a more fundamental dichotomy behind many of these constructs: the East versus the West. As noted above, all four of the theologians we discussed received their doctorates from academic institutions in the West, and they have all returned to the West in pursuing their teaching and research careers. This fact alone certainly does not disqualify them from writing for those in the East, and many of these scholars do recognize their own present socioeconomic context.[52] Some Asian writers have, however, found their christologies ironically as products of the Western liberal academia. In his review of Song's works, for example, the Indian scholar G. R. Singh has noted how Song's "ideas are steeped in the categories of Western thought."[53] The influences of Western thinkers on these christologies are also recognized by others.[54]

A deeper problem behind this insistence on the East-West dichotomy lies in the failure to appreciate both the complexity of the Christian gospel and the contemporary global church. Those who reject the Pauline writings, for example, as products of Western obsession with individual status and ontology fail to appreciate how Paul himself

---

[50]See, in particular, *An Asian Theology of Liberation* (Maryknoll, NY: Orbis, 1988); *Love Meets Wisdom: A Christian Experience of Buddhism* (Maryknoll, NY: Orbis, 1989); and *Fire and Water: Basic Issues in Asian Buddhism and Christianity* (Maryknoll, NY: Orbis, 1996).

[51]Aloysius Pieris, "Does Christ Have a Place in Asia? A Panoramic View," in *Any Room for Christ in Asia*, ed. Leonardo Boff and Virgil Elizondo (London: SCM, 1993), 43. Pieris is also correct in asserting that "christology is the first casualty of this new ecclesiology, while proselytism is the second" (43).

[52]Jung Young Lee, e.g., is now writing consciously as an Asian American. Others also do not pretend to fully represent the audience whom they address.

[53]G. R. Singh, "Christian Mission in Reconstruction—An Asian Attempt," *Religion and Society* 23 (1976): 117.

[54]Cf. Larry W. Caldwell, "Third Horizon Ethnohermeneutics: Re-Evaluating New Testament Hermeneutical Models for Intercultural Bible Interpreters Today," *Asia Journal of Theology* 1 (1987): 314–33.

navigated between Jewish and Greco-Roman thought worlds. And to classify Paul either as a Jewish or a Hellenistic thinker is itself a "Western" invention.[55] The complex and rich development of early Christianity should also not be reduced to a Western phenomenon. To consider the gospel message that survives in the geographical West simply as a product of Western ideology is to ignore the first fourteen hundred years of the history of the church.[56] Moreover, to identify Western missionaries in the modern era simply as colonial political instruments is to fail to consider the varied indigenous responses to the gospel message where political goodwill is lacking.[57]

Those who insist on the East-West dichotomy often adopt a static view of culture that fails to explain the contemporary global reality.[58] The spread of the gospel in Asia and its encounter with the "Western" powers are to be considered strong influences on contemporary culture in many parts of Asia, even where the Christian population is still negligible.[59] To strip the gospel of its Western clothes may then not only strip away its power; this act may also render the gospel unintelligible even in the Asian world.

Contributions of Asian New Testament Scholars
Though rejected by many who are involved in the construction of Asian christologies, Asian New Testament scholars do make significant

[55]See, e.g., the helpful survey in Dale B. Martin, "Paul and the Judaism/Hellenism Dichotomy: Toward a Social History of the Question," in Troels Engberg-Pedersen, ed., *Paul Beyond the Judaism/Hellenism Divide* (Louisville: Westminster John Knox, 2001), 29–61, who concludes that "the Hellenism/Judaism dichotomy is recent and has a limited geographical range. It was invented in nineteenth-century Germany and imported into British and North American usage mainly from there" (58).

[56]See, e.g., the discussion in Kwame Bediako, *Christianity in Africa: The Renewal of a Non-Western Religion* (Edinburgh: Edinburgh University Press, 1995), 89–187. In his recent work, Mark Noll (*The New Shape of World Christianity: How American Experience Reflects Global Faith* [Downers Grove, IL: InterVarsity, 2009], 191) likewise points to the fact that "Christianity began as Jewish; before it was European, it was North African, Syrian, Egyptian and Indian. While in recent history it has indeed been American, it has also been Chilean, Albanian, Fijian and Chinese."

[57]See Lamin Sanneh, *Whose Religion Is Christianity? The Gospel beyond the West* (Grand Rapids: Eerdmans, 2003), 21–77.

[58]See, e.g., Emiko Ohnuki-Tierney, "Against 'Hybridity': Culture as Historical Processes," in *Dismantling the East-West Dichotomy: Essays in Honour of Jan van Breman*, ed. Joy Hendry and Heung Wah Wong (New York: Routledge, 2006), 11–24.

[59]Jason H. Yeung, "Indigenized Chinese Theology—Viewed from the Cultural Perspective," *China Graduate School of Theology Journal* 31 (2001): 125–44. See also Noll, *New Shape of World Christianity*, 27, who points to specific examples of how in many non-Western regions "the Christian message, fully indigenized in local languages, has become part of local cultures."

contributions to issues related to such constructions. Sampling a few of these works will be sufficient to show that these contributions are relevant to the current discussion despite their focus primarily on the New Testament text rather than the contemporary contexts in which the text is to be received. These studies may not provide the final word in this christological discussion, but their relevance shows that the issues they treat are not limited to one ethnic context. Though not writing particularly for "Asians," these Asian voices should also be heard in the construction of a christology for Asians.

The Political Jesus?

In responding to the current trend in New Testament scholarship that focuses on the anti-imperial agenda of Jesus and Paul,[60] Seyoon Kim's recent work *Christ and Caesar* provides a helpful correction.[61] Drawing from the Gospel of Luke, Kim argues, "Jesus' redemptive work did not consist in altering the political, economic, and social structures of the day to bring Israel political freedom, economic prosperity, and social justice."[62] This does not mean, however, that Jesus was unaware of the evils of the Roman imperial system.

> Yet he did not regard it as the only manifestation of Satan's rule but rather as one of the many diverse forms, such as physical and spiritual illness, various forms of sins . . . social alienation, and poverty. Therefore, as the messianic bearer of the Kingdom of God Jesus was determined to overcome the reign of Satan, the root cause of all these forms of evil and suffering.[63]

Refusing to define "evil" simply in political and structural terms, this reading argues against a reductionist reading that distorts the true gospel message, thus rendering it impotent against spiritual forces that plague human beings.

Kim's reading not only aims at criticizing those who see Jesus primarily as a political Messiah; he also points to the inherent prob-

---

[60]See, in particular, Richard A. Horsley, *Jesus and the Spiral of Violence: Popular Jewish Resistance in Roman Palestine* (San Francisco: Harper & Row, 1987); Horsley, *Jesus and Empire: The Kingdom of God and the New World Disorder* (Minneapolis: Fortress, 2002); and N. T. Wright, *Paul: In Fresh Perspective* (Minneapolis: Fortress, 2005), 40–58.

[61]Seyoon Kim, *Christ and Caesar: The Gospel and the Roman Empire in the Writings of Paul and Luke* (Grand Rapids: Eerdmans, 2008).

[62]Ibid., 147.

[63]Ibid., 147–48.

lems of seeing the Roman imperial system as the only target of Jesus' mission.

> Luke clearly thinks that the Roman Empire has its evil side, as it essentially represents the reign of Satan, and therefore has to be replaced by the Kingdom of God at the *parousia* of the Lord Jesus Christ. But in this the Roman Empire is not alone. *All* the kingdoms of the world have the same character (Luke 4:5–7; cf. also 22:24–27). According to Luke, Jesus was opposed to his contemporary Jewish revolutionaries because he saw that the kingdom of David or Israel that they aspired to establish through their fight against the Roman imperial system would be no exception.

In noting Jesus' criticism against all evil powers, Kim's reading provides a helpful critique of contemporary readings of the "Asian Jesus" that identify the colonial powers as the primary embodiment of satanic forces and thus downplay the idolatrous act of identifying indigenous political expressions as the fulfillment of the kingdom of God.

In situating the church's struggle in history within the wider plan of God in history, Kim further points to the inadequacy of any christology that limits Christ to a political or ethnic context.

> While seeking to materialize the salvation of the Kingdom of God in terms of promotion of justice, freedom, peace, environmental health, and so on, the church must acknowledge the proleptic or provisionary character of such materialization in history, and maintain the eschatological vision for the consummation of salvation in terms of a trans-historical and transcendental reality.[64]

Salvation-Historical Framework

Kim's note concerning the "eschatological vision for the consummation of salvation" points to the need to situate christology within the wider salvific plan of God. In his detailed study of Jesus' evocation of the Zion traditions in explicating his own eschatological mission,[65] Kim Huat Tan argues against Herrman Samuel Reimarus, who saw Jesus as a revolutionary intent on liberating the Jews:[66]

---

[64]Ibid., 202–3.
[65]Kim Huat Tan, *The Zion Traditions and the Aims of Jesus*, SNTSMS 91 (Cambridge: Cambridge University Press, 1997).
[66]See Charles H. Talbert, ed., *Reimarus: Fragments*, trans. R. S. Fraser (Philadelphia: Fortress, 1970).

Jesus' reticence in the entry and his action of protest against the Jewish authorities and not against the Romans in the temple incident would suggest that his motivations behind these actions were far from an intended coup. Instead, he was motivated by his understanding that God's restorative programme for Zion had dawned.[67]

Noting the striking absence of the concern for the "Land" in Jesus' teachings, one that is often connected to Zion traditions, Tan rightly emphasizes that Jesus aims at transcending the sociopolitical realm in proclaiming the fulfilling of God's promise to his people.

> The importance of Jesus' relationship to his social world is not denied, but we would want to emphasize that, for Jesus, theology overrides societal constraints and informs his relationship to the social world. Hence, many aspects of his ministry are religious first even though they certainly have societal roots.[68]

Tan concludes that Jesus' mission must be understood in light of the promise of God in the Old Testament, and in light of the divine plan of God for his people. To reduce Jesus to a first-century Palestinian Jew who is reacting to the political situation of his time is to fail to understand his self-conscious mission to bear the cross.

Tan's conclusion, reached by his careful exegetical work, is affirmed by another Third-World New Testament scholar, Teresa Okure:

> The biblical perspective calls for awareness that the question of the global Jesus needs to be situated first and foremost within the context of biblical history and faith where it rightly belongs, and from which it derives its fundamental identity. Put differently, all efforts to understand and appreciate the global nature of Jesus are to be located within biblical history. More specifically, it relates to the biblical accounts of creation and fall (protology) as well as salvation and redemption (soteriology), seen comprehensively as God's work of love and mercy for humanity.[69]

---

[67]Tan, *Zion Traditions and the Aims of Jesus*, 234–35.

[68]Ibid., 236–37.

[69]Teresa Okure, "The Global Jesus," in *The Cambridge Companion to Jesus*, ed. Markus Bockmuehl (Cambridge: Cambridge University Press, 2001), 237.

Tan's conclusion also leads him to criticize those who see Jesus merely as a moral teacher, for this reading likewise fails to explain why Jesus went to Jerusalem.[70] It is to this image of Jesus that we shall now turn.

Jesus the Wisdom Teacher

As noted above, Jesus is often considered a sage in Asian christologies. This image evokes one who works among the people and whose teaching is often more important than his deeds or his unique status. While it is true that Jesus is portrayed as a teacher in the canonical Gospels, the teacher that one encounters in these Gospels is often quite different from the one that surfaces in these christologies. Focusing on the Gospel of Matthew, where Jesus is "most extensively and most distinctively" portrayed as a teacher, John Yieh examines the significance of this imagery within Matthew's program.[71] Yieh situates this portrayal within the ancient context by comparing the Matthean Jesus with the teacher of righteousness in the Qumran scrolls[72] and Epictetus the Greek Stoic philosopher.[73] His conclusion points to two distinct emphases in the Gospel portrayal.

First, Jesus stands out from these two figures in his consciousness of his self-identity.

> The Teacher of Righteousness claims to be a teacher of the law and revealer of eschatological mystery endowed with the knowledge of all prophetic revelation. Epictetus impresses his pupils and visitors as a moral teacher gifted with philosophical insights and practical advice. In contrast, Jesus claims to be the Prophet like Moses who comes to speak all the words of God. His instruction fulfills the law and the prophets, and his words reveal God's will concerning the coming of the kingdom, the criteria of final judgment, and the ethics for the interim period of time.[74]

Jesus grounds his claim "to be the one and only teacher worthy of listening and honor"[75] in his unique place in salvation history, as he

---

[70]Tan, *Zion Traditions and the Aims of Jesus*, 235–36.
[71]John Yueh-Han Yieh, *One Teacher: Jesus' Teaching Role in Matthew's Gospel Report*, BZNW 124 (New York: de Gruyter, 2004), 327.
[72]Ibid., 95–184.
[73]Ibid., 185–236.
[74]Ibid., 329.
[75]Ibid., 327.

is the climactic and final revelation of God. To ignore this significant self-understanding is to fail to understand his role as the ultimate "teacher."

In light of this self-understanding, Jesus claims to possess final authority.

> The Teacher of Righteousness prepares his followers at Qumran to await the coming of the two messiahs, but Jesus is claimed to be the Messiah. . . . Epictetus considers himself a witness of God summoned to be a scout for God, but Jesus is believed to be the Son of God. With an intimate relationship with God the Father, he alone has direct access to divine revelation.[76]

As such, Jesus emphasizes that "he is the only teacher in the church, just as there is only one God the Father in heaven."[77] This reading reminds the audience that the contemporary contextual reading of Jesus has to be situated within the ancient contexts through which the uniqueness of Jesus the teacher is made clear.

In such studies, one again finds the necessity to ground the gospel portrayals of Jesus within their wider theological context, which highlights his role in the redemptive plan of God.[78] Moreover, reading with such a context in view will show that the Jesus proclaimed in the gospel is not distinct from the one proclaimed in the early church.

Jesus of History and the Christ of Faith

Behind various forms of Asian christologies one finds the insistence on the separation between the Jesus of history and the Christ of faith. This is reflected in the overwhelming focus on portions of the Synoptic Gospels over against the Johannine and Pauline writings. In her painstaking comparison of the Pauline statement "faith that can

---

[76]Ibid., 329–30.

[77]Ibid., 330.

[78]Another example that examines a commonly misunderstood Matthean image of Jesus can be found in Young S. Chae, *Jesus as the Eschatological Davidic Shepherd: Studies in the Old Testament, Second Temple Judaism, and in the Gospel of Matthew*, WUNT 2/216 (Tübingen: Mohr Siebeck, 2006). Instead of simply seeing Jesus as a popular leader or shepherd, Chae rightly emphasizes the eschatological role of this shepherd, one who is identified as "the eschatological Shepherd (YHWH), the smitten Shepherd, the Davidic Shepherd/King/Judge in the future, and currently the Davidic Shepherd Prince/Leader/Teacher for the eschatological one flock comprised of both Israel and the nations" (387).

remove mountains" (1 Cor. 13:2) with the synoptic saying, "your faith has healed/saved you" (Matt. 9:22; Mark 5:34; 10:52; Luke 7:50; 8:48; 17:19; 19:42), Maureen Yeung[79] challenges the assertion of William Wrede that "Paul is to be regarded as the second founder of Christianity,"[80] thereby questioning the basic dichotomy between Jesus and Christ, accepted by many since Martin Kähler.[81] After a careful comparative study, Yeung concludes:

> The major contribution of Paul, namely, the doctrine of salvation by faith in Jesus Christ, is beyond doubt indebted to the teachings of Jesus. This doctrine is at the same time so close an echo of Jesus' inclusion of the ritually impure into the Kingdom of God through faith in himself, of Jesus' understanding of the descendants of Abraham and of Jesus' own claim of his special identity in relation to God, and yet so far away from Second Temple Judaism and other New Testament writings, that it is difficult for us not to draw a line of continuity from Jesus to Paul.[82]

The significance of assertions such as this is not missed by other Asian New Testament scholars who critically interact with Asian christologies.[83] In light of these studies, it becomes clear that general assertions that support the entire enterprise need to be evaluated critically in light of the New Testament evidence. Only *a priori* ideological commitment can justify the rejection of a significant portion of New Testament evidence in building a christology for communities of God's people.

Criterion of Dissimilarity to Investigators

Finally, Hyeon Woo Shin's *Textual Criticism and the Synoptic Problem in Historical Jesus Research*[84] warrants mention because of both

---

[79]Maureen W. Yeung, *Faith in Jesus and Paul: A Comparison with Special Reference to "Faith That Can Remove Mountains" and "Your Faith Has Healed/Saved You,"* WUNT 2/147 (Tübingen: Mohr Siebeck, 2002).

[80]William Wrede, *Paul,* trans. Edward Lummis (London: Philip Green, 1907), 179.

[81]Martin Kähler, *The So-Called Historical Jesus and the Historic Biblical Christ,* trans. Carl E. Braaten (Philadelphia: Fortress, 1964).

[82]Yeung, *Faith in Jesus and Paul,* 292. On this continuity between Jesus' and Paul's concept of faith, see also Akira Ogawa, "Action-Motivating Faith: The Understanding of 'Faith' in the Gospel of Matthew," *Annual of the Japanese Biblical Institute* 19 (1993): 53–86.

[83]See, e.g., Takashi Onuki, *Heil und Erlösung: Studien zum Neuen Testament und zur Gnosis,* WUNT 165 (Tübingen: Mohr Siebeck, 2004), 115–51.

[84]Hyeon Woo Shin, *Textual Criticism and the Synoptic Problem in Historical Jesus Research: The Search for Valid Criteria,* CBET 36 (Leuven: Peeters, 2004).

its direct relevance for historical Jesus studies and a wise cautionary note contained in its concluding remarks. Shin examines criteria used in text-critical and synoptic studies and applies them to historical Jesus research. Shin comes to the conclusion that some criteria for authenticity should not be applied in historical Jesus research, among them the "criterion of quality," "criterion of the shorter saying," "criterion of the less theologically developed saying," and "criterion of vividness."[85]

In discussing the criterion of dissimilarity that has often been applied in evaluating the historical Jesus against his first-century contexts, Shin wisely voices the need to apply this criterion to contemporary constructions:

> If EC [early Christianity] could distort the picture of the HJ [historical Jesus], modern scholars probably do so as well, and perhaps even more. On the basis of this assumption, another criterion needs to be formulated, "the criterion of dissimilarity to investigators": The construction of a historical Jesus which ends up being dissimilar to the investigator's Zeitgeist or ideological emphasis has a greater claim to authenticity than a reconstruction which is not dissimilar to the investigator's Zeitgeist or ideological emphasis.[86]

Contemporary scholars, Asian or otherwise, would do well to heed this cautionary note.

Conclusion

The brief and fragmentary survey of works by Asian New Testament scholars above is sufficient to show the relevance of such research for a construction of a christology that is both powerful and relevant for Asians. The conclusions reached by these works may not be "ground breaking" in New Testament scholarship, and these scholars neither write as Asian scholars nor intend to address a particular Asian audience. These works, among others, do exemplify the contributions of Asian New Testament scholars interacting with wider biblical scholarship and providing helpful critiques of their fellow pilgrims as they search for a gospel that is both authentic and relevant for communities

---

[85]Ibid., 201–6.
[86]Ibid., 220.

within various contextual constraints. After all, in this age of global Christianity, we need to be "eager to learn from one another, to correct and to be corrected by one another, provided only that there is a principled submission to God's gracious self-disclosure in Christ and in the Scriptures."[87]

---

[87]Carson, *Gagging of God*, 552.

12

New Testament Studies in Europe

ROBERT W. YARBROUGH

N
o. I would not know where to begin." Those were the (no doubt sagacious) words of a veteran European New Testament scholar when asked to write an essay on New Testament studies in Europe in recognition of D. A. Carson, whose near-native language (Canadian French), paternal heritage (Irish), and doctoral degree (Cambridge) all connect him with the European sphere. His speaking, students, and publications, too, give him extensive connections with New Testament studies in Europe and those involved in or affected by it at various levels. This is all the more true given that, as will be shown below, New Testament scholarship in North America at the high level Carson is known for is inherently intertwined with its counterpart in Europe. It is fitting that this Festschrift include a look at New Testament studies in that quarter of the globe.[1]

The task of commenting briefly and meaningfully on New Testament studies originating in or closely associated with that mass of

---

[1]I wish to thank assistants Craig Long and Carl Park for their bibliographic labors. Thanks also to Richard Hess, editor of *Bulletin for Biblical Research*, for permission to quote portions of my book reviews published in that journal.

nations we call Europe is indeed daunting. The region includes some fifty countries encompassing a population of well over seven hundred million. It extends from Iceland in the northwest to Armenia in the southeast. The English language is, of course, dominant in the British Isles and widely utilized for commercial purposes across Europe as a whole, but this will often be found to be a thin linguistic veneer, with large segments of populations at local levels having little need or understanding of it. There can hardly be said to be, then, a true single "bridge" language. This has implications for New Testament studies in that published conversations proceed that are occasionally not very cognizant of discussions in other languages, resulting in parochial publications—not necessarily a bad thing, as local views deserve airing, and local issues have to be addressed. The vernacular, not the going lingua franca, may well be the best means of achieving those ends.

But the Europe-wide situation is complex. Some of the national tongues hail from disparate language groups and in certain cases (Finnish, Hungarian) are relatively anomalous. This is not to mention numerous non-European languages (Turkish, Arabic, Chinese, etc.) increasingly spoken in Europe among immigrant populations, among whom are sure to be found those who study and write about the New Testament. Not only languages but also national cultures and identities in the broader sense are often divergent, sometimes drastically so. This has caused or resulted in bitter conflict in past eras. All of this presents challenges for a clear and concise picture of New Testament studies as it may be carried on across the region *in toto*.

Moreover, while with the dissolution of classical antiquity Christianity gradually grew to dominate Europe, that faith in its ecclesial expression assumed increasingly numerous and divergent forms, not only with the parting of East and West (formalized by AD 1054) but particularly since the Reformation (sixteenth century). Today, extreme variety is not seldom present even within the same country—with "Christian" in, say, Romania meaning significantly contrasting things depending on whether one speaks of Orthodox, Reformed, Catholic, Uniate, Baptist, or Pentecostal manifestations (and other forms of faith expression are found). New Testament studies proceeding under the auspices of these varying confessional (or anticonfessional) loyalties may be expected to exhibit fairly significant differences.

It should also be noted that non-Christian views of New Testament figures and teachings are an increasingly common feature of the academic and social landscape—a recent study published in the Netherlands essentially simply recounts the view of Jesus propounded by two Islamic thinkers (Ibn Hazm [994–1064] and Al-Ghazali [1058–1111]) about a thousand years ago.[2] Or, views are Christian in orientation, but the definition of "Europe" is stretched. How European is a study about Scripture and evangelization published in Italy by a professor at the Pontifical University of Urbaniana—given that the professor is Nigerian and his observations pertain mainly to Africa?[3]

In view of the diversity and complexity of virtually anything found across all or much of Europe, this essay will attempt no more than to venture six descriptive propositions that may help capture the flavor of selected features of the topic at hand. Focus will be primarily on western and northern Europe, with some reference to former Eastern bloc nations; this is not because New Testament studies does not exist in predominately Catholic southern Europe but because this author is less cognizant of the history and heritage of New Testament scholarship in those regions, and space constraints for this essay do not permit unlimited coverage. Also, Catholic biblical scholarship in the modern sense did not really get underway, as far as papal sanction is concerned, until midway through the twentieth century. This is not the place to attempt to chronicle that particular chain of events and how those events are playing out today, though Catholic scholars and scholarship are by no means absent from discussion below.

New Testament studies in Europe is too complex for facile summation.

The point already mooted above deserves further explication. If the international research tool *New Testament Abstracts* is a reasonably reliable indicator, just the journals published regularly in Europe and containing works that *Abstracts* editors regard as pertinent to "New Testament studies" is impressive (see table 2).

---

[2]B. Duran, "The Prophet Jesus in Islamic Theology," *Studies in Interreligious Dialogue* 18, no. 1 (2008): 55–62. From a different viewpoint see J. M. Mutei, "The Bible: Classical and Contemporary Muslim Attitudes and Exegesis," *Evangelical Review of Theology* 31, no. 3 (2007): 207–20.

[3]F. A. Oborji, "The Bible and Evangelisation of Africa: A Missiological Appraisal," *Euntes Docete* 61, no. 3 (2008): 47–82.

Table 2. Geographical analysis of journals covered by *New Testament Abstracts*

	Total Number of Journals	Places of Publication and Number of Journals
Europe (Continent only)	178	Germany 44 Italy 32 France 24 Spain 21 Belgium 17 Netherlands 11 Switzerland 7 Austria 6 Poland 6 Norway 3 Sweden 2 Czech Republic 1 Denmark 1 Greece 1 Malta 1 Portugal 1
United Kingdom, Ireland	55	Great Britain 50 Ireland 5

In 2009 alone, *New Testament Abstracts* gave notice of some twenty-one hundred published periodical items worldwide. Perhaps half of these or more were of European origin, whether by virtue of place of publication or national origin of author. As to topics, *New Testament Abstracts* groups articles under five headings (as of 2009) (see table 3). For nonspecialists in particular, this listing will dramatize the breadth and complexity of what "New Testament studies" entails.

As far as books, *New Testament Abstracts* lists them under the same five headings. In 2009, in excess of five hundred books that dealt with some aspect of New Testament studies were published by European publishers or authors.

To the mass of hundreds of journals, articles, and books must be added the complicating factor that these appear in numerous languages, most commonly (after English) German, French, Italian, and Spanish, but with notable numbers in other languages, too, including Dutch, Swedish, Norwegian, Danish, and Czech. A number of articles appear in Afrikaans; the orientation and subject matter of many of these may be more European than African. Many items by Asians are likewise more European, whatever (Western) language they may publish in (a matter touched on in David Pao's essay above). One bibliography of biblical studies items published since World War II lists in excess

Table 3. The breadth and complexity of New Testament studies

The New Testament: General	Epistles–Revelation
Canon	Epistles (General)
Interpretation	Paul
Textual Criticism	Romans, 1–2 Corinthians
Biblical Linguistics and Philology	Galatians–Philemon
Biblical Translation	Hebrews
Computer-Assisted Research	Catholic Epistles
Scholars	Revelation
Bulletins	**Biblical Theology**
Gospels–Acts	Christology
Gospels (General)	Church and Ministry
Jesus	Various Themes
Passion and Death	**The World of the New Testament**
The Resurrection	General
Synoptics	Archaeology
Matthew	Dead Sea Scrolls
Mark	Jewish World
Luke	Rabbinics
John	Greco-Roman World
Acts of the Apostles	Early Christianity
	Gnosticism

of twenty-three thousand items—*in Polish alone.*[4] More will be said about the Polish contribution below.

An important overarching consideration is that, hermeneutically speaking, there are really multiple Europes. The world of Roman Catholic discussion and scholarship has its own history and conventions and often proceeds as if no other Christian group exists. No less distinct, frequently, are studies emanating from Protestant centers of thought, Protestantism itself being variegated (and sometimes as exclusivist in tone as its Catholic counterpart). Eastern Orthodoxy (some of whose centers, of course, are located outside Europe) has never been as involved in New Testament studies as either Catholics or Protestants, but this is increasingly changing.[5] British scholarship, whether by Anglicans or others, is typically both derivative of and distinct in orientation from its counterparts

---

[4]See Z. J. Kapera, "Two New Polish Biblical Serials," *Polish Journal of Biblical Research* 8, no. 1 (2009): 51–60. This does not count encyclopedia or dictionary articles.

[5]See, e.g., K. Nikolakopoulos, "An Orthodox Critique of Some Radical Approaches in New Testament Studies," *Greek Orthodox Theological Review* 47, no. 1–4 (2002): 339–55. More broadly, see Theodore G. Stylianopoulos, *The New Testament: An Orthodox Perspective* (Brookline, MA: Holy Cross Orthodox Press, 2004). But this may be more indicative of a North American than of a European Orthodox perspective.

elsewhere, including its European counterparts.[6] A Polish scholar reports the variegated and eclectic nature of biblical studies in that nation:

> Our country's past favoured an interest in others; we lived for centuries in a multi-national and multi-confessional environment. Polish culture willingly adopted foreign ideas. . . . Nevertheless, no single source of inspiration was preferred. We tend to be selective, taking something from France, something from Germany, something from the Eastern Churches, something from Jewish interpretation, and recently something from American and British intellectual life. . . . On the other hand, the number of original contributions is increasing. In the world of biblical scholarship our role would be a modest, but visible one.[7]

By now it should be clear why anyone familiar with the field—sorry, fields—of New Testament studies might reasonably decline to attempt a synthetic comment on them. Yet the fact that European New Testament studies defies facile summation does not mean that no synthetic statements can be made about the enterprise at all.

New Testament studies in Europe is part of an international network, interlocking particularly with North America.

The upshot of that assertion is that New Testament studies in Europe have already to some degree been described by Craig Blomberg in his essay above on New Testament studies in North America. In each of the categories into which he subdivides New Testament studies—the historical Jesus and the Synoptic Gospels; John and Acts; Pauline studies; Hebrews through Revelation; hermeneutical methods and approaches—it would be possible to compile long lists of European scholars and publications reflecting research that is intertwined with the North American discussion, sometimes to the point of virtual symbiosis. An example of such close international cooperation is seen, for example, in essays presented at a symposium held in Eisenach,

---

[6]The classic work depicting an English view of New Testament studies historically is Stephen Neill and Tom Wright, *The Interpretation of the New Testament 1861–1986*, 2nd ed. (Oxford: Oxford University Press, 1988).

[7]M. Wojciechowski, "Biblical Studies in Poland," *Expository Times* 119, no. 11 (2008): 542.

Germany, in 2005.[8] Eleven were written in English, the rest in German. Five contributors were scholars resident in Germany: Ulrich Busse, Rainer Hirsch-Luipold, Silke Petersen, Folker Siegert, and the editor Ruben Zimmermann. Five were from faculties in the US: Paul N. Anderson, Harold Attridge, R. Alan Culpepper, Craig Koester, and Marianne Meye Thompson. Two scholars were from Swiss universities (Uta Poplutz, Jean Zumstein), two from South Africa (D. Francois Tolmie, Jan G. Van der Watt), and two from Belgium (Petrus Maritz and Gilbert Van Belle, who cowrite their chapter). Rounding out the participants were scholars teaching in Denmark (Jesper Tang Nielsen) and Australia (Mary L. Coloe).

This interplay is seen also in certain major New Testament commentary series like the International Critical Commentary. It covers the whole of the New Testament and was written primarily by British authors (with some American representation) beginning over a century ago.[9] Its production continues with fresh replacements of older volumes by newer scholars, still both British and American. For example, Howard Marshall (British) and Philip Towner (American)[10] collaborated to replace the older volume on the Pastoral Epistles by Walter Lock (British).[11] C. E. B. Cranfield (British) contributed two volumes on Romans, but these bear a marked Swiss and German flavor, Cranfield having much appreciation for Karl Barth.[12] Few commentary series have done more to uphold the style and substance of British New Testament commentating in learned North American circles, carrying forward into the twenty-first century an association that was already robust due to North American affection for the work

---

[8]Jörg Frey, Jan G. van der Watt, and Ruben Zimmermann, eds., in collaboration with Gabi Kern, *Imagery in the Gospel of John: Terms, Forms, Themes, and Theology of Johannine Figurative Language* (Tübingen: Mohr Siebeck, 2006).

[9]See, e.g., Alfred Plummer, *A Critical and Exegetical Commentary on the Gospel According to S. Luke* (London: T&T Clark, 1896); W. Sanday and Arthur C. Headlam, *A Critical and Exegetical Commentary on the Epistle of the Romans*, 3rd ed. (New York: C. Scribner's Sons, 1897); Marvin Richardson Vincent, *A Critical and Exegetical Commentary on the Epistles to the Philippians and to Philemon* (New York: C. Scribner's Sons, 1897); Charles Bigg, *A Critical and Exegetical Commentary on the Epistles of St. Peter and St. Jude* (Edinburgh: T&T Clark, 1901). Plummer, Sanday, Headlam, and Bigg were British; Vincent was American.

[10]I. Howard Marshall and Philip H. Towner, *A Critical and Exegetical Commentary on the Pastoral Epistles* (New York: T&T Clark, 2004).

[11]Walter Lock, *A Critical and Exegetical Commentary on the Pastoral Epistles* (Edinburgh: T&T Clark, 1924).

[12]C. E. B. Cranfield, *A Critical and Exegetical Commentary on the Epistle to the Romans*, 2 vols. (New York: T&T Clark, 1975).

of British scholars J. B. Lightfoot, B. F. Westcott, and F. J. A. Hort from the nineteenth century. At the same time there has been a (more limited) reverse dissemination of scholarly style and substance across the Atlantic west to east.

In more recent times, Continental New Testament scholarship has affected New Testament interpretation in North America at the same scholarly level through the Hermeneia series. Whether U. Luz (Swiss) on Matthew (3 volumes, 2001–2007), F. Bovon (French) on Luke (1 volume to date, 2002), or G. Strecker (German) on 1–3 John (1996), this Augsburg Press series has for decades mediated European scholarship to North America through numerous volumes, often written in a European language and translated into English. Some volumes, however, were written by North Americans themselves, whether Paul Achtemeier (1 Peter, 1996), Robert Jewett (Romans, 2006), or Richard Pervo (Acts, 2008). This illustrates that for at least a generation now, rough parity has obtained between North American and European New Testament scholarship. W. Kahl even states that today "essential impulses in theology generally and in the exegetical disciplines in particular are established primarily in the USA,"[13] not Germany or elsewhere. At any rate, until a couple of decades after World War II, leading lights in Britain (e.g., C. H. Dodd) and Germany (notably Rudolf Bultmann, his student Ernst Käsemann, or others from the Bultmann "school") clearly were the pacesetters internationally. The ongoing strong influence of figures from Europe (e.g., the late F. F. Bruce and now N. T. Wright in Britain; the late Martin Hengel in Germany) on North America is a permanent and rightful fixture on the international scene (see below). The movement is not always reciprocal in a given subfield, however: Schnelle's recent New Testament theology[14] does not even list the equivalent English-language works by Howard Marshall and Frank Thielman.[15] In turn, it is rather less than more common for North American New Testament scholars to interact extensively with works published in non-English European languages.

---

[13] W. Kahl, "Akademische Bibelinterpretation in Afrika, Lateinamerika und Asien angesichts der Globalisierung," *Verkündigung und Forschung* 54, no. 1 (2009): 57.
[14] *Theology of the New Testament*, trans. M. Eugene Boring (Grand Rapids: Baker, 2009), on which D. A. Carson has commented trenchantly: "Review Article: Locating Udo Schnelle's *Theology of the New Testament* in the Contemporary Discussion," *JETS* 53, no. 1 (2010): 133–41.
[15] I. Howard Marshall, *New Testament Theology: Many Witnesses, One Gospel* (Downers Grove, IL: InterVarsity, 2004); Frank Thielman, *Theology of the New Testament: A Canonical and Synthetic Approach* (Grand Rapids: Zondervan, 2005).

Another place where the highly interactive nature of European and North American scholarship may be seen is in educational cross-fertilization. An American like Larry Hurtado may occupy a chair in a Scottish university (Edinburgh). The influence on North American (and international) scholarship exerted by the late Krister Stendahl (Swedish) over four decades of teaching at Harvard was extensive. The same can be said for the career of Hans Dieter Betz (German) at the University of Chicago or Helmut Koester (also German) at Harvard. Germans Eckhard Schnabel (Trinity Evangelical Divinity School) and Thorsten Moritz (Bethel Seminary) occupy chairs in North American seminaries; both earned their doctorates in Britain (Schnabel, at the University of Aberdeen; Moritz, at King's College, London).[16] The same is true of German Hans Bayer, who teaches at Covenant Theological Seminary in St. Louis; his doctorate is from Aberdeen.[17] Over the years, several Dallas Theological Seminary professors earned their doctorates (or in some cases second doctorates) in Britain, including the University of Aberdeen (e.g., Darrell Bock) or Cambridge (the late Harold Hoehner).[18] New Testament faculty in the Talbot School of Theology associated with Biola University in California have doctorates from Aberdeen (Clinton Arnold, Andy Draycott), St. Andrews (Edward Klink III), and Oxford (David Horner, Moyer Hubbard). Many, if not most, evangelical seminaries in North America have New Testament faculty with European[19] and particularly British doctorates.

Korean American scholar Sydney Park teaches New Testament at Beeson Divinity School and earned her doctorate at Aberdeen;[20] here is a melding of not just two but three continents. This would also describe the road followed by distinguished New Testament scholar Seyoon Kim at Fuller Theological Seminary (Korean with Manchester

---

[16]Schnabel plays a key role not only in the US but also in Germany, coediting the New Testament commentary series Historisch-Theologische Auslegung Neues Testament, jointly published by R. Brockhaus and Brunnen, with contributions so far by Schnabel (1 Corinthians), Heinz-Werner Neudorfer (1 Timothy), Gerhard Maier (James), and Hans Bayer (Mark).

[17]Bayer teaches not only in North America (and internationally) but also, as the previous note indicates, publishes in Germany.

[18]John D. Hannah, *An Uncommon Union: Dallas Theological Seminary and American Evangelicalism* (Grand Rapids: Zondervan, 2009), 241, 362n55.

[19]E.g., Scott Hafemann, at Gordon-Conwell, earned his doctorate at Tübingen; David Alan Black, at Southeastern Baptist Theological Seminary, earned his at Basel.

[20]See her published dissertation *Submission within the Godhead and the Church in the Epistle to the Philippians: An Exegetical and Theological Examination of the Concept of Submission in Philippians 2 and 3* (New York: T&T Clark, 2007).

doctorate). Also at Beeson, and also with an Aberdeen doctorate, is Osvaldo Padilla, a native of the Dominican Republic.[21] Austrian Andreas Köstenberger, New Testament professor at Southeastern Baptist Theological Seminary and editor of the *Journal of the Evangelical Theological Society*, earned his New Testament doctorate from Trinity Evangelical Divinity School in the US, but his first doctorate (in economics) was taken in the leading city of his native country, the Vienna University of Economics.

Interplay between the British system of doctoral studies and North American New Testament scholarship is seen in a recent volume to which D. A. Carson contributed. Of the eighteen scholars who collaborated on *Commentary on the New Testament Use of the Old Testament*,[22] twelve earned their doctorates in Britain.[23] The intertwining of Continental, British, and North American scholarship is highlighted in a recent anthology dealing with the Gospel of Thomas.[24]

New Testament studies in Europe remains tethered to leading luminaries.

In Craig Blomberg's chapter above, North American scholarship was analyzed effectively along topical lines. This reflects the approach of a more detailed, book-length survey of the same subject from the previous generation.[25] In important respects, European New Testament study is more readily grasped not in topical categories but in terms of dominant figures whose legacy at some point came to reign within a discipline or subdiscipline and continues into the present. Sometimes, this dominance emerged in the scholar's own lifetime; this was true for Rudolf Bultmann (1884–1976), whose work in Gospels studies, Paul, New Testament theology, and hermeneutics was of towering significance internationally by the 1950s. In other cases, the influence is posthumous, as with Hermann Samuel Reimarus (1694–1768); his impact on life of Jesus studies was felt most fully over a century after his death, when in the early twentieth century Albert Schweitzer high-

---

[21]See his published dissertation *The Speeches of Outsiders in Acts: Poetics, Theology and Historiography* (Cambridge: Cambridge University Press, 2008).
[22]Ed. G. K. Beale and D. A. Carson (Grand Rapids: Baker; Nottingham: Apollos, 2007).
[23]I.e., from Aberdeen (5), Cambridge (4), Edinburgh (1), Manchester (1), and St. Andrews (1).
[24]Jörg Frey, Enno Edzard Popkes, and Jens Schröter, eds., with assistance from Christine Jacobi, *Das Thomasevangelium. Entstehung—Rezeption—Theologie* (New York: de Gruyter, 2008).
[25]E. J. Epp and G. W. MacRae, eds., *The New Testament and Its Modern Interpreters* (Atlanta: Scholars Press, 1989).

lighted him in *The Quest of the Historical Jesus*.[26] In either case, leading figures (most often German) frequently have been, and sometimes
still are, determinative for the direction and flavor of New Testament
studies in Europe. B. Sixtus observes that D. F. Strauss's (1808–1874)
"hermeneutics of critical distance" "still provides the basic framework
within which academic biblical scholarship is mainly construed and
conducted."[27]

When Larry Hurtado surveys twentieth-century New Testament
studies[28]—in whose shadow we still stand—the dominance of particular
individuals is notable. Johannes Weiss and Albert Schweitzer in the
areas of Jewish eschatology and the life of Jesus; Adolf Deissmann
in New Testament backgrounds and Greek language; Walter Bauer
in lexicography and the history of the early church; Ernst Lohmeyer
in Pauline and historical studies; Gustaf Dalman in archaeology and
geography; Karl Schmidt and Martin Dibelius along with Bultmann
in form criticism—in category after category particular individuals
establish a hegemony of outlook that is then maintained for decades.
He could have added F. C. Baur (1792–1860), H. J. Holtzmann
(1832–1910), William Wrede (1859–1906), and others. In French
and Roman Catholic scholarship, Hurtado points to Alfred Loisy
(1857–1940) and Marie-Joseph Lagrange (1855–1938).[29] Another
significant French voice was Joseph Bonsirven (1880–1958).[30] F. Bovon
points to Jacques Dupont (1915–1998).[31] Perhaps as the result of
national-ethnic-historical consciousness that is established in Europe
in ways it is not in North America, New Testament studies in Europe is
often steered by the material contribution or at least effective memory
of particular great figures of the past.

One indication of this is the way German New Testament scholars
(or scholars whose work bears on New Testament interpretation) are
the subject of dissertations that review their legacy and seek to restate

[26]German edition 1906.
[27]B. Sixtus, "Bridging the Gap? On Some Suggestions towards Solving the Normative Problem
in Ecclesial Exegesis," *Scottish Journal of Theology* 58, no. 1 (2005): 13–38.
[28]L. W. Hurtado, "New Testament Studies in the 20th Century," *Religion* 39, no. 1 (2009):
43–57.
[29]Ibid., 48.
[30]J. N. Clayton, "Bonsirven, Joseph," in *Dictionary of Major Biblical Interpreters*, ed. D. McKim
(Downers Grove, IL: InterVarsity; Nottingham: Inter-Varsity, 2007), 207–10.
[31]F. Bovon, "Dupont, Jacques," in *Dictionary of Major Biblical Interpreters*, ed. McKim,
394–96.

their significance for the present time. Whereas in North America, New Testament study tends to a synchronic focus—what are the current important views?—the European outlook is frequently diachronic— what have past scholars established that ought to continue to steer research? This comes to the fore, for example, in a recent study of Reimarus.[32] While the scholarship of this volume marks it as indispensable for future interaction with this pivotal figure, some will find puzzling the author's positive commendation of Reimarus as a faithful upholder of a post-Reformation theological tradition that is to be continued on the basis of declaring itself bankrupt and starting afresh with something like the vision championed by Reimarus. Is it really the case that "one of the abiding tasks of theology" today is to "engage with the theological legacy"[33] of Reimarus? Or consider a recent biography of Bultmann.[34] On the one hand, this is an inexhaustible trove of Bultmann fact and lore set amid the unfolding of times still of importance for biblical interpretation today. On the other, it is a loss for scholarship that Hammann did not do more to characterize criticisms of Bultmann's views, which he either ignores or curtly disparages (see, e.g., his dismissal of Marburg professor Ernst-Wilhelm Kohls's misgivings[35]). Apparently Hammann is comfortable with Bultmann's core notion that his demythologization program is (still!) for our time what justification through faith alone was for Luther's.[36] But many readers will lament the absence of critical interaction. Granted, much of this literature has appeared in English-language publications. But these are largely absent from the book's discussion and even bibliography—out of over two hundred monographs listed,[37] only six are in English, and none is fundamentally critical of Bultmann. This illustrates once more that sophisticated European scholarship can at the same time have its parochial dimensions.

Recovery of solid insight from the past is a legitimate enterprise in any field of study. This is recognized on both sides of the Atlantic.[38]

---

[32]Dietrich Klein, *Hermann Samuel Reimarus (1694–1768). Das theologische Werk* (Tübingen: Mohr Siebeck, 2009).
[33]Ibid., 279.
[34]Konrad Hammann, *Rudolf Bultmann: Eine Biographie* (Tübingen: Mohr Siebeck, 2009).
[35]Ibid., 507.
[36]Ibid., 427.
[37]See ibid., 520–27.
[38]For North America, see *Dictionary of Major Biblical Interpreters*. For a voice that is both British and Continental, see Marcus Bockmühl, *Seeing the Word: Refocusing New Testament*

The observation being made here is simply that in New Testament studies in Europe, figures of the past often wield imposing authority in and even over current discussion.[39] This is illustrated by a volume reproducing "landmarks in the search for the Jesus of history."[40] With the exception of Spinoza, all the scholars anthologized are either German or Swiss: Troeltsch, Reimarus, Strauss, Wrede, Ritschl, J. Weiss, Schweitzer, Kähler, Bultmann, Barth, and Käsemann. L. T. Johnson has shown how this dynamic worked in the question of authorship of the Pastoral Epistles;[41] the (Teutonic) "consensus" that Paul did not write them "resulted as much from social dynamics," including the authority of leading figures like Schleiermacher, F. C. Baur, and Holtzmann, "as from independent assessment of the evidence by each independent scholar."[42]

While the dominance of luminaries can be stultifying,[43] it can also be productive when the dominance liberates subsequent generations of researchers rather than imprisoning them with a paradigm that turns out to be overly restrictive. The recognition of mature or recently deceased New Testament interpreters of stature is an important index of the movers and shakers in European New Testament studies. Recent years have seen well-deserved tributes to the likes of Bernard Orchard, Martin Hengel, Eduard Schweizer, Maurice Wiles, and C. K. Barrett.[44] Barrett's greatness lies partially in the fact that although Morgan places him at the pinnacle of a research trajectory established

---

Study (Grand Rapids: Baker, 2006), who among other things stresses the value of history of interpretation even for "critical" New Testament study, and even extending to "precritical" times and thinkers. For a largely positive assessment of Bockmühl, see P. Doble, "So What Has Athens to Do with Jerusalem. . . ?," *Expository Times* 118, no. 9 (2007): 400–22.

[39]Cf. H. Bärend, "Schutz vor Beliebigkeit," *Zeitzeichen* 6, no. 11 (2005): 30–32.

[40]The quoted words are the subtitle of Gregory Dawes, ed., *The Historical Jesus Quest* (Louisville: Westminster John Knox, 2000; Leiderdorp: Deo, 1999).

[41]L. T. Johnson, *The First and Second Letters to Timothy*, AB 35A (New York: Doubleday, 2001), 42–58.

[42]Ibid., 55.

[43]Cf. B. Hägglund, "Vorkantianische Hermeneutik," *Kerygma und Dogma* 52, no. 2 (2006): 180, who notes the loss of an adequate theological dimension in much historical-critical exegesis.

[44]Anonymous, "Dom Bernard Orchard May 3, 1910–November 28, 2006," *Scripture Bulletin* 37, no. 1 (2007): iii–iv; R. Deines, "Martin Hengel: Ein Leben für die Christologie," *Theologische Beiträge* 37, no. 6 (2006): 287–300; L. W. Hurtado, "Martin Hengel's Impact on English-speaking Scholarship," *Expository Times* 120, no. 2 (2008): 70–76; U. Luz, "Eduard Schweizer zum Gedenken: 18.4.1913–27.6.2006," *Evangelische Theologie* 66, no. 5 (2006): 323–24; J. Macquarrie, "The Theological Legacy of Maurice Wiles," *Anglican Theological Review* 88, no. 4 (2006): 597–616; R. Morgan, "A Magnificent Seven: C. K. Barrett at 90," *Expository Times* 119, no. 6 (2008): 226–28.

by six preceding figures—F. C. Baur, J. B. Lightfoot, Edwyn Clement Hoskyns, Bultmann, Barth, and Käsemann—Barrett maintained his capacity for independent judgment and fresh direction. This may in fact be regarded as an important element of much British scholarship over the decades and a primary reason why young scholars are drawn to Britain to pursue doctoral studies. To a significant degree, independence of thought is valued and promoted, and not so much the confirmation and extension of views of a *Doktorvater*.

New Testament studies in Europe remains tethered to dominant traditions, both national and confessional.

All of Europe's dozens of nations, which sustain various forms of New Testament studies, have their own individual histories of development. B. Ericsson notes Sweden's former relative isolation. But by the beginning of the twentieth century, European biblical scholarship was making its presence felt, with "German exegetical tradition . . . dominating."[45] Sweden has made a signal contribution to New Testament studies through the work of Anton Fridrichsen (a Norwegian who eventually settled in Sweden), Krister Stendahl (who eventually migrated to Harvard), Bo Reicke, Hugo Odeburg, and many others. Fridrichsen's legacy has received fresh attention in a recent multiauthor work.[46] Other Scandinavian countries have also made significant contributions. An example is the work of Troels Engberg-Pedersen at the University of Copenhagen,[47] along with associated colleagues at other universities of the region, or the Finnish interpretation of Luther with its implications for interpretation of Paul.[48] The Norwegian Nils Dahl (1911–2001) influenced generations of New Testament students at the University of Oslo and then from 1965–1980 at Yale.[49]

[45]B. Ericsson, "Religious Studies in Sweden during the 20th Century," *Polish Journal of Biblical Research* 4, no. 2 (2005): 161–65.

[46]Sven-olav Back and Tom Holmen, eds., *The Institutions of the Emerging Church* (New York: T&T Clark, 2009).

[47]Cf., most recently, Troels Engberg-Pedersen, *Cosmology and Self in the Apostle Paul: The Material Spirit* (New York: Oxford University Press, 2010).

[48]See Carl Braaten and Robert Jenson, eds., *Union with Christ: The New Finnish Interpretation of Paul* (Grand Rapids: Eerdmans, 1998).

[49]See H. Moxnes, "Dahl, Nils Alstrup," in *Dictionary of Major Biblical Interpreters*, ed. McKim, 344–47.

Turning to Poland, as late as the mid-twentieth century, not one Polish commentary on a book of the Bible had ever been published,[50] though there had been numerous Bible translations into Polish dating back to the immediate post-Reformation era.[51] Until the twentieth century, "wars, anarchy and partitions of Poland among three major powers in the end of the eighteenth century . . . made it nearly impossible" for "academic and intellectual life" to flourish.[52] Despite many disruptions, biblical scholarship grew in volume and quality during the twentieth century. Even under Communist pressure, student numbers in theological faculties of Poland's universities increased: "Thirty years ago there were perhaps 400 lay students of theology in Poland" and about 4,000 seminarians; "biblical studies participated in this development."[53] Since the fall of Communism in 1989 growth has continued:[54] "At present there are about 7,000 lay students," though the number of seminarians remains unchanged.[55] The number of biblical and theological scholars in Poland has roughly doubled in the past fifteen years.[56] Wojciechowski summarizes the focus of (predominantly Catholic) scholarship in Poland as follows:

> Biblical theology prevails over exegesis itself and history. The influence of the Pontifical Biblical Institute leads many scholars to concentrate on a philological and literary approach, rather than on historical methods. The interest in New Testament background is worth mentioning, with a considerable number of studies on Qumran.[57]

By way of summary,[58] in Poland there is an unprecedented growth and volume of biblical publications. Many Polish scholars are publishing outside Poland and in languages accessible to international audiences. New institutions for biblical research have arisen; all seem to want their own academic journal, and the level of new publications

---

[50]Z. J. Kapera, "A Guide to Polish Biblical Research (Review Article)," *Polish Journal of Biblical Research* 5, no. 2 (2006): 138.
[51]Wojciechowski, "Biblical Studies in Poland," 539.
[52]Ibid.
[53]Ibid., 540.
[54]Cf. Kapera, "A Guide to Polish Biblical Research," 139.
[55]Wojciechowski, "Biblical Studies in Poland," 540.
[56]Ibid.
[57]Ibid., 541.
[58]For the following profile see Kapera, "Two New Polish Biblical Serials," 51–53.

may be suffering as a result. Still, such growth and interest can hardly be detrimental in the long run to New Testament studies.

Another significant yet largely disregarded site for New Testament studies is Hungary. György Benyik voices displeasure that the Hungarian heritage of certain biblical scholars seems to be suppressed; he names Géza Vermes, Dénes Farkasfalvy, and Elisabeth Schüssler-Fiorenza as Hungarians whose ethnicity is too little known.[59] Biblical studies in Hungary dates at least as far back as the eleventh century.[60] There have been about two hundred translations of the Hungarian Bible to date.[61] Hungarian history has been complex, fascinating, and often detrimental to maintenance of a healthy tradition of biblical studies,[62] whether because of intra-European conflict or Turkish incursion. Both Lutheran and Reformed branches of Protestant churches were severely persecuted, for example, by Catholic forces of the Counter-Reformation. There had been some growth by the time of Communism's encroachment after World War II. But at that time "the sciences of classical philology and theology" were condemned by Marxist ideology as "retrograde sciences."[63] Soviet troops looted and intentionally destroyed library and archival resources; Hungarian scholars and scholarship were cut off from international connection,[64] though eventually some interchange with colleagues in other Soviet bloc countries was permitted.[65] In the wake of the fall of Communism, by 1995 the international congress of the Society of Biblical Literature was able to convene in Budapest.

Today, biblical studies proceeds at a healthy pace, though hampered by lack of library resources and sometimes by lack of knowledge of foreign languages by Hungarian scholars.[66] One example of a Hungarian New Testament scholar with an international readership is Peter Balla of the Károli Gáspár Reformed University in Budapest. Fluent in Hungarian, German, and English, Balla published his Edinburgh PhD thesis (supervised by J. C. O'Neill) as *Challenges to New Testa-*

---

[59]G. Benyik, "Biblical Studies in Hungary Today and in the Past," *Communio Viatorum* 50, no. 3 (2008): 300.
[60]Ibid., 301.
[61]Ibid.
[62]Ibid., 302–6.
[63]Ibid., 306.
[64]Ibid., 306–7.
[65]Ibid., 307.
[66]Ibid., 309.

ment Theology: An Attempt to Justify the Enterprise.[67] This was an effort to reaffirm New Testament theology's legitimacy in the wake of attacks upon it by the likes of William Wrede (German), Heikki Räisänen (Finnish), and James Robinson (US). Balla's *Habilitationsschrift* entitled *The Child-Parent Relationship in the New Testament and Its Environment* appeared in 2006.[68] Balla also won Hungarian government grants to publish (1) a New Testament introduction and (2) a commentary on Galatians, both now in print in Hungarian for a national readership.

In addition to the interpretive traditions associated with particular nations, as sketched in a few cases above, New Testament studies in Europe proceeds under the aegis of the three great Christian communions: Roman Catholic, Protestant, and Eastern Orthodox. Henry Wansbrough comments helpfully on biblical scholarship in Europe over the past forty years from his own British and Catholic vantage point.[69] He notes the proliferation of publications and "the perceived need of academics to publish regularly, whether they have something new to say or not."[70] He summarizes as follows:

> For Catholics in particular it has been a period of return to the Bible, initiated by the encouragement of Vatican II, and marked by the enhanced importance of the Bible in the liturgy and in ecclesiastical studies, the widespread use of the Bible by the laity in praying the Prayer of the Church both publicly and privately, and the growing practice of *lectio divina*. The increased use of the Bible for prayer and meditation is not, of course, identical with study; it does, however, naturally lead to and grow from the enrichment of biblical study.

Wansbrough traces developments in three domains—historical Jesus, Synoptic Gospels, and New Perspective on Paul. In historical Jesus studies he goes back to Bultmann, whose authority for decades "it was felt almost impossible to contradict."[71] Skepticism of any sure knowledge of Jesus peaked in the North American Jesus Seminar and

---

[67]Peabody, MA: Hendrickson, 1998.
[68]Peabody, MA: Hendrickson. Both of Balla's monographs appeared first in Germany as WUNT monographs published by Mohr in Tübingen.
[69]H. Wansbrough, "Forty Years of Biblical Study," *Scripture Bulletin* 39, no. 1 (2009): 3–16.
[70]Ibid., 3.
[71]Ibid., 7.

in "the apogee of this method" as articulated by Gerd Lüdemann.[72] He feels the work of E. P. Sanders, N. T. Wright, and John P. Meier contradicted such skepticism, even assuming the relative legitimacy of the (generally skeptical) form-critical starting point. But Wansbrough notes the different historiography employed by Berger Gerhardsson, James Dunn, Kenneth Baily, and now Richard Bauckham.[73] "The way may be opening to a return to a wider acceptance of the accuracy of the gospel tradition."[74]

In summarizing "English Catholic Biblical Studies," with stress on New Testament studies, since his essay commemorates the late (English Catholic) New Testament scholar R. C. Fuller (born 1908), Wansbrough sees a succession of scholarly milestones achieved by Catholic scholarship. These include *The Catholic Commentary* (1953), *The Jerusalem Bible*, and *A New Catholic Commentary on Holy Scripture* (1969). In conclusion, however, Wansbrough states:

> Perhaps the most significant development of all in Catholic biblical studies of the last forty years is that Catholics are now prepared to trust non-Catholic biblical scholarship. The bibliographies of the first edition of the Catholic Commentary on Holy Scripture asterisked non-Catholic works; this was no longer the case for the New Commentary. Such a change betokens both trust and self-confidence. Catholics do not abnegate their own judgment and beliefs in assessing either non-Catholic or Catholic writing.[75]

Wansbrough's summary nicely dramatizes the point of this section: New Testament studies in Europe reflects, and in some respects is inexplicable apart from, both its national and confessional location. Even where New Testament (or biblical) studies seeks to break free of all constraints except for, say, the conventions of the postmodern secular university,[76] time will doubtless show that there were national and

---

[72]Wansbrough points to Lüdemann's *Jesus after 2000 Years* (Amherst, NY: Prometheus, 2001).

[73]On Bauckham, see the German assessment of R. Riesner, "Die Rückkehr der Augenzeugen: Eine neue Entwicklung in der Evangelienforschung," *Theologische Beiträge* 38, no. 6 (2007): 337–52. See also M. F. Bird, "Bauckham's *The Gospel for All Christians Revisited*," *European Journal of Theology* 15, no. 1 (2006): 5–13.

[74]Wansbrough, "Forty Years of Biblical Study," 10.

[75]Ibid., 15–16.

[76]See Oda Wischmeyer, *Hermeneutik des Neuen Testaments: Ein Lehrbuch* (Tübingen: A. Francke, 2004). Exegesis of the New Testament must be liberated from reliance on theological or biblical-

confessional elements in the mix, however surreptitiously. That is the nature of New Testament studies, in Europe and everywhere, though its European forms will naturally exhibit their own distinct and even unique features, only a few of which could be touched on above.

New Testament studies in Europe is challenged by and benefits from changes in world Christianity.

New Testament studies as a professional guild has its insular features. In Europe this has meant dominance by past luminaries and traditions (see above). New Testament studies in Europe has at times given the impression that most significant knowledge of New Testament matters begins with the European Enlightenment and is pretty much comprehensively limned by developments proceeding since that time and on that basis.[77]

But religious historians underscore that larger geopolitical developments, and especially the growth of (largely) Bible-believing Christianity that is sweeping the globe, have dramatic entailments that do and will affect everyone.

> The impression that Christianity in its essence is either European or American is . . . simply false. Christianity began as Jewish; before it was European, it was North African, Syrian, Egyptian and Indian. While in recent history it has indeed been American, it has also been Chilean, Albanian, Fijian, and Chinese. The gospel belongs to every one in every culture; it belongs to no one in any one culture in particular.[78]

This has implications for New Testament studies in Europe. True, when historians move from their position of specialists in knowledge of the past to giving futuristic pronouncements, they are on shaky

---

theological considerations. New Testament interpretation must rather proceed under the rule of "the contemporary state of those sciences whose task it is to understand and interpret texts" (197). This program is worked out comprehensively in Oda Wischmeyer, ed., *Lexikon der Bibelhermeneutik* (Berlin: de Gruyter, 2009).

[77]This outlook is explicit in, e.g., W. G. Kümmel, *The New Testament: The History of the Investigation of Its Problems*, trans. S. McLean Gilmour and H. C. Kee (Nashville: Abingdon, 1972). Contrast the very different view of the subfield of synoptic studies in David Dungan, *A History of the Synoptic Studies* (New Haven, CT: Yale University Press, 1999). Kümmel leaves no inkling of the comprehensive and fruitful investigation of the synoptic phenomena that Dungan documents well back into the Patristic era and culminating in Augustine's significant synthesis.

[78]Mark Noll, *The New Shape of World Christianity* (Downers Grove, IL: InterVarsity, 2009), 191.

ground. But writing of Europe in particular, Philip Jenkins projects a less than despairing scenario in coming decades. From Britain, David Ford has substantially affirmed the outlook Jenkins proposes.[79] It is true that Islam is burgeoning, internationally and in Europe.[80] It is also true that leading New Testament lights like Bultmann disparaged foundational New Testament affirmations such as Jesus' bodily resurrection, and European scholars (along with others internationally) routinely discount (from a historic Christian standpoint) biblical authority and aspects of Christian faith, like miracles.[81] J. C. Poirer restates James Barr's skeptical approach to canon and a Christian view of Scripture,[82] while D. C. Parker doubts not only that there is an authoritative New Testament text but that we can know what the New Testament writers wrote in the first place.[83] Skeptical biblical scholarship displays the tendency to regard itself as the sole and sovereign arbiter of New Testament meaning and significance,[84] whatever credit such scholarship may deserve for freeing Scripture from ecclesial or other shackles.[85] But Jenkins sees elements of recovery of traditional Christian voices in Europe. And he asserts, focusing on the Roman Catholic Church:

> The church's strong European roots mean that tactics and movements that originate here are likely to spread to other parts of the world, so that as in earlier centuries [when the existence of Christian faith seemed doomed], European Catholicism provides a creative laboratory of faith. The opportunities to interact with Islam give lessons

---

[79]David F. Ford, "God and Our Public Life: A Scriptural Wisdom," *International Journal of Public Theology* 1 (2007): 81.

[80]See, e.g., Efraim Karsh, *Islamic Imperialism: A History* (New Haven, CT: Yale University Press, 2007).

[81]For an updating and helpful taxonomy of the debate see Bernd Kollmann, "Glaube—Kritik—Deutung: Gängige Deutungsmuster von Wundergeschichten in der Bibelwissenschaft," *Bibel und Kirche* 61, no. 2 (2006): 88–93.

[82]J. C. Poirier, "The Canonical Approach and the Idea of 'Scripture,'" *Expository Times* 116, no. 11 (2005): 366–70.

[83]D. Parker, "Textual Criticism and Theology," *Expository Times* 118, no. 12 (2007): 583–89. For a vigorous refutation see J. C. Poirier, "Living Text or Exquisite Corpse?," *Expository Times* 119, no. 9 (2008): 437–39.

[84]Ralf Huning, "Bibelwissenschaft und Bibelpastoral: Mehr als eine Einbahnstrassen-Kommunikation," *Bibel und Kirche* 63, no. 1 (2008): 42. See also L. T. Johnson, cited by Sixtus, *Scottish Journal of Theology* 58, no. 1 (2005): 32n105; Johnson points to how historical criticism "makes 'hegemonic' claims to being the only legitimate way of interpreting Scripture."

[85]See, e.g., the brief commendation by Christof Gestrich, "Schriftauslegung und Macht—ein unerledigtes Problem von 'sola scriptura,'" *Berliner Theologische Zeitschrift* 22, no. 2 (2005): 262–63.

learned in Europe still wider applicability. And the presence of so many Christian immigrants makes it all the more probable that solutions devised in Europe will spread around the world.[86]

The future Jenkins projects for Catholics in Europe has already arrived for others. In Germany alone, in the past two decades about eight hundred independent African immigrant congregations have arisen, most of them Pentecostal. "On the basis of such migration, globalization is leading to the transformation of all concerned."[87]

Observers of biblical studies note that "the scientific investigation of the OT and NT is presently in upheaval."[88] Australian scholar Elaine Wainwright writes from her post at the University of Auckland that we live

in a world context in which difference and differentiation have become hallmarks. This has been manifest in biblical studies in which methodologies and hermeneutics have multiplied over the past two or three decades and hence diverse interpretations of biblical story-telling and meaning-making abound.[89]

Biblical studies, accordingly, is "a changed and changing discipline."[90]

Voices at the local level clamor for theological and ecclesial renewal.[91] New Testament studies needs to transcend limits imposed by former historical-critical strictures and restrictions.[92] Feminist voices from black North American, Latin American, Asian, and African quarters call for a critical hermeneutic to supplement, if not supplant, methods that have reigned in the academy for generations.[93] But feminist exegesis itself is far from monolithic, being characterized today by more detailed attention to various themes rather than veneration

[86]Philip Jenkins, *God's Continent: Christianity, Islam, and Europe's Religious Crisis* (Oxford: Oxford University Press, 2007), 288.

[87]W. Kahl, "Akademische Bibelinterpretation in Afrika, Lateinamerika und Asien angesichts der Globalisierung," *Verkündigung und Forschung* 54, no. 1 (2009): 57.

[88]Werner Kahl, "Die Bibel unter neuen Blinkwinkeln: Exegetische Forschung im Umbruch," *Bibel und Kirche* 61, no. 3 (2006): 166.

[89]E. Wainwright, "'Many Have Undertaken . . . and I Too Decided': The One Story or the Many?," *Concilium* 2006, no. 2 (2006): 46.

[90]Ibid.

[91]See, e.g., with its theme of *Aufbruch* (renewal) the rudimentary explorations of the journal of Tübingen's Albrecht Bengelhaus, *Theologische Orientierung* 157 (Jan.–Mar. 2010).

[92]Kahl, "Die Bibel unter neuen Blinkwinkeln," 170.

[93]Marie-Theres Wacker, "Auf dem Weg zu einer geschlechtergerechten Bibelwissenschaft: Neue Tendenzen," *Bibel und Kirche* 63, no. 2 (2008): 102–5.

of grand syntheses.[94] Roman Catholic calls for more attention to the Bible have not seen sufficiently successful implementation; too many elements found in the Bible still seem to be interpreted in the light of old hierarchical forces.[95]

Evangelical coalitions in both Britain and Germany publish scholarly works that in method, outlook, and result often challenge older skeptical hegemonies. In Britain, the Cambridge-based Tyndale House Library offers one of the world's best venues for accessing biblical studies publications and online resources. Its journal, *Tyndale Bulletin*, has for decades published cutting-edge research across the full range of New Testament topics. In Germany, the *Jahrbuch für evangelikale Theologie* has, since the late 1980s, published essays and reviews chronicling and furthering New Testament studies (along with numerous other biblical studies and theological fields). A recent issue, for example, explored the christology of an important Islamic sect, papyrological and astronomical data regarding the star of Bethlehem, and new monographs on Luke-Acts.[96] It also contained over fifty pages of reviews of books in the field of New Testament studies.[97]

From a number of directions, and championing a wide range of intents, subgroups are currently moving New Testament studies in Europe into new shapes and terrains, in large measure owing to developments in world Christianity as these affect the European scene.

New Testament studies in Europe will continue to sustain vibrant discussion over its charter document.

One of D. A. Carson's more recent major publications is *Collected Writings on Scripture*.[98] The topic of the Bible, its origin, its meaning, and its application have always been at the forefront of Carson's speaking and writing activity. It is fitting that this brief glimpse of New Testament studies in Europe conclude by observing that discussion of the Bible seems, if anything, more spirited and prominent in

---

[94]M. Grohmann, "Feministische/Gender-faire Exegese: Geschichte—Hermeneutik—Themen," *Protokolle zur Bibel* 14, no. 2 (2005): 86.
[95]H. Frankemölle, "Fortschritte und Stillstand: Entwicklungen seit 1965," *Bibel und Kirche* 60, no. 3 (2005): 173–77.
[96]See in *Jahrbuch für evangelikale Theologie* 22 (2008): Ralf-Dieter Krüger, "Die Christologie der Ahmadiyya Muslim Jamaat," 15–35; Hans R. Pruppacher, "Der Stern von Bethlehem und die Geburt Jesu: Ein Versuch eines Gesamtbildes," 57–68; Christoph Stenschke, "Neue Monographien zum lukanischen Doppelwerk," 68–105.
[97]*Jahrbuch für evangelikale Theologie* 22 (2008): 202–53.
[98]Wheaton, IL: Crossway, 2010.

New Testament studies literature today than at any other time in recent decades.

When a new translation of the Bible appeared in Germany (Bibel in gerechter Sprache), a firestorm ensued. An English-language account of the translation's history and distinctives hardly does justice to its marginal aspects and the gravity of scholarly criticisms against it.[99] While some defend it as fomenting helpful discussion,[100] Karin Bornkamm speaks for many others in using words like "crass" and "coarse" of key renderings.[101] Of its handling of justification language in Romans she writes, "These are ponderous questions; they extend to the very core of the Christian faith. Here one must speak of a coarse, theologically misleading alteration of the text. It is intolerable even as a paraphrase, much less a translation."[102] U. Wilckens's critique is extended and blistering.[103] Klaus Haacker cites the appearance of this translation as a reason why theological and pastoral students need training in original languages: to defend themselves and those they teach from the deleterious effects of bad theology based, in this case, on a faulty Bible translation.[104]

In Britain likewise it is hard to find a significant aspect of the study of the New Testament (and the Bible more generally) to which substantial publications are not constantly being devoted. Lee Gatiss discusses recent books on biblical authority by British writers John Stott, Alister McGrath, and J. I. Packer.[105] S. Plant looks back at the respective legacies of A. S. Peake and Dietrich Bonhoeffer and how

---

[99] See Luzia Sutter Rehmann, "What Is the Bibel in gerechter Sprache? Assumptions, Process, and Goals of a New German Bible Translation," accessed April 30, 2010, http://www.sbl-site.org/publications/article.aspx?articleId=761.

[100] E.g., E. Bohle, "Der Widerstand fremder Erfahrung," *ZeitZeichen* 8, no. 9 (2007): 55–57; also M. Köhlmoos, "Ewig blüht der Mandelzweig: Anmerkungen zu den 'Grundlagen' des Projekts 'Die Bibel—übersetzt in gerechte Sprache,'" *Theologische Rundschau* 71, no. 2 (2006): 247–57. Köhlmoos apparently thinks that since "every translation from start to finish is led by hermeneutical principles," and "no original text can be carried over one-to-one into a target text," every translation is to be welcomed. Many reviewers, as well as the German Protestant church (EKD) itself, strongly disagree.

[101] Karin Bornkamm, "Vermisst: der Menschensohn," *ZeitZeichen* 8, no. 4 (2007): 19, 17.

[102] Ibid., 17.

[103] U. Wilckens, "'Bibel in gerechter Sprache,'" *Theologische Beiträge* 38, no. 3 (2007): 135–51.

[104] K. Haacker, "Was zählt im Studium des Neuen Testaments? Blicke zurück und nach vorn," *Theologische Beiträge* 39, no. 4 (2008): 235n5.

[105] L. Gatiss, "Biblical Authority in Recent Evangelical Books," *Churchman* 120, no. 4 (2006): 321–35.

each regarded Scripture.[106] He finds that Peake overvalued biblical criticism, reacting to the rising fundamentalist movement of his day. Bonhoeffer, however, who was actually trained in stringent critical exegesis, rightly saw its limits and arrogance. Plant avers that biblical criticism has changed today.[107] Theology and historical criticism can and should be talking to each other.[108] R. S. Briggs reviews books on Scripture by John Webster, N. T. Wright, Telford Work, and Brenda Watson.[109] He longs for and welcomes the time when questions of historical accuracy will not dominate discussion of Scripture, when hermeneutical and theological fruitfulness will be the main concern of interpreters.[110]

H. Kremers argues against traditional views of inspiration but shows how Enlightenment thought debunks itself and leaves room for Scripture to exercise an inspiring function.[111] R. J. Hill grapples with similar issues.[112] Oliver O'Donovan wrestles with Scripture, and particularly Psalm 119, in its implications for Christian living.[113]

It becomes evident that like some cagey beast that refuses to be tamed and shut up out of sight however powers and people conspire, Scripture and the New Testament in particular call forth attention from some of the best minds and energies of this generation. Admittedly much study of the New Testament in Europe is far removed from the hermeneutical and theological concerns we have majored in above. But much is not. From the Catholic side there is redoubled effort for Scripture to receive its due in the life and mission of the Polish church; Henryk Witczyk's statement is among the most searching and convicting to be found.[114] In Poland, Scripture is read, but this is "a 'trampoline' serving to pass onto a secular topic, not at all related with the Word of God and the Holy Eucharist. This shows the crisis in

---

[106]S. Plant, "'In the Bible It Is God Who Speaks': Peake and Bonhoeffer on Reading Scripture," *Epworth Review* 33, no. 4 (2006): 7–22.

[107]Ibid., 19.

[108]Ibid., 21.

[109]R. S. Briggs, "Perspectives on Scripture: Its Status and Purpose: A Review Article," *Heythrop Journal* 48, no. 2 (2007): 267–74.

[110]Ibid., 273.

[111]H. Kremers, "Nicht vom Himmel gefallen," *ZeitZeichen* 8, no. 4 (2007): 39–41.

[112]R. J. Hill, "Reading Symbols, and Writing Words: A Model for Biblical Inspiration," *New Blackfriars* 89, no. 1019 (2008): 22–38.

[113]O. O'Donovan, "Scripture and Christian Ethics," *Anvil* 24, no. 1 (2007): 21–29.

[114]H. Witczyk, "The Word of God in the Life of the Church in Europe with Particular Attention to Poland," *Euntes Docete* 61, no. 3 (2008): 129–49.

the proclamation of the Word, which is still continually present in our pastoral ministries."[115] He indicts old-style historical-critical seminary training.[116] He calls for duly gifted and trained biblical teachers "to give professional support to Biblical renewal, in such a way that the Bible will in reality become the daily nourishment and God's wellspring for all the faithful."[117]

R. Slenczka has published a scarcely less searching statement from a Protestant perspective.[118] He asks whether the Bible is only partially authoritative, as he finds it to be under the Roman Catholic magisterium; or is it God's word in the words of people, as in liberal Protestantism; or is it the revealed word of the triune God, as in confessional Protestantism? He closes with a preamble and seven theses detailing what he takes to be a biblically grounded approach to the question of the nature and authority of Scripture.[119]

However numerous Christians in Asia or the global South become, and however successful North American entrepreneurs may be in keeping New Testament issues in this or that public spotlight, Europe will continue to occupy a sheet-anchor position in the research and interpretation of the New Testament. If Philip Jenkins is correct, Europe's importance will spiral upward as challenges to Christian existence increase in coming years. Even if this proves to be not the case to the extent or in the way Jenkins projects, the momentum of history and the vigor of current discussion make it unlikely that the vast sweep of European nations, resources, and interests will be eclipsed anytime soon, as all who have a stake in the New Testament's import exert their respective wills in making their understanding of it known.

---

[115]Ibid., 130.
[116]Ibid., 140.
[117]Ibid., 147.
[118]R. Slenczka, "Die Heilige Schrift, das Wort des dreieinigen Gottes," *Kerygma und Dogma* 51, no. 3 (2005): 174–91.
[119]Ibid., 189–90.

APPENDIX

D. A. Carson

His Life and Work to Date

ANDREAS J. KÖSTENBERGER

W hile many know D. A. Carson for his mind and his impressive scholarly writings, fewer have an intimate acquaintance with the heart that produces those works.[1] Carson's inner disposition is particularly apparent in such writings as *How Long, O Lord? Reflections on Suffering and Evil* and *A Call to Spiritual Reformation: Priorities from Paul and His Prayers*, which reveal a deeply personal faith.

Though Carson is a rather private person, those who know him well attest to his devotion to family and his true pastor's heart. The noted scholar Colin Hemer, a personal friend, died in Carson's arms. Carson's eulogy for Hemer provides a moving testimony to his deep

---

[1]The present essay represents a reworked, updated, and expanded version of "D. A. Carson," in *Bible Interpreters of the 20th Century: A Selection of Evangelical Voices*, ed. Walter A. Elwell and J. D. Weaver (Grand Rapids: Baker, 1999), 423–33.

care for the spiritual welfare of those close to him.[2] Similarly, after hearing of the death of his mentor, Barnabas Lindars, Carson was genuinely moved, reminiscing at the beginning of a class for quite a while about his studies and personal conversations with Lindars while at Cambridge.

The intensity of his beliefs is evident in an autobiographical section of *How Long, O Lord?*, where Carson writes, "I would rather die than end up unfaithful to my wife; I would rather die than deny by a profligate life what I have taught in my books; I would rather die than deny or disown the gospel."[3] To understand the true depth of D. A. Carson's faith, it is important to recount in some detail his godly heritage.

His Godly Heritage

The second of three children, Donald Arthur Carson was born on December 21, 1946, to Thomas Donald McMillan Carson (Aug. 26, 1911–Oct. 26, 1992) and his wife Elizabeth Margaret (née Maybury; Jan. 6, 1909–Dec. 31, 1989).[4] In *How Long, O Lord?*, Carson describes the "just under the poverty line" type of family in which he grew up.

> The father and mother love each other. They serve the Lord in a low-paying job where they feel they can exercise real ministry. Their modest (and rented) home is characterized by gratitude; their children are disciplined for ingratitude and shown by example how the Lord provides for his own. There is time to read and think and discuss. There is moral and emotional support (and sometimes material support as well) from the local church, and even an adventurous challenge to see how much can be invested in the "bank of heaven" (Matt. 6:19–21). I grew up in such a home. I did not find out how "poor" we were until I left home to go to university (funded by scholarships and part-time work; my parents certainly could not afford to send me).[5]

[2] D. A. Carson, "Colin John Hemer: *In Memoriam*," *Forum for the Association of Christians in Higher Education* (Fall 1987): 56–60.

[3] D. A. Carson, *How Long, O Lord? Reflections on Suffering and Evil* (Grand Rapids: Baker, 1990), 120.

[4] For a moving biography of Don Carson's father written by Don himself, see D. A. Carson, *Memoirs of an Ordinary Pastor: The Life and Reflections of Tom Carson* (Wheaton, IL: Crossway, 2008).

[5] Ibid., 56; see also D. A. Carson, "Growing Up a 'PK,'" *Evangel* 2, no. 4 (1984): 16–18.

Yet Carson would not want anyone to think that his family heritage was one of "unmitigated godliness and joy."[6] He qualifies his family "success" story by disclosing times of dramatic illness, financial strains, and moral and spiritual pressures: "The family quiet time was not always brilliant and scintillating; indeed, during particularly stressful periods of our lives it could disappear for days at a time."[7] Yet these difficulties notwithstanding, Carson recollects the advantages of growing up in a home with parents who were "genuine and self-consistent." He learned humility from his father, common sense from his mother, and value and proportion from both as they eked out a meager income on limited resources. In the end, Carson is forced to conclude that, "looking back on certain crucial turning points in the family's life, a thoughtful historian would have to conclude that apart from the grace of God all three of us children could have turned out quite another way."[8]

Tom Carson, Don's father, was born in Carrickfergus, near Belfast, Northern Ireland, and immigrated with his family to Ottawa, Canada, in 1913. There Tom grew up under the influence of Calvary Baptist Church. In 1933, at the height of the Great Depression, he entered Toronto Baptist Seminary. During his years there, Tom developed an interest in evangelism and church planting in the province of Quebec. He graduated in 1937 and married in 1938. After a few years of service in an English-speaking congregation, Tom moved to Drummondville in 1948, where he established a bilingual church, Faith Baptist Church. The fifteen years spent in ministry in Drummondville were times of persecution, hardships, and a scarcely visible harvest. From 1963 until his death in 1992, Tom Carson continued serving in various forms of local church ministry, primarily at the Montclair Church in Hull, where the Carsons had moved.

In his moving tribute on the occasion of his father's funeral, D. A. Carson expressed his gratitude for his father's perseverance, his life of prayer, his uncomplaining spirit, and his generosity. "When Dad died," Carson wrote,

> there were no crowds outside the hospital, no notice in the papers, no announcements on the television, no mention in Parliament, no

---

[6]Ibid., 2.
[7]Ibid.
[8]Ibid.

notice in the nation. In his hospital room there was only the quiet hiss of oxygen, vainly venting because Dad had stopped breathing and would never need it again. But on the other side, all the trumpets sounded. Dad won admittance to the only throne-room that matters, not because he was a good man or a great man, but because he was a forgiven man.[9]

His Career to Date

D. A. Carson attended McGill University in Montreal from 1963 to 1967, graduating with a bachelor's degree in chemistry and mathematics. He was determined to make his mark as a chemist, though during a short tenure in a lab in Ottawa, Canada, Carson recalls that his imagination began to be captured by the challenges of a fledgling church plant up the valley where he had been volunteering. He remembers, as a significant turning point in his vocational calling, the words of a chorus he sang as a child playing incessantly in his mind:

> By and by when I look on his face—
> Beautiful face, thorn-shadowed face—
> By and by when I look on his face,
> I'll wish I had given him more.[10]

As a result of a message preached on Ezekiel 22:30—"I looked for someone among them who would build up the wall and stand before me in the gap on behalf of the land" (NIV)—Carson recalls the intense conviction, stating, "It was as if God by his Spirit was compelling me to say, 'Here, please send me!'"[11]

He then earned a master's in divinity from Central Baptist Seminary in Toronto. From 1970 to 1972 he pastored Richmond Baptist Church in Richmond, British Columbia, where he was ordained in 1972. The years 1972–1975 were spent in doctoral studies at Cambridge University under Barnabas Lindars. Carson's doctoral dissertation bore the

---

[9]D. A. Carson, "Thomas Donald McMillan Carson: A Tribute," *Banner of Truth* 356 (May 1993): 24. See also Carson, *Memoirs of an Ordinary Pastor*, 148 et passim.

[10]D. A. Carson, "The Scholar as Pastor," 5. This is a lightly edited manuscript of a talk originally delivered on April 23, 2009, at Park Community Church in Chicago (available online at http://s3.amazonaws.com/tgc-documents/carson/2009_scholar_as_pastor.pdf; accessed May 3, 2010). The audio and video can be viewed on the websites of the Henry Center, Desiring God Ministries, and The Gospel Coalition.

[11]Ibid.

title "Predestination and Responsibility: Elements of Tension-Theology in the Fourth Gospel against Jewish Background."[12]

During his time in Cambridge, Carson, like another well-known author before him, was "surprised by Joy." To the amazement of Carson's friends, who thought him too devoted to serious scholarship to be sidetracked by romance, Carson's attraction to Joy Wheildon, a British schoolteacher, quickly grew, and on August 16, 1975, the two were married in Cambridge. For the next three years Carson served at Northwest Baptist Theological College in Vancouver, the first year as associate professor of New Testament, the following two years as the founding dean of the seminary.

A significant turn of events occurred when Kenneth Kantzer, the dean of Trinity Evangelical Divinity School in Deerfield, Illinois, heard Carson present a paper at a theological conference and asked him to join the Trinity faculty, where he has served for over thirty years. From 1978 until 1982 as an associate professor, from 1982 until 1991 as professor, and since 1991 as research professor of New Testament, Carson has bloomed into one of the most respected evangelical scholars in the early twenty-first century. The breadth of his writing is apparent in the bibliography following this essay.

The Reception of Carson's Biblical Scholarship

C. S. Lewis once remarked, "A man is ill-advised to write a book on any living author. There is bound to be at least one person and there are probably several who inevitably know more about the subject than ordinary research will discover. Far better to write about the unanswering dead."[13] Reasons why the present essay is preliminary and limited could be multiplied. Thus readers should not view with any degree of finality the present attempt to assess D. A. Carson's contribution to evangelical biblical scholarship to date.

Decades ago, Mark Noll, in his survey of evangelical scholarship, singled out Richard Longenecker and D. A. Carson as doing "the most seminal New Testament work by contemporary evangelicals."[14] This assessment is becoming increasingly justified by the year. In the past,

[12]A revised and simplified form was published as D. A. Carson, *Divine Sovereignty and Human Responsibility: Biblical Perspectives in Tension* (Atlanta: John Knox, 1981).
[13]Quoted in Brian Sibley, *C. S. Lewis through the Shadowlands* (Old Tappan, NJ: Revell, 1985), 11.
[14]Mark A. Noll, *Between Faith and Criticism*, 2nd ed. (Grand Rapids: Baker, 1991), 136.

Carson's productivity was made possible in part by Trinity's generous sabbatical policies, which allowed him to spend every third year at Tyndale House, a research center for biblical studies in Cambridge, which Carson regards as his ultimate academic home. Apart from affording Carson time and opportunity to write, these sabbaticals also enabled him to maintain a truly international scope for his teaching and scholarship. He blends well into the academic setting in Britain and is accepted and sought after in university circles there. This involvement, together with his worldwide travels, has helped him to surmount the isolation from the rest of the world that continues to characterize much of North American biblical scholarship.

His Prodigious Output and Strategic Influence

Many stand in awe at Carson's prodigious output ("he makes us all look like sluggards," one of his colleagues at Trinity, himself a respected author, remarked), though Carson is not one to allow academic expectations to set the primary agenda for his writing. Rather than operating solely in the vein of a seminary professor, Carson perfectly embodies the role of a pastor-scholar, exploiting the tools of scholarship in his expansive efforts to minister the gospel.[15] In this regard, Carson's emphasis on theological integration and biblical synthesis has helped to mend not only the fragmented character of biblical scholarship, but also its dislocation from the church.

His substantial contribution to popular evangelicalism notwithstanding, Carson's name has continued to appear on several important projects addressing current issues in biblical studies such as linguistics,[16] the relationship between biblical and systematic theology,[17] the New Testament use of the Old,[18] and the New Perspective on Paul.[19] What all these publications have in common is Carson's role as editor and

---

[15]See the talks by John Piper and D. A. Carson, "Pastor as Scholar" and "The Scholar as Pastor," originally given on April 23, 2009. An audio and video of Carson's talk is most easily accessible at http://thegospelcoalition.org/resources/a/The-Scholar-as-Pastor.

[16]See, e.g., D. A. Carson and Stanley E. Porter, eds., *Linguistics and the New Testament: Critical Junctions* (Sheffield: JSOT, 1999).

[17]See T. Desmond Alexander, Brian S. Rosner, D. A. Carson, and Graeme Goldsworthy, eds., *New Dictionary of Biblical Theology* (Leicester, UK: Inter-Varsity, 2000).

[18]G. K. Beale and D. A. Carson, eds., *Commentary on the New Testament Use of the Old Testament* (Grand Rapids: Baker, 2007).

[19]D. A. Carson, Peter O'Brien, and Mark A. Seifrid, eds., *Justification and Variegated Nomism: A Fresh Appraisal of Paul and Second Temple Judaism*, 2 vols. (Grand Rapids: Baker, 2001, 2004).

contributor, and his collaboration with other notable scholars in the execution of a given task. In fact, the list of contributors to these volumes is a veritable *Who's Who* of contemporary biblical scholarship. The breadth of knowledge required for any one of these subjects would be enough to keep a scholar busy for a lifetime. Yet Carson, it appears, has grasped and perfected the strategic value of forging scholarly coalitions. In so doing, he has succeeded in making significant contributions to numerous areas of biblical studies in a relatively short period of time without compromising excellence in scholarship.[20]

In his two-volume work *Justification and Variegated Nomism*, for example, Carson demonstrates his ability to step outside traditional evangelical circles in order to recruit distinguished specialists from a variety of academic backgrounds.[21] What is particularly worthy of note in this regard is Carson's willingness to grant these scholars a measure of latitude with regard to methodology and presentation. Though some of Carson's own conclusions in this volume have predictably drawn criticism,[22] his ability to marshal a considerable array of scholars and to make their collaborations subservient to a common goal has served to launch a major reappraisal of Paul's view of justification.

His Conservative Reputation
The reception of Carson's commentary on John's Gospel provides a representative case study as to the varied responses to his own work. Hailed in evangelical circles as the epitome of lucidity and thorough scholarship,[23] the work has not been received quite as favorably by scholars in the larger Christian community.[24] However, it should be

---

[20]On the subject of scholarly excellence, see my forthcoming volume *Excellence: The Character of God and the Pursuit of Scholarly Virtue* (Wheaton, IL: Crossway), including also reminiscences of studying under Don Carson.

[21]Some of these scholars are candid about the necessity of drawing distinct boundaries between confessional theology and secular biblical studies. See especially Philip Davies, *Whose Bible Is It Anyway?*, 2nd ed. (London: T&T Clark, 2004).

[22]See, e.g., Don Garlington, in a review article posted online at http://www.thepaulpage.com /Variegated_Nomism.pdf, who claims that Carson's conclusions are at odds with the essayists but nonetheless commends the methodological diversity as a means of saving the project from predictability and redundancy (see p. 6 and n16 for references to other reviewers). The review is also included in Don Garlington, *Studies in the New Perspective on Paul: Essays and Reviews* (Eugene, OR: Wipf & Stock, 2008).

[23]See, e.g., Moisés Silva, review of *The Gospel according to John*, by D. A. Carson, *WTJ* 54 (1992): 376–78.

[24]See, e.g., David Ball, "Some Recent Literature on John: A Review Article," *Themelios* 19, no. 1 (1993): 13–18.

expected that any effort to defend the historicity of John's Gospel will be criticized in our day.[25] Moreover, it does not endear Carson to more critical scholars that he gives short shrift to source and redaction theories[26] and that he maintains a healthy skepticism regarding the many contemporary literary techniques invading biblical scholarship.[27] Thus Carson has critiqued such Johannine scholars as R. Alan Culpepper[28] and J. Louis Martyn, disputing the validity of their "mirror" and "two-level" readings of John's Gospel.[29] As a result, some in the academic world see Carson as unduly conservative and as too far to the right. As one Oxford professor remarked in personal conversation, "He is too clever to be a fundamentalist," but still "far too conservative" to be seriously engaged by scholars in certain circles. Also very revealing is correspondence with a senior British scholar on the nature of Scripture that Carson included in *The Gagging of God*.[30]

Although Carson is viewed by some of his scholarly colleagues as rather conservative, this assessment does not do adequate justice to his work. He is often unconventional and more than ready to break new ground. For example, he essentially embraced the "verbal aspect theory" that one of his students, Stanley Porter (Carson was his external examiner at Sheffield), forcefully advocated at a time when few colleagues had even heard of this theory on the function of the Greek verb.[31] Carson's forthcoming commentary on the Johannine Epistles

---

[25]See Ben Witherington, review of *Jesus as God*, by Murray Harris, *Themelios* 19, no. 1 (1993): 28–29.

[26]See D. A. Carson, "Current Source Criticism of the Fourth Gospel: Some Methodological Questions," *JBL* 97 (1978): 411–29; Carson, "Historical Tradition and the Fourth Gospel: After Dodd, What?," in *Gospel Perspectives*, ed. R. T. France and David Wenham, vol. 2 (Sheffield: JSOT, 1981), 83–145; and for more general treatments see Carson, "Redaction Criticism: On the Legitimacy and Illegitimacy of a Literary Tool," in *Scripture and Truth*, ed. D. A. Carson and John D. Woodbridge (Grand Rapids: Zondervan, 1983), 119–46; and D. A. Carson et al., "Redaction Criticism: Is It Worth the Risk?," *Christianity Today* 29, no. 15 (1985): 1–10.

[27]See Carson's survey articles on Johannine studies in *Themelios* 9, no. 1 (1983): 8–18; and 14, no. 2 (1989): 57–64; or "Gundry on Matthew: A Critical Review," *TrinJ* n.s. 3 (1982): 71–91.

[28]D. A. Carson, review of *Anatomy of the Fourth Gospel*, by R. Alan Culpepper, *TrinJ* n.s. 4 (1983): 119–21; Carson, *The Gospel according to John* (Grand Rapids: Eerdmans, 1991), 63–68.

[29]D. A. Carson, review of *Overcoming the World*, by David Rensberger, *Themelios* 17, no. 1 (1991): 27–28; and Carson, review of *Peter and the Beloved Disciple*, by Kevin Quast, *Themelios* 17, no. 2 (1992): 21–22.

[30]See D. A. Carson, *The Gagging of God: Christianity Confronts Pluralism* (Grand Rapids: Zondervan, 1996), 158–63.

[31]Stanley E. Porter, *Verbal Aspect in the Greek of the New Testament* (New York: Peter Lang, 1989).

promises to be the first consistent effort to integrate verbal-aspect theory into a full-fledged commentary. As the general editor of a series entitled Studies in Biblical Greek, Carson has also had a hand in the publication of seminal studies on the topic.[32]

His Scope and Stature

D. A. Carson may one day be remembered as one of the last great Renaissance men in evangelical biblical scholarship. In an age of increasing specialization and fragmentation, Carson, to the admiring disbelief of many of his colleagues, persistently refuses to limit his interests. His publications cover a vast range of subjects: New Testament Greek, Bible translation, hermeneutics, contextualization, the New Testament use of the Old, preaching, various aspects of New Testament and biblical theology, major commentaries on Matthew and John (with more to come), and even poetry. Carson's fielding of questions subsequent to a presentation at the 1993 annual meeting of the Institute for Biblical Research showed glimpses of his competence in a vast array of fields. As a reviewer of one of his books put it:

> Professor Carson possesses qualities which are not often found in combination. He is a New Testament scholar who sees the Bible as a whole; a biblical scholar with a concern for both the theological and the practical implications of the Bible's teaching; a blunt writer with a pastoral heart; and (perhaps rarest of all) an academic with a clear, vigorous, occasionally even slangy style.[33]

In the light of these qualities, it is understandable that some compare Carson favorably with other evangelical scholars such as F. F. Bruce (with whom he almost studied)[34] and I. Howard Marshall. While Bruce, unlike Carson, had a background in classical Greek, Carson may exceed Bruce in his exegetical and theological grasp. Significantly, Carson is not just a New Testament exegete but also a biblical theologian who synthesizes materials that other scholars leave unrelated. Moreover, he is abreast of the latest developments in fields as diverse as

---

[32]E.g., K. L. McKay, *A New Syntax of the Verb in New Testament Greek* (New York: Peter Lang, 1994).

[33]Paul Ellingworth, review of *How Long, O Lord?*, by D. A. Carson, *Evangelical Quarterly* 64 (1992): 361.

[34]Per Carson's oral reminiscences in his talk "The Scholar as Pastor," online at http://thegospel coalition.org/resources/a/The-Scholar-as-Pastor.

computer technology and linguistics. At the same time, some see Carson as taking over the mantle from John Stott as an evangelical leader and spokesman respected worldwide. That Carson can be compared with evangelical figures as diverse and influential as Bruce, Marshall, and Stott is in itself a tribute to his versatility and increasing stature.

What is more, this notion of synthesis extends even beyond Carson's wide range of interests to the dynamics of his relationships, not only within the varied landscape of evangelicalism, but also at the broader level of mainstream academia. Increasingly over the course of his career, there is a discernible effort on Carson's part to unite evangelicals around the essential truths of the faith and to reach out to the larger world of scholarship. In the often polemical atmosphere of biblical studies, Carson serves as an example of one who is at once conciliatory and yet focused on "the main thing," forcefully advocating the gospel without sacrificing strength of conviction. This does not alter the fact that, as mentioned, there remains a group of scholars outside evangelicalism who do not share his conservative evangelical views on Scripture and apparently believe they can safely ignore his writings. Some are only beginning to give Carson's views the attention they deserve.

Carson and the Love of God

In this context, it may be interesting to note that one of Carson's driving motivations has been his understanding of the love of God and its implications for the Christian life and scholarship. In two relevant volumes, *The Difficult Doctrine of the Love of God* and *Love in Hard Places*, Carson counters the "vapid sentimentalism with which Western culture is so heavily afflicted."[35] Applied to God, Carson contends, this perception "generates a deity with all the awesome holiness of a cuddly toy, all the moral integrity of a marshmallow."[36] Applied to Christians, it fosters the expectation that "whatever else Christians should be, they should be *nice*, where 'niceness' means smiling a lot and never ever hinting that anyone may be wrong about anything (because that isn't nice)."[37] Thus anyone who would accurately assess Carson's work will do well to remember his conviction that the superficial character

---

[35] D. A. Carson, *Love in Hard Places* (Wheaton, IL: Crossway, 2002), 9.
[36] Ibid., 11.
[37] Ibid., 12.

of a sentimental view of love does not accurately reflect the profound character of true love, biblically conceived.

The depth of Carson's compassion is evident from what served as a major catalyst for conceiving *Love in Hard Places*. In the wake of the tragic events of September 11, Carson writes that he felt compelled to move the discussion from a purely conceptual level to one that wrestled biblically with the practical issue of loving one's enemies. In all this, Carson demonstrates his capacity to merge biblical exegesis with practical application, the scholarly enterprise with the needs of the church, and his love for the Scriptures with compassion for a world that is bound to perish apart from Christ.

The state of contemporary biblical scholarship betrays a critical need for scholars who are willing to build bridges. Such persons should be sufficiently conservative to operate within the overall theological matrix of evangelicalism. They should be practical enough to connect the contributions of biblical scholarship with the needs of the church. Their theology ought to be broad enough to synthesize apparent incongruities within the biblical canon. They ought to be conversant with recent scholarly contributions in a variety of related fields. They should be sufficiently open-minded to remain in dialogue with nonconfessional scholarship. Finally, they must be passionate enough to communicate the relevance of scholarly advances to practitioners in the church. D. A. Carson is such a scholar, and brings to the scholarly task a rare combination of qualities that render him uniquely qualified to occupy a leadership role in both academic and ecclesiastical circles.

No Signs of Retirement: Current and Future Projects

Despite the fact that he is about to reach formal retirement age—the occasion for this present volume!—Carson shows no signs of slowing down. In a recent 9Marks interview, he evidences awareness of the inevitable reality of aging, yet remains optimistic that barring some debilitating infirmity, he will be able to continue his ministry, for the good of the church, for many years to come.[38] His prayer is to know when to cut back and what tasks to shed as energy levels and the ability to multitask may diminish.

---

[38] Available online at http://media.9marks.org/2008/11/25/observing-evangelicalism-with-don-carson.

At present, Carson has a number of monographs on the horizon that promise to make a significant contribution. In his work *Evangelicalism: What Is It and Is It Worth Keeping?*, for example, Carson evaluates the biblical and theological foundations of this elusive label and offers a cogent argument for its enduring relevance within the broader landscape of contemporary Christianity. Nevertheless, Carson makes clear that it is of little interest for him to defend evangelicalism—his overwhelming concern is with the *evangel*, the gospel, in our day.

Likewise, in *Scandalous: The Cross and Resurrection of Jesus*, Carson captures the inherent peculiarity of the death and resurrection of Christ, giving special attention to both the history and the theology of the work of Christ and stressing its profound implications for the way Christians live their lives. To the ongoing discussion on the nature of Scripture, Carson adds his *Collected Writings on Scripture*, a compilation of several essays and book reviews from the past thirty years. Carson hopes this volume will serve as a catalyst for a 2012 project tentatively titled *The Scripture Project*. This two-volume set, with over thirty-five contributors, professes to represent a "robust confessionalism" of the doctrine of Scripture working through "fundamental biblical, theological, historical, and philosophical issues."[39]

Other future projects include two more volumes in Carson's devotional set *For the Love of God*. Also, we can only hope that Carson will follow through with his desire to write a two-volume work on the unity of the canon, centered on the joint issues of mystery and fulfillment in Scripture. This topic, incidentally, invokes fond memories of my first doctoral seminar with Don Carson at Trinity in the fall of 1990, which bore the title "Mystery in the New Testament." As I was stunned to discover on the first day of class, the syllabus included works in German, French, and Italian on the reading list, and the course was taught at such a high academic level that I could only hold on to my seat belt in order not to be utterly blown away by Carson's massive erudition. (I also recall distinctly that temperatures in Deerfield were so cold that winter that your coffee would almost freeze on the short walk from the White Horse Inn to the Aldeen classroom building.)

---

[39]Carson, *Collected Writings on Scripture*, 11.

Characteristics of Carson's Biblical Scholarship
An International Ministry

Carson grew up in the Baptist tradition. To this day, while in England he associates with and worships in a Baptist church. However, during his doctoral studies and his regular sabbaticals at Tyndale House he has functioned in an interdenominational context. He moves freely in Anglican circles in Britain and in Australia, and his counsel is sought on a wide range of biblical and pastoral issues by church leaders from various confessional backgrounds. Ultimately, Carson's ministry is channeled not through denominations but through individuals and institutions that invite him to minister in their respective contexts.

For a number of years, Carson served with the Faith and Church Study Unit of the Theological Commission of the World Evangelical Fellowship, an involvement that is indicative of his concern for the universal church and of his commitment to cooperation among evangelicals worldwide. His contacts in Britain and the fact that his command of French enables him to function as a liaison to French-speaking Africa place Carson in a strategic position to facilitate such collaboration. He himself has lectured all over the world. Operating in a global context, with a commitment to first-rate evangelical scholarship, Carson has been engaged for a considerable amount of time in nurturing those who in turn train other Christian leaders. Indeed, Carson places a high priority on mentoring gifted students. Craig Blomberg, Stanley Porter, and many others (including some of the contributors to this volume) can attest to his formative influence on their scholarly careers.

While Carson chaired the Faith and Church Study Unit, the group strove to make the ideal of a worldwide scope for the World Evangelical Fellowship a reality. Nigerians, Japanese, Indians, Indonesians, continental Europeans, and delegates from other parts of the world struggled to produce global solutions for important issues facing the church worldwide. In the past, those with adequate resources would have done all the writing. Under Carson's leadership, however, scholars from the Two-Thirds World, despite the lack of materials in their native contexts, were encouraged to participate fully in the discussions and writing. Carson ensured that every contributor was given bibliographical assistance and suggestions for improvement. Thus helpful insights on important subjects found their way to Japan, Hong Kong, Indonesia, and many other places. Eventually Carson would edit the submitted contributions for publication. In this way he promoted significantly both the coming of age of scholarship in the Two-Thirds World and global evangelical partnership.[40]

A High View of Scripture

As already indicated, assigning D. A. Carson a distinct place in the field of evangelical theology is a rather complex undertaking. He himself has great admiration and respect for the fathers of the evangelical movement in the United States, Kenneth Kantzer and Carl Henry. Indeed, he had the privilege of interviewing these two men for the video *Know Your Roots* in 1991. His own scholarly career has been characterized by a significant degree of independence from other scholars' views, a bedrock commitment to the authority of Scripture,[41] and use of all the resources available to the modern scholar to interpret it.

Carson considers a high view of the Scripture's integrity a nonnegotiable for his own work.[42] Thus in a speech given during a luncheon at Tyndale House, he once remarked that anyone who arrives at a conclusion at odds with the traditional evangelical positions about the authority of the Bible should have the integrity to stop claiming to be an evangelical.[43] At the same time, Carson is not a fundamentalist in the sense of interpreting Scripture fideistically and literalistically. He uses intelligent, detailed biblical study as the basis for theological construction and application. This general procedure was already visible in his dissertation on God's sovereignty and human responsibility. It has been refined over the years and was further elaborated upon in his lecture on biblical theology at the 1993 meeting of the Institute for Biblical Research.[44] What is more, while Carson is committed to

---

[40]Peter O'Brien, interview by author, September 1994. The volumes produced during Carson's term with the Faith and Church Study Unit include *Biblical Interpretation and the Church*, *The Church in the Bible and the World*, *Teach Us to Pray*, *Right with God*, and *Worship*.

[41]See D. A. Carson, "Three Books on the Bible: A Critical Review," *JETS* 26 (1983): 337–67; Carson, "Recent Developments in the Doctrine of Scripture," in *Hermeneutics, Authority, and Canon*, ed. D. A. Carson and John D. Woodbridge (Grand Rapids: Zondervan, 1986), 1–48; Carson, *Collected Writings on Scripture*.

[42]D. A. Carson, "The Role of Exegesis in Systematic Theology," in *Doing Theology in Today's World*, ed. John D. Woodbridge and Thomas E. McComiskey (Grand Rapids: Zondervan, 1992), 54–56.

[43]Interview with Peter Comont, a former pastor at Eden Baptist Church in Cambridge.

[44]D. A. Carson, "Current Issues in Biblical Theology: A New Testament Perspective," *BBR* 5 (1995): 17–41.

biblical theology, he does not therefore eschew systematic theology.[45] To the contrary, he is highly concerned about the contextualization of the Christian faith in the pluralistic Western world of today, as well as in cross-cultural contexts.[46]

Owing to its breadth, Carson's scholarship is not easy to categorize. His treatment of the emergent church movement, for example, is driven as much by his commitment to Scripture, and the belief that its truth is both objectively knowable and absolute, as it is by his conviction that the gospel is foundational and worthy of proclamation.[47] Insofar as he believes that proponents of the emergent church movement are within the bounds of evangelicalism, he is driven by his concern for the fidelity of the church. Though his own broad perspective on the relationship between Christianity and culture differs markedly,[48] Carson's approach to this movement is at once critical of its inimical aspects and yet sympathetic toward its ideals. Like a wise father admonishing a child, he prefaces his criticisms with a series of affirmations. Yet in the end, Carson is not afraid to come down hard on what he believes to be unwarranted dichotomies. He concludes rather sternly, "Damn all false antitheses to hell, for they generate false gods, they perpetuate idols, they twist and distort our souls, they launch the church into violent pendulum swings whose oscillations succeed only in dividing brothers and sisters in Christ."[49] His passion is unmistakable and reflects, above all, a zeal for unity within the church.

On the whole, as any careful review of Carson's plethora of writings will readily reveal, his high view of Scripture is the basis for all his theological inquiry. There are certain recurring expressions in his description of Scripture that disclose his conviction that the Bible, with

---

[45]See D. A. Carson, "Unity and Diversity in the New Testament: The Possibility of Systematic Theology," in *Scripture and Truth*, ed. Carson and Woodbridge, 65–95; Carson, "Role of Exegesis," 39–76.

[46]See especially D. A. Carson, "Christian Witness in an Age of Pluralism," in *God and Culture*, ed. D. A. Carson and John D. Woodbridge (Grand Rapids: Eerdmans, 1993), 31–66; Carson, "Church and Mission: Reflections on Contextualization and the Third Horizon," in *The Church in the Bible and the World*, ed. D. A. Carson (Grand Rapids: Baker, 1987), 213–57; Carson, "A Sketch of the Factors Determining Current Hermeneutical Debate in Cross-cultural Contexts," in *Biblical Interpretation and the Church*, ed. D. A. Carson (Grand Rapids: Baker, 1993), 11–29; Carson, *Gagging of God*; and Carson, ed., *Telling the Truth: Evangelizing Postmoderns* (Grand Rapids: Zondervan, 2000).

[47]D. A. Carson, *Becoming Conversant with the Emerging Church* (Grand Rapids: Zondervan, 2005).

[48]See D. A. Carson, *Christ and Culture Revisited* (Grand Rapids: Eerdmans, 2008).

[49]Carson, *Becoming Conversant with the Emerging Church*, 234.

all its diversity, remains a robust and nourishing source of absolute truth. His approach to any controversial issue or innovative movement, then, is to determine its scriptural warrant, giving special attention to the key junctures in biblical theology.

This methodology is the most defining element of the New Studies in Biblical Theology series. As series editor, Carson continues to accentuate the unity within the diversity of Scripture, maintaining that within the canonical boundaries of the Bible, with all its rich diversity, there is one Mind from which emerges "a unified thought and vision."[50] Yet within these constraints, he allows for a measure of methodological flexibility. Contributors can trace themes across the canon, or work within a book or corpus, as long as their approach remains inductive, allowing the categories to emerge from within the text. While this approach is not new, Carson has had a key role in leading the recent resurgence of biblical theology.

Commitment and Ministry to the Church

For all his erudition, D. A. Carson insists that scholarship and personal faith must not be kept separate. Rather, a deep evangelical faith should undergird a person's effort to search the Scriptures as diligently and penetratingly as possible. Especially commendable is Carson's strong commitment to serving the needs of the evangelical church today. Indeed, Carson is a symbol for many that competent biblical scholarship and evangelical orthodoxy can go together. Pastors and other committed Christians can turn to his commentaries and biblical studies for help when interpreting difficult passages or confronting controversial issues. It is significant that several of his books are based on sermons or letters to a church or parachurch context (e.g., *The Sermon on the Mount* and *Showing the Spirit*). Carson's deep concern for the spiritual state of the church today can be seen in his *Call to Spiritual Reformation*, which begins with an impassioned plea for and practical tips on prayer.[51] He has also strongly advocated the need for biblical expository preaching and regular time with God.[52]

---

[50]See the IVP interview with D. A. Carson, http://www.ivpress.com/spotlight/2600.php.

[51]See also D. A. Carson, ed., *Teach Us to Pray* (Grand Rapids: Baker, 1990); and Carson, "A Church That Does All the Right Things, But . . . ," *Christianity Today* 23, no. 18 (1979): 28–31.

[52]D. A. Carson, "Accept No Substitutes: Six Reasons Not to Abandon Expository Preaching," *Leadership* 17 (1996): 87–88; Carson, "Preaching That Understands the World," in *When God's Voice Is Heard*, ed. Christopher Green and David Jackman (Leicester, UK: Inter-Varsity, 1995),

Unafraid to speak out on controversial issues, Carson considers it his responsibility to contribute discerningly and constructively to current debates within the church. In *Showing the Spirit* and in his essay "The Purpose of Signs and Wonders in the New Testament,"[53] Carson addresses the contemporary charismatic movement; in "Reflections on Christian Assurance"[54] he deals with the "lordship salvation" debate; in *How Long, O Lord?* he provides a courageous discussion of AIDS;[55] and in *The King James Version Debate* and *The Inclusive Language Debate* he seeks to adjudicate between two sides of important issues.[56] However, by maintaining a biblical focus, Carson continually rises above mere polemics.

Perhaps one of Carson's greatest strengths is his ability to appreciate the merits of opposing views and to incorporate the best of both into a balanced mediating position. For example, on the issue of charismata, Carson is not a cessationist, arguing that 1 Corinthians 13 appears to preclude such a position. On the issue of divine sovereignty and human responsibility, Carson holds to "compatibilism"; on the issue of Christian assurance, Carson seeks to balance carefully the believer's security with the biblical injunctions for perseverance in the Christian faith.

Carson has never been one to retreat into academic subculture. He is sensitive to cultural trends and current affairs, and quick to address the needs of the body of Christ with a seasoned word. Though Carson is a practicing Baptist, he is more inclined to step out of the confines of his own tradition in order to apply the fruits of his biblical scholarship in a more universal setting. In his book *Worship by the Book*, Carson addresses the need for reformation in the church based on a biblical-theological understanding of worship. In this endeavor, he exhibits a synthesis of various elements that set this project apart from others on the subject. First, he balances theological reflection with practical implementation. He offers a concise yet sufficiently

---

145–59; Carson, *For the Love of God*, 2 vols. (Wheaton, IL: Crossway, 1998 and 1999); and Carson, "The Difficult Doctrine of the Love of God," a four-part series starting in *Bibliotheca Sacra* 156 (1999): 3–12.

[53]D. A. Carson, "The Purpose of Signs and Wonders in the New Testament," in *Power Religion*, ed. Michael S. Horton (Chicago: Moody Press, 1992), 89–118.

[54]D. A. Carson, "Reflections on Christian Assurance," *WTJ* 54 (1992): 1–29.

[55]But see the critique by Ellingworth, review of *How Long, O Lord?*, 362–63.

[56]D. A. Carson, *The King James Debate* (Grand Rapids: Baker, 1979); Carson, *The Inclusive Language Debate* (Grand Rapids: Baker, 1999).

thorough construction of a biblical theology of worship integrated into complete service outlines. Second, he preserves the fidelity of biblical instruction while remaining attentive to the need of contextualizing patterns of worship in other cultures. Third, he interacts with his own tradition while remaining sensitive to the diversity of worship styles represented in evangelicalism.

Carson's commitment to the church extends beyond the narrow focus of denominational traditions. His high view of Scripture, his focus on the gospel, and his commitment to the ministry of the church converge in his passion to integrate Christianity and culture. In his important book *Christ and Culture Revisited*, Carson addresses the tension between the believer's call to be separate from the world and the cultural implications of the Great Commission. Once again, he approaches a complex situation by canvassing the prevailing responses and assessing each of these models in light of the biblical teaching on the subject. His unwavering belief that Scripture holds the key to understanding truth is no better illustrated than by his own conclusion:

> To pursue with passion the robust and nourishing wholeness of biblical theology as the controlling matrix for our reflection on the relations between Christ and culture will, ironically, help us to be far more flexible than the inflexible grids that are often made to stand in the Bible's place. Scripture will mandate that we think holistically and subtly, wisely, and penetratingly, under the Lordship of Christ— utterly dissatisfied with the anesthetic of the culture.[57]

From this emerges Carson's conviction regarding Scripture as the only sure guide for truth. Contrary to those who think of the Bible as either hopelessly incongruous or inflexibly rigid, Carson maintains that Scripture provides an exceedingly rich resource for theological reflection, and he unapologetically bases on this foundation his ministry to the church.

While many in the scholarly guild consciously or unconsciously drive a wedge between pastoral ministry and scholarship, Carson remains an exemplar of how the two can, and should, be held together. For those who gravitate to the scholarly side, he cautions against being owned by the agenda of publishers: "If you are a pastor-scholar, you ought to be asking yourself what might be especially helpful at the

---

[57]Carson, *Christ and Culture Revisited*, 227.

present moment, what work of scholarship is crying out to be tackled, what popularization would benefit the Lord's people."[58] Even more important is the crucial balance between pursuing knowledge and preserving love. In this regard, Carson warns that "nothing is quite as deceitful as an evangelical scholarly mind that thinks it is especially close to God *because* of its scholarship rather than because of Jesus."[59]

Carson, for his part, seems to gravitate toward the other side of the continuum, claiming that the most serious temptations to leave his academic post have come, not from other teaching opportunities, but from the prospect of returning to full-time pastoral ministry.[60] His advice to the scholar to "avoid becoming a mere quartermaster" (one who provides the supplies to the frontlines during battle)[61] reflects his own resolve not only to equip those engaged in practical Christian ministry but also to take his place alongside them: "This means engaging the outside world at a personal level, at an intellectual and cultural level; it means working and serving in the local church; it means engaging in evangelism."[62]

Focus on the Gospel

What is not always understood but nonetheless crucial for a true appraisal of his driving motivation is that Carson, for all his scholarly writings, is first of all a minister of the gospel, not an academician. He is a gospel-centered man, not a theoretical scholar.[63] It appears that academia has not mastered him—he has mastered academia. Why, then, is Carson so deeply involved in scholarship? Doubtless he recognizes his God-given gifts and desires to be faithful to his calling. Also, Carson believes that people are built up by the faithful exposition of Scripture and by the defense of the gospel. Well aware that too often liberals have held sway in the defining moments of debate, he recognizes that the task of the evangelical is not exhausted by the assertion of truth; it also extends to the responsibility to expose and confute error.

---

[58]Carson, "The Scholar as Pastor," 15.
[59]Ibid., 3.
[60]Ibid., 5–6.
[61]Ibid., 6.
[62]Ibid.
[63]See *Evangelicalism: What Is It and Is It Worth Keeping?* (Wheaton, IL: Crossway, forthcoming).

367

The centrality of the gospel has always been the centerpiece of Carson's scholarship. Yet with the onslaught of postmodernism, the traditional modes of communicating this message have grown increasingly archaic and ineffective. Carson, in response, has been on the front lines grappling with the relevance of the gospel in an increasingly pluralistic culture.[64] In his book *Telling the Truth: Evangelizing Postmoderns*, for example, Carson is critical of mere relational evangelism, underscoring the essential nature of the gospel message. According to Carson, "the crucial question is whether the Christian witness has a clear, relatively simple, straight-forward grasp of what the Bible's story line is. How it must give form to worldview, and how the wonderful news of the gospel fits powerfully into the true story. . . ."[65] This quote bears telling testimony to Carson's commitment to proclaiming the gospel in a way that is relevant to today's culture yet without losing sight of the timeless message of the gospel.

No account of Carson's influence within evangelicalism is complete without reference to his latest role in the formation of the Gospel Coalition (http://thegospelcoalition.org), a nondenominational network of North American evangelicals committed to the proclamation of the gospel. All the characteristics of Carson's scholarship converge in this ministry. The theological vision of the coalition addresses epistemological, hermeneutical, and contextualization concerns, but its central focus is promoting a fully integrated gospel-centered ministry that is designed to permeate the evangelical churches of North America.[66] In this endeavor, Carson's synthesis of scholarship and faith is perhaps most evident; and sound, responsible scholarship forms the foundation for a profound and enduring impact on the advance of God's kingdom on earth.

Conclusion

But how would D. A. Carson himself like to be remembered? When his mother died and he struggled as to whether he should fulfill a commitment to speak at a large missionary conference, he was led to reflect on his priorities: "Sometimes when I look at my own children, I wonder if, should the Lord give us another thirty years, they will

[64]E.g., Carson, *The Gagging of God.*
[65]D. A. Carson, *Telling the Truth*, 398.
[66]See "Theological Vision for Ministry," http://thegospelcoalition.org/about/foundation-documents/vision.

remember their father as a man of prayer, or think of him as someone distant who was away from home rather a lot and who wrote a number of obscure books."[67]

It is appropriate to conclude with Carson's poem "The Finitude of Man," which puts the entire human quest to understand God in its proper perspective:

> I understand that matter can be changed
> To energy; that maths can integrate
> The complex quantum jumps that must relate
> The fusion of the stars to history's page.
> I understand that God in every age
> Is Lord of all; that matter can't dictate;
> That stars and quarks and all things intricate
> Perform his word—including fool and sage.
> But knowing God is not to know like God;
> And science is a quest in infancy.
> Still more: transcendence took on flesh and blood:
> I do not understand how this can be.
> The more my mind assesses what it can,
> The more it learns the finitude of man.[68]

[67]D. A. Carson, *A Call to Spiritual Reformation* (Grand Rapids: Baker, 1992), 26.
[68]D. A. Carson, *Holy Sonnets of the Twentieth Century* (Grand Rapids: Baker, 1994), 97. I would like to acknowledge my gratitude to my assistant Jake Pratt for his assistance in updating this essay.

Selected Writings of D. A. Carson

ANDY NASELLI

AND ANDREAS J. KÖSTENBERGER

The listing of books authored, coauthored, edited, or coedited by D. A. Carson below is exhaustive until the spring of 2010. In keeping with the nature of the present volume, the listing of Carson's other works focuses on his scholarly contribution to New Testament studies (not including book reviews). For an exhaustive listing of resources, see www.thegospelcoalition.org.

Books

Basics for Believers: An Exposition of Philippians. Grand Rapids: Baker, 1996.

Becoming Conversant with the Emerging Church: Understanding a Movement and Its Implications. Grand Rapids: Zondervan, 2005.

Biblical Greek Language and Linguistics: Open Questions in Current Research. Edited by D. A. Carson and Stanley E. Porter. SNTG 1. JSNTSup 80. Sheffield: JSOT, 1993.

Biblical Interpretation and the Church: Text and Context. Edited by D. A. Carson. Exeter: Paternoster, 1984.

A Call to Spiritual Reformation: Priorities from Paul and His Prayers. Grand Rapids: Baker, 1992.

Christ and Culture Revisited. Grand Rapids: Eerdmans, 2008.

The Church in the Bible and the World: An International Study. Edited by D. A. Carson. Grand Rapids: Baker, 1987.

Collected Writings on Scripture. Wheaton, IL: Crossway, 2010.

Commentary on the New Testament Use of the Old Testament. Edited by G. K. Beale and D. A. Carson. Grand Rapids: Baker, 2007.

The Cross and Christian Ministry: An Exposition of Passages from 1 Co-rinthians. Grand Rapids: Baker, 1993. Repr. *The Cross and Christian Ministry: Leadership Lessons from 1 Corinthians.* Grand Rapids: Baker, 2004.

The Difficult Doctrine of the Love of God. Wheaton, IL: Crossway, 2000.

Discourse Analysis and Other Topics in Biblical Greek. Edited by D. A. Carson and Stanley E. Porter. SNTG 2. JSNTSup 113. Sheffield: JSOT, 1995.

Divine Sovereignty and Human Responsibility: Biblical Themes in Tension. Atlanta: John Knox, 1981. 2nd ed. *Divine Sovereignty and Human Responsibility: Biblical Perspectives in Tension.* Grand Rapids: Baker, 1994.

Evangelicalism: What Is It and Is It Worth Keeping? Wheaton, IL: Crossway, forthcoming.

Exegetical Fallacies. Grand Rapids: Baker, 1984. 2nd ed. 1996.

The Farewell Discourse and Final Prayer of Jesus: An Exposition of John 14–17. Grand Rapids: Baker, 1980.

For the Love of God: A Daily Companion for Discovering the Riches of God's Word. 2 vols. Wheaton, IL: Crossway, 1998, 1999.

From Sabbath to Lord's Day: A Biblical, Historical, and Theological Investigation. Edited by D. A. Carson. Grand Rapids: Zondervan, 1982.

From Triumphalism to Maturity: An Exposition of 2 Corinthians 10–13. Grand Rapids: Baker, 1984. Repr. *A Model of Christian Maturity: An Exposition of 2 Corinthians 10–13,* 2007.

The Gagging of God: Christianity Confronts Pluralism. Grand Rapids: Zondervan, 1996.

God and Culture: Essays in Honor of Carl F. H. Henry. Edited by D. A. Carson and John D. Woodbridge. Grand Rapids: Eerdmans, 1993.

God with Us: Themes from Matthew. Ventura, CA: Regal, 1985.

The Gospel According to John. PNTC. Grand Rapids: Eerdmans, 1991.

Greek Accents: A Student's Manual. Grand Rapids: Baker, 1985.

Hermeneutics, Authority, and Canon. Edited by D. A. Carson and John D. Woodbridge. Grand Rapids: Zondervan, 1986.

Holy Sonnets of the Twentieth Century. Grand Rapids: Baker, 1994.

How Long, O Lord? Reflections on Suffering and Evil. Grand Rapids: Baker, 1990. 2nd ed. 2006.

The Inclusive-Language Debate: A Plea for Realism. Grand Rapids: Baker, 1998.

Introducing the New Testament: A Short Guide to Its History and Message. By D. A. Carson and Douglas J. Moo. An abridgment of *An Introduction to the New Testament.* Edited by Andrew David Naselli. Grand Rapids: Zondervan, 2010.

An Introduction to the New Testament. By D. A. Carson, Douglas J. Moo, and Leon Morris. Grand Rapids: Zondervan, 1992. 2nd ed. 2007 by D. A. Carson and Douglas J. Moo.

It Is Written: Scripture Citing Scripture. Essays in Honour of Barnabas Lindars, SSF. Edited by D. A. Carson and H. G. M. Williamson. Cambridge: Cambridge University Press, 1988.

Justification and Variegated Nomism: A Fresh Appraisal of Paul and Second Temple Judaism. 2 vols. Edited by D. A. Carson, Peter T. O'Brien, and Mark A. Seifrid. WUNT 2/140, 181. Tübingen: Mohr Siebeck; Grand Rapids: Baker, 2001, 2004.

Letters Along the Way: A Novel of the Christian Life. By D. A. Carson and John D. Woodbridge. Wheaton, IL: Crossway, 1993.

Linguistics and the New Testament: Critical Junctions. Edited by D. A. Carson and Stanley E. Porter. SNTG 5. JSNTSup 168. Sheffield: Sheffield Academic Press, 1999.

Love in Hard Places. Wheaton, IL: Crossway, 2002.

"Matthew." In *The Expositor's Bible Commentary,* 8:1–599. Grand Rapids: Zondervan, 1984. Rev. ed. 2009.

"Matthew." In *Zondervan NIV Bible Commentary,* edited by Kenneth L. Barker and John L. Kohlenberger III, 2:1–135. Grand Rapids: Zondervan, 1994.

Memoirs of an Ordinary Pastor: The Life and Reflections of Tom Carson. Wheaton, IL: Crossway, 2008.

New Bible Commentary: 21st Century Edition. Edited by D. A. Carson, R. T. France, J. A. Motyer, and G. J. Wenham. Downers Grove, IL: InterVarsity, 1994.

New Dictionary of Biblical Theology. Edited by T. Desmond Alexander, Brian S. Rosner, D. A. Carson, and Graeme Goldsworthy. Downers Grove, IL: InterVarsity, 2000.

New Testament Commentary Survey. 6th ed. Grand Rapids: Baker, 2007.

Right with God: Justification in the Bible and the World. Edited by D. A. Carson. Grand Rapids: Baker, 1992.

Scandalous: The Cross and Resurrection of Jesus. Wheaton, IL: Crossway, 2010.

Scripture and Truth. Edited by D. A. Carson and John D. Woodbridge. Grand Rapids: Zondervan, 1983.

The Sermon on the Mount: An Exposition of Matthew 5–7. Grand Rapids: Baker, 1978.

Showing the Spirit: A Theological Exposition of 1 Corinthians 12–14. Grand Rapids: Baker, 1987.

Teach Us to Pray: Prayer in the Bible and the World. Edited by D. A. Carson. Grand Rapids: Baker, 1990.

Telling the Truth: Evangelizing Postmoderns. Edited by D. A. Carson. Grand Rapids: Zondervan, 2000.

When Jesus Confronts the World: An Exposition of Matthew 8–10. Grand Rapids: Baker, 1987.

Worship: Adoration and Action. Edited by D. A. Carson. Grand Rapids: Baker, 1993.

Worship by the Book. Edited by D. A. Carson. Grand Rapids: Zondervan, 2002.

Articles, Essays, and Other Contributions

"Acts." Translation in the New Living Translation.

"Adam in the Epistles of Paul." In *In the Beginning . . . : A Symposium on the Bible and Creation*, edited by Nigel M. de S. Cameron, 28–43. Glasgow: Biblical Creation Society, 1980.

"The Apocryphal/Deuterocanonical Books: An Evangelical View." In *The Parallel Apocrypha*, edited by John R. Kohlenberger III, xliv–xlvii. New York: Oxford University Press, 1997.

"Approaching the Bible." In *New Bible Commentary: 21st Century Edition*, 4th ed., edited by D. A. Carson, R. T. France, J. A. Motyer, and G. J. Wenham, 1–19. Downers Grove, IL: InterVarsity, 1994.

"Atonement in Romans 3:21–26." In *The Glory of the Atonement: Biblical, Historical, and Practical Perspectives: Essays in Honor of Roger R. Nicole*, edited by Charles E. Hill and Frank A. James III, 119–39. Downers Grove, IL: InterVarsity, 2004.

"The Biblical Gospel." In *For Such a Time as This: Perspectives on Evangelicalism, Past, Present and Future*, edited by Steve Brady and Harold Rowdon, 75–85. London: Evangelical Alliance, 1996.

"Biblical Theology." In *Dictionary of Biblical Criticism and Interpretation*, edited by Stanley E. Porter, 35–41. London: Routledge, 2007.

"Brother/comrade, companion, friend [ἑταῖρος]," "Cry [κράζω]," "Cunning [πανουργία]," "Escape, Flee [φεύγω]," "Flow [ῥέω]." In *New International Dictionary of New Testament Theology*. Vol. 1, *A–F*, edited by Colin Brown, 259–60, 408–10, 412–13, 558–59, 682–83. Grand Rapids: Zondervan, 1975.

"The Challenge of the Balkanization of Johannine Studies." In *John, Jesus, and History*. Vol. 1, *Critical Appraisals of Critical Views*, edited by

Paul N. Anderson, Felix Just, and Tom Thatcher, 133–59. Society of Biblical Literature Symposium Series. Atlanta: Society of Biblical Literature, 2007.

"Christological Ambiguities in the Gospel of Matthew." In *Christ the Lord: Studies in Christology Presented to Donald Guthrie*, edited by Harold W. Rowdon, 97–114. Downers Grove, IL: InterVarsity, 1982.

"Current Issues in Biblical Theology: A New Testament Perspective." *BBR* 5 (1995): 17–41.

"Current Source Criticism of the Fourth Gospel: Some Methodological Questions." *JBL* 97 (1978): 411–29.

"Divine Sovereignty and Human Responsibility in Philo: Analysis and Method." *Novum Testamentum* 23 (1981): 148–64.

"Divorce: A Concise Biblical Analysis." *Northwest Journal of Theology* 4 (1975): 43–59.

"Do the Prophets and the Law Quit Prophesying Before John? A Note on Matthew 11.13." In *The Gospels and the Scriptures of Israel*, edited by Craig A. Evans and W. Richard Stegner, 179–94. JSNTSup 104. Studies in Scripture in Early Judaism and Christianity 3. Sheffield: Sheffield Academic Press, 1994.

"Five Gospels, No Christ: In their attempt to rescue the Bible from conservatives, scholars in the Jesus Seminar became liberal fundamentalists." *Christianity Today* 38, no. 5 (1994): 30–33.

Foreword to *Encountering God's Word: Beginning Biblical Studies*, edited by Philip Duce and Daniel Strange, 7–8. Leicester: Apollos, 2003.

"The Function of the Paraclete in John 16:7–11." *JBL* 98 (1979): 547–66.

"Historical Tradition and the Fourth Gospel: After Dodd, What?" In *Gospel Perspectives*. Vol. 2, *Studies of History and Tradition in the Four Gospels*, edited by R. T. France and David Wenham, 83–145. Sheffield: JSOT, 1981.

"Historical Tradition in the Fourth Gospel: A Response to J. S. King." *JSNT* 23 (1985): 73–81.

Introduction by D. A. Carson and G. K. Beale to *Commentary on the New Testament Use of the Old Testament*, edited by G. K. Beale and D. A. Carson, xxiii–xxviii. Grand Rapids: Baker, 2007.

"An Introduction to Introductions." In *Linguistics and the New Testament: Critical Junctions*, edited by D. A. Carson and Stanley E. Porter, 14–22. SNTG 5. JSNTSup 168. Sheffield: Sheffield Academic Press, 1999.

Introduction to *The Complexities of Second Temple Judaism*. Vol. 1 of *Justification and Variegated Nomism*, edited by D. A. Carson, Peter T. O'Brien, and Mark A. Seifrid, 1–5. WUNT 140. Tübingen: Mohr Siebeck; Grand Rapids: Baker, 2001.

"An Introduction to the Porter/Fanning Debate." In *Biblical Greek Language and Linguistics: Open Questions in Current Research*, edited by D. A. Carson and Stanley E. Porter, 18–25. SNTG 1. JSNTSup 80. Sheffield: JSOT, 1993.

"Is the Doctrine of Claritas Scripturae Still Relevant Today?" In *Dein Wort ist die Wahrheit Beiträge zu einer schriftgemäßen Theologie* [FS, Gerhard Maier], edited by Eberhard Hahn, Rolf Hille, and Heinz-Werner Neudorfer, 97–111. Wuppertal: Brockhaus, 1997.

"James, 1–2 Peter, 1–3 John, Jude." In *Commentary on the New Testament Use of the Old Testament*, edited by G. K. Beale and D. A. Carson, 997–1079. Grand Rapids: Baker, 2007.

"Jesus and the Sabbath in the Four Gospels." In *From Sabbath to Lord's Day: A Biblical, Historical, and Theological Investigation*, edited by D. A. Carson, 57–97. Grand Rapids: Zondervan, 1982.

"The Jewish Leaders in Matthew's Gospel: A Reappraisal." *JETS* 25 (1982): 161–74.

"Johannine Perspectives on the Doctrine of Assurance." *Explorations* 10 (1996): 59–97.

"The Johannine Writings" and "The Johannine Letters." In *New Dictionary of Biblical Theology*, edited by T. Desmond Alexander and Brian S. Rosner, 132–36 and 351–55. Downers Grove, IL: InterVarsity, 2000.

"John and the Johannine Epistles." In *It Is Written: Scripture Citing Scripture. Essays in Honour of Barnabas Lindars, SSF*, edited by D. A. Carson and H. G. M. Williamson, 245–64. Cambridge: Cambridge University Press, 1988.

"The Limits of Functional Equivalence in Bible Translation—and Other Limits, Too." In *The Challenge of Bible Translation: Communicating God's Word to the World: Understanding the Theory, History, and Practice* [FS, Ronald F. Youngblood], edited by Glen G. Scorgie, Mark L. Strauss, and Steven M. Voth, 65–113. Grand Rapids: Zondervan, 2003.

"Love." In *New Dictionary of Biblical Theology*, edited by T. Desmond Alexander and Brian S. Rosner, 646–50. Downers Grove, IL: InterVarsity, 2000.

"Matthew 11:19b/Luke 7:35: A Test Case for the Bearing of Q Christology on the Synoptic Problem." In *Jesus of Nazareth: Lord and Christ. Essays on the Historical Jesus and New Testament Christology* [FS, I. Howard Marshall], edited by Joel B. Green and Max Turner, 128–46. Grand Rapids: Eerdmans, 1994.

"Mystery and Fulfillment: Toward a More Comprehensive Paradigm of Paul's Understanding of the Old and New." In *Justification and Variegated Nomism*. Vol. 2, *The Paradoxes of Paul*, edited by D. A. Carson, Peter T.

"Reflections on Salvation and Justification in the New Testament." *JETS* 40 (1997): 582–608.

"The Role of Exegesis in Systematic Theology." In *Doing Theology in Today's World: Essays in Honor of Kenneth S. Kantzer*, edited by John D. Woodbridge and Thomas Edward McComiskey, 39–76. Grand Rapids: Zondervan, 1991.

"Selected Recent Studies of the Fourth Gospel." *Themelios* 14, no. 2 (1989): 57–64.

"'Silent in the Churches': On the Role of Women in 1 Corinthians 14:33b–36." In *Recovering Biblical Manhood and Womanhood: A Response to Evangelical Feminism*, edited by John Piper and Wayne Grudem, 140–53, 487–90. Westchester, IL: Crossway, 1991.

"Summaries and Conclusions." In *Justification and Variegated Nomism*. Vol. 1, *The Complexities of Second Temple Judaism*, edited by D. A. Carson, Peter T. O'Brien, and Mark A. Seifrid, 505–48. WUNT 2/140. Tübingen: Mohr Siebeck; Grand Rapids: Baker, 2001.

"Syntactical and Text-Critical Observations on John 20:30–31: One More Round on the Purpose of the Fourth Gospel." *JBL* 124 (2005): 693–714.

"Systematic Theology and Biblical Theology." In *New Dictionary of Biblical Theology*, edited by T. Desmond Alexander and Brian S. Rosner, 89–104. Downers Grove, IL: InterVarsity, 2000.

"The Three Witnesses and the Eschatology of 1 John." In *To Tell the Mystery: Essays on New Testament Eschatology* [FS, Robert H. Gundry], edited by Thomas E. Schmidt and Moisés Silva, 216–32. JSNTSup 100. Sheffield: JSOT, 1994.

"Understanding Misunderstandings in the Fourth Gospel." *TynBul* 33 (1982): 59–91.

"Unity and Diversity in the New Testament: The Possibility of Systematic Theology." In *Scripture and Truth*, edited by D. A. Carson and John D. Woodbridge, 65–95, 368–75. Grand Rapids: Zondervan, 1983.

"The Vindication of Imputation: On Fields of Discourse and Semantic Fields." In *Justification: What's at Stake in the Current Debates*, edited by Mark Husbands and Daniel J. Treier, 46–78. Downers Grove, IL: InterVarsity, 2004.

"When Is Spirituality Spiritual? Reflections on Some Problems of Definition." *JETS* 37 (1994): 381–94.

"Why Trust a Cross? Reflections on Romans 3:21–26." *Evangelical Review of Theology* 28 (2004): 345–62.

"Worship Under the Word." In *Worship by the Book*, edited by D. A. Carson, 11–63. Grand Rapids: Zondervan, 2002.

"'You Have No Need That Anyone Should Teach You' (1 John 2:27): An Old Testament Allusion That Determines the Interpretation." In *The New Testament in Its First Century Setting: Essays on Context and Background in Honour of B. W. Winter on His 65th Birthday*, edited by P. J. Williams, Andrew D. Clarke, Peter M. Head, and David Instone-Brewer, 269–80. Grand Rapids: Eerdmans, 2004.

Contributors

Craig L. Blomberg is Distinguished Professor of New Testament at Denver Seminary.

Mark Dever is Senior Pastor of Capitol Hill Baptist Church in Washington, DC.

Andreas J. Köstenberger is Director of PhD Studies and Senior Professor of New Testament and Biblical Theology at Southeastern Baptist Theological Seminary.

Douglas J. Moo is Blanchard Professor of New Testament at Wheaton College.

Peter T. O'Brien is Emeritus Member of Faculty at Moore Theological College, Sydney, Australia.

Grant Osborne is Professor of New Testament at Trinity Evangelical Divinity School.

David W. Pao is chair of the New Testament Department and Professor of New Testament at Trinity Evangelical Divinity School.

Stanley E. Porter is President, Dean, and Professor of New Testament at McMaster Divinity College, Canada.

Eckhard J. Schnabel is Professor of New Testament at Trinity Evangelical Divinity School.

John D. Woodbridge is Research Professor of Church History and the History of Christian Thought at Trinity Evangelical Divinity School.

Robert W. Yarbrough is Professor of New Testament at Covenant Theological Seminary.

Bible Permissions

General Index

Abraham, 166–71, 177, 185, 208
accommodation, 112–13
Acton Publishers (Nairobi), 268
Acts of the Apostles, 287–89
Africa, New Testament studies in,
    249–76
Africa-in-the-Bible approach, 273
Aguilar, Mario, 274
Akper, Godwin, 269, 274
Aktionsart, 48, 52–53
Alexandria, Egypt, 272
Al-Ghazali, 326
allegorical approaches, 66, 67, 272
Allen, R. Michael, 162n1
Allison, Dale, 283
already/not yet, 186–90, 191n80,
    193n84
amillennialism, 295
Anabaptists, 69
analogia fidei, 687
analogia Scripturae, 68
Anderson, Paul, 286
angels, 202
animal sacrifices, 210
antithetical possibilities, 56, 57
apartheid, 252, 264, 275
Apocalypse of Abraham, 143, 144
apocalyptic literature, 143–46
apographa, 116
apostasy, 210
Apostles' Creed, 68, 85, 107n6
apostolicity, of the church, 91
application, 299
Aristotle, 123n55
Arnold, Clinton, 332
Asian christologies, 300–315, 320–21

Asian New Testament scholars, 315–23
"as it is written," 198
aspectual value, 46–47, 50–52, 53, 54
assembly, church as, 89
assurance, 365
Astruc, Jean, 130
Athanasian Creed, 107n6
Augustine, 64, 67, 110–13, 114, 118,
    133
authorial intent, 64, 71–77
author-text-reader trialogue, 76
autographa, 116
Avalos, Hector, 280

Baconianism, 115n27
Baily, Kenneth, 341
Balla, Peter, 339–40
Balmer, Randall, 134
baptism, 91, 92–93
   mode of, 93
   subjects for, 93
"baptism of suffering," 243–44
baptize (term), 218–46
Barr, James, 19, 26, 78, 128n76, 343
Barrett, C. K., 336
Barth, Karl, 78, 125n65, 330, 336, 337
Bartholomew, Craig, 80
Bauckham, Richard, 287, 341
Bauer, Walter, 21–22, 28, 33–35, 36,
    334
Baugh, S. M., 187n68
Baur, F. C., 334, 336, 337
Bayer, Hans, 332
Bayle, Pierre, 128
Beale, Greg, 298
Beardsley, Monroe C., 71

Beaugrande, Robert de, 40
Bediako, Kwame, 261
Bellarmine, Robert, 126
Bengel, J. A., 116
Benyik, György, 339
Berkhof, Louis, 89, 94
Betz, Hans Dieter, 332
Bible
    authority of, 346–47, 362
    God's speech in, 198–200
    inerrancy of, 105–10, 134
    infallibility of, 114, 117, 120, 126, 134
    inspiration of, 347
    and tradition, 68–69, 86
    translation of, 9
    unity within diversity of, 364
biblical chronology, 128
biblical theology, 64, 70, 82, 362–64
    and systematic theology, 354
    and theological interpretation, 78–81, 85
bishops, 99
Bizer, Ernst, 125
Black, D. A., 41–42
black theology, 275
Blocher, Henri, 189
Blomberg, Craig, 329, 333, 361
Bock, Darrell, 281, 332
Bonhoeffer, Dietrich, 346–47
Bonsirven, Joseph, 334
Borg, Marcus, 278–79
Bornkamm, Karin, 346
Botha, Jan, 250
Botha, J. Eugene, 264–65, 271
Bovon, F., 334
Brethren, 69
Bridges, Charles, 103
Briggs, R. S., 347
"brothers and sisters," 204
Brown, Gillian, 40
Bruce, F. F., 201, 331, 357–58
Brunner, Theodore, 24
Bultmann, Rudolf, 331, 333, 335, 336, 337, 340, 343
Burton, Keith, 261

Calvin, John, 68, 125, 134, 176
Campbell, Constantine, 46–54, 60

Campbell, Douglas A., 183n55, 184
canonical criticism, 78–79
canonical reading, 63
"canon within a canon," 70
Carson, D. A., 9–10, 19–20, 63, 78, 84, 142, 156, 195, 217–18, 298, 299, 324, 345
    life and work, 349–69
Carson, Thomas Donald McMillan, 350–52
catholic, church as, 90
"Catholic modernists," 120
ceremonial cleansing, 222–23
cessationism, 365
Chalcedonian Creed, 107n6
Chalmers, Thomas, 134
Chantraine, Pierre, 48
Chaput, Charles J., 121
charismatic movement, 365
Charlesworth, James H., 283
Chicago Statement on Inerrancy, 107n5
children, of God, 211
Childs, Brevard, 78–79
China, 312
Chomsky, Noam, 38, 40, 43, 44
Christianity, as corporate, 95
Christian water baptism, 226, 229–41, 245
church, 87–89, 366
    attributes of, 90–91
    marks of, 91–94
church discipline, 92, 100, 101–2
church dogma, 66
church fathers, 64, 66, 81
church membership, 92, 94–98, 101
church-reading-centered hermeneutic, 65
circumcision, 174
Clackson, James, 48, 51
Coleridge, Samuel Taylor, 131–32
Collinge, N. E., 45
Combrink, H. J. B., 262
Common Sense Realism, 115n27
Communism, 339
community of interpretation, 72, 85
comparative approach, 272–73
compatibilism (free will), 365
complementarianism, 297n106
Comrie, Bernard, 49, 51

consumerism, 87
context, 27
contextual constraints (lexicography), 30–31
contextualization, 299
contextual methods, 272
conventional constraints (lexicography), 30
conversion, 175n32
Coptic Orthodox Church, 272
Cotterell, Peter, 41
Council of Trent, 69, 118, 134
Counter-Reformation, 339
covenant nomism, 192
Cranfield, C. E. B., 236, 330
Cranmer, Thomas, 122–23
creeds, 64, 68
critical scholarship, 65, 67
Crossan, Dominic, 278–79, 283
crusading, 308
Cruse, Alan, 27, 28, 29–30, 31
Culpepper, R. Alan, 356
culture, 366
Curtius, Georg, 48n97

Dahl, Nils, 337
Dalman, Gustaf, 334
Daneau, Lambert, 125
Danker, Frederick, 21–22, 28, 33–35, 36
Danove, Paul, 24
Da Vinci Code, 282
Dayton, Donald, 130n86
decentering, reading as, 74–75
Decker, Rodney, 48
deconstruction, 74
Deissmann, Adolf, 334
Dei Verbum, 121–23
demythologization, 335
denominations, 361, 366
Derrida, Jacques, 74
descent into hades (Apostles' Creed), 68, 85
de Villiers, Pieter G. R., 262, 264
diachronic approach (New Testament studies), 335
diachronic linguistics, 37, 59
Diaspora, 143, 148
Dibelius, Martin, 334

Didache, 69, 235n62
Dietrich, Walter, 300
discipleship, 160
discipline, 211, 214
discourse analysis, 39, 40–43
divine sovereignty, and human responsibility, 195, 365
divorce, 297n106
doctrine, 100
Dodd, C. H., 331
Donfried, Karl, 187n69
Draycott, Andy, 332
Dube, Musa, 268
Dunn, James D. G., 181, 190n77, 193n84, 223, 238, 288, 291, 341
Dupont, Jacques, 334
dynamic construal approach (lexicography), 30–31
dynamic equivalence, 329

East-West dichotomy, 314–15
Eck, Johannes, 113–15, 124, 127
edification, 103
egalitarianism, 297–98
Ehrman, Bart, 280–81, 282
Eichhorn , Johann Gottfried, 130
elasticity, 56
elders, 99, 101
El-Hassan, Shahir, 48
embedded kernels, 56, 57
emergent church, 10, 363
Engberg-Pedersen, Troels, 337
Enlightenment, 62, 116, 117, 342, 347
Erasmus, 113–14, 122, 124, 127
Ericsson, B., 337
eschatology, 190, 192
Essenes, 226, 228
Ethiopian's baptism, 234–35
ethnochristologies, 301
Europe, 324–48
    and North America, 329–37
    and world Christianity, 342–45
evaluative approach (inculturation), 273–74
evangelical approaches to Scripture, 68
evangelicalism, 9, 360
    approaches to Scripture, 68
    unity within, 358, 361–62
evangelism, and social concern, 269

evangelization, 103
Evans, Craig, 281
Evans, Trevor, 49, 51n105
evidence, of faith, 194
evil, 272, 316
excommunication, 102
exegesis, 85
    and theological interpretation, 85
    and theology, 62–63, 64, 67
experience, 84
expository preaching, 364

faith, 168–69
    and law, 179–80
    and scholarship, 364–67, 368
    and works, 182–84, 194
faithfulness, 183
faith of Christ, 166n10, 183–84
false teachers, 100
Fanning, Buist, 46
Farkasfalvy, Dénes, 339
Fatio, Olivier, 125
fellowship, 96
feminism, 260, 268, 274–75, 297–98,
    344
Ferguson, E., 226, 228, 243n91
Fernandez, Paula Lorente, 48
Fillmore, Charles, 24, 38
Filología neotestamentaria, 38
fire, 242
Fish, Stanley, 75
Fitzmyer, Joseph A., 237n70, 240n82
flesh, 185
Foley, Toshikazu, 48
Ford, David, 343
fourfold sense of Scripture, 64–67
4 Ezra, 143, 145–47
Fourth Lateran Council, 123n55
Fowl, Stephen, 71–72, 75
France, R. T., 225
Fredriksen, Paula, 281
Fridrichsen, Anton, 337
Friedrich, Paul, 48
fruit of the Spirit, 194–95
Fuller, R. C., 341
Fuller Theological Seminary, 104, 105
fundamentalism, 133, 362
    and inerrancy, 104–5, 106, 108, 121
Fung, Ronald, 186

"fusion of horizons," 72
future justification, 188–89, 192–93
futurism, 295

Gadamer, Hans-Georg, 72
Gaffin, Richard B., Jr., 190n78
Galadima, Bulus Y., 264
Galatians, justification in, 161–95
Garlington, Don, 184n59
Gathercole, Simon, 174, 189n76,
    190n77
Gatiss, Lee, 346
General Epistles, 294–95
genocide, in Africa, 254
Gentiles, 157, 184
    in apocalyptic literature, 144–47
    inclusion in people of God, 173, 178
    judgment upon, 147
George, Timothy, 106, 187n68
Gerhardsson, Berger, 341
German Pietists, 130
Gifford, Paul, 265–66
Gilkey, Langdon, 78
Gleason, Henry, 46
global South Christians, 253, 260, 313,
    348
Gnostic Gospels, 281
God
    as consuming fire, 213
    glory of, 103
    love of, 142, 155–57, 158, 358–59
    pathos of, 302–3
    promises of, 208
    speech of, 197–98, 214–16
good works, 184, 194–95
Gorman, Michael, 291
gospel, 9, 267–68, 360
Gospel Coalition, 368
grace, 165, 185
Grafton, Anthony, 128
Graham, Billy, 135–36
Great Commission, 157, 366
Greek genitive case, 54–60
Greek lexicography, 19–20, 21–37
Greek perfect tense, 46–54

Haacker, Klaus, 237, 346
halakha, 280, 290
Hammann, Konrad, 335

Hays, Richard, 183n53
Hazard, Paul, 128
Hebrews, 196–216, 294
heirs, 169
Hellenism/Judaism dichotomy, 315n55
Hemer, Colin, 349
Hengel, Martin, 287, 331, 336
Henry, Carl F. H., 104–5, 106, 135,
    137–38, 362
Hermeneia series, 331
hermeneutical circle/spiral, 84
higher criticism, 115, 119, 130
Hill, R. J., 347
Hippolytus, 69
historical criticism, 65, 270
historical-grammatical exegesis, 65
historical Jesus, 279–85, 320–22, 334,
    336, 340–41
historical theology, 64, 77–78, 83
Hodge, A. A., 108–9, 117, 133–35
Hodge, Charles, 113, 135
Hoehner, Harold, 332
Holden, Henry, 122
holiness, of the church, 90
holistic ministry, 269
Holtzmann, H. J., 334, 336
Holy Spirit
    in Galatians, 171
    outpouring of, 242–43, 246
homonymy, 34
hope, 96, 186–87
Horner, David, 332
Horrell, David G., 170n23
Horton, Michael, 83n68
Hoskyns, Edwyn Clement, 337
Hubbard, Moyer, 332
Hungary, 339–40
Hurtado, Larry, 332, 334
Huxley, Thomas, 132–33, 134

Ibn Hazm, 326
Ignatius of Antioch, 90–91
"illegitimate totality transfer," 78
immerse, immersion, 220–21, 230–41,
    244, 246
"in Christ," 169, 176–78, 179, 183
inclusion, in people of God, 171
"incorporation into Christ," 237
inculturation, 270–71, 272–74

indeterminacies, of text, 73
indicative and imperative, 170n23
indigenous interpretation, 264, 266,
    269, 272, 315
individualism, 87
inheritance, 169
International Critical Commentary, 330
intratextual echoes, 81, 82
intuition, 309
Irenaeus, 64, 69
Isaac, 208
Iser, Wolfgang, 73
Islam, 326, 343
Israel
    election of, 147
    ethnic, 146–47, 152, 153, 154, 156,
        158
    wilderness wanderings of, 241

Jackson, Glenna, 269–70
James, and Paul, 184
Jenkins, Philip, 260, 313, 343–44, 348
Jerome, 111
Jerusalem, destruction of, 142, 144,
    147, 156, 159
Jesus Christ
    crucifixion of, 155, 157, 232, 238
    death and resurrection of, 256, 360
    exaltation of, 155
    as final word, 200–201, 213
    as High Priest, 207
    immersion practice of, 227–28
    "lifting up" of, 151, 155, 156, 157,
        158
    sacrifice of, 210
    as Son of God, 211, 304
    subordination of, 305
    as wisdom teacher, 307, 319–20
Jesus Seminar, 269–70, 278–79, 340
Jewett, Robert, 237n67
Jewish immersion rites, 221–27
Jews, unity with Gentiles, 142
John, Gospel of, 285–87
Johnson, Keith, 63
Johnson, Luke Timothy, 199, 336
John the Baptist, 223–27, 229, 231
judgment, 211, 212, 215
justification, 160–78, 190–95, 355
    means of, 178–86
    time of, 186–90

Kahl, W., 331
Kähler, Martin, 321, 336
Kairos document, 275
Kantzer, Kenneth, 353, 362
Käsemann, Ernst, 175n33, 331, 336, 337
Katongole, Emmanuel, 252–53
Keener, Craig, 283
Kelber, Werner, 265
Kim, Seyoon, 332
King, Karen, 281
kingdom of God, 89, 150–51, 153, 158, 317
Klink, Edward, III, 332
Knox, John, 134
Koester, Helmut, 332
Kohls, Ernst-Wilhelm, 335
Köstenberger, A., 228, 333
Koyama, Kosuke, 302–3, 308–9
Kremers, H., 347
Kugel, James L., 123–24
Küng, Hans, 110
Kuss, O., 237

Lagrange, Marie-Joseph, 334
Lammenais, 122
Lane, Anthony, 69
language, 26
law, 168, 179–82. *See also* works of the law
lawcourt metaphor, 173
Laws, Curtis Lee, 108
Le Clerc, Jean, 128, 129–30, 132
Lee, John, 21
Lee, Jung Young, 305–6, 312
Leithart, Peter, 162n1
LeMarquand, Grant, 251, 267–68
Leo XIII, Pope, 117–20
Lessing, G. E., 132
Lessius, 122
Levine, Amy-Jill, 283
Lewis, C. S., 353
lexicography, 19–20, 21–22, 27–36, 60–61
liberation, 260, 272, 274, 296–97, 304, 309, 311
Lietzmann, H., 237
Lightfoot, J. B., 337
limited inerrancy, 118, 120

Lindars, Barnabas, 350, 352
linguistics, 19–20, 25–26, 37–43, 60–61, 354, 358
literary criticism, 298
local congregation, 99–101
Lock, Walter, 330
Locke, John, 128
logos, 206n20
Lohmeyer, Ernst, 334
Loisy, Alfred, 120, 122, 334
Longenecker, Richard, 353
Lord's Day, 97
Lord's Supper, 91–92, 93–94, 102
Louw, Johannes, 22–23, 28, 33–35, 46, 47, 48, 60, 262
love, 98, 306
lower criticism, 112, 116
Lüdemann, Gerd, 341
Luther, Martin, 68, 113, 122, 124–25, 134, 161
Lutherans, 161
Lyons, John, 20, 26, 27, 28, 49

Marcus, J., 226
Marcuse, Harold, 110n12
margins, and center, 301, 306, 308
Marsden, George, 115n27
Marshall, I. Howard, 79, 243n91, 330, 331, 357–58
Marty, Martin, 108
Martyn, J. Louis, 178–79, 183n55, 356
Marxist theory, 274, 339
Masoga, M., 264, 266
Mateos, Juan, 23
Matthews, Peter, 60
Mbiti, John, 266, 267, 274
McGrath, Alister, 69, 346
McKay, Ken, 46, 47, 48
meaning, 29, 30, 31, 34, 45, 56–57, 61, 71
meditation, 309
Meier, John P., 279, 341
Melchizedek, 207
Messianic Jewish movement, 290
methodological fragmentation, in North American academy, 298
metonymy, 35
Meyer, Wilhelm, 270
Michaelis, John David, 130

Michaelis, Laura, 48
Mingdao, Wang, 313
minimalist formalized semantics,
    44–46, 54, 60, 61
miqveh, 233
mission, 156–57
Mitchell, T. F., 48
modernism, 62, 120
modularity, 35–36
monosemy, 31–35, 36
Moo, D. J., 236
Moritz, Thorsten, 332
morphology, 44–45, 54
Morris, Leon, 237n71
Mugambi, J. N. K., 273
Muller, Richard, 83, 113, 125–26
Muthengi, J., 269

name of Jesus, 231, 234
neoorthodoxy, 125
new atheism, 280
new birth, 151, 154, 159
new covenant, 208–9, 212, 214–15
new creation, 89
New Perspective on Paul, 160, 180–81,
    289–91, 340, 354
new temple, 143, 152–53, 159
New Testament, use of Old Testament,
    298, 354
New Testament Abstracts, 256–58,
    326–27
New Testament Society of South Africa,
    262
Nicene Creed, 90, 107n6
Nicodemus, 149–51, 153, 158, 159
Nida, Eugene, 22–23, 28, 33–35, 39, 60
Nigerian Association for Biblical
    Studies, 263, 268
Njoroge, Nyambura J., 253–54
Noll, Mark, 261, 353
North America, 278–99
Nyende, Peter, 265
Nzimbi, Benjamin, 255

obedience, 184
Odeburg, Hugo, 337
O'Donovan, Oliver, 347
Ohlers, Clinton, 134
Okure, Teresa, 267, 318

Old Testament, use in the New, 298,
    354
Orabator, Agbonkhianmeghe E., 251,
    255
Orchard, Bernard, 336
ordinances, 92
Origen, 67, 272
original autographs, 109, 120, 134–35
original meaning, 63, 67
Orthodox approach to Scripture, 68
otzar, 233

Packer, J. I., 346
Padilla, Osvaldo, 333
Pagels, Elaine, 281
Pan-African Association of Biblical
    Exegetes, 268
Park, Sydney, 332
Parker, D. C., 265, 343
Patristic interpretation, 272
Paul, and James, 184
Pauline studies, 289–94
Peake, A. S., 346–47
Pearson, Charles W., 134
Peláez, Jesús, 23
Pentecostalism, 266, 297, 344
people of God, 88–89, 171, 173–75,
    178
persecution, 214
perseverance, 205, 365
Pervo, Richard I., 288–89
Peterson, Margaret Kim, 297n106
Peyrère, Isaac de La, 122, 128–29
Pharisees, 221–23
Pieris, Aloysius, 314
Piper, John, 193
Pius XII, Pope, 120–21
Plant, S., 346–47
pluralism, 305
Pobee, John, 267
Poirer, J. C., 343
Poland, 338, 347
polemics, 365
polysemy, 34
pools, in Jerusalem, 232–34
Popkin, Richard, 129
Porter, Stanley, 47, 48, 152, 356, 361
postcolonialism, 260, 268, 296–97,
    306, 310–11, 317

postmillennialism, 295
postmodernism, 10, 341, 368
poststructuralism, 73
poverty, 304n12
practical wisdom, 86n76
pragmatics, 32–33, 45, 61
preaching, 91, 92
precritical interpretation, 64–67, 81
premillennialism, 295
presbytery, 99
preterism, 295
progressive revelation, 83
prophets, 199
proselyte baptism, 225–26, 228
Protestants, on justification, 160, 161,
    163
Prothero, Stephen, 281
prototype theory, 29–30, 31
"public scribes hypothesis," 129
Punt, Jeremy, 252n12
purification, 228, 232–33, 234, 245
purification rites, 219

Qumran community, 225–26

racism, 275
Rainbow, Paul, 295
Räisänen, Heikki, 79, 240
Raitt, Jill, 125
reader-response criticism, 74
reason, 84
reception history, 109–10
reconciliation, 272
Reformation tradition, on justification,
    175, 184, 192, 194
Reformers, 69
regeneration, 150
regula fidei, 68
Reicke, Bo, 337
Reimarus, Hermann Samuel, 280, 317,
    333, 335, 336
Reinitzer, Heimo, 124–25
relevance theory, 39
Reno, R. R., 81
repentance, 102, 232
rest, 205–6
revelation, 196–97
Revelation (book), 295
Ricoeur, Paul, 73

righteousness, 167, 172, 175, 178n39,
    186–87, 191
    forensic vs. moral, 162, 165, 169,
        175, 176, 187
Ritschl, Albrecht, 336
ritual, 245
ritual purification, 226, 227–28
Robinson, James, 340
Robinson, John, 286–87
Rohrbaugh, Richard, 271
Roman Catholics
    biblical scholarship of, 340–41,
        343–45
    on inerrancy, 115–22, 135
Roman Empire, 296, 316–17
Rosner, Brian, 81
Ruhl, Charles, 32–36
"ruled reading," 63, 66
Rule of Faith, 64–66, 68, 81, 82
Rwanda, 274

Saayman, Willem, 275
Sabatier, Louis Auguste, 131–32, 134
Sabbath rest, 205–6
sacraments, 91, 92
Said, Edward, 271
salvation history, 158, 159, 179, 183,
    184–86, 203, 317–18
same-sex relations, 252
Sandeen, Ernest, 108–10, 122, 134–35
Sanders, E. P., 175n32, 177n39, 291,
    341
Sanneh, Lamin, 261
Saussure, Ferdinand de, 26, 28
Scandinavia, 337
Schleiermacher, Friedrich, 336
Schmidt, Karl, 334
Schnabel, Eckhard, 332
Schnelle, Udo, 178n39, 331
scholarship, and faith, 364–67, 368
Scholasticism, 125
Schreine, T. R., 237
Schüssler-Fiorenza, Elisabeth, 339
Schweitzer, Albert, 177–78n39, 281,
    333, 334, 336
Schweizer, Eduard, 336
science and religion, warfare between,
    129
Scripture. *See* Bible

2 *Baruch*, 143, 144–45
Second Helvetic Confession, 134
Second Temple Judaism, 222, 232
secular culture, 88
seed of Abraham, 169, 171, 177
semantic-field theory, 22–23, 26
semantic maximalism and minimalism, 32
semantics, 31–33, 45, 61
semi-Pelagianism, 186
Semler, Johann Salomo, 130, 132
sentimentalism, 358–59
Shembe, Isaiah, 259
Shin, Hyeon Woo, 321–22
Silva, Moisés, 26–27, 28–29, 107n5
Simon, Richard, 115–17, 122, 127–28, 129–30, 132, 135
Singh, G. R., 314
Sixtus, B., 334
Slenczka, R., 348
Smit, Dirkie, 251–52
sola fide, 192
sola gratia, 192
sola Scriptura, 85
Song, Choan-Seng, 303–5, 309, 312
Soskice, Janet Martin, 70
South Africa, 262–64
southern shift, in world Christianity. *See* global South Christians
speech-act theory, 75, 76
Spinoza, 129, 336
spirituality, 271
spiritual nourishment, 102
Sprinkle, Preston M., 182n51, 185n63
sprinkling, 235n62
Spurgeon, C. H., 95
stativity, 48
Steinmetz, David, 65
Stendahl, Krister, 332, 337
Stott, John, 346, 358
Strauss, D. F., 334, 336
Stuhlmacher, Peter, 190n77
Sudan, 256
suffering, 211, 214, 302–3
   of Africans, 253–54
   of Asians, 304
suffering servant, 155
Sugirtharajah, Rasiah S., 306–8, 309–10

Summer Institute of Linguistics, 39
Sweden, 337
synchronic approach (New Testament studies), 335
synchronic linguistics, 37, 59
Synoptic Gospels, 278–85, 340
syntax, 41
systematicity, 35–36
systematic theology, 64, 77–78, 83, 84

Tan, Kim Huat, 317–19
technical meaning, 217–18, 226
temple, destruction of, 143, 144, 153, 156, 159
temple clearing, 148, 152
Templeton, Chuck, 136
Tennent, Timothy, 261
Tertullian, 64, 69
text, as art, 73
text-centered understanding, 73
"textual cleansing," translation as, 310
textual criticism, 265
textual meaning, 75
"theo-drama," of Word, 85
theological "indigestion," 312
theological interpretation, 62–64, 67, 70, 77–86
   and authorial intent, 71–77
   and biblical theology, 78–81
Thesaurus Linguae Graecae (TLG), 24–25
Thielman, Frank, 331
Thiselton, Anthony, 25–26, 28–29, 35
Thomas Aquinas, 123n55
Thompson, Alden, 146
Thompson, Michael B., 68
Tiénou, Tite, 259, 267
torah obedience, 170, 174, 179–82, 185, 188, 191
Towner, Philip, 330
tradition, 67–71, 83–86
   and interpretation, 65, 72
   and Scripture, 86
transformation, 175, 177
translation, 39
   and meaning, 46–47
   in postcolonial context, 310–11
transubstantiation, 123n55
Treier, Daniel, 67, 71–72, 80, 162n1

Trinitarian mission, 156
Trinity, 64
Trinity Evangelical Divinity School, 353
Troeltsch, Ernst, 336
Turner, Max, 41, 242–43n89
Tutu, Desmond, 275
two-covenants theory, 290
Tyndale House, 345, 354, 361
Tyndale, William, 89
typology, 67

Ukpong, Justin, 272, 273
Ullmann, Stephen, 34
unfaithfulness, 205
union with Christ, 177–78
unity, of the church, 90
universal church, 90, 99
Ussher, James, 128

van Aarde, Andries, 269
van Eck, Ernest, 267
Vanhoozer, Kevin, 76, 85–86
van Huyssteen, Wentzel, 69
van Voorst, Robert, 280
Vatican II, 121–23
Vendryes, J., 27
verbal aspect, 39, 46, 356–57
Verkuyl, Henk, 48
Vermes, Géza, 339
Vincent of Lerins, 107n6
vindication, 172, 191–92
Vulgate, 118–19

Wainwright, Elaine, 344
walking in the Spirit, 195
Wall, Andrew, 249
Wall, Robert, 65
Wallace, Daniel, 40–43, 54–60
Wansbrough, Henry, 340–41
Warfield, B. B., 108–9, 117, 133–35
water, 245
Watson, Brenda, 347
Watson, Francis, 63, 78n54, 84, 180n46
Waweru, Humphrey Mwangi, 271
Webb, R. L., 226
Webb, William, 299
Webster, John, 347
Weiss, Johannes, 334, 336

Wells, David, 108
Wenham, David, 277
Wesley, John, 134
West, Gerald, 259, 269
West, influences in Africa, 260
Westerholm, Stephen, 182
Western scholarship, and African interpretive communities, 266–68
Westminster Confession of Faith, 109, 134
Whitaker, William, 126–27
Whitefield, George, 134
Wilckens, U., 237, 346
Wiles, Maurice, 336
Wimsatt, W. K., 71
witchcraft, 271
Witczyk, Henryk, 347–48
Witherington, Ben, 281
Wittgenstein, Ludwig, 29
Wojciechowski, M., 338
Wolterstorff, Nicholas, 75, 76
Woodbridge, John, 108
Word of God, 92, 198, 206–7
  as living, 215
  as personal, 215
  as trustworthy, 215–16
Work, Telford, 347
works, 185
works of the law, 165, 166–67, 174, 180–82
works righteousness, 191
world, 151–52, 156
World Evangelical Fellowship, 361
worship, 103, 365–66
Wrede, Wilhelm, 177–78n39, 321, 334, 336, 340
Wright, N. T., 77, 173–75, 181n46, 186, 190, 192n81, 194, 289, 331, 341, 347
Wuest, K. S., 236, 238, 240

Yeung, Maureen, 321
Yieh, John, 319
Ysebaert, Joseph, 245n98
Yule, George, 40

Ziesler, John, 162
Zion traditions, 317–18

Scripture Index

Genesis
1:3—197
2:2—205–6
12—88
12:2–3—208
12:3—157
12:7—157
13:15—157
15:5—208
15:6—157, 166–67, 172, 175
17:5—200
18:18—157
22—152
22:16–17—208
22:18—157
24:7—157
38:26—172
44:16—172

Exodus
15:13–16—88
15:26—166n10
19:5—166n10
19:18—212
23:7—172
23:22—166n10
33:14–16—101

Leviticus
11:44–45—90, 101
18:5—182n51, 185n63
19:2—90, 101
20:7—90, 101

Numbers
21:8–9—151, 155, 159

Deuteronomy
11:13—166n10
11:22—166n10
14:2—90
15:5—166n10
25:1—172
28:1—166n10
28:2—166n10
31:6–8—213
32—211n29
32:35—210
32:36—210

Joshua
1:5—213
3:11—90
3:13—90

1 Samuel
15:22—166n10

2 Samuel
7:14—201n14, 202n16
22:45—166n10

1 Kings
8:32—172

2 Kings
(as 4 Kings)
5:14—219n7

1 Chronicles
12:32—9

2 Chronicles
6:23—172

Psalms
2:7—201, 202n16, 207, 214
2:8—200
22:22—204, 214
27:4—96
40:6–8—209, 214
40:8—198n5
45:6–7—202n16
63:5—231n50
82:3—172
84—95–96
84:4—96
84:10—96
94:17—268
95—198n7, 205–6
95:3—205
95:4—205
95:5—205
95:7—205
95:7–8—205
95:7–11—204, 214
95:11—205
97:5—90
97:7—202n16
102:25—197
102:25–27—202n16
104:4—202n16

105:3—231n50
110—201–2
110:1—202n16
110:4—207, 208n, 214
118:6—213
119—347
119:25—207
129:8—231n50
133—97

Proverbs
3—211
3:11–12—211
3:34—276

Isaiah
5:23—172
8:17—204, 214
8:18—204, 214
21:4—219n7
40–55—172, 174
46–55—190–91
49:1–7—172
50:8—172
51:6—172
51:8—172
52:13–14—155
52:13–53:12—172
54:1—172
54:14—172
55:11—207

Jeremiah
3:11—172
5:14—137
17:24—166n10
23:24—90
23:29—137, 207
31—208–9
31:31–34—199, 209,
    214

Ezekiel
16:51–52—172
22:30—352
37—92

Joel
2:28—242

Micah
4:13—90

Habakkuk
1:4—168
1:13—168
2:4—157, 167, 172

Haggai
2:6—212

Zechariah
4:14—90

Matthew
2—114
3:1—223n20, 231n51
3:5–6—224
3:6—223n23, 227,
    231n51
3:7—223n23, 231n51
3:11—223n23, 231n51,
    242, 243n90
3:13—223n23, 231n51
3:14—223n23, 231n51
3:16—223n23, 227n38,
    231n51
5:16—102
5:20—176
6:1—35
6:19–21—350
7:3–4—221
9:22—321
10:37—89
11:11—223n20, 231n51
11:12—223n20, 231n51
12:37—190n77
14:2—223n20, 231n51
14:8—223n20, 231n51
14:30—221
16:14—223n20, 231n51
17:13—223n20, 231n51
18—102
18:15–17—99
21—89
21:25—224n23, 231n51
21:43—89
23—277
24:14—157

26:29—93
28:18–20—93
28:19—157, 229n42,
    230
28:19–20—230

Mark
1:4—223n21, 223–
    24n23, 224n24
1:4–5—224
1:5—223n23, 227
1:8—223n23, 242
1:9—223n23, 227n36
1:10—227n36
1:21–22—82
1:23–26—82
1:27—82
1:44—222
3:31–35—89
5:34—321
6:14—223n21, 223n23
6:24—223n21, 223n23
6:25—223nn20–21
7:3—68
7:3–4—223–24
7:4—222n18
7:5—68
7:8—68
7:9—68
8:28—223nn20–21
10:29–30—103
10:38—238n76, 243–44
10:39—243
10:52—321
11:30—224n23
14:25—93
16:16—229n42

Luke
1:5—223
1:75—176
2:22—222
3:3—224n23
3:7—223n23
3:12—223n23
3:16—223n23, 242,
    243n90
3:21—223n23
4:5–7—317

5:7—221
5:14—222
6:13—91
7:20—223n20
7:29—223–24n23
7:30—223n23
7:33—223n20
7:50—321
8:48—321
9:19—223n20
11:37–38—222
11:38—222n18
12:50—243
16:24—220
17:19—321
19:42—321
20:4—224n23
22:17—93
22:19—93
22:24–27—317
23:26—254n20
24:47—157

John
1—92
1:10—151n29
1:11—154
1:11–13—154
1:12—154–55
1:12–13—154
1:14—143, 149n21, 152
1:18—47, 149n21, 152
1:19–36—152n33
1:25—223n23
1:26—223n23
1:28—223n23
1:29—152
1:31—223n23
1:33—223n23, 242
1:41—47
1:51—143
2:1–4:54—148n19
2:6—222
2:13—148
2:13–22—148, 159
2:13–25—152n33
2:13–3:21—148, 153
2:14–22—143
2:18—148–49

2:19—149
2:20—149
2:20–22—149
2:23—148–49
2:23–25—149
2:23–3:21—148
2:25—149
3:1—149
3:1–15—149
3:2—148–49
3:3—150–51, 157
3:4—154
3:5—150, 157
3:5–7—151
3:9—151
3:12—149n21
3:13—149n21
3:14—149, 155
3:14–15—151, 153
3:15—149n21, 153,
    155n38
3:16—141–43, 147n16,
    148, 149n21, 151–59
3:16–21—149
3:17—152
3:18—148n18, 149n21,
    152
3:21—149n21
3:22—148, 228
3:23—223n23
3:24—149n21
3:25–26—227–28
3:27–30—149n21
3:31–36—149n21
3:36—148n18, 155n38
4:1—228n38
4:2—228n38
4:8—149n21
4:9—149n21
4:14—155n38
4:19–24—143
4:21–24—153, 156
4:22—158
4:36—155n38
4:42—152
4:44—149n21
4:45—149n21
5:24—155n38
5:24–30—148n18

5:39—155n38
6:1–14—152n33
6:22–71—152n33
6:27—155n38
6:37—92
6:40—148n18, 155n38
6:47—155n38
6:54—155n38
6:64—149n21
6:68—155n38
7:7—151n29
7:22—47
8:23—151n29
8:24—148n18
8:28—155
8:31–59—154
8:37—154
8:42—154
8:44—154
8:56—154
9:38—143
9:39—151n29
10:16—154n37
10:28—155n38
10:40—223n23
11:9—151n29
11:25–26—148n18
11:47–12:8—152n33
11:48—150
11:50—154
11:51–52—154
11:52—154n36
12:25—155n38
12:32—155
12:33—155
12:34—149n21, 155
12:48–50—148n18
12:50—155n38
13:1–17:26—152n33
13:11—149n21
13:26—220
13:29—149n21
13:34–35—97–98
14:6—106, 151
14:17—151n29
14:22—151n29
14:26–27—82
14:27—151n29
14:30—151n29

15:12–17—97
15:13—155
15:18–19—151n29
15:19—156
15:26—82
15:26–27—156
16:8—151n29
16:12–15—82
16:20—151n29
16:33—151n29
17:2–3—155n38
17:6—151n29
17:9—151n29
17:11—231n53
17:14—151n29
17:20—91, 156
17:20–23—154n36
18:36—150, 151n29
19:13–42—152n33
19:14—152n33
19:29—152n33
19:31—149n21, 152n33
19:36—149n21
19:36–37—152n33
20:9—149n21
20:21—156
20:22–23—156
20:28—143
20:31—148n18, 153
21:7—149n21

Acts
1:5—223n23, 242,
   243n91
1:15—233
1:22—224n23
2:1—233
2:9–10—254n20
2:14–36—232
2:36—234
2:37–41—231
2:38—229, 230n47,
   232n54, 234
2:39—158
2:41—229n42, 232n54,
   234
2:42—96
4:32—90
6:9—94

7:4—71
7:38—89
8:12–13—229n42
8:16—229n42, 230n47
8:26–40—254n20
8:36—229n42, 235
8:36–39—234
8:37—235n63
8:38—229n42, 235
8:39—235
9:18—229n42
10:35—176
10:37—224n23
10:47—229n42
10:48—229n42, 230n47
11:16—223n23, 242,
   243n91
13:24—224n23
15:9—232n54
16:15—229n42
16:33—229n42
17:21—77
17:24—96
18:8—229n42
18:25—224n23
19—89
19:3—224n23
19:4—224n23
19:5—229n42, 230n47
19:32—89
19:39—89
19:41—89
20:28—88, 102
22:16—229n42
28:26–28—89

Romans
1:1–2—157–58
1:16—158
1:16–17—158
1:17—172
2—290
2:13—190n77
3:20—190n77
3:21—158
3:21–22—172
3:21–5:21—239
3:30—190n77
4—183n55

4:1–25—157
4:9–15—157
5—188, 193n84
5:1—175n32, 185, 187,
   189
5:2—186n67
5:8—157
5:9—175n32, 187, 189
5:19—190n77
6:1—239
6:1–5—93
6:1–11—238–39
6:2—238–39
6:3—229n42, 230n47,
   236–39
6:3–5—235, 236n64
6:3–6—238
6:3–11—239
6:4—238–39
6:5—238
6:6—239
6:12–19—94
6:12–8:30—239
6:13—176
6:16—176
6:18—176
6:19—176
6:20—176
7:23—94
8—193n84
8:19—187n70
8:23—187n70
8:25—187n70
8:29–30—187
8:30—189
8:33—172, 190n77
8:35—55
9–11—158
10:3—172
10:4—82
10:16—166n10
10:17—92
12:4–5—94
12:9–10—97
12:16—98
12:19—210n27
13:8–10—97
14:19—98

1 Corinthians

1:7—187n70
1:13—229n42
1:14–17—229n42
1:15—229n42
1:18–2:4—290
4:1—98
4:5—207
4:16—98
5—102
5–6—90
5:5—100
5:7—100
5:11—100
5:13—100
6—193n84
6:11—175n32, 187
6:15—94
10:1–2—241
10:2—236, 241
11:1—98
11:2—68
11:23—68
11:24—93
12:12–27—94, 97–98
12:13—229n42, 239–40, 242
12:17—166n10
13—365
13:2—321
13:7—98
15:3—68
15:29—229n42

2 Corinthians

1:20—89
2:6–8—101
5:21—172
6:14–7:1—90
12:20—98
13:5—87

Galatians

1:1–2:14—164
1:6—165
1:8—100
1:11–12—68
1:11–16—178
1:15—165

1:15–17—68
1:22—177
1:23—183
2:4—177
2:5—174
2:7—182
2:8—165
2:11–14—164, 173
2:14—111, 164, 174
2:15—164n, 165, 170n21, 185
2:15–16—164, 172–73
2:15–21—164, 176
2:16—163–67, 171, 173–74, 179–82, 183n55, 185, 188
2:16–4:31—170
2:17—165, 177, 179, 188
2:17–18—165
2:19–20—165, 177, 179
2:20—182
2:21—162n2, 163, 165, 174, 185n64, 188, 192, 192n83
3—166n10, 170n21, 183n55
3:1—164n, 165n9
3:1–5—166, 174, 183n55, 188–89
3:1–6—168
3:1–9—183
3:1–4:12—165n9
3:1–4:20—165
3:1–5:12—164–65
3:2—166, 171, 177, 180, 182
3:3—166, 171, 185
3:5—166, 171, 177, 180, 182
3:6—163, 166, 166n10, 169, 175, 179, 182, 188
3:6–9—157, 191
3:6–11—165
3:6–4:7—171
3:7—167–69, 171, 179, 182
3:7–9—167–69

3:8—163, 167–69, 179, 183, 188, 190n77
3:8–9—157
3:9—167–69, 171, 179, 183
3:10—167–68, 180–81
3:10–14—167
3:11—164, 167–69, 179, 183, 188, 190
3:12—167–69, 179, 182–83, 185n63
3:13—168
3:13–14—177, 179
3:14—167–69, 171, 177, 183
3:14–18—157
3:15–18—168
3:15–25—169
3:16—157, 167, 169, 177
3:17—169
3:18—165, 167, 169
3:19—168–69
3:21—163, 165, 168–69, 188
3:22—168–69, 179, 182–83
3:23—169, 183
3:23–25—169, 185n62
3:24—163, 165, 169, 179, 183, 185, 188, 190n77
3:25—169, 183
3:26—169, 171, 177, 183
3:26–29—169, 177
3:27—169, 177, 229n42, 230n47
3:28—169, 177
3:28–29—157
3:29—167, 169, 171, 177
4:1–7—169
4:3—170
4:5–7—171
4:6—171
4:7—171
4:8–9—170
4:8–20—166, 169

4:9–11—165n9
4:11—165n9
4:12–20—165n9
4:21—170
4:21–30—169
4:22—167
4:27—172
4:28–31—171
4:29—171
4:30—170
5:1—170
5:2—170n21
5:2–4—170, 193
5:2–6—170, 174
5:3—182
5:4—163, 165, 171,
    179–80, 188, 192
5:4–5—165
5:5—163, 170–71, 183,
    186–88
5:5–6—170–71
5:6—177, 183–84
5:7–12—170
5:13–6:10—176–77
5:13–6:18—164
5:15—97
5:16—195
5:22—183
5:22–23—194
5:24—177, 179
5:25—195
6:7–9—194
6:10—97, 183
6:14—177, 179
6:15—157

Ephesians
1:15—97
1:18—186n67
2:4–5—157
2:11–22—142
2:14–15—157
3:10–11—103
4:1–16—99
4:3–6—98
4:4—186n67
4:5—93
5:9—176

Philippians
2:3—98
2:9—231n53
3—178n
3:17—98
3:20—187n70

Colossians
1:23—186
1:27—186n67
2:6–7—68
2:8—68
3:11—157

1 Thessalonians
1:3—186n67
2:13—166n10
2:16—89
4:1–2—68
5:8—186n67
5:13—98

2 Thessalonians
2:15—68
2:16—157
3:6—68
3:11—98

1 Timothy
3:15—91
3:16—192
6:11—176
6:20—68

2 Timothy
1:14—68
4:3—100, 166n10
4:4—166n10

Titus
1:2—186n67
3:5—157
3:7—186n67

Hebrews
1—203
1:1—199
1:1–2—196, 207, 213
1:1–4—200, 202

1:2—197, 200–201, 203,
    209, 211n30, 215
1:2–4—200, 213
1:3—197–98, 201–2
1:4—201n14
1:5—197–99, 201–2,
    211n30
1:5–6—199
1:5–13—202, 214
1:5–14—201n14, 203
1:6—197–99, 202
1:7—197–99, 202
1:8—197, 202, 211n30
1:8–9—198, 202
1:10—197
1:10–12—202
1:13—197, 199, 202
2—203
2:1—199, 203
2:1–4—202, 210, 214
2:2—197, 206n20
2:2–3—197
2:3—203, 215
2:4—197, 203
2:5—201
2:10—197, 209, 214–15
2:10–18—211
2:11—197, 204
2:12—89
2:12–13—197, 199, 204,
    209, 214
2:14—209
2:14–18—204
2:16—204
2:17—204, 209
3:1—203, 214
3:1–4:11—206
3:4—198
3:5—197
3:6—211n30
3:7—197, 199, 205–6
3:7–11—205, 214
3:7–19—205
3:7–4:11—206, 210
3:7–4:13—204–5
3:11—197, 205
3:12—198
3:13—205
3:15—197, 199, 204–5

3:16–18—205
3:16–19—205
3:18—197
3:19—205
4—205
4:1—206
4:1–11—205
4:2—197, 206n20
4:3—197–99, 204
4:4—197, 199
4:6—197
4:7—197, 199
4:8—197
4:9—206
4:11–16—294
4:12—137, 197–98, 200, 206
4:12–13—199, 205, 215
4:13—199, 206
4:14—211n30
4:16—201
5:1–10—207
5:5—197, 199, 207, 211n30, 214
5:5–6—199, 207
5:6—197, 199, 207, 214
5:8—211n30
5:11—199
5:13—206n20
6:1—206n20
6:4–8—210
6:5—197
6:6—211n30
6:7—198
6:9—199
6:13—197, 208
6:13–14—199, 208
6:14—197, 208
6:15—208
6:16—208
6:17—197, 208
7:3—211n30
7:8—197
7:13—197
7:17—197
7:20—197
7:21—197, 199, 207, 214
7:27—201

7:28—197, 206n20, 211n30
8:1—199
8:5—197
8:7–10:18—208
8:8—197, 199, 208–9
8:8–12—199, 209, 214
8:8–13—208
8:9—197, 209
8:10—197
8:13—197
9:8—197, 199, 204
9:10—222n18
9:14—198, 201
9:26—198
10—210
10:5—197, 199, 209
10:5–7—204, 209
10:7—197, 198n5, 209–10, 214
10:8—197, 210
10:9—197, 210
10:12—201
10:15—197, 199, 204, 208–9, 214
10:15–17—208
10:16–17—214
10:19–25—294
10:23—197
10:25—96
10:26–31—210
10:29—211n30
10:30—197, 199, 210
10:31—198
10:36—197
11:3—197
11:4—197
11:5—197
11:7—197
11:8—197
11:11—197
11:16—204
11:18—197
11:39—197
12:2—201, 216
12:5—197
12:5–6—199, 211, 214
12:7–11—211
12:19—197, 206n20

12:22—198
12:22–24—204, 212
12:25—197, 215
12:25–26—212
12:25–27—198
12:26—197, 199, 215
12:27—197
12:28—212
12:29—213
13—98
13:1–6—212
13:4—213n
13:5—197, 199, 212–13
13:6—213
13:7—98, 197, 206n20
13:15—213
13:20—99
13:20–21—197
13:22—197, 200, 211

James
1:20—176
2—193, 195n88
2:21—195n88
2:21–25—190n77
2:24—195n88
2:25—195n88
3:18—98
4:6—276
4:11—98

1 Peter
1:3—157
1:14–16—90, 101
1:22—97
1:23—157
2:12—102
2:17—97
3:8—97
4:8—97
5:4—99

1 John
2:2—152
3:16—97
4:7–12—97
4:14—152
4:20—87

Revelation
1:10—97
2–3—90
3:21—201
15:3—90
19:13—220
19:15—206n21
19:21—206n21
21:24—295

Apocrypha
Judith
12:7—219n7

Sirach
31:30—219n7

Pseudepigrapha
Apocalypse of Abraham
21:1–22:5—144

22:4–5—144
27:1–6—144
31:3—144
31:5—144
32:1–4—144

2 Baruch
5:1—144
13:6—145
13:11—145
21:21—144
48:20—145
48:23—145
70:10–71:1—145
72:2–6—145
78:3—144

4 Ezra
3:7—145
3:20–22—145

3:26—145
5:23–27—147n13
5:33—147n13
7:17–18—146
7:17–25—146
7:45–48—146
7:45–74—146
7:62–69—146
7:116–26—146
7:118—145
7:132–8:3—146
8:37–62—146
8:47—146n9
9:22—146n9
12:10–34—146
13:33–38—146
13:39–50—146
13:48–50—146